720 STE
00 868

D0997209

HISTORY OF ART LIBRARY
BRADFIELD COLLEGE

Bradfield College
WITHDRAWN

HISTORY OF ART LIBRARY
BRASFIELD COLLEGE

MODERN
CLASSICISM

7 20,01 STER

MODERN CLASSICISM

ROBERT A.M. STERN

WITH RAYMOND W. GASTIL

RIZZOLI
NEW YORK

Frontispiece: Masterplan for Washington DC.
Leon Krier, 1984–5. Unbuilt project.
Washington, *painting by Rita Wolff, 1986.*

This edition first published 1988 by
Rizzoli International Publications Inc.,
597, Fifth Avenue,
New York,
NY 10017

Copyright © 1988 Robert A. M. Stern

All rights reserved. No part of this publication
may be reproduced or transmitted in any
form or by any means, electronic or
mechanical, including photocopy, recording
or any information storage and retrieval
system, without permission in writing from
Rizzoli International Publications Inc.

A John Calmann and King book.

ISBN 0–8478–0848–3

LC 87–43251

This book was designed and produced by
John Calmann and King Ltd., London

Designed by Karen Stafford
Typeset by Wyvern Typesetting Ltd,
Bristol
Printed in Hong Kong by
Mandarin Offset

CONTENTS

*"... history is essential for architecture,
because the architect, who must now deal
with everything urban, will therefore always be
dealing with historical problems—with the past and,
a function of the past, with the future. So the architect
should be regarded as a kind of physical historian,
because he constructs relationships across time:
civilization in fact. And since civilization is based
largely upon the capacity of human beings to remember,
the architect builds visible history. ..."*

Vincent Scully

American Architecture and Urbanism (New York: Praeger, 1969): 257

MODERN ARCHITECTURE, MODERNISM AND MODERN CLASSICISM

". . . the historical sense involves a perception not only of the pastness of the past, but of its presence; the historical sense compels a man to write not merely with his own generation in his bones, but with a feeling that the whole of the literature of Europe from Homer and within it the whole of the literature of his own country has a simultaneous existence and composes a simultaneous order. This historical sense, which is a sense of the timeless as well as of the temporal . . . together, is what makes a writer traditional. And it is at the same time what makes a writer most acutely conscious of his place in time, of his contemporaneity."[1]

Today, the first international style of Modern architecture — the Classical style — after half a century of ahistorical Functionalist Modernism is again perceived as useful if not essential to the practice of the art of architecture. Regarded as moribund as recently as ten years ago, today, Classicism is the fulcrum about which architectural discourse balances. For many, Classicism is the *new* architecture, providing a generation raised in the tradition of an endlessly evolving Modernist present with the shock of the old. Yet closer examination of the evolution of architecture in the twentieth century suggests that Classicism has played a far greater role than generally acknowledged. This role cannot only be measured in superb, if seemingly *retardataire*, buildings that ignored the Modernist revolution and employed the Classical language with as much skill and artistic vision as those in previous centuries but also in the fact that the Classical tradition has continued to be the yardstick by which the various counter-Classical impulses of Modernism are measured, even by Modernists themselves.

The purpose of this book is to explain the continuing appeal of Classicism throughout the Modern period and to investigate in some detail the various directions in which Classicism manifests itself at present. While not a history of Modern Classicism, this book uses history to marshal its arguments on behalf of Classicism and the Classical ideal in architecture.

The representative, symbolic power of Classicism has never been equaled in Western architecture by any other formal language. Like the Gothic, it has within it a spiritual dimension, celebrating man's individual glory in a wider sphere. Like ahistorical Modernism it transcends the individualities of place and time to address universals. But where Modernism confines us to an "eternal present", to use Sigfried Giedion's chilling phrase, Classicism propels us into a conversation between an idealized Ancient world and an evolving present. The relationship between the Classical and the Modern is a profound one, and they are ideals which have flourished more often together than apart for the past five hundred years.

Classicism, as I see it, is the formal expression of Modern (i.e. Post-Medieval) secular institutions in the West. Classicism inherently represents the public and institutional realm of the Modern world. Classicism has traditionally been used to transcend or modify the vernacular of local technologies and local cultures in order to draw people together in their diversity; it brings the republican spirit of Washington to the county courthouses of the South and Midwest, just as it brought the authority of Ancient Rome to cities meant to symbolize a Modern nation — Leningrad, New Delhi, Paris, and Washington. The public realm, however, extends beyond great squares, museums and seats of government to encompass all levels of shared space. Classicism is not inherently identified with or tainted by any particular ideology, but has served rather as a distillation of the best that society can achieve. It is a tradition and a point of view. If, as some have suggested, even the Classicism of Jefferson's Monticello is marred by the memory of slaves, what of Bacon's Lincoln Memorial, whose testament to emancipation draws strength from a particular but nonetheless compelling interpretation of Greek democracy, and is further sanctified by memories of Marian Anderson and Martin Luther King, each of whom chose it as a forum? Great works of architecture — as surely as those of literature, painting, and music — transcend the particular social or political situation in which they were created. To say otherwise requires that we dismiss all art of the past, and indeed the present moment, and idly wait for social conditions to improve.

Classicism is the only codified, amplified, and perennially vital system of composition bringing order to the process of architectural design. It is also the only codified, amplified, and perennially vital language of architectural form. Gothic is equally representational and is widely admired, but it was a comparatively short-lived, geographically confined language of form inextricably connected to a comparatively narrow set of largely spiritual associations, and without a fully developed compositional system of its own. Classicism is at once a tradition and a language incorporating rules of syntax and rhetoric; it provides a methodology to establish composition and character; it operates on a spiritual as well as secular plane.

Classicism, as Lutyens argued, is "the high game" of architecture. It presents the designer with a system of symphonic complexity for relating the smallest detail to the overall structure. It is the most abstract and complex language that architecture can speak, but it has that virtue which Ruskin termed "superabundance:" it is at once a source of intellectual pleasure to the initiate and of sensuous delight to the layman. A fundamental concern with the relationship of public and private space to human scale is inherent in Classicism and in no other architectural tradition. That concern enhances the sheer beauty of mouldings and ornament which provide Classical building with layers of detail, enriching people's experience as they pause for second and third moments to appreciate the play of light on carved surfaces, the formalized naturalism of acanthus leaves, wreathes and garlands, the literary text of inscriptions, or the empathetic thrust of a column. Classicism — taken as a language of form — embraces all that richness, moreover it embodies it: it has it built in.

MODERNISM AND THE MODERN

What can be called the "Modern period" of Western architecture begins in the fifteenth century with the birth of Humanism. Although Classical forms persisted throughout the Medieval era, and there was, indeed, a serious revival of the Antique under Charlemagne at Aachen in the late eighth and early ninth centuries, the Renaissance in the early 1400s is the first of the stylistic phases of Modern Classicism; the Baroque and the Rococo are subsequent styles of Modern Classicism.

It is important not to confuse "Modern" with "Modernism," a movement that proposed a break with history and a repudiation of traditional aesthetics in favor of self-referential, functionally and technologically determined form. Many proponents of the various Modernist styles of the mid-twentieth century (the so-called International style, Constructivism, De Stijl, and others) claim that they stand apart as a parallel tradition to Western Humanism and Classicism, and indeed, that Modernism is *the* Modern style, at last emerging from the pretenses to modernity of all that went before it, from the Renaissance through the Belle Epoque. They thus appropriate the word "Modern," limiting its meaning to a representation of the urge to produce new artistic work that eschews all known form language in favor of a new language of form whose principal cultural responsibility is towards its moment in time. Modernism — as this movement is properly called — sees each work of art as a manifestation of its own immediate culture. In the most oversimplified terms, it represents a moralistic application of superior value to work that is not only new but also independent of all previous production. Modernism views the present as a state of continuing existential crisis; it sees history only as a record of experiences, a body of myth, but not as objective truth. Modernism, moreover, is apocalyptic in its relationship to the future.

Modernism, its advocates maintained, would replace the succession of styles with a unified cultural order that would somehow be always the same yet always fresh, always new. But with the reaction against Modernism in the 1960s, it is now clear that Modernism is not the way beyond style, or even the style to end all styles, but simply one of the succession of styles in the Modern continuum which began with the Renaissance.

THE COMPLEXITY OF MODERN CLASSICISM

In the Modern world the rise of the bourgeoisie, and ultimately the emergence of mass democracy, brought in their wake a range of building types and a variety of patrons and institutions unprecedented in either the Ancient or Medieval world — blurring the hierarchical distinction between "architecture," which previously applied only to monumental buildings designed by architects working in the Classical tradition, and "building," which described more modest structures, realized by builders in a variety of vernacular traditions. As the distinction between monumental and everyday building types blurred, so did the boundary between Classical and vernacular architectural expression. By the eighteenth century, there was a vast middle ground of building, Classical in its overall organization and detail yet vernacular in its means of production and in its process of design — by builders rather than architects — that was exemplified by the red-brick Georgian architecture of London. This overlap of Classical and vernacular modes would be further complicated when industrialization began to make an impact on construction.

By the nineteenth century, three aesthetic paradigms had emerged and, I would argue, still exist today: the Classical paradigm, the vernacular paradigm, and the process or production paradigm.

The Classical paradigm is concerned with the grammar, vocabulary, and rhetoric of the Classical language. The Classical paradigm takes the compositional methods and the basic forms of Greco-Roman architecture as the model for Modern architecture that attempts to be at once rational and humanistic, both a construct of human intelligence and as inevitable as a phenomenon of nature.

The vernacular paradigm that emerged in the nineteenth century posits both the tradition of modest "building" and highly evolved regional styles, such as the various Gothic medieval styles, including the High Gothic modes of France or England, or the much more informal and localized modes of expression, such as Elizabethan, Tudor, or French Norman, as models for Modern architecture rooted in place and history. Because vernacular buildings necessarily grow out of conditions largely pertaining to a particular locale, they are perceived in relation to the political, religious,

and social aspirations of that locale. For these reasons they have also been considered by many nineteenth and twentieth century reformers as "honest" and "natural" relative to Modern Classical buildings which were held to be untainted by self-conscious scholarship. The evident irony is that the very concept of the vernacular as an ideal — a self-conscious compositional strategy — puts it on the same level of supposed artifice as Classicism.

The process paradigm represents an attempt to establish a model for those conditions peculiar to the Modern era, which many people consider synonymous with the industrialized world. Industrialization has made it possible to think of the act of building in new terms: what had been an act of construction became an act of assembly. Modernism tended to value this paradigm above the other two and, in the case of extreme apologists, to value it as a replacement for them. But looking at the Modern period as a whole, it seems fair to argue that all these paradigms coexist and that the relative importance that Modern architects assign to the three paradigms in the design process gives Modern buildings their character. That these paradigms can coexist, indeed must for a vital architecture, is a principal thesis of this essay.

Contrary to the anti-traditional argument of Modernism, the exploration of Classical themes in the nineteenth century did not thwart architecture's ability to come to terms with either the new processes of production or the new types of building programs required. On the contrary, by using known models and Classical grammar and vocabulary architects were able to conceptualize some of the most functionally and technologically complex works ever built and also to make those works comprehensible to the public at large. Furthermore, the pioneers of Modernism were not only thoroughly grounded in Classicism but also, as Colin Rowe, Reyner Banham, and others have suggested, preoccupied with its grammar, or composition, while they struggled to free themselves from its specific vocabulary of forms (content). Banham's *Theory and Design in the First Machine Age* (1960) revealed that many Modernist designs of the early twentieth century which in their time were believed to be determined by new materials and technology were, in fact, affected by any number of artistic sources, including those of Classicism, which Banham disparagingly calls Academicism. Reviewing the masterpieces of the International Style, specifically Mies van der Rohe's Barcelona Pavilion (1929) and Le Corbusier's

Villa Savoye (1929–31), Banham writes, "The theory and aesthetics of the International Style were evolved between Futurism and Academicism, but their perfection was only achieved by drawing away from Futurism and drawing nearer to the Academic tradition. . . ."[2]

Colin Rowe's essay "The Mathematics of the Ideal Villa" (1947) underscored the Classical compositional techniques of Le Corbusier's canonic villas of the 1920s, arguing that their grids, strip windows, and asymmetries could be understood only in the context of the symmetry, proportion, and hierarchy of Classical and specifically Palladian designs. In a later essay, "Neo-'Classicism' and Modern Architecture II" (1956), Rowe pointed out the parallels and differences between Mies van der Rohe's American designs, such as Crown Hall (1956) at the Illinois Institute of Technology, and Palladio's Villa Rotonda. Rowe observed that Crown Hall was "symmetrical, four square, and approached by

an elevated platform which might suggest the podium of some yet unbuilt portico," adding that "it is surely not by accident that it invites the parallel to be drawn."[3] Taken together, Rowe's and Banham's analyses demonstrate that much of the most aesthetically and intellectually satisfying "advanced" Modernist work represents not a break with the past but a continuation of the search for a synthesis of the Classical and process paradigms that will stand as a distinctly Modern form of Classicism.

The recognition that Modernist designs are often Classically derived is only the beginning of a re-evaluation of Classicism in this century. Equally important is the belated recognition that some of the best architecture of the past ninety years has been by architects committed to the Classical tradition, including the firm of McKim, Mead, & White, responsible for such monuments as New York's former Pennsylvania Station (1902–11, demolished 1963), Edwin

Lutyens (1869–1944), who with Herbert Baker (1862–1946) designed the capital buildings in New Delhi (1912–31), and John Russell Pope (1874–1937), architect of the National Gallery in Washington (1937–41). Until the Second World War, Classicism remained the principal architectural language of civic and large-scale commercial and residential building, and its masters are only now being recognized for their contribution to Modern architecture as a whole.

It should be pointed out that efforts to break completely with the past and create purely Modernist forms in architecture — notably Futurism, Constructivism, and Expressionism — have failed, even more than in other arts, to establish themselves as enduring form languages, although they have produced individual works of compelling interest. It seems essential, today, to examine why and how Classicism has survived as the primary basis of architecture in the Modern world.

THE RISE OF MODERN CLASSICISM

Modern Classical architecture, like Modern history, began in the Renaissance, when two Florentine polymaths, Filippo Brunelleschi (1377–1446) and Leon Battista Alberti (1404–72), recalled Western architecture to its Classical origins and dedicated it to equaling in modern terms the architectural splendor of the ancient world. Brunelleschi, trained as a goldsmith and proficient as a sculptor and scientist, made his

1 *Foundling Hospital, Florence. Filippo Brunelleschi, 1419–24.*

most enduring contribution as an architect. His dome for the Cathedral of Florence, the design for which he began in 1417 and saw through to its virtual completion in 1436, marks the beginning of Modern architecture, a fully conscious attempt to equal and surpass Ancient architecture. Pointed rather than hemispheric, the dome is hardly Classical in appearance, but its size — $138\frac{1}{2}$ feet (42 meters) across — and its constructional techniques place it in the Ancient, specifically Roman tradition. Brunelleschi had studied Roman construction during several sojourns in Rome, where he had measured the extant monuments of antiquity and undertaken rudimentary archeological excavations.

In several other of his buildings, especially the Foundling Hospital (1419–24) and the Pazzi Chapel (c. 1430), both in Florence, Brunelleschi went much further toward reviving the Classical language. The Foundling Hospital's arcaded loggia has the Classical elements of round arches, Corinthian capitals, columns, and pilasters. The second-story windows have pedimented surrounds. More complex and also more archeologically-minded is Brunelleschi's Pazzi Chapel. Both designs present an image of

lucid geometric wholeness generally uncharacteristic of Medieval design. Articulate and symmetrical, they embody the ideal of comprehensible form which Humanist scholars considered the essence of Classical art. Every part relates to every other part in a proportional system, from the form of a single column to the form of the entire building.

Although belonging to a rich Florentine merchant family, Leon Battista Alberti had been born in exile, and he visited Florence for the first time in 1428. There he met Brunelleschi and probably also the artists Donatello and Ghiberti. In 1436 Alberti wrote, in a prologue to his essay "On Painting," that Brunelleschi and his contemporaries had equalled the achievements of the Classical world.[4]

However, Alberti differed sharply from Brunelleschi in his approach to the Classical past. He, too, had examined Roman ruins, but he was less interested than Brunelleschi in structural questions or even in the particular forms of the Classical language. Alberti's primary interest in the Classical past lay in his belief that it had discovered the enduring, universal principles of architectural composition.

2　*Pazzi Chapel, Florence. Filippo Brunelleschi, c.1430.*

For Alberti, the architect's task had as much to do with representation as it did with reality, function and structure, which had to be balanced against ideal visual principles — aesthetics. Alberti laid out his theories in a work first completed in 1452, which he revised until his death twenty years later. *De re aedificatoria* ("Ten Books on Architecture"), published posthumously in 1485, is the foundation of Modern Classical theory. In it, Alberti codified the new definition of the architect exemplified by Brunelleschi's career. The architect was no longer a relatively anonymous master mason working within a local tradition but, rather, a self-conscious artist who designed with reference to an ancient ideal:

. . . It is not a carpenter or a joiner that I thus rank with the greatest masters in the other sciences: the manual operator being no more than an instrument to the architect. Him I call an architect, who by sure and wonderful art and method, is able, both with thought and invention, to devise, and, with execution, to complete all those works, which, by means of the movement of great weights, and the conjunction and the amassment of bodies, can, and with the greatest beauty, be adapted to the uses of mankind.[5]

The "sure and wonderful art and method" was

not the one passed down from medieval master to apprentice but, rather, the method found in the architecture of ancient Greece and Rome — the Classical. Alberti used the first century AD text of Vitruvius, *De Architectura*, as his guide in interpreting Classicism for his contemporaries. Vitruvius's text, which may have been known in the Middle Ages, was rediscovered in about 1415 by the Humanist scholar Poggio Bracciolini. It included technical information as well as artistic principles, but was also riddled with unintelligible passages and sections of dubious authorship. Alberti's treatise set out both to make sense of Vitruvius and to explain the principles that he had derived from ancient precedent.

Alberti began with Vitruvius's essential definition of architecture as the art of building according to *utilitas, firmitas,* and *venustas,* translated in the seventeenth century by the English poet and diplomat, Henry Wotton, as commodity, firmness, and delight.[6] In order to render "delight" or "beauty," according to Alberti's reading of Vitruvius, an architect had to learn the principles of primary, perfect geometric forms, which, as Vitruvius described them, related to the human form itself. Leonardo da Vinci's well-known drawing of a man spread-eagled within a circle and a square (1490) is based on a passage in Vitruvius in which a well-made man with arms and legs

extended is said to fit these perfect geometric forms.[7] To compose a building in accord with these perfect forms, an architect, Vitruvius and Alberti wrote, had to maintain a uniform system of proportion throughout all parts of a building.

The uniform proportional systems were derived from the Orders, the proportional modes developed by the Ancients. The Greeks used three Orders: the Doric, Ionic, and Corinthian; the Romans added the Tuscan. A fifth Order, the Composite, which combined elements of the Ionic and Corinthian, was employed on the third story of the Colosseum in Rome and re-discovered during the sixteenth century. The Orders form the essential grammar of Classicism and made it, argued Alberti, a living language that could be used by architects in fresh expressions, by combining and re-combining its elements "with thought and invention." As Sir John Summerson has written in his essay *The Classical Language of Architecture*: ". . . the great achievement of the Renaissance was not the strict imitation of Roman buildings . . . but the reestablishment of the grammar of antiquity as a universal discipline — *the* discipline, inherited from the remote past of mankind and applicable to all honourable building enterprises whatever."[8]

For Alberti, the Orders were the manifestation of divine reason, as irrefutable as musical harmony, and the pleasure afforded by contemplating Classical architecture was not due to any arbitrary admiration for the antique. Classical architecture expressed a universal ideal of harmony:

". . . I shall define beauty to be a harmony of all the parts, in whatsoever subject it appears, fitted together with such proportion and connection, that nothing could be added, diminished or altered, but for the worse."[9]

Alberti regarded architecture as but one aspect of the body of Humanist knowledge, believing that the "secret argument" of architectural harmony corresponded to an objective ideal of beauty which could be verified by direct human experience — both musical and architectural harmony give pleasure — and by mathematical proofs.

Alberti realized his principles in the 1440s, when he was commissioned by Sigismondo Malatesta, the ruler of Rimini, to rebuild a Medieval church as a monument to himself. For the west front of the Tempio Malatestiano (1446), Alberti adapted the tripartite composition of a Roman triumphal arch to the higher dimensions of the existing medieval church by adding a second story in much the same mould as the first. (This part was never completed, and Alberti's intentions are derived from the fragment that exists and from a medal cast in 1450.) In so doing he made it clear that the monuments of the Classical past were not to be slavishly imitated but were to serve as examples of a living language which was capable of fresh interpretation and invention. Alberti established the fundamental historicizing position of Modern architecture: although the past-ness of the past is indisputable, it represents a coherent tradition which serves as a critical reference point for the work of the present.

The inherent logic and the compelling beauty of its forms has made the Classical tradition the standard of reference in virtually every architectural discussion in the West ever since. From the time of its revival in late fifteenth-century Italy, Classicism has been seen as a grammar and vocabulary susceptible to evolution. The five Orders may have been considered to be divinely inspired, but the individual architect could take it upon himself to decide their exact proportional and decorative attributes and then present his decisions to the world.

Following upon Alberti's writings, other significant architectural treatises were published by the painter and architect Sebastiano Serlio in 1537 and by the architects Giacomo da Vignola and Andrea Palladio in 1562 and 1570 respectively. In these writings, as in architectural practice itself, the Classical language was acknowledged to be capable of development for both practical and aesthetic reasons. The functional requirements of a church or a Renaissance

4 *Palazzo del Tè, Mantua. Giulio Romano, 1526–34.*

theater, for example, entailed modifying the forms, such as temples, inherited from antiquity; so, too, did technological advances. But the received language of Classicism was also challenged on the grounds not only of aesthetics but of "individual talent" — a concept increasingly valued at this time.

Several sixteenth-century architects specifically rejected the ideal of harmonic repose advocated by Alberti. The confident expression of the unity of man and nature of the early Renaissance was superseded in the work of later artists by the portrayal of man and nature in conflict — further testimony to Classicism's capacity for representation. This new trend can clearly be seen in buildings by Giulio Romano (1492 or 1499–1546). Giulio used elements of ancient architecture neglected by Alberti and wreaked havoc with Vitruvian norms. At the Palazzo del Tè (1526–34), in Mantua, Giulio's courtyard façades are essays in insecurity: triglyphs slide out of the entablature into the wall surface below; keystones break through arch and cornice; columns are irregularly spaced; rusticated and smooth surfaces compete with — rather than balance — each other. It is sophisticated and high-minded play, evidence that Giulio felt that he, and any colleagues who might visit the summer palace, knew the Orders well enough to break their rules for effect. A further complication to the possible interpretations was that the effect of the design could be seen as similar to that of a ruin, in which the keystones would actually have slipped; or its rusticated walls might be evidence that the construction was left unfinished, a romantic impression that

emphasized the continuities between antiquity, the present, and the future. Alberti had looked to Classical precedent for the rules of perfect architecture; Giulio, who had the instincts of a scenographer, sought emotional effects.

Michelangelo Buonarroti (1475–1564) was fundamentally bolder than Giulio, and less playful in assuming the prerogatives of an individualistic artist in his exploration of the Classical tradition. His architectural masterpiece, the vestibule of the Laurentian Library (begun 1524) in Florence, takes liberties with the proportions and forms of Classical elements established by Vitruvius and Alberti in order to create a room that is a virtual repudiation of the inherited canon while being irrefutably Classical in spirit. The room itself defies conventional proportions

5 *Laurentian Library, Florence. Michelangelo Buonarroti, begun 1524. Vestibule and staircase.*

3 *Tempio Malatestiano, Rimini. Leon Battista Alberti, 1446.*

by being much higher than it is wide or long. The walls are treated as exterior façades, complete with window surrounds and a giant Order. Inverting the traditional idea of articulation, in which columns stand away from the wall, Michelangelo cut out recesses and pushed the paired columns — still fully articulated — back into the wall. Ignoring the hierarchies and proportions of the Orders, which generally represented some form of structural logic— though not necessarily any structural function — he supported the paired columns on pairs of huge console brackets.

The compositional strategies explored in the Laurentian Library, like those pursued in the Palazzo del Tè, have been described as Mannerist, a convenient enough art-historical term, coined early in this century to describe the approach to Classicism that challenged ideal harmonies. Mannerism stands at one point in the perennial cycle of Classicism; it is a call to aesthetic freedom that follows the call to aesthetic order of a purer, more canonic generation that precedes it.

QUINTESSENTIAL MODERN: PALLADIO

Like Giulio and Michelangelo, Andrea Palladio (1508–80) to some extent shared the Mannerist impulse. Yet at the same time he believed in a strict application of Vitruvian principles. The ambiguity of Palladio's point of view brings into sharp focus the essential Modern position, in which architecture walks a tightrope between the demands of the old and the new: between inherited formal traditions and the inventions of individual architects.

Palladio's treatise, *I Quattro Libri dell'Architettura* ("The Four Books of Architecture", 1570)[10] represents the first fully articulated conception of Modern architecture, seeking as it does a synthesis between tradition and modernity and in the process appropriating the sacred symbols of Ancient architecture for the comparative banalities of contemporary profane life.

Christened Andrea Pietro della Gondola, Palladio was born in 1508 in Padua and worked as a stone-carver in Vicenza, where he was eventually taken into the circle of the pre-eminent intellectual of Vicenza, Count Giangiorgio Trissino, and embarked on a new career as an architect. An amateur architect himself, Trissino had first met della Gondola when the thirty-year-old stonemason came to work on a new

6 *Basilica, Vicenza. Andrea Palladio, 1546–9, completed 1617.*

loggia. Trissino gave him the name Palladio suggesting the wisdom of Pallas Athene, and directed his reading in subjects close to architecture. The result, according to the historian, James S. Ackerman, was not so much a "universal" man as "an early precursor of the modern expert with a penetrating knowledge of the practice and the literature in one discipline, and a casual acquaintance with some others."[11]

Palladio went to Rome in 1541, 1547, and 1554, and travelled relentlessly elsewhere in Italy and in Provence to see Classical architecture firsthand. In 1554, he published a guidebook to the Roman ruins and standing monuments that he had measured and sketched, *Le antichità di Roma* ("The Antiquities of Rome"). In addition to studying the ancients, Palladio — as his designs and sketchbooks show — paid close attention to the architecture of his own century, particularly that of Donato Bramante and Giacomo da Vignola.

The first commission to bring Palladio fame was a renovation. In his design for Vicenza's town hall or Basilica (1546–9, completed in 1617), Palladio masked the form of the existing hundred-year-old Medieval building with grandly Classical façades. For Palladio, the vernacular, asymmetrical form of the existing hall was not architecture; it was merely building. Accordingly, he wrapped it with a two-story loggia which buttressed the original, structurally weakened building while camouflaging its humble origins and endowing it with the civic importance that he believed only Classicism could convey. The first floor of Palladio's loggia employs the Doric Order, the second the Ionic; and the spaces between the giant piers with their attached columns are filled with large arches supported by smaller columns in the arch-lintel combination invented by Bramante and popularized by Serlio but best-known as a

Palladian or Venetian motif. Surmounting the balustrade human figures celebrate the fundamental humanity of the Classical ideal.

Palladio's entire *oeuvre* demonstrates his role in defining Modern Classicism as a response to the increasing complexity of purpose and variety of patronage that are among the hallmarks of post-medieval civilization. Recognizing the enhanced status of the secular realm in relation to the Church, he accorded the highest place in the hierarchy of building types equally to civic programs, like that of the Basilica, and ecclesiastical ones, such as the Church of San Giorgio Maggiore (1565–1610) in Venice, giving them fully articulated Classical façades, often in a giant order, in the "noble" material of stone. At the domestic end of the spectrum, he designed farm buildings in accord with an aesthetic that realized simple Classical shapes — that of a gabled temple, for example — in local "vernacular" materials, such as rubble covered with stucco, with only sparing use of ornament.

In his urban palaces in Vicenza, Palladio's designs demonstrate the belief that private clients have a responsibility to embellish the public realm. For example, the Palazzo Chiericati (1550) and the Palazzo Barbarano (1569–70), both built with open colonnades over a sidewalk, show that whether Palladio misunderstood Roman precedent or, more positively, understood Modern conditions, he had cast aside the tradition of the internalized, anonymous Roman house to make each residence a celebration of the owner's personal greatness on the public stage of the street.

Palladio's integration of grand public gestures with private programs reached its apogee in his country villas. Unlike his monumental urban buildings, these country houses were usually constructed of relatively modest vernacular materials: brick, covered in stucco. Even the columns, which in the grand buildings of antiquity had been carved from blocks of stone, were made of brick. Having a professional's knowledge of the time and cost entailed in stone-carving, Palladio reserved it for the refined details. His earliest country house, the Villa Godi at Loneto (1537), designed before Palladio had been to Rome, used the principles of Classical composition but almost none of the details, and the house's plain cubic mass is opened up only by a slightly recessed triple-arched entrance. After his first visit to Rome in 1541, however, Palladio decided to give the country house the representational grandeur of a temple or semi-public palace by applying a temple front to the villas that he designed. He was one of the first architects to express a very Modern confidence in the seemingly unlimited applicability of Classical form. The Villa Barbaro (1557–8), at Maser, was a new type of building, a house-temple melding vernacular building techniques with a full-blown Classical vocabulary of forms. Palladio's *apologia* for this practice shows his pragmatically-reasoned approach to design:

In all the buildings which I have made in the country, and also in some of those in towns, I have always placed the pediments before, where the principal gates are; because they make the principal entry to the house more observable, and contribute very much to the magnificence and nobleness of the buildings. This gives the forepart a great advantage over the others, and therefore it must be made higher; besides that it is much properer to put there the arms of the owner, which are commonly placed in the middle of them. The ancients employed them also in their works, as it is to be seen in the old remains of temples and other public buildings; from which it is probable, as I have observed in the preface to my first book, that they borrowed the contrivance and proportions of private houses.[12]

While Palladio's innovation would profoundly affect the future, it was probably, as the historian Peter Murray points out, based on a mistake: "[Palladio's] knowledge of temples and public buildings led him to believe, quite erroneously, that the ancients 'very probably took the idea and the reason [of a portico] from private buildings; that is, from houses,' and he therefore designed all his villas with an impressive entrance portico."[13]

In the interiors of his houses Palladio showed an understanding of the expressive limitations of architecture, and, like the Romans of the Imperial Age, he used allusion and illusion to transform his often boxlike rooms. The most notable example of this is the Villa Barbaro, where the painter Paolo Veronese (1528–88) was commissioned to break open the box with Arcadian landscapes, portraits, and allegories and scenes from mythology, all framed by a painted architecture of Classical columns and entablatures.

The contrast between the luxury of Veronese's murals inside the villa and the straightforward appearance of the wings flanking it makes Palladio's synthesis of Classical splendor and the everyday even more impressive. The temple front is a representation of grandiloquent intention, a public statement about the Barbaro family, their house, and the land. Yet the two wings, given over to the homely purposes of a working farm, served as the stables and storehouses. They take the villa further toward the public realm, extending it far enough so that the drive it faces becomes a street. The villa and its dependencies can be interpreted as a town center: the open arcades recall the sidewalk loggia of the palaces in Vicenza or the stoa of a Classical agora, and face onto a "piazza." The "town" also includes a second monumental Classical building, the Tempietto Church (1580) to the south-east.

After Palladio, every Modern architect, confronted with even the most humble task, was perforce obliged not only to design the new building in relation to its purpose and physical context, but also to position it in relation to a hierarchy of building types and to choose the correct elements of expression and construction materials in order that its character be appropriate to its social role. Equally important, Palladio raised the aesthetic stakes, demanding by his

8 *Villa Barbaro, Maser. Andrea Palladio, 1557–8. Interior.*

example that the realities of everyday life be expressed in terms of the highest Classical ideals.

CLAUDE PERRAULT AND THE TRADITION OF REFORM

In 1664 the Roman architect Gianlorenzo Bernini (1598–1680) was invited by Louis XIV to design a new wing for the Louvre. After completing two schemes in Rome, Bernini travelled to Paris, where he completed a third scheme, for which the foundation stone was laid three days before he returned to Italy in the autumn of 1666. But Bernini's design pleased neither the King nor his ministers; and after a year's delay it was rejected, ostensibly on practical grounds, by Jean-Baptiste Colbert, chief minister to the king and Superintendent of Buildings, who complained that Bernini had provided for ballrooms but no better lodging for the king. In reality, the French objected to the scheme because they found it — and its designer — unsympathetic to the existing palace buildings and to French taste in general.

Accordingly, in 1667 the king set up an all-French council to complete a new design for the Louvre. The council consisted of his First Architect, Louis Le Vau (1612–70), his First Painter, Charles Lebrun (1619–90), and Claude Perrault (1613–88), a doctor, scientist, and amateur architect. Credit for the final design, completed seven years later, is variously attributed to the three members of the committee and their assistants, but Claude Perrault's claim is generally given the most weight.[14]

7 *Villa Barbaro, Maser. Andrea Palladio, 1557–8.*

The east front of the Louvre is remarkable for its austerity and its understatement — its repetitious, almost antique peristyle, only mildly emphasized center, and cubic corner pavilions. Set against the exuberantly personal interpretations of the Classical by Baroque architects such as Bernini and Francesco Borromini (1599–1667), the new Louvre was seen by many as a reform, a return to first principles. It was, like Brunelleschi's Foundling Hospital, a new beginning, a purification, an exemplar of Classicism as the true and the simple and the universal. It was also, and perhaps most significantly, a demonstration not only that the Classical tradition could extend beyond the Italian peninsula but also that it was not inherently a product of Italian culture. In short a French building, for example, designed by a French architect could be more purely or strictly Classical than one designed by an Italian and yet remain quintessentially French. The Classical tradition belonged to no one nation; although not a vernacular architecture, it could take on the characteristics of particular places, through an admixture with local building vernaculars, as in the case of Palladio's villas, or through the sheer imposition of intellect and will, as in the case of Perrault's design for the Louvre.

For the French, the Classicism of seventeenth-century Italy was decadent. In his writings, Perrault, whose archeological knowledge undoubtedly inspired the "correct" aspect of the Louvre's otherwise remarkably unprecedented screen of coupled Corinthian columns, advocated a return to the Ancients in order to create an at once purer and more appropriate — that is a more Modern — Classical architecture. In 1673, the year before the east front of the Louvre was completed, Perrault published his French translation of Vitruvius's ten books, accompanied by illustrations of his own reconstructions of ancient edifices, as well as designs for new buildings. French architects could now return to Classical precedent without the intervention of Alberti or his Italian successors, and a decade later they could also develop the five Orders in accord with French taste, using Perrault's *Ordonnance des cinq espèces de colonnes selon la méthode des anciens* ("A Treatise of the Five Orders of Columns in Architecture", 1683).[15]

Perrault's return to the primary sources of Classical architecture — Vitruvius's text and ancient Roman examples — was a reform rather than a revolution. Like Vitruvius, who wanted to reform what he considered illiterate Roman variations on Greek models, and Palladio, who wanted in part to return more closely to the architecture of the Romans, Perrault was bent on reforming Classical architecture within the context of an ongoing tradition. He did not subscribe to Alberti's belief that the Orders were the expression of perfect harmony in accord with natural, God-given laws. Alberti was a man of the Renaissance, intent on endowing architecture with transcendental, religious values; Perrault belonged to the Enlightenment and, like generations of architects after him, sought to invest architecture with the intellectual rigor of a science. Perrault tried to discipline the five Orders to one overall modular system. At the same time, he had some respect for the Gothic style, admiring its structural articulation. Above all, he believed that architecture should be literal rather than representational; for example, columns, which are, or can be, loadbearing, were preferable in his view to pilasters, which are merely decorative. This approach has come to be described somewhat misleadingly as "rational," as free of artifice as possible, literal rather than scenographic, yet unlike many of his rationalist successors, Perrault had a balanced view of architecture's relationship to art and science, demonstrated by his theory of positive and arbitrary beauty. Positive beauty had the objectivity of everyday reason: it depended on good materials, precise execution, size, and symmetry. Arbitrary beauty, however, had the subjectivity of art and custom and depended on proportional systems and decorative schemes. For Perrault, custom was reason enough to continue to use the proportional systems and decorative elements of the five Orders, and an architect's real talent lay in his manipulation of them in response to circumstantial realities.

9 *Louvre, Paris. Claude Perrault, begun 1667. East front.*

THE SEARCH FOR ORIGINS

The Ancient World and the Primitive Hut

Architects of the eighteenth century, after Perrault, searched for a new style through a precise reappraisal of antiquity. The motivation of many was not simply to obey the Ancients but to obey the principles on which their work had been based. By the mid-eighteenth century Classical architecture had been established as the accepted mode of building in Europe. That is to say, Classical architecture was Modern architecture. As we have seen, it was essentially Roman in derivation, although, through Vitruvius, some knowledge of the architecture of Etruria and Greece was current; but most importantly, the accumulated experience of over 300 years of post-medieval culture constituted an almost independent tradition. A number of new trends now began to expand and deepen the interpretations of Modern Classicism. On the one hand, travel to Rome became relatively commonplace for English and French architects; but more significantly some went on to southern Italy, where remains of Greek colonial building remained, and even to Greece itself.

As a result of this increased knowledge, modern Europeans began to see the Classicism of the Ancients not as an Italian or even a Roman phenomenon but as a fundamental characteristic of Mediterranean culture, extending backward in time and outward in geography to encompass the Greeks, the Etruscans, and even the Egyptians. Above all others, the Greek achievement was seen as paramount. In particular, it was considered a purer form of Classicism (a judgment made in ignorance of the fact that the blazing white Pentelic marble of the Parthenon had originally been painted).

This increased knowledge of the origins of Classicism paralleled another trend: a growing awareness of the need to align architecture with the increasing materialistic nationalism that went with the public works programs (canals, bridges etc.) and soon thereafter, industrialized manufacture. All of these factors combined to push Modern Classicism toward yet another set of reforms, perhaps as profound and far-reaching as those that marked the break with Medievalism in the fifteenth century.

This movement of the late eighteenth century, known as Neo-Classicism, was not a break with the Classical tradition, but an attempt to peel away the layers of Modern reinterpretations of Classicism in order to get to its essence. Neo-Classicism embodied a search for origins in the Ancient civilizations of the Mediterranean world, and even further back, to Biblical times.

The most eloquent theorist of Neo-Classicism in architecture was Abbé Marc-Antoine Laugier (1713–69), an outspoken Jesuit priest and distinguished man of letters, who determined to return architecture to its true Classical roots. In his *Essai sur l'Architecture* ("Essay on Architecture," 1753; second edition 1755)[16] Laugier presented what he considered a rational proof of the natural origins of Classical architecture. Much of the essay drew heavily upon the writings of an earlier French architectural theorist, Jean-Louis de Cordemoy (1631–1713), who, like Perrault, had advocated freeing Classical architecture from Baroque excesses.[17] But Laugier added his own compellingly succinct principles to Cordemoy's, and he also provided the visual image that perfectly expressed the mixed ideals of his era: the "primitive hut." In this hypotheti-

cal precursor of the Greek temple, living trees served as free-standing columns, boughs laid across the trees were beams, and the pediment of a pitched roof of logs rose above.

Laugier's hut first appeared as the frontispiece to the second edition of his *Essai*. Asserting that the fundamentals of architecture were all in the illustration of the hut, he further argued that Modern architecture should also be based on these same simple structural forms, or should at least express this essential construct as closely as possible.

An ideal architecture, then, would be all columns and beams — that is, trabeated — and not based on walls. Practical considerations forced Laugier to admit the necessity of walls — but only if these were handled in the barest possible way; decorative elements such as pilasters, pedestals, broken entablatures, and pediments (unless directly expressing a roof) were to be cleansed from the vocabulary of architecture. Even the Orders were open to criticism and capable of improvement, both the Tuscan and the Composite were rejected and in some projects the three canonic Orders themselves might be thrown out altogether and replaced by a compositional method based solely on modular grids. Thus, for Laugier, Classical architecture, released from the bondage of accrued tradition in the Modern as well as the Antique age, and cleansed of the impurities and frivolities of artistic invention, could be as it was in the beginning, natural and rational — essential.

After wrecking the edifice of over 300 years of architectural history — but significantly not that of the Classical tradition itself — Laugier outlined the major directions of a reformed architecture that would, first, return to original principles by literally re-creating the earliest examples of Classical architecture, many recently uncovered by archeology; second, employ the principles of Classicism but not necessarily the forms of Ancient architecture, thereby opening the door to stylistic eclecticism; and third, would explore the invention of a wholly Modern style, not based on any historical precedent, provided that the style adhered to the essential elements of the primitive hut.

Although intended to liberate architecture from the arbitrary and return it to the essential, Laugier's theory was suffused with the intoxicating influence of early Romanticism. With its overtones of a primitive golden era, the hut is immediately recognizable as the natural home of Jean-Jacques Rousseau's "Noble Savage." Of

10 *Frontispiece*, Essai sur l'Architecture. *Abbé Marc-Antoine Laugier, second edition, 1755.*

course, as anthropology and archeology have shown, both of these concepts are illusory.

While it surely did not resemble the pre-monumental arch of Ancient Greece Laugier's hut does look like a Greek temple, returned to its presumed origins in the wooden architecture of the pre-Classical era. Taking his cue from Vitruvius's explanation of the Doric Order as a translation of wooden structure into stone, Laugier worked backward from an ideal Classical form. Vitruvius had declared the superiority of Greek architecture; Laugier did the same: "Architecture is only under moderate obligation to the Romans, and . . . it owes everything that is valuable and solid to the Greeks alone."[18] And whereas the Renaissance had only Vitruvius's word on Greek architecture, the eighteenth century had rich new knowledge of Greek, and Roman, precedent. It should be noted, however, that for most Neo-Classical designers, the vaunted superiority of Greek art did not preclude the use of Roman models. The antiquities of Rome were assessed anew; the ancient monuments of Greece, for the first time.

The libraries of Europe now possessed a wealth of archeologists, architects, and illustrators. Among these was Julien-David Le Roy (1724–1803), a young French architect who succeeded in publishing the first illustrations of Classical Greek buildings in 1754 in *Ruines des plus beaux Monuments de la Grèce*. Two Englishmen, James Stuart (1713–88) and Nicholas Revett (c. 1721–1804) undertook a much more rigorous examination of Greek architecture, spending from 1751 to 1755 in Athens. Their publishing schedule was painfully slow, however, the first volume of *The Antiquities of Athens* only coming out in 1762. The monuments of Hellenic and Hellenistic Greece were not the only new source of inspiration. In a celebrated example, Robert Adam, a young Scottish architect, led an expedition that resulted in the publication of *Ruins of the Palace of the Emperor Diocletian at Spalato in Dalmatia* in 1764.

A third major influence on Neo-Classical design, in addition to Laugier's call for structural honesty and the ever-richer catalogue of available forms collected by archeology, was in the grandiose visions of the architect-illustrator Giambattista Piranesi (1720–78), whose drawings and engravings introduced the possibility of an architecture unbound by constraints of economics or cultural will, and that offered a heroic view of Roman Classicism. Spurred by patriotic indignation at the spate of pro-Greek and anti-Roman architectural treatises in the mid-eighteenth century, Piranesi published a volume of etchings entitled *Della Magnificenza ed Architettura de Romani* ("On the Magnificence and Architecture of the Romans," 1761), loaded with evidence of Rome's architectural preeminence. In a later work, *Parere su l'Architettura* ("Thoughts on Architecture," 1765), he combined his archeological knowledge with a fantastic imagination, devising sections and elevations for near-impossible buildings incorporating archeological fragments. Piranesi argued that the architect-artist should design according to his genius, not within the "natural" and "rational" confines of Laugier's system, and with a consciousness of the widest range of architectural precedent. In short, the architect was to become a genius-archeologist.

Two French architects, Etienne-Louis Boullée (1728–99) and Claude-Nicolas Ledoux (1736–1806) proposed a new, elemental architecture derived from both the rationalism of Laugier and the romanticist sublime. Whereas Boullée

was most active as a teacher, Ledoux began as a busy practitioner with a government career during the last years of the *ancien régime*; but both would finish their careers by undertaking visionary designs for vast buildings and utopian cities. The underlying principles behind these extraordinary visions were born in the age of Louis XVI, yet they only evolved fully after the shock of the French Revolution of 1789. They represent the final working-out of the archeological, eclectic, and essential or "un-Ordered" possibilities for architecture made available by Laugier's argument, and made socially "relevant" by the political climate of the time.

Boullée had been appointed an official architect for the French government in the late 1770s. In 1782, however, he resigned his position in order to evolve a more personal and essential concept of architecture, in which primary architectural forms were as fundamental as the physical laws of the universe outlined by Newton. The shape of a sphere, the form Boullée chose for his project of a cenotaph to Newton (1784), was, in his view, the most perfect: "[Of all bodies] it offers the largest surface to the eye, and this lends it majesty. It has the simplest form: beauty that comes from its uninterrupted surface; and joined to all these qualities that of grace, because the outline of this body is as soft and as flowing as it is possible to imagine."[19] Boullée also envisioned colossal pyramids and truncated cones, all fulfilling his passion for an essential architecture of unmodulated mass. These imaginary buildings were designed according to the reductive "architecture of shadows" which Boullée felt he had invented, a theory in which he declared himself anti-Vitruvian: "Shall I, like Vitruvius, define architecture as the art of building? No, for this would be to confuse causes and effects."[20] For Boullée, the effects were the crucial issue, and "the effects [of architecture] are caused by light."[21]

Equally adventurous and, in his later career, equally visionary, Claude-Nicolas Ledoux expressed his own ideas of essentialized forms in his *barrières* (tollhouses) ringing Paris. Constructed on the eve of the French Revolution, between 1785 and 1789, they showed a brilliant capacity to create monumental mass by combining primary architectural shapes. A striking example is the Barrière de la Villette, in which a cylinder is placed four-square on a rectangular base. Ledoux surpassed the boldness of this compositional strategy in the almost perverse means he employed in articulating the design, such as the square columns of the portico. In

11 *Proposal for Newton's Cenotaph. Etienne-Louis Boullée, 1784. Cross-section.*

Ledoux's built work one senses a deliberate attempt to get Classical architecture wrong. For example, in the Barrière d'Enfer, he carried the sixteenth-century detail of a banded column to an extreme; the standard tripartite arched entryway has columns whose great horizontal blocks of stone, which actually bind the end pairs, completely drain the composition of verticality.

Ledoux's essentialist view of architecture was most clearly expressed in his designs for the imaginary city of Chaux, which grew out of the new saltworks in Arc-et-Senans on which he had worked from 1773 to 1779. Ledoux imagined that the saltworks, which were partially realized, would form the center of an ideal, circular city designed for a disciplined version of the good life. The plan was published in 1804 as part of his *L'Architecture Considérée sous le Rapport de l'Art, des Moeurs et de la Législation* ("Architecture Considered in Respect of Art, Morals, and Law"). The geometric order of Chaux was meant to embody a matching social organization, with schools, temples, marketplaces, workplaces and brothels logically disposed.

Ledoux probably completed most of the designs, and definitely completed the text of

12 *Barrière de la Villette, Paris. Claude-Nicolas Ledoux, 1784–7.*

L'Architecture Considerée, in the late 1790s, when he built nothing. During the Terror, he had been imprisoned as an architect and bureaucrat of the *ancien régime*: it is perhaps not surprising that he devoted himself to designing an ideal, ordered society after his experience.

The most revolutionary designs for Chaux went beyond the *barrières* in their independence from the Orders. Employing basic shapes for the various buildings, Ledoux at once accepts Laugier's interdiction on ornamental architecture, and goes beyond it by matching the shape of his buildings to their purpose or — in the case of dwellings — to the *métier* of the inhabitants, thereby introducing a kind of psychological functionalism. For the charcoal burners, for example, he proposed a dome supported by tree trunks; for the water authority, a gigantic cylinder like a water pipe, a sphere for a shepherd. Like the visionary drawings and text of Boullée, the designs exhibit a remarkable faith in the power of architectural forms to communicate on their own without the traditional narrative elements of applied decoration, painting and sculpture. In so doing, Ledoux sought to replace the aristocratic conventions of Classical taste with something more direct and comprehensible. In Ledoux's opinion architecture since the Renaissance had failed to communicate to most of its viewers. He wrote: "The palaces that are reflected in the limpid waters of the Brenta; the palaces respected by the vexing seasons; these masses corrected by the impassive scruple of knowledge; the details saved from the barbarian deluge, resuscitated for the instruction of happy ages: What have they produced for the numerous class? Nothing."[22]

CLASSICISM AND THE SEARCH FOR MEANING IN A SECULAR MASS SOCIETY

Ledoux posed the problem that would plague nineteenth-century architects: how to create architecture with meaning for a society in which the traditional sources of patronage — Church, monarchy, and aristocracy — were either gone or at least in decline, and in which traditional forms of building were being challenged. His answer, however, placed him at the end of the first stage of Modern architecture. Ledoux's vision was one of the last of many efforts made since the Renaissance to synthesize the vernacular and Classical models into an essential archi-

tecture that would convey the sense of the Classical past without slavishly depending upon its forms; it came just as a new paradigm, that of mass production, of process, began to emerge to confuse the scene further. Perhaps more importantly, for those who would see Ledoux as a proto-twentieth-century figure, he misapprehended the nature of what he called the "numerous class," imagining them as the citizens of a utopian, authoritarian, probably socialist society. Instead, the "numerous class" which was to determine the course of architecture in the nineteenth century consisted of members of the burgeoning middle class in countries that were liberal and capitalist.

The first answers to the question of how to create meaningful architecture in an age of mass society came not in France but in the United States. America was an unprecedented phenomenon, a new place, beyond the old geographical boundaries of the Western Humanist tradition, yet inextricably part of that tradition, as much by a conscious act of will as by inheritance. In America, a new society was inventing itself on a sparsely populated continent whose only history — at least in the eyes of European settlers — appeared to be natural rather than human. Central to that story of America's self-invention is the figure of Thomas Jefferson (1743–1826), whose conception of architecture was in exact accord with the ideals he helped to incorporate in the Constitution. In America, as Jefferson saw it, the values of the Ancient Classical world would be re-established free of their Modern European corruptions.

As a man of the Enlightenment, trained in

law, but also provided with the standard education of an eighteenth-century English gentleman in philosophy, history, the arts, and languages, Jefferson had a profound admiration for Classical civilization — in particular for the sober republic of pre-Augustan Rome. Throughout his political career, he sought to provide the laws and leadership that would engender a society of virtuous, democratic citizen-farmers.

While working to imbue the new republic with the spirit of ancient Rome, Jefferson also strove, as an architect, to give that spirit tangible form. He began with his own house, which was to be built on the hilltop of his 6,000-acre (2,430-hectare) estate near the frontier town of Charlottesville, Virginia, in the foothills of the Appalachians. In his first design (begun in 1767) the influence of Palladio, as interpreted by the English architects of Lord Burlington's (1694–1753) circle, is paramount.[23] Conventional though the design was compared to the great work of Jefferson's maturity, it nonetheless hinted at the liveliness of its architect's imagination. Indeed, Jefferson's designs for the first Monticello stretched the fashionable Palladianism of the day to its limits. Its proportions were extraordinarily refined; the interlocking polygonal rooms of its plan more interesting and varied than the boxlike rooms characteristic of Georgian houses; the details more scholarly than in the typical Virginia plantation house. Yet the first Monticello was to seem completely provincial to Jefferson once he had experienced the treasures of France, where he served as American Minister Plenipotentiary between

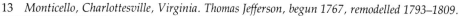
13 *Monticello, Charlottesville, Virginia. Thomas Jefferson, begun 1767, remodelled 1793–1809.*

1784 and 1789. In France Jefferson was able to study masterworks of Western architecture first-hand and share ideas with the great architects of his time.

Like most architect-theorists before him, Jefferson wanted to go back to first principles and begin anew, to create a pure Classicism untrammeled by the necessarily compromised work of its post-medieval revival. His first public architectural project was conceived as an almost literal recycling of a Roman precedent. For the Virginia State Capitol in Richmond (1785–97), he chose as his model a first-century AD Roman temple in Nîmes, the so-called Maison Carrée, believed to be the best-preserved example of Ancient architecture. By giving the new legislative building the form of a Classical temple (albeit of Imperial, not Republican, vintage), Jefferson not only helped to establish Classicism as the architectural form for the new Republic but also implicitly elevated democratic statecraft to the status of religion.

At the same time, Jefferson had also augmented and to a considerable extent reconstructed the fundamental meaning of the Modern Classical ideal, transforming the Renaissance conception of Classicism as a humanistic expression of spiritual values into an equally humanistic expression of a purely secular, democratic society. Thus it can be said that with Jefferson Modern architecture, and with it Modern Classicism, entered a second phase.

Jefferson's sojourn in Europe stimulated his decision to reconstruct Monticello (1793–1809). Whereas the first Monticello was the work of a devoted student of Palladio, the second version would be that of a colleague across time — one

14 *Maison Carrée, Nîmes. First century AD.*

15 *University of Virginia, Charlottesville. Thomas Jefferson, 1817–26. Library.*

who shared Palladio's indebtedness to Roman models. With increased self-confidence, Jefferson became a rather eclectic designer, whose synthesis of conventional elements was frequently inspired if not entirely resolved. In this sense his was the model not only for American Classical architecture but also for the Modern Classicism of the nineteenth and twentieth centuries. For it is not in the specific elements of Jefferson's Monticello, or of his University of Virginia campus (1817–26), that we look for originality; rather, it is in the way those elements were put together. As a Modern Classicist, Jefferson would not invent a new language, but he would struggle to say new things.

Jefferson's reconfiguration of Monticello took the form of a Classical temple surmounted by a noble if somewhat incongruous dome, from which two long parallel wings project to embrace a U-shaped courtyard. Like Palladio's Villa Barbaro, Monticello's Classicism is rendered in the local dialect. Palladio used red tile roofs and stucco-covered brick walls; Jefferson covered his roof in shingles, sheet iron and tin and built his walls of red brick trimmed with white-painted wood.

The campus of the University of Virginia is the most eloquent demonstration of Jefferson's belief in Classical architecture as *the* architectural language of the new society. Here he employed the Classical idiom to create a new form of University complex, which he called an "academical village." Jefferson saw this as a great improvement over the College of William and Mary in Williamsburg (1695–8), which he had attended. The College was only an element within the larger composition of the town, while the University could be approached as an ideal village complete within itself. At the head of the

university's village green, the Lawn, Jefferson placed a rotunda — a half-scale adaptation of the Pantheon in Rome — built to house the university's library. The monumental scale of the Rotunda and its central, dominant position announced the single-minded intent and focus of the enterprise with then-revolutionary clarity. The Rotunda was devoted not to the worship of the gods or even to a monotheistic religion but, rather, to the common purpose of the village — learning. Through grandly scaled features, such as its Corinthian columns (realized in the affordable and available materials, cast iron and wood, assembled and whitewashed to resemble marble; its form, derived from the pure geometric figure of a sphere; and its evocation of a temple, the Rotunda implicitly stated that secular learning, rather than religion, was the essence of the university. And, in a further break with the cloister-like tradition of English college planning and a reaffirmation of its founder's faith in the future of the new nation, the Lawn was not closed in as a quadrangle; from the Rotunda, across the Lawn, a view beyond lay open to the continental empire that Jefferson believed to be America's destiny.

The architecture of the entire academical village was meant as a model for the instruction of the students in the Classical tradition. Jefferson managed to combine the expressive, communicative ideal of Ledoux's Chaux with a fairly strict adherence to Classical language. As he wrote to Benjamin Latrobe (1764–1820), the English-trained architect who advised him in the design of the buildings, the faculty houses in particular were meant to be "models of taste and correct architecture — and of a variety of appearance, no two alike, so as to serve as specimens of orders for the architectural lectures."[24] The specimens, however, in the tradition of Palladio, Perrault, and most Neo-Classical architects, were designed with "thought and invention," rather than in strict conformity to Vitruvian rules. Jefferson's liberal approach to Classicism is evident not only in the overall conception — two rows of house-temple classrooms with individual two-story porticoes establishing a giant Order linked by a continuous one-story colonnade — but also in his treatment of the individual buildings. The domed apsidal entry of Pavilion IX, for example, is modelled on a Neo-Classical, rather than an Ancient precedent, Ledoux's Hôtel Guimard (1770–74) in Paris, making it perfectly clear that Jefferson saw Classicism as an evolving language.

To Jefferson, the new democratic programs, such as free, state-run universities, enhanced the expressive possibilities of Classical architecture. The English architect John Soane (1753–1837) and the German architect Karl Friedrich Schinkel (1781–1841) perceived similar opportunities for a Modern Classical language in their industrializing, increasingly middle-class (if still relatively undemocratic) societies.

John Soane took Classicism far further toward a highly personal formal language than did Jefferson. Whereas Jefferson was an amateur, whose fundamental preoccupation was politics, Soane was a professional architect. Early in his career he spent three years (1778–80) in Italy as a Travelling Student, sponsored by the Royal Academy; but even before going to Italy, he had mastered the elements of the Classical language, as demonstrated in his design for a Triumphal Bridge (1776), which won the Royal Academy's Gold Medal. When he returned to England after his Italian sojourn, Soane executed a number of modest Palladian villas. Then in 1788 he was appointed surveyor to the Bank of England, a position he retained for forty-five years, during which time he created a remarkable series of rooms which inventively transformed their Greek and Roman sources into an entirely new, simplified, distinctive version of the Classical language. The Bank Stock Office (1792–3) included a sidelit circular lantern and replaced the detailed articulation of pilaster and entablature with grooved strips and simplified ornament. Soane later added the Consols Office (1798–9), in which, again, the combination of grooved patterns replacing pilasters and schematic ornament showed Soane's readiness to dispense with full-blown Classical Orders.

In its design, the Bank of England reflects a

16 *Bank of England, London. Sir John Soane, 1788–1833, Consols Office, 1798–9.*

vision much different from Ledoux's ideal city of Chaux or Jefferson's University of Virginia. Whereas Ledoux and Jefferson offer variety within a highly-disciplined geometric whole, the overall plan of the Bank of England, as Soane developed it over nearly half a century, reflects an empirical, experiential sense of planning, thoroughly at odds with the symmetrical rigors of the French tradition, and suggests that utopian order is neither possible nor desirable. Within the confines of the Bank's exterior wall,

17 *Bank of England, London. Sir John Soane, 1788–1833. Plan.*

Soane devised a great complex of buildings — offices, courtyards, and banking halls. Soane's Bank (now demolished) was more inherently Roman than anything the Modern world had yet seen. It was like the plan of a city, Imperial Rome itself, miniaturized, or like an elaborate villa such as the one the Emperor Hadrian had built in the second century AD. The bank design was full of picturesque effects, such as grand entrances that led to minor corridors and Greek Doric entrance vestibules incongruously barrel-vaulted.

Soane achieved the fullest expression of his intensely personal Classicism in the house he built for his own use at 12–14 Lincoln's Inn Fields in London (1792–1824), which he bequeathed to the British people as a museum. An advertisement both for architecture and for Soane himself as an architect, the house is permeated with tradition and individual talent. Its relationship to the Georgian buildings elsewhere in the square is much like its relationship to the Classical tradition as a whole. In the façade Soane approaches the Classical tradition in three ways. First, Classical elements are reproduced in a mechanical way, as in the balustrades on the *piano nobile*. Second, fragments of Classical architecture (and a few pieces of the Gothic) are set out almost as icons on the façade: the column capitals, and, most poignantly, the caryatid figures which visually support the cornices of the adjoining buildings. Thus, an explicitly human quality is introduced

18 *Sir John Soane's Museum, London. Sir John Soane, 1792–1824. Breakfast room, 1812.*

into the architecture, bringing the viewer naturally into the argument of the building. The incised mouldings and the more austere composition of the façade on the third-floor level exemplify Soane's third approach to the Classical language: a free interpretation of its grammar and vocabulary, much as he had done at the Bank of England. Soane looks to the past to take us into the future within the context of a perennially meaningful set of forms.

In the interior, Soane handled Classical forms with even greater vigor. Here a modest townhouse expands to become a Classical villa by means of deft proportions and lighting. Perhaps no effect is more successful than the dome room in the back of the house, where Soane showed his special capacity to re-invent Classical forms with the help of new technology. One can imagine Soane drawing up the dome, and thinking, "What would the architect of the Pantheon have given to be able to have done the dome in glass and the oculus as a big rosette hung as though from the sky?" Here can be seen the new possibilities of architecture in the nineteenth century — revolutionary relationships between solid and void, hand-made and machine-made; and yet the continuity of the form, based on Roman precedent, makes the change all the more vivid, all the more explicit. This solid rosette floating in glass caused all the domes in history suddenly to be considered in a new way. By bringing so much together in one place, by making us acutely aware of the possibilities of architecture and comprehending the "pastness" of the Classical tradition in the use of antique fragments, obviously from the past, set like pieces in a museum, at the same time

19   *Sir John Soane's Museum, London. Sir John Soane, 1792–1824. Cross-section.*

20   *Park Crescent, London. John Nash, designed 1811.*

demonstrating its "presentness" by reinterpreting Classical forms and rendering them in new materials, Soane reveals its unbroken, endlessly self-renewing character.

Soane's contemporary John Nash (1752–1835) had the opportunity to build on an urban scale, in a series of projects around Regent's Park in London. First designed in 1811, and largely completed in the decade after the defeat of Napoleon (1815–25), Nash's scheme for 500 acres (203 hectares) placed private villas and townhouses around a picturesquely landscaped park and connected the new development to the West End with a new street, Regent Street, running north-south. The result was an impressive synthesis of the vernacular and the monumental Classical. Townhouses along the park were united behind the façade of a Classical palace — as in Cumberland Terrace (1825) behind whose central Ionic temple front stood residences no more luxurious than those of the flanking, less imposing wings. By contrast, in Park Village West the streets were curved to invoke the *ad hoc* planning of country roads and the houses were highly individual versions of Italian villas.

At about the time Nash's scheme was nearing completion in 1826, Karl Friedrich Schinkel (1781–1841), the most prominent German architect of the time, travelled to England to see the latest developments in technology and design. Schinkel had been the supervisor and designer of all royal, civic, and religious buildings in Prussia since 1810, and following the final defeat of Napoleon in 1815, had been busy with commissions for the state. Like Jefferson's University of Virginia, Schinkel's designs were exemplars of the new building types required by the increasingly culture-conscious middle class. Public libraries and museums, as well as

theaters and concert halls were to be important projects in monarchies as well as democracies.

Before going to England, Schinkel had completed his first major public building, the National Theater (*Schauspielhaus*, 1819–23). The increasingly secular values of the early nineteenth century were boldly articulated by the theater's siting: its Ionic portico, at the head of a grand staircase (high above the actual entrance), dominated a square already flanked by two Corinthian temple-fronted eighteenth-century churches.

Schinkel was busy with the construction of his second major public building, Berlin's Altes Museum (1823–30), when he visited England. There, he examined the progress on Robert Smirke's British Museum (1823–47), whose east range, housing the King's Library, was near completion. In designing the 300 foot- (90 meter) long, two-story-high main room, Smirke used cast-iron structural elements but clothed them in Classical masonry. Schinkel admired the museum and its technology, but in his later designs he went further than Smirke, re-creating for many of the details of his museum the elements of typically lithic Classical architecture in cast iron.

Set across from the royal palace on the Lustgarten, and adjacent to the city's Lutheran cathedral, the Altes Museum had a higher place than the *Schauspielhaus* in the city's hierarchy of sites. Schinkel ranked eighteen immense Ionic columns *in antis*, to recreate the Stoa Poikile of Hellenic Athens. At the center of this colonnade a great loggia contains a double-winged staircase leading to the second floor. Ascending the staircase, the visitor looks out at the Lustgarten and royal palace through the colossal columns. The arrangement was an ennobling setting for a

21   *Altes Museum, Berlin. Karl Friedrich Schinkel, 1823–30. Drawing.*

22 *Schloss Charlottenhof, Potsdam. Karl Friedrich Schinkel, 1826. View from the east.*

popular ritual of the new middle class — museum-going.

In the Altes Museum, Schinkel used iron for only a few decorative elements, such as railings, but in several later projects he employed iron for a wide range of structural purposes as well. In the Classicizing modernizations of Baroque palaces for Prince Karl (1827) and Prince Albrecht (1829), Schinkel realized Classical staircases in cast iron.

Schinkel's admiration for Classicism was not absolute. He was equally at ease with Gothic, as is evident in the Kreuzberg War Memorial (1821) in Berlin, where he recreated Gothic tracery in cast iron, and in his use of various vernacular modes, which he reserved for humbler projects such as the wooden Swiss Cottage (1825) on Berlin's Pfaueninsel.

In many of his greatest buildings, Schinkel freely combined Classical and vernacular elements with contemporary technology to create Modern buildings that resonated with historical

23 *Prince Albrecht Palais, Berlin. Karl Friedrich Schinkel, 1829. Cast-iron staircase.*

nuances. In his design for Schloss Charlottenhof, at the edge of the park of Sanssouci in Potsdam (1826), Schinkel transformed an existing building into an antique villa whose prominent feature was a Doric temple front overlooking a terrace bound by a pergola and enlivened by basins and fountains. The picturesque hillocks and winding paths lay beyond, as did the steam pressure machine that operated the fountains. The boiler was hidden, but the chimney, directly on an axis with the villa's portico, was visible and, in Schinkel's vision, worthy of being treated as architecture. He described the chimney as "in the form of a candelabrum which decorates the landscape."[25] For Schinkel, the art of architecture, Classical in its principles of symmetry, order and proportion, could accommodate the asymmetry and decorative variety of the vernacular and the new materials of the Industrial Revolution. Utility was only the beginning of architectural design; "the fine arts" were its end.

FORM AND FUNCTION

While Soane and Schinkel reveled in the rich possibilities and unprecedented technological and stylistic freedom of architecture in the nineteenth century, many others had a narrower vision. Jean-Nicolas-Louis Durand (1760–1834), professor of architecture at L'École Polytechnique in Paris, slammed down the ruler of reason on what he saw as idle aesthetic and associational play. Laugier's mythical primitive hut was a joke to Durand, who argued that the imitation of nature had nothing to do with architecture. In his masterworks, the presentation of his course at L'École Polytechnique, *Précis des Leçons d'Architecture Données à l'École Polytechnique* ("Précis of Architectural Lessons Given at the Polytechnic School", 1802–5)[26] and the *Recueil et Parallèle des Édifices de Tout Genre* ("Survey and Comparison of Buildings of All Types"),[27] Durand established his position. Like Boullée, he believed in an architecture of simple geometrical forms, yet he went further. As far as Durand was concerned the Vitruvian formula of firmness, commodity and delight could be rewritten as firmness + commodity = delight:

Whether we consult our reason, or examine ancient monuments, it is evident that the primary purpose of architecture has never been to please, nor has architectonic decoration been its object. Public and private usefulness, and the

happiness and preservation of mankind, are the aims of architecture.[28]

Durand argued that to strive to please was futile, whereas a functional approach would yield beauty: ". . . in architecture economy, far from being, as is generally believed, an obstacle to beauty, is on the contrary the most fruitful source."[29]

In Durand's theory, the architect's job was to design with the same functionalist credo as an engineer. Representation was futile; what mattered was primarily how the building worked and, secondly, the way in which it was constructed. A building, in Durand's argument, became a machine which could be made Classical if that proved convenient, but which was not necessarily so.

THE GOTHIC

The structural rationalism articulated by Laugier and the functionalism advocated by Durand constitute the two most important ideals in the formation of the paradigm of mass production fundamental to the Modernist movement in architecture. In an era of new building techniques and new building programs, any culturally responsible architect inevitably had to consider whether literal Classical forms were appropriate. Much of the force and resonance of the argument for a "new" architecture came from the joining of enduring material and functional realities with cultural and political ideals. Thus the movement toward Modernism begins with a startling paradox — a revival of the Gothic style of architecture justified by rationalism.

A complex set of ideals, including religious and social reform, nationalism and Romanticism, generated the Gothic Revival. The Gothic style had been revived in eighteenth-century England for the charm of its association with pre-Modern history and the picturesque pleasures of its massing and detail. In the nineteenth century, its proponents assigned it much loftier values: in their eyes it was the embodiment of a virtuous society, a necessary spiritual antidote to the crass materialism of the industrialized world.

In England, France, and Germany, Gothic architecture was advocated as the proper nationalistic style, yet the ironies of varying claims are evident: in Germany, Schinkel saw his design for a Gothic mausoleum for Queen

Louise (1810) as an appropriately patriotic gesture, in honor of a Queen who had just returned from French-imposed exile, yet he would go on to design the great public buildings of Berlin in a style derived in part from the French Classical tradition; in France, too, the Gothic was eventually declared the proper national style, demoting the Louvre and Versailles and promoting the cathedrals as national symbols; in England, the pursuit of a Gothic architecture sprung from the native soil was somewhat compromised by a national taste for the Italian Gothic.

The argument for the Gothic styles was consistently a moral one, conflating extra-architectural issues of nationalism and religion with those of structural rationalism and functionalism. Gothic architecture was perceived as "natural" — and, in moral terms, "honest." The great cathedrals were regarded in large measure as structurally straightforward building machines, designed to incorporate the maximum height and light possible. This view prevailed well into the twentieth century, and the moral force of the argument has been so powerful that science has only finally chal-

24 *Illustration from* Contrasts. *Augustus Welby Pugin, 1836.*

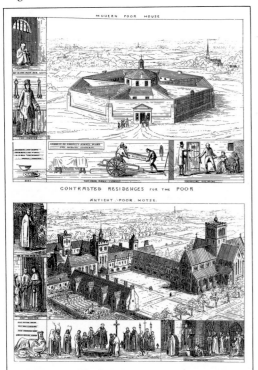

lenged it in the twentieth century, disproving much of it by contemporary structural analysis which shows that many of the specific elements, such as finials and vault ribbing, serve only as decoration.[30]

In England, Augustus Welby Pugin (1812–52) was the first architect and critic to convince the public and the architectural profession of the necessity of morality — and by extension, the Gothic Style — in architecture. The original thrust of Pugin's argument was from the point of view of social reform rather than structural rationalism; where Neo-Classicists had extolled Greek and Roman civilization as the Golden Age, Pugin reveled in a dream of the glory of the medieval Catholic Church. But after the publication of his book *Contrasts* in 1836, which had eighteen illustrations showing the hard, greedy life of a Modern Georgian town and the gentle, generous life of a Gothic town, Pugin decided to argue from reason rather than association. In a Protestant country, it behooved him to campaign for Gothic architecture on the basis of something more palatable to the public than the glories of Catholic civilization. In *The True Principles of Pointed or Christian Architecture*, published in 1841, Pugin argued for the superiority of the Gothic style on the grounds of its honest structural expression.

Pugin and his supporters condemned the Classical style as abstract, intellectualized, and generally elitist. The supposed moral imperatives of the attack made the public debate particularly bitter, most famously in the "Battle of the Styles" fought over the commission to design the new Foreign Office. In 1857, a competition was held for the new building, and out of a field of 218 the winner was a design in the "Renaissance" style. However, the architect of a Gothic style design which had taken third place, George Gilbert Scott (1811–78), so energetically pursued his claim to the prize by lobbying in Parliament and writing letters to newspapers that he persuaded the Minister of Works to give him the commission. "The Battle of the Styles" scandal erupted as the Classicists, led by the architect Charles Robert Cockerell (1788–1863), strove to stop the Gothicists. Lord Palmerston, the Prime Minister, eventually accepted Scott's dubious right to the commission, while at the same time refusing to let him build in the Gothic style. Scott, shamefaced but richer, accepted these conditions, and hired Matthew Digby Wyatt (1820–77) to embellish the building in the Renaissance manner.

Despite the shabby episode of the Foreign

Office commission, the power of a moralist ideal in architecture continued, especially under the influence of the British art critic John Ruskin (1819–1900), whose ideas helped the Gothic Revival to evolve into a broader architectural movement, which respected a variety of non-Classical sources, including the Romanesque, Byzantine, and native British vernacular. Ruskin advocated an architecture antithetical to the Classical taste of the early part of the century and yet he was somewhat at odds with the Gothic Revival. For Ruskin, buildings should have polychromy, arcades, massiveness, and, again, "honesty," as he argued in *The Seven Lamps of Architecture* (1849) and *The Stones of Venice* (1851–3). The designer and theorist William Morris (1834–96) took the ideas of Ruskin and applied them to a philosophy and practice of design that was steeped in a Romantic ideal of the Middle Ages, yet not Gothic revivalist. The artist, Morris believed, had to become a craftsman again, and the craftsman an artist, or man would be destroyed by the new machine culture. The Arts and Crafts Movement of the late 1800s, inspired largely by Morris and Ruskin, saw the full flowering of this craft ideal.

In France, the attack on the Classical Style followed a similar path at first, beginning with the Gothic Revival and its emphasis on honesty and handicraft, then turned to a faith in engineering as the highest aesthetic. Beginning as a Romantic rejection of everything represented by the Academies, the attack was led by the architect, historian, critic, and court reporter Eugène Emmanuel Viollet-le-Duc (1814–79). Like Pugin, Viollet considered medieval buildings the highest expression of architectural art. In his *Dictionnaire Raisonné de l'Architecture Française du XIe au XVIe Siècle* ("Rational Dictionary of French Architecture from the 11th to the 16th Century," ten volumes, 1854–68), he set out to prove, much more exhaustively and with more compelling logic than Pugin, that every aspect of Gothic architecture could be justified on technological and functional grounds.

As a young man, Viollet was entrusted with the plum responsibility of restoring Gothic and Romanesque buildings, including Notre-Dame de Paris, and from that time he pursued a public career of strenuous accomplishment and commensurate recognition. Later, he became court architect to Napoléon III, and provided Gothic sets for royal fêtes and a Gothic railway car for the imperial train. He was not, however, a strict Gothic revivalist, and he had few illusions about the moral superiority of one style or another.

Although Viollet's view of architecture may have been colored by a predilection for the medieval, he had a clear grasp of the role industrial building materials might play in Modern architecture. In his *Dictionnaire* and his *Entretiens sur l'Architecture* ("Discourses on Architecture," 1863–72)[31], Viollet proposed that the structural systems of the Gothic style be reinterpreted in new materials; for example, cast-iron columns could replace the stone piers of a church's nave.

NEITHER GOTHIC NOR CLASSICAL

Architecture Speaking for Itself

Viollet called for a new architecture derived from the new structural possibilities of the industrial age. He could never convincingly demonstrate his ideas in his designs, but by the time of his death in 1879, the impact of new industrial processes in building on aesthetics was the principal focus of architectural debate. One side of that debate called for revolutionary new buildings constructed of mass-produced industrial components such as the Halles Centrales in Paris (1853–7), designed by Victor Baltard (1805–74) and Félix-Emmanuel Callet (1792–1854), while the other side proclaimed the value of traditional, representational Classicism. The Halles was a huge marketplace consisting of pavilions linked by internal streets, lined by cast-iron arcades and lit by the roof's glazed central portion and clerestory windows. The Classical details, such as Corinthian capitals in iron, were few; and to the novelist Émile Zola, Les Halles, which he described in *Le Ventre de*

25　*Les Halles, Paris. Victor Baltard and Félix-Emmanuel Callet, 1853–7.*

Paris ("The Belly of Paris," 1874) was ". . . not copied from anything and . . . had grown naturally out of the soil of the age."[32]

This idea that technology constituted a pattern that would replace historically-derived architecture — that is, replace high-style Classicism as well as the Gothic and the craft-based vernacular — married Durand's concept of functionalism and rationalism to the materialist positivism of late nineteenth-century thought. Zola's praise was in accord with Viollet-le-Duc's belief that the changes in building technology since the beginning of the Industrial Revolution warranted a new form of architectural expression. The architect, it was argued, should work with reference to an ever-progressing technology, not a tradition that alienated architecture and architects from their own times. Only an architecture of glass and iron, a new vernacular sprung from the "soil" of industrialized Europe, could restore architecture to its primordial responsibility of shelter, leaving symbolism to less practical arts, and especially to literature, which cheap printing had made available to the masses.

The advocates of a vernacular of craft and of a vernacular of the machine both denied the essential fact of Modern architectural experience emphasized by Alberti — the split between craft and art. The machine, by distancing man the maker from man the designer, merely carried the distinction further. The craft of the arched masonry construction of ancient Rome was separate from the art of its columns and entablatures and pediments. A craftsman could provide firmness and commodity in any technology, whether in masonry construction or in iron and glass. An architect brought the rhetoric of art to articulate the inherent structure of a building and to relate the building to the wider issues of culture. As Geoffrey Scott put it in *The Architecture of Humanism*: "It [the Renaissance] realized that, for certain purposes in architecture, fact counted for everything, and that in certain others, appearance counted for everything. And it took advantage of this distinction to the full."[33]

Even more than Les Halles, the Crystal Palace (1850–51) in London has often been praised as building sprouted from the "soil of the age." Yet it was deeply rooted in architectural tradition, although this aspect of its derivation is usually overlooked or dismissed as irrelevant. Its designer, Joseph Paxton (1801–65), began his career only after gaining the commission for the Crystal Palace. Before that, he had been the

26　*Crystal Palace, Hyde Park, London. Joseph Paxton, 1850–51.*

Duke of Devonshire's gardener at Chatsworth, where he had designed a large iron, glass, and wood conservatory (1837–40).

When the competition was opened for the design of an exhibition hall that would house an unprecedentedly large display of industrial products from around the world, 245 architects submitted plans. None of their designs was deemed satisfactory by the selection committee. With only nine months left before the scheduled opening, they chose a scheme offered by Paxton (who had taken eight days to work out his ideas). With the help of Charles Fox, a railway engineer, Paxton erected a building that was unquestionably a product of its time: a machine-made building of vast scale, put up in six months with prefabricated parts of iron and glass (and wood, fabricated by a steam-driven sash-cutting machine) composed into a new kind of structure with a skeleton of cast- and wrought-iron girders, and, as some historians delight in pointing out, some timber construction.[34] Perhaps the most salient feature of the structure of the Crystal Palace was its mutability. A machine made up of interchangeable parts, it was dismantled with relative ease in 1852 and reassembled at a new site, in Sydenham, the next year. (It was destroyed by fire in 1936).

Despite the absence of any explicit reference to the Orders, the Crystal Palace was a work of Modern Classicism, as was evident in the symmetrical plan; the axial, barrel-vaulted nave, and the symmetrical elevations of evenly-stacked stories, it was, in fact, a version of a Roman basilica, such as that of the Emperor Constantine (reigned AD 310–13).

Paxton used the Roman paradigm to make it obvious that his exhibition hall was a grand public building, despite its new materials. It was in effect a people's palace, designed for a new kind of event: a temporary exhibition of mass-produced objects intended for mass consumption.

Taking the Crystal Palace as an outstanding example of Modern architecture at the first maturity of the Machine Age, it is clear that many of the nineteenth century's best architects saw technology as a tool capable of expanding the scale and thereby the cultural "reach" of traditional building types, and of accommodating the new program of a democratic society within a historical framework. To this end, they adopted a synthesizing and syncretic approach, reasserting their belief in Classicism as a living architectural language.

Perhaps the most brilliant achievement in this vein was that of Henri Labrouste (1801–75), who managed to combine Viollet-le-Duc's sense of the structural naturalness inherent in the Gothic with the compositional clarity and symbolic appropriateness of the Classical. Going much further than Schinkel, Labrouste accommodated both the traditional craft and the industrial age production vernaculars in cultural monuments which were, essentially, Classical. Labrouste had won the École des Beaux-Arts' Grand Prix in 1824, and duly went to Rome to continue his studies. Then, in 1828, he shocked his masters with his fourth-year *envoi*, or project, in which he chose not only to illustrate Greek rather than Roman architecture, but also to reconstruct theoretically the three Doric temples at Paestum according to his "realistic" interpretation of how they had once looked, rather than according to Vitruvian and Renaissance ideals. In his reconstruction Labrouste envisioned temples covered with polychrome ornament and graffiti. In his reconstruction of the Temple of Hera I, Labrouste deleted the pediment and put on a hipped roof, arguing that the building was not a temple at all but, rather, a civic structure. Labrouste's position was radical because he was asserting that Greek architecture was *not* simply the imperfect prelude to Roman

27 *Bibliothèque Sainte-Geneviève, Paris. Henri Labrouste, 1838–50.*

architecture, but an independent and less rule-bound style. Furthermore, he argued that every feature of the temples could be explained by the demands of material, site, and program. A realist in the most profound sense, he combined a functionalist analysis with a socially motivated belief that art exists in the context of cultural circumstances. Most egregiously, in the eyes of the Academicians, Labrouste did not speculate on the relationship of the temple's Doric Order to the Roman Doric Order. He also neglected the foundation of French Classical rhetoric, considering the temples at Paestum as specific, individual monuments that need not be compared to the ideal Orders.

Labrouste's fifth-year *envoi* added insult to injury. Instead of the traditional fully-articulated Classical design showing that the Academy's *pensionnaire* in Rome had finally mastered the forms of correct architecture, Labrouste presented a severe, skimpily ornamented bridge, with two single-arched triumphal entries, still Classical in their engaged columnar order yet with decorative elements so thin that they rose in relief against the blank walls like brittle icons. Intended as an Alpine link between France and Italy, the bridge was a declaration of architectural purism, suggesting that the parade of traditional decorative motifs and even the Orders themselves should not be allowed across the border into a France that had strayed from its tradition of elemental Classicism. For Labrouste, the Classical language should not be spoken for its own sake, but only to convey culturally conditioned, functionally rationalized intentions.

Labrouste returned to Paris on the eve of the July Revolution of 1830, which led to the installation of Louis-Philippe, the "Citizen King." Although still *persona non grata* with the Académie, whose Secrétaire Perpétuel, Antoine Quatremère de Quincy (1755–1849), was to use his power to ensure that no important commissions came his way for the next eight years, Labrouste found himself a hero among young architects. Eventually the new political climate gave him ample opportunity to demonstrate his architectural principles. The first of these opportunities was the commission, in 1838, for the Bibliothèque Sainte-Geneviève (1843–50). Here he argued that the very meaning of a library had changed in an age of cheap printing, and called for an entirely fresh approach. Responding to this challenge and to the demands of a wide but shallow site across the street from Jacques-Germain Soufflot's (1713–

28 *Bibliothèque Sainte-Geneviève, Paris. Henri Labrouste, 1838–50. Interior.*

80) Panthéon (1756–90), one of the purest expressions of French Classicism, Labrouste produced a brilliant, readable, Classical machine, a work of architectural alchemy that distills a wholly Modern design from elements of Greek, Roman, and Renaissance Classicism. The first story, a stone wall pierced by small arched windows, evoking a Renaissance palazzo, has a frieze of garlands beneath its moulding which echoes that of the Panthéon across the street. Above this, a two-story-high arcade is punctuated by vestigial pilasters, a Renaissance Classical arrangement without a Classical Order. The arcade is glazed at the top and filled in, except for small rectangular windows at the base. Rather than leave the surface blank, Labrouste inscribed it with the names of 810 authors chosen to represent the progress of learning. The names, stacked like so many titles in a catalogue or like books on library shelves, literally refer to the goods inside the building. The decorative program, decided on in 1848, was inspired by the Positivist philosophy of Auguste Comte, who argued that man's intellectual and social progress could be charted by empirical scientific analysis of every field of human endeavor. Labrouste's representation of the temple of Hera I had had graffiti scratched onto its surface; the inscribed names on his Parisian library looked as though a machine had stamped them out or printed them. For Labrouste, each of these structures represented a phase of "organic" architecture, expressing a coherent system of beliefs. In his novel *Notre Dame de Paris* (1832), Victor Hugo had argued that the narrative function of architecture had been lost since the invention of the printing press. According to Hugo, the book had killed the building; whereas a Gothic cathedral had been the translucent and universal vessel of

Medieval culture, after Gutenberg buildings had become decadent and meaningless. In the chapter as written, Hugo saw no hope for a revival of architecture, yet in his "Note" accompanying the definitive edition of 1832, he wrote that there was hope for the future. As the historian Neil Levine has suggested, Hugo's more positive prognosis for architecture may have been based on his discussions with Labrouste, who introduced him to the latest architectural thinking.[35] Labrouste, in turn, seems to have taken heed of Hugo's analysis and attempted to reverse it by creating a building that embodied its program, a building that was, in essence, a wall of books.

The interior actually abounded in machine-made parts, carrying the implied metaphor of the printing press into reality, as exposed cast-iron arches and columns were carried on stone bases. Despite their machined repetitiousness, the columns are not neutral utilitarian posts, but fluted, attenuated columns with capitals that synthesized the Orders. The overall decoration has an almost Pompeiian tone, while at the room's midpoint, at the staircase's landing, Labrouste commissioned a replica of Raphael's "The School of Athens." Striving to be of his time and still within the wider tradition of Classical architecture, Labrouste provided one of the most convincing answers to the dilemma of creating meaningful architecture in the age of machinery.

In a strikingly different way, Jean-Louis-Charles Garnier (1825–98) did the same in his Paris Opéra (1862–75), the quintessential statement of nineteenth-century Classicism. Unconcerned with technological realism though it was, Garnier's design was as surely "grown out of the soil of the age" as Les Halles. More than any other building, the Opéra exemplifies the materialism of its age, not only in the physicality of its elaborately decorated surfaces, but also in the extraordinary machinery that made

29 *The Opéra, Paris. Jean-Louis-Charles Garnier, 1862–75.*

30 *The Opéra, Paris. Jean-Louis-Charles Garnier, 1862–75. Grand staircase.*

the backstage into a model of efficiency for generations to come.

Imperial though it is, Garnier's design did not please the Empress Eugénie, perhaps because, although a synoptic work of Classicism, it was too firmly locked in its moment. In a celebrated exchange, she complained, "Qu'est-ce cela, ce n'est pas un style; ce n'est ni du Louis XIV, ni du Louis XV, ni du Louis XVI," to which Garnier replied, "Madame, c'est du Napoléon III, et vous vous plaignez."[36] ("What is this, it is not a style, it is neither Louis XIV, nor Louis XV, nor Louis XVI." Garnier replied, "Madame, it is Napoleon III, and you complain.") As much as Labrouste, Garnier broke with the academicism of his predecessors; he impudently invoked the rhythms of the Baroque and stretched the language of Classicism to create a new, powerful architectural idiom.

Attending the Opéra in Paris constituted one of the great rituals of late nineteenth-century culture, and Garnier organized the building as a showcase for both the actors on the stage and the audience. The basic architectural volumes and the ornate decorative program conspired to create an architecture of motion, in which the operagoer moves from the exterior, through vestibules, and up the principal flights of the grand staircase and to the auditorium in a seamless sculptural sequence.

MODERNITY AND THE MODERN

In the history of Modern architecture, few events are more often condemned as destructive

to the orderly development of art in relationship to culture than the World's Columbian Exposition in Chicago of 1893. Until recently the standard evaluation of the "White City" of Classical colonnades on the shores of Lake Michigan began and ended with the disgruntled comment, made thirty-one years later by the architect Louis Sullivan (1856–1924), that the "damage wrought by the World's Fair will last for half a century . . . if not longer."[37] The "damage" that Sullivan saw — the use of explicitly Classical architectural language in American architecture and urban planning — now appears as an extraordinarily beneficial influence on the American city in the first half of the twentieth century. In addition, it is possible today, almost a century after the Chicago fair, to see that the relationship between the Classical language that Sullivan denounced and the elements of the new architecture that he championed is closer and more complex than Modernist polemics against the fair and against Classicism in general have acknowledged. Modernism, which once seemed a permanent, radical break with the past, now appears to be one of many cyclical returns within the Modern architectural tradition to sources within and without the Classical canon in order to refresh a language from time to time perceived as exhausted.

The architecture and planning of the Chicago fair was, in its own time, almost universally heralded as progressive, in that it provided what seemed a genuine alternative to the aesthetic and functional chaos of the industrialized, late nineteenth-century city. The focus of the Exposition was the White City, a group of Classical buildings set around a 350-foot (105-meter)-wide, 1,100-foot (330-meter)-long basin. Consistent in height and incorporating a nearly continuous colonnade, the buildings were characterized by a robustly spectacular, exuberantly detailed Classicism. All of this had

31 *World's Columbian Exposition, Court of Honor. 1893.*

to be realized as quickly as the iron-and-glass Crystal Palace of forty-two years earlier. Metal skeletal frames were clad in a temporary substitute for masonry – staff, a mixture of jute, cement, and plaster. At the head of the basin stood the Administration Building designed by Richard Morris Hunt (1827–95), composed of four Doric corner pavilions and a lofty, open, Ionic colonnade, culminating in a 250-foot (75-meter)-high dome. Four years before, at the Paris Exhibition of 1889, Gustave Eiffel's naked metal tower had dominated the fairgrounds. Hunt's dome, without any exposed structural framework in sight, was a deliberate challenge to the French effort to monumentalize pure engineering. At Chicago's fair, technology and history were not seen as opponents; rather each was treated as means to a shared cultural ideal: that of establishing a vigorous, increasingly powerful America as the inheritor of the Western European Classical tradition from a decadent, polyglot Europe of competing national interests.

A century's perspective enables us to appreciate the White City on the Lake for what it was: a model for the reconstruction of the American city from a dull commercial grid built up haphazardly in a variety of styles to one of grand plans and coordinated public architecture.

The impact of the Chicago fair was enormous; not only was it the single greatest attraction America had ever seen, visited by 27,000,000 people in six months, but it also spawned a host of imitations around the country. After ridiculing the fair in 1893, even France tacitly reversed its view with the Exposition Universelle, held in Paris in 1900. No longer infatuated with the engineer's aesthetic of the 1889 exposition, the French too built a White City, and developed for it a robust Classicism which enlarged upon the work of Charles Garnier but did not ignore the countervailing naturalistic anti-Classical style known as Art Nouveau. In such temporary buildings as the Château d'Eau and permanent buildings like the Grand Palais (Henri Deglane, Albert Louvet, and A.-E.-T. Thomas, 1895–1900) and Petit Palais (Charles Girault, 1895–1900), a new synthesis emerged, a Modern French Classicism which has been less than charitably dubbed Beaux-Arts Baroque, a style that perfectly suited the effulgent culture of the Belle Epoque. Its critics called it *cartouche* architecture, bemoaning its voluptuous ornament, which a more sympathetic observer might see as suited to a clientele that enjoyed excessive display, gastronomy, and girth.

32   *Gare du Quai d'Orsay, Paris. Victor Laloux, 1898–1900.*

Different though they were, both the Chicago and Paris (1900) expositions shared the critical premise that coherent, consistent, Modern metropolitan architecture — at once functional, grand, and expressive of national character — was not only necessary to bind up the urban wounds inflicted by industrialization, but also possible. In France, this vision was perhaps best fulfilled by a building erected in connection with the fair: the Gare du Quai d'Orsay (1898–1900), designed by Victor Laloux (1850–1937) for a site facing the Seine opposite the Tuileries. The station (now a museum) took advantage of the new technology of smokeless, electrically-powered engines which enabled the railroads to penetrate to the very heart of the capital. Laloux combined the train shed and the waiting rooms into one building, in which the trains emerged from their tunnels into a grand, light-filled room, a public hall of unprecedented scale vaulted over in iron, plaster, and glass. Laloux's vault was a spectacular hybrid: between the glass and iron he placed narrow bands of acanthus-centered coffers to create a completely contemporary synthesis of traditional Classicism and modern engineering. At the west end, in front of a taut wall of glass, he placed a clock dripping with scrolls and garlands. On the exterior façade fronting the Seine, Laloux showed off his genius with an arcade in which paired Doric pilasters framed massive, rusticated arches that rose to lion-headed keystones, while above them the attic story erupted into sculptures and escutcheons. For the traveller, the Gare d'Orsay offered incontrovertible evidence that he had arrived in a permanent,

twentieth-century metropolitan environment as efficient, lavishly ornamented, and exuberant as the one celebrated in the temporary nearby exposition.

At the same time, in the United States, Charles Follen McKim (1847–1909) led an architectural movement which had by the late 1890s adopted a more scholarly, even archeological approach to the forms of the past. Scientific Eclecticism (also known as Academic Eclecticism), the more-or-less authentic reproduction of elements and even entire compositions from the past, was the dominant stylistic trend of the revival of Classicism in the plastic arts from 1890–1915 known as the American Renaissance. Its proponents believed that traditional Western European architecture was a repository of aesthetic and cultural meaning to be drawn upon for the creation of a mature American civilization.

The closest an American city came to building a permanent incarnation of the 1893 Chicago fair and the ideals of the American Renaissance was in Washington, DC, where Daniel Burnham (1846–1912), working with McKim and the sculptor Augustus Saint-Gaudens (1848–1907), determined to realize fully the Classical splendor of L'Enfant's original plan. In the Senate Parks Commission Plan, which they prepared in 1902, the reconstituted Mall became a *tapis vert* 300 feet (90 meters) wide, flanked by cultural institutions and monuments. At the end of the Mall's axis, the Lincoln Memorial (1912–17) by Henry Bacon (1866–1924) was to be a marble temple based loosely on the Parthenon, while at the end of the cross-axis formed by the

33 *National Gallery, Washington DC. John Russell Pope, 1937–41.*

already-existing White House and Washington Monument, another monument was proposed, and was realized as the Jefferson Memorial (1934–43), a design after the Pantheon by John Russell Pope (1874–1937). The Mall became an American main street and a front lawn for palaces of government and culture. The greatest of these was Pope's National Gallery (1937–41), which surpassed its twentieth-century Classical contemporaries in its austere dignity and functional perfection. Enclosed in subtle, sparely ornamented exterior walls of Tennessee marble, relieved only by an Ionic portico leading to a pantheonic entrance rotunda, 100 feet (30 meters) in height and diameter, the National Gallery is a superbly thought-out working organism, endowed from the outset with advanced technology of lighting and climate control.

The renewed capital city also had a new portal, Union Station (1903–8), designed by Burnham's firm after the design by Charles B. Atwood (1848–95) for the train station at the Chicago fair.

34 *Pennsylvania Station, New York. McKim, Mead & White, 1902–11.*

The grandest American railroad station, however, was built in New York, the financial capital of the new world empire. A less exuberant and more implacably reasoned gateway to a modern metropolis than Laloux's Gare d'Orsay, McKim, Mead and White's Pennsylvania Station (1902–11; demolished 1963) is still perhaps unparalleled in its resolution of technologically sophisticated urban life and Classical architecture. Technological progress was its reason for being. For years, trains had come to a halt at the New Jersey side of the Hudson River, after which passengers and freight had to be ferried to Manhattan Island. Railroad bridges had long been proposed but were rejected as expensive and impractical because of the Hudson's width and the sharply different heights of its opposite banks. With the development of engines run on electricity rather than steam, a tunnel beneath the river was at last feasible, and western train lines could now bring travelers into the heart of the city.

Charles McKim, who designed the station, chose to celebrate this feat of engineering in a monument whose very Classicism made it clear that the railroad was not merely a business but a public service. McKim wrapped the waiting rooms in a low yet monumental building which formed a perimeter wall around the two combined city blocks. Like the Paris Opéra, Pennsylvania Station had carefully modulated entrances for pedestrians and for those who

35 *Pennsylvania Station, New York. McKim, Mead & White, 1902–11. Ticket room.*

arrived in vehicles. Pedestrians entered through the colossal portico facing Seventh Avenue and proceeded along a marble-lined internal street to the trains. Those in cars, or, for a few years still, carriages, also entered through porticoes leading to covered ramps that descended from the two Seventh Avenue corners to the center of the block. To board the trains, all travelers passed through the vast ticket room, whose floor was sunken below the level of the street and whose travertine-covered walls rose above the perimeter buildings to a groin-vaulted ceiling, the plaster ribs and coffers of which clad a steel frame. Light poured in from eight thermal windows modelled on the tepidarium of the Baths of Caracalla. Just beyond the waiting room was its skeletal double, where the steel structure stood exposed in a concourse enclosed by steel and glass vaulting.

For McKim, the various historical modes of Classicism carried specific cultural meanings that could help convey the meanings of new buildings to the public. Whereas the architecture of imperial Rome served as his sourcebook for a colossal train station, or for the library of an urban university like Columbia in New York, he was capable of working in any style. Whatever the architectural style language, McKim and his disciples approached the project with a scholar's intelligence and an artist's eye, even if the compositional rigor of the French academic tradition, in which they had been trained, was sometimes sacrificed.

Although the values of the American Renaissance gradually lost favor after the First World War, the movement persisted, especially in government commissions, until the Depression of the 1930s. American architects and their patrons rediscovered the truth in Jefferson's perception that Classical architecture was one way to forge a homogeneous national culture out of the ethnic and social mélange of polyglot mass democracy. To be sure, there was a dark side to this movement. Cultural minorities were perceived as threats to the prevailing Anglo-Saxon ethic, and traditional architecture served as a valuable tool in preserving the values of the traditional ruling class. Yet although the call for a uniform Classicism was fueled by nostalgia for the social and architectural decorum of the nation's colonial and early republican past, it was also a way to emblazon the values of a new nation in full confidence, to realize in stone and mortar the vision that had inspired so many Europeans to crowd the steerage of transatlantic steamers and sail for the "promised land."

The first tangible indication of the coming American Renaissance, the Statue of Liberty, expressed the fundamental optimism of Modern Classicism in the nineteenth century and the cultural cosmopolitanism of the era. This massive sculpture in New York's harbor, designed by Frédéric Auguste Bartholdi (1834–1904), was dedicated in 1886, a year before work began on the Eiffel Tower. In fact, the iron skeleton of the statue was itself the work of Gustave Eiffel (1832–1923); but here, Eiffel's engineering skills were subordinated to Bartholdi's art, which clad the skeleton with the copper plates of an idealistic sculpture, the first colossus since those of the ancient world. Fittingly, the statue's granite and concrete base was designed by Richard Morris Hunt, the first American to attend the École des Beaux-Arts in Paris, who provided a Classical pedestal for this symbol of the New World as the hope of Western civilization.

Yet in America, as in Europe, there were many architects and critics who considered Classicism, no matter how ennobled by cultural sentiment or how synthesized with advanced technology, as architecture in chains, shackled by historical precedent. Although they often accepted the need for a unifying architectural order, the advocates of a modern, ahistorical style denied the expressive relevance of traditional forms, preferring instead to create *de novo* an architectural language that would monumentalize the machine in a way comparable to the glorification of handicraft characteristic of the medieval age. But whereas the medieval era was intensely spiritual as well as intensely material, the Modernist impulse of the late nineteenth century carried with it no such transcendent mission. Rather, its obsession was to celebrate the present in all its naked realism, without reference to the past, or concern for the future.

The generation of architects born in the 1860s and 1870s — here called the generation of 1870 — rebelled against academic Classicism, rejecting the textbook of rules derived from the encyclopedia of masterworks. This rebellion took many forms, some of which genuinely abandoned the Classical tradition, yet I would argue that despite innumerable polemics, the evidence of the actual buildings designed by this generation of "moderns" had at its heart a sense of a renewal of traditional architecture, of a return to a more essential expression of the Classical ideal.

The "modern" architecture of the period that extends from the *belle époque* to the First World War was cryptically Classical. It was the first important stylistic movement to grow up simultaneously in Europe and America. In Vienna, the Secession was founded in 1897 by a group of architects and artists determined to open Austria to the innovations in the plastic arts that were sweeping Europe, especially Art Nouveau. Among the leading Secessionists were two architects, Josef Hoffmann (1870–1956) and Josef-Maria Olbrich (1867–1908), as well as Jože Plečnik (1872–1957) and (briefly) Adolf Loos (1870–1933), and the artists Koloman Moser (1868–1918) and Gustav Klimt (1862–1918), all of whom took architecture and the arts away from orthodoxy to freer, more essential exploration of Classical and proto-Classical themes. In Germany, Peter Behrens (1868–1940), a contemporary of Hoffman and Olbrich, first trained as a painter and, coming to architecture only after 1900, followed a similar path, as did Heinrich Tessenow (1876–1950).

In France, two star pupils of the École des Beaux-Arts, Tony Garnier (1868–1948) and Auguste Perret (1874–1954), vied to create an architectural style for the modern, industrialized metropolis within the rationalist tradition by using the structural facts of building as the principal source of architectural expression. In England, Charles Holden (1875–1960) did much the same, yet often returned to an overtly Classical expression, while Edwin Lutyens (1869–1944) shifted from the English vernacular to the Classical as his career shifted from country houses to large public commissions, in which he varied from a fully articulated and often Mannerist Classical language to a stripped-down essentialist one. In Scandinavia and Finland, the brief flowering of National Romanticism, characterized by the early work of the Finnish architect, Eliel Saarinen (1873–1950), was followed by the stripped Classical work of Johan Sigfrid Sirén (1889–1961) in Finland, Hack Kampmann (1856–1920) in Denmark, and Eric Gunnar Asplund (1885–1940) and Ivar Tengbom (1878–1968) in Sweden. In America the retreat from academic Classicism was carried furthest by Frank Lloyd Wright (1867–1959), although Bernard R. Maybeck (1862–1957), Irving Gill (1870–1936), and Bertram Grosvenor Goodhue (1869–1924) also contributed to the evolution of a style characterized by abstract masses and stripped Classical details, best described as crypto-Classicism. The French-born-and-educated Paul Philippe Cret (1876–1944) led the American development of stripped Classicism.

Behind all of these stand the towering figures of Louis Sullivan (1856–1924) and Otto Wagner (1841–1918). Sullivan challenged academic Classicism at the site of its greatest triumph in America, the World's Columbian Exposition. In addition to the Court of Honor, the fairgrounds also included a picturesque lagoon, laid out according to naturalistic principles by Frederick Law Olmsted (1822–1903) and his associate Henry Codman (1859–93), and bordered by buildings in a variety of national vernaculars. These represented not only Western but also non-Western cultures — most influentially the Japanese, exemplified by the Ho-o-den temple on the lagoon's island, which inspired Wright. At the north shore of the lagoon stood the most perfect example of American academic Classicism, the Palace of Fine Arts, designed by Atwood in a Greek Ionic order. Sullivan's challenge to this prevailing style, standing on the south-west shore of the lagoon, was a Classical building of a different order from Atwood's and those facing the Court of Honor. Despite his claims to the contrary — and his argument that an organic architecture was by definition a non-Classical architecture — Sullivan's Transportation Building was in essence a disciplined synthesis of Classical composition and Romanesque and Moorish detail, culminating in the ornate, semicircular archway of its "Golden Doorway." But in the minds of many it represented the kernel of an idea that Sullivan would powerfully, if confusingly, advance in his writings, that America must create an architecture naturally expressive of a modern technological democracy.

The gap between Sullivan's rhetoric and his actual design, and the inconsistency within his writings, bring into question how "progressive" the Transportation Building was in Sullivan's

36 *Transportation Pavilion, World's Columbian Exposition. Louis Sullivan, 1893. Entrance.*

37   *Transportation Pavilion, World's Columbian Exposition. Louis Sullivan, 1893. View from lagoon.*

own terms. Sullivan's building is as historicist as, if less archeological than Hunt's Administration Building — not only in its specific forms but also in the fundamental Classicism of its composition, manifested in its emphatically emphasized center and end pavilions. On a smaller scale, Sullivan's tombs for the Ryerson and Getty families in Graceland Cemetery in Chicago exhibit a similar ambiguity, resembling the excursion of a Classical architect into the proto- and para-Classical modes of the Egyptian (in the case of the Martin Ryerson tomb of 1887) and of the Moorish-Romanesque (the Carrie Eliza Getty tomb of 1890).

38   *Ryerson tomb, Graceland Cemetery, Chicago. Louis Sullivan, 1887.*

39   *Getty tomb, Graceland Cemetery, Chicago. Louis Sullivan, 1890.*

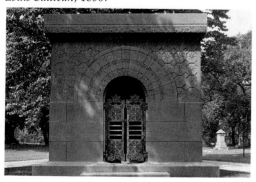

The ideal opportunity for Sullivan to demonstrate his theory of ahistorical architectural design for a Modern, industrial democracy came, not with the fair buildings or the tombs, but with the tall office building. This was a genuinely new building type, a direct result of technological innovation — notably the development of the elevator and steel-frame construction — and a distinct representation of modern culture, a building type virtually without precedent. In his essay "The Tall Office Building Artistically Considered" (1896), Sullivan asked: "How shall we proclaim from the dizzy height of this strange, weird, modern housetop the peaceful evangel of sentiment, of beauty, the cult of a higher life?"[38] The question itself divorces Sullivan from a strictly functionalist solution. His answer, as embodied in his work, takes him far from materialism to the distant shores of aesthetics and mysticism.

Although Sullivan was opposed to Classical detail in tall buildings, the elevations of his skyscrapers suggest the Classical division of a column into base, shaft, and capital. In addition to this horizontal tripartite division, a strong vertical emphasis was, he insisted, essential to the tall building. His designs for tall buildings, from the Wainwright Building in St. Louis (1890) onward, for the first time resolved the new building type, distilling it into its essence as a column and gracing it with visual subtleties in the form of intercolumniations and ornamental detail comparable in inventiveness to the visual embellishments initiated in the sixth century BC, when the Greeks distilled the wooden architecture of prehistory into the Doric order. With his Bayard Building in New York (1898), Sullivan lifted the type to the heights of spirituality: piers rise in perfect register to an arcade of angels, their arms stretched out to the heavens.

The Bayard Building was lauded at the time by critics such as Montgomery Schuyler, who wrote that it was "the nearest approach yet

made, in New York . . . to solving the problem of the skyscraper."[39] Despite the novel ornament, Sullivan's basic approach was Classical. What Sullivan objected to was not Classical composition, which was natural, but Classical detail, which he felt was culturally derived and inappropriate, therefore, as codified into a canon for modern times. Thus, it can be argued that, rhetoric apart, Sullivan's search for an organic architecture for Modern American democracy was not a break with Classicism but a search for a more Modern form of Classicism, an astylar Classicism, a Classicism that conflated the handicraft and technological processes to create what his disciple Frank Lloyd Wright would brilliantly describe in a speech of 1901 as "The Art and Craft of the Machine."[40]

Sullivan's potential influence on the course of American architecture was seriously impaired by his mercurial personality, his hyper-romanticism, and his ambivalent attitudes towards commercialism. By contrast, his Viennese near-contemporary, Otto Wagner, gradually emerged as patriarch of architectural reform for the entire generation of 1870. Wagner was a curious leader for an anti-establishment movement. Born in 1841, by the late 1880s when he began to advocate aesthetic reform, he was an established architect and developer, a comfort-loving bourgeois, totally unlike the stereotypical member of the radical avant-garde. Wagner belonged to the Ringstrasse generation, the rising liberal middle class who defined the culture of Vienna from 1848 until the turn of the century. Their shining civic monument was the Ringstrasse, a broad, tree-lined avenue built, beginning in 1859, over the old city's fortifications. Lined with the institutions of the rising bourgeoisie — university, museum, theater, opera — and with bourgeois apartment houses, the Ringstrasse was a veritable encyclopedia in stone of traditional Classicism.

As a developer-architect, Wagner reaped the benefits of capitalist expansion beginning in the 1860s, although he was not sufficiently respected to be awarded a commission for one of the important civic buildings. Though his early work was very much part of the received Classical tradition, he began to record dissatisfaction with its limitations in the late 1880s when he designed his own villa (1886–8). A suburban retreat fit for the highly cultivated life of a late nineteenth-century aesthete, it has a stately Classical layout with a central Ionic colonnade flanked by loggias. Though the Orders were rigorously observed there was also a crisp

40 *First Villa Wagner, Vienna. Otto Wagner, 1886–8.*

minimalism in the detailing that suggested reaching out for the authority of the elemental Classicism of the late eighteenth and early nineteenth centuries.

Wagner's attack on the prevailing Classicism of the Ringstrasse began in earnest in 1893, when he finished his winning competition entry for the development of Vienna beyond the Ringstrasse. The city had just incorporated a wide belt of suburbs, and Wagner saw the new city plan as a turning point for Vienna, as important as the beginning of the Ringstrasse more than thirty years before. The essence of Wagner's plan (largely unexecuted) was transportation — a system of ring and radial roads which would permit, in theory, infinite expansion. Wagner's enthusiasm for this efficient, technologically advanced metropolis is evident in the inscription he gave his design, *Artis sola domina necessitas* ("Necessity is art's only mistress"), a motto borrowed from the German architect and rationalist theorist of industrial art Gottfried Semper (1803–79).

Appointed professor of architecture at the Vienna Academy of Fine Arts in 1894, Wagner was now in a position to campaign for an antihistorical, functionalist architecture. His short theoretical textbook published the next year, *Moderne Architektur* (1895), was prefaced with the statement: "One idea inspires the whole book; namely, that the whole basis of views of architecture prevailing today must be displaced by the recognition that the only possible point of departure for artistic creation is modern life."[41]

By 1900 Wagner had freed himself from traditional Classicism to create innovative, yet still essentially Classical, buildings for the Modern city. He inveighed against what he viewed as the decadent *Stilarchitektur* ("style architecture") of his day. In his role as architect of the Vienna

City Railway system, from 1894 to 1901, he had a remarkable opportunity to realize his vision of the swiftly moving metropolis unhindered by history. Wagner's railway designs balanced a nascent functionalist aesthetic of exposed construction with suave Classicizing composition and detail, from the miles of guardrails in the Roman-inspired square-and-diagonal module to the iron-framed station entrances flanked by stone pavilions.

With the Imperial and Royal Post Office Savings Bank (1904–6), Wagner at last achieved a commission almost comparable in importance to those of the Ringstrasse. For the Post Office Bank he balanced new materials and decorative forms with the Classical composition that remained essential to his architecture. The main façade, concluding the axis of the Georg Coch Platz, off the Stuben Ring, has a rusticated base and is covered above in thin sheets of marble cladding bolted in place, surmounted by a strong concluding cornice and attic. But in its details the façade comes alive, with natural and alloyed materials assembled in a brilliant, articulate, structurally expressive manner which Viollet-le-Duc might have endorsed. Skinny aluminum columns set on stone pedestals support the canopy of the entrance porch. Aluminum bolts hold the thin sections of white marble to the frame, creating a constructionally rational yet highly decorative pattern. Exposed steel girders project to support the main cornice in place of traditional stone consoles. Crowning the attic, two aluminum-winged Victories evoke archaic Greek sculpture and proclaim a return to the fundamentals of Western art and architecture.

In the interior of the bank, the public services

41 *Imperial and Royal Post Office Savings Bank, Vienna. Otto Wagner, 1904–6.*

42 *St. Leopold Church, Steinhof. Otto Wagner, 1902–7. Altar.*

are arranged around a glazed courtyard, covered by a glass-and-steel curved vault. Here the tradition of Classical interior space is completely restudied in terms of a vocabulary based on engineering: beneath the glass ceiling, the air is warmed by radiators in the shape of columns — a simplified order for the machine age.

Whereas the Post Office Savings Bank seems the perfect fulfillment of Wagner's philosophy, the program and purpose of the St. Leopold Church for the mental hospital at Steinhof (1902, built 1902–7) liberated him from his own rhetoric. Wagner had entered the competition for the design of the mental hospital in 1902, and although his general plan was accepted, his design for the individual pavilions was not. Ironically, the great functionalist was given the most symbolic building, the church, rather than the practical hospital buildings to design. The Post Office Savings Bank, designed at roughly the same time, was materialist, international architecture for the deracinated modern urbanite; the church was mystic, redolent of history and place, built for the inmates of an asylum at the edge of a forest. However, the Steinhof church does have many affinities with the bank's modernity — once again, thin sheets of marble are held to the frame with exposed bolts, metal and tile provide the ornament, and the composition appears reduced to primary forms — yet at every turn, Wagner reached for traditional symbols to express the program. The hemispherical copper dome was originally gilded, evoking the domes of Eastern Orthodox churches, thus making a comment on Vienna's position at the center of Europe, between East and West. The free-standing colonnade allies the church to the tradition of the Classical temple, while the transept windows are serlianas (also known as Venetian or Palladian windows) from the Italian Renaissance. In the interior, Wagner rejected the obvious rationalistic gesture of exposing the interior of the hemispheric dome, choosing instead to suspend a vault over the crossing.

Despite the apparent contradictions between the design of the Steinhof church and his own rhetoric, Wagner continued to argue for a functionalist urban architecture. On the eve of the First World War, he reissued his text *Moderne Architektur* with a new title, *Die Baukunst unserer Zeit* ("The Building Art of Our Time," 1914)[42] — the use of the word *Baukunst* underscoring his renunciation of the Academic, historical styles associated with the word "architecture." In his essay, *Die Grozstadt* ("The Metropolis," 1911), Wagner reasserted his vision of a capitalist metropolis, a theoretically infinite world populated by managers and clerks, who would live and work in buildings that were nominally Classical and uniform in height and bulk.

Wagner built a second villa for his own use, allowing himself to go the full distance away from stylistic orthodoxy. The house is a smooth-surfaced cube, its walls decorated with a minimum of geometric ornament, with unframed windows punched through with machine-like regularity. The overt Classicism of the first villa has gone, replaced by blunt, blocky forms and sketchily symbolic ornaments of circle and line, with a general absence of bilateral symmetry. Nonetheless, this second Villa

43 *City plan of* Die Grozstadt, *published 1911. Otto Wagner.*

44 *Secession building, Vienna. Josef-Maria Olbrich, 1897–8.*

Wagner is a fundamentally Classical design, encoding a traditional composition and decorative scheme into a new crypto-Classicism which could be inferred from the striated ("rusticated") base, the tile pattern between the tall narrow windows (a "colonnade" between the windows of the *"piano nobile"*), and the heavy cornice with coffers under the eaves.

Although it was Wagner who laid the groundwork for a stripped-down Modern Classical architecture, it was the younger Secessionists of the 1870 generation who carried this abstraction of traditional forms and details to its limit, producing a true crypto-Classicism. At first, the reforming impulse of these turn-of-the-century Viennese architects was driven by two almost contradictory impulses: on the one hand to develop a rich new decorative style, and on the other, to return to an architectural vocabulary of fundamental forms. The Secession Building (1897–8), by Josef-Maria Olbrich, designed to exhibit the works of the newly formed Secessionist group of artists, exemplifies both of these impulses. The new decorative style is explicit in the Mycenaean swirls of the urns flanking the entrance, the laurel-leaf pattern incised in the plain stucco surfaces, the writhing-snake moulding, and the magnificent perforated dome, a lattice of metal laurel leaves, suspended above the entrance between four battered (inclined) pylons. The composition of the building, however, is less radical. Try as one would like to make an argument for the Secession Building as a radical break with the past, it is, in essence, a traditional design, a proto-Classical temple for the new religion of art. The front elevation is a tripartite composition of two cubic blocks flanking a recessed entrance: there is still a base, middle, and top, ending in frieze and cornice, and the mouldings — other than the snakes which project into space — are still

related to Classical orders. Often seen as the immediate precursor of Modernism, the Secession Building can with equal, if not greater, validity be seen as yet another reform of Classicism from within, comparable to the Revolutionary Classicism of the late eighteenth and early nineteenth centuries which, as we have seen, tried to get behind traditional details to a more fundamental conceptual truth, an essential Classicism of circle and square, sphere and cube. The goal shared by the Revolutionary Classicists and the Secessionist architects might thus be seen as a purification in which forms would be stripped to their essence, a physical reflection of the spiritual search for the origins of Classical culture.

The fundamental Classicism of Olbrich's Secession Building was probably more the result of the design sketch by the painter Gustav Klimt (1862–1918) than of Olbrich's own inspiration. Yet aesthetic fundamentalism became the dominant theme of the architect's work. Olbrich further developed the mystical, pan-German utopianism of the Secession Building in his designs for Darmstadt, where he had moved in 1899 to help found an artists' colony sponsored by the Grand Duke Ernst Ludwig of Hesse. His Ernst Ludwig House (1901), which contained studios and exhibition space, was, like the Secession Building, a proto-Classical temple, with a high, blank façade and an ornate circular entrance flanked by huge male and female nudes. By the time of Olbrich's premature death, in 1908, he had evolved, among other styles, a personal Classicism exemplified by the Haus Feinhals, in Köln-Marienburg (1908).

Olbrich's contemporary and former associate in Vienna, Josef Hoffmann, followed a similar course, moving from free-style composition and decorative pattern-making toward an abstract, cubic geometry and finally to a crypto- or stripped Classicism. After Olbrich's departure for Darmstadt in 1899, Hoffmann became the leading progressive architect in Vienna. In his Purkersdorf Sanatorium (1903) he went further toward an ahistorical Modernism than Otto Wagner. But his masterpiece, the Palais Stoclet in Brussels (1905–11), was more complex — the ultimate product of the craft and design of the Viennese Secession disciplined to a crypto-Classicism of composition and form. The Stoclet House is clad in a skin of thin sheets of marble, whose smooth planes seem to be held in place by the bands of bronze mouldings running along the perimeters of the cubic volumes that make up the whole. The bronze ornament

45 *Palais Stoclet, Brussels. Josef Hoffmann, 1905–11.*

46 *AEG Turbine Factory, Berlin. Peter Behrens, 1909.*

becomes more and more concentrated as the house rises to its blocky tower, surmounted by four Atlas figures guarding the laurel dome, the symbol of the Secession lifted from Olbrich's design for the building in Vienna. The Secessionists' belief in expressing instinct and passion erupts in the dining room's gold-flecked mosaic mural, "The Kiss," by Gustav Klimt; and the entire design of the house exhibits the same dramatic tensions as a stage play in which passion and reason, asymmetry and symmetry are enacted, a conflict expressed perhaps most eloquently by the Doric columns in the garden, staid Classical symbols, representative of rational, trabeated construction, turned into fountains, representing the renewal of life.

Hoffmann was unable to sustain this level of dramatic conflict in his later designs. In his house for Eduard Ast in Vienna (1911), he created the impression of a giant order of pilasters by fluting the wall between the windows. Above, he placed a heavy cornice to create an effect nearly as articulate as a traditional Classical order, yet with each surface covered with languorous carved foliage. For the Rome International Art Exhibition (1911), Hoffmann designed the Austrian pavilion as a Classical stage set, a stripped-down little temple.

The reacceptance of Classical syntax and, to a remarkable extent, Classical vocabulary after the excursion into the aesthetic freedom of the Secession and its German counterpart, the *Jugendstil*, was carried even further by Peter Behrens, a young German painter and graphic designer who came to the Darmstadt art colony in 1899. Behrens added an essential ingredient that had been largely absent from the Viennese work — that of mass production, adapting the English Arts and Crafts ideal that had been promulgated in German by Hermann Muthesius'

appeal for the importance of a native craft culture in *Das Englische Haus* ("The English House," published in 1904), to the industrial demands of mass production. In his position as principal of the Düsseldorf school of arts and crafts, and as a founder of the Deutsche Werkbund ("Work Union") in 1907, Behrens was well placed to carry out the program of modern metropolitan architecture and design, proposed a decade earlier by Wagner and enthusiastically supported by Muthesius in Germany. With his appointment as architect and designer for the German General Electrical Company (AEG), Behrens had the power to improve the design of all sorts of products, from posters to metal fans to architecture. The image of twentieth-century German industrial and architectural design that he projected was both Modern and Classical, a marriage of engineering and art, whether in the temple-like design for the assembly hall of the AEG Turbine Factory in Berlin (1909) or in the colossal "order" of rounded brick piers of the AEG Small Motor Factory, also in Berlin (1910–13).

For the German Embassy in St. Petersburg

(1911–12) Behrens sought a simpler, more monumental effect through a more conventional Classicism strongly evocative of Schinkel's Altes Museum. The embassy's façade has an engaged colonnade of Doric columns, stretched three stories from a minimal base to the building's cornice. Like Schinkel's Altes Museum, Behrens's design uses heavy, square piers to emphasize the corners of the main block. At the center, Behrens compacted the central plinth of the Altes Museum, bringing closer together the paired statues of Castor and Pollux (Dioscuri). Throughout the design, Behrens also referred to the tradition of the palazzo, as in the contrast of the smooth granite columns with the highly rusticated wall surface behind them.

Heinrich Tessenow preferred a more synthetic approach, attempting to fuse artisanal, vernacular architecture with the symbolic representationalism of Classicism. The basis of the *Heimat* ("homeland") style proposed by Tessenow was the suburban equivalent of Wagner's theory of Modern urban architecture and, like it, advocates a shift from the historicist styles of *Architektur* to the astylar, rational forms of *Baukunst* ("building art"). As his designs for large *Siedlungen* (suburban housing developments) reveal, Tessenow came as close as any to creating by fiat the vernacular townscape that had grown naturally over time in the pre-industrial past. But Tessenow's vernacular was in no way sentimentalized. Unlike Ruskin and Morris, who celebrated the idiosyncratic detail as an expression of identity, Tessenow virtually eliminated such detail in favor of simple geometric volumes and regularly proportioned windows which gave humble single-family houses the symmetry and monumentality of temples. Tessenow's bond of Classical and vernacular was explicit in an early project, the

47 *Festival Hall, Dalcroze Institute, Hellerau. Heinrich Tessenow, 1910.*

Dalcroze Institute in Hellerau on the outskirts of Dresden (1910), the center of a community devoted to eurhythmics, a system of gymnastic movement invented by Émile Jaques Dalcroze (1865–1950), the Swiss composer. Although the smaller buildings of the Institute followed a strictly delimited traditional vocabulary, the Festival Hall's façade, a square-columned porch beneath a low gable, is unmistakably a reinterpretation of a Classical temple's portico.

The architect who summed up the Austro-Germanic quest for a normative, Modern Classical architecture that could apply to anything from a temple to a barn was the Viennese architect and vitriolic essayist Adolf Loos. Born in Brunn (now Brno, Czechoslovakia), Loos was the son of a sculptor-stonemason, who inculcated the craft ideal in his son at an early age. After attending school, with no great distinction, Loos left for America, where his primary destination was the 1893 Chicago World's Fair. Moving on to New York, he worked as a mason, journalist, dishwasher, and draftsman. Following a brief sojourn in London he returned to Vienna in 1897; there he found a job with an architect and also immediately threw himself into the other real work of his life, the writing of critical essays.

Loos first associated himself with the Secession, publishing two articles in their magazine *Ver Sacrum* in 1898, but he soon broke with them, mocking their *Gesamtkunstwerk* ("total work of art") ideal in a fable called "The Story of the Poor Rich Man" (1900), in which a client is humiliated and crippled by his architect's insistence on controlling every element in a house. Loos himself was obsessed with every detail, however small, of his own designs, yet he proclaimed that the eccentric, individualistic elements of the Secessionists' designs should be replaced by typical, understated objects, as urbane and unobtrusive as the dark English suit, which he advertised in his short-lived periodical *Das Andere* ("The Other"), in 1903. Loos's disdain for the ornamental excesses of the Secession reached its peak in 1908, when he penned his notorious essay "Ornament and Crime," in which he baldly stated that "the evolution of culture is synonymous with the removal of ornament from utilitarian objects."[43] Loos argued that ornament was typical of lower cultures, which practised tattooing and other such customs. In the high culture of twentieth-century Vienna, Loos believed, ornament should be regarded in the same way as tattoos — that is, as savage. It was excusable only for those who did

not share in the city's high cultural life, such as his cobbler, who could take his aesthetic pleasure only in the intricate stitching of his craft. For the others, such as those reading "Ornament and Crime," life was sterner: "After the toils and troubles of the day we go to Beethoven or to Tristan . . . anyone who goes to the *Ninth Symphony* and then sits down and designs a wallpaper pattern is either a confidence trickster or a degenerate."[44] Loos anticipated the thesis of "Ornament and Crime," in his design for the American (Kärntner) Bar, executed in 1907. The tripartite marble façade was conspicuously unornamented, while the "entablature" consisted of an American flag in stained glass. In the interior, a tiny space, 8 by 15 feet (2.4 by 4.5 meters), Loos offered what he saw as the quintessence of a modern civilized bar, with the fine materials and perfect, understated craft respected by the son of a stonemason. Its only "ornament," a coffered marble ceiling, is Classical, and serves as a symbol of the cavernous Classical clubrooms of New York, Chicago, and London.

In 1910 Loos wrote his most polemical essay on the state of architecture in his time. In "Architecture" he concurred in part with the growing ideology of *Baukunst* that Tessenow epitomized, and expanded upon Alberti's essential dichotomy, arguing that "Only a very small part of architecture belongs to art: the tomb and the monument. Everything else, everything that fulfils a function is to be excluded from the domain of art."[45] Loos railed against the "art" which he believed destroyed the harmony of the vernacular landscape:

May I take you to the shores of a mountain lake? The sky is blue, the water is green and everything is at peace . . .

What is the discord, that like an unnecessary scream shatters the quiet? . . . a villa . . . Why does the architect, the good one as well as the bad one, desecrate the lake? The architect, like almost every urban dweller, has no culture. He lacks the certainty of the farmer who possesses culture. The urban dweller is an uprooted person.[46]

Loos offered no remedies for this situation — in the country it was possible to go back to vernacular harmony, as he did in one of the last of his designs, the Kuhner House, Kreuzberg, Payerbach, Austria (1930) — but for the deracinated city dweller the very least one could do was provide an architecture of essentialized, Classi-

cal clarity. Like most theorists of Classical architecture before him, Loos was in many ways a conservative, calling for a *retour à l'ordre*:

But every time the minor architects who use ornament move architecture away from its grand model, a great architect is at hand to guide them back to antiquity.[47]

Loos's built answer to the problem of urban architecture in his day was the Goldman & Salatsch Building, now known as the Looshaus, prominently located on a corner of the Michaelerplatz in Vienna (1909–12). In this building he stripped the Viennese apartment house type down to what he saw as its Classical essence: shops for the first story and mezzanine, apartments above, and a clear division between the two. The main entrance is a Classical portico, four unfluted Doric columns *in antis*. Like the rest of the base, the columns are made of green veined marble, brought from a Greek quarry that had just been reopened after 2,000 years. Above the marble and glass base, the smooth stucco walls have square windows, punched through without any surrounds, continuing up to the minimal cornice. A rationalistic display of construction was not the point: the design does not reveal or even express its reinforced concrete frame. Instead, the building is the image of Loos's belief in an architecture with the elegant, standardized economy he perceived in the English-style dinner jackets and tweed suits in which the building's principal tenants specialized.

48 *Goldman & Salatsch building, Michaelerplatz, Vienna. Adolf Loos, 1909–12.*

49   *Proposal for department store, Alexandria. Adolf Loos, 1910. Drawing.*

Loos's pursuit of normative Classical architecture continued in projects as various as a department store in Alexandria, Egypt (1910) — an unbuilt vision of Ptolemaic splendor including a giant order of Ionic pilasters — and the sugar-

50   *Proposal for The Chicago Tribune Building. Adolf Loos, 1922. Drawing.*

refining factory in Rohrbach, Czechoslovakia (1916–19), where the structural brick pillars are rounded to create a colossal industrial order.

Loos's most striking analysis of the relationship of Classicism to modern building types came in his project for the Chicago Tribune Competition in 1922. Once considered a joke, it can now be seen for what was intended — a sardonic comment on the nature of the American skyscraper, which Loos knew well from his years in Chicago and New York. He proposed that the Tribune's tower be organized as an incipient column composed of base, shaft, and capital. The competition had called for "the most beautiful and distinct office building in the world."[48] Loos responded with the radical conformity shown at the Looshaus, providing a primary Classical monument, a Trajan's column, which was at once an homage to the skyscraper as column and a witty comment on newspapers and their columnists.

For Loos the dilemma of Modernity was the crisis of architecture, and his "Classical" typologies the only answer to the building needs of the deracinated urbanite. The French architects Tony Garnier and Auguste Perret felt a similar drive to create a rational, Modern architecture based on Classicism. Garnier's project for a Cité Industrielle (1904–17), his fifth year *envoi* after winning the Prix de Rome in 1899, was as radical as that submitted 61 years earlier by Henri Labrouste. In its new vision of Classicism the domestic buildings were simple cubic blocks, as in the Greek vernacular, and the major public buildings resembled the crypto-Classicism of Otto Wagner's designs for the *Grozstadt*. Garnier, who worked for the municipal government of his home town of Lyons from 1904 to 1939, was able to build only a few components of

52   *Notre-Dame du Raincy, Paris. Auguste Perret, 1922–4. Interior.*

his ideal city; these include his step-gabled Slaughterhouse (1908–24), Municipal Stadium (1913–18), and housing for the États-Unis quarter (1920).

For Auguste Perret, reinforced concrete construction was an opportunity to reappropriate the trabeated stone construction of ancient Greece and Rome. Perret's thinking owed much to Auguste Choisy (1841–1909), a professor at the Beaux-Arts, who argued, like Viollet-le-Duc, that the best architectural styles followed the logical consequences of building technique. Perret followed this ideal, one that had preoccupied French architects since the eighteenth century, in reinforced concrete buildings that articulated their structure — among them his Rue Franklin apartment building in Paris (1903) and his church of Notre-Dame du Raincy (1922–4).

51   *Proposal for Assembly Hall, Cité Industrielle. Tony Garnier, 1904–17. Drawing.*

Toward the end of his career, Perret had the opportunity to rebuild the bombed-out port of Le Havre according to an infinitely repeatable, adaptable geometric system which reduced the principles of Classical architecture to their lowest common denominator.

In England, Charles Holden (1875–1960) was equally determined to express the industrial age; but whereas Perret had tried to invent a new, trabeated world of perfect order, Holden was concerned more with expressing issues than with tectonics. In an article for *Architectural Review* in 1905, Holden asked:

Why should we architects live in such perpetual rebellion with the present? . . . if we could only build with the same fitness, the same science, the same *unchallenged acceptance of modern material and modern conditions*, and the same sincerity; if we could only think of our building as an entirely modern problem without precedent (and it is an entirely modern problem without precedent), just as the railway engine is; then, without a doubt, the same beauty, the same serene dignity would inevitably accompany our efforts, and the ruins of the past might crumble to dust, but the architectural tradition would remain with us still.[49]

Although Holden's article declared that designing a "modern" building had no more to do with historical precedent than designing a machine, his design for the British Medical Association Headquarters in London (1906–8) revealed a much more complicated historical sensibility.

53 *British Medical Association Headquarters (now Zimbabwe House), London. Charles Holden, 1906–8.*

54 *Arnos Grove Underground Station, London. Charles Holden, 1932.*

The first two stories refer to a building by C. R. Cockerell (1788–1863) that had stood on the site, rather than to the "modern problem," which emerges on the third story, in the series of sculpted nudes by Jacob Epstein (1880–1959), vaguely linked to the theme of "The Seven Ages of Man." The sculptures shocked the public by their frankness and lack of adherence to the tradition of idealist Classical sculpture. The architecture was equally bold, framing the sculptures with chunky vertical elements which rise in a staccato rhythm to the roof.

By the 1930s Holden had welcomed the functionalist palette of materials, yet he continued to ally himself formally to the Classical tradition. His Arnos Grove Underground station (1932), like many of Otto Wagner's train stations for Vienna, encases its new materials and function in a Classical envelope; in this case, the station's form is a cylinder emerging from a square in brick and glass, reminiscent of the Barrière de la Villette by Ledoux. In his Senate House buildings for the University of London (1936–40), Holden explored a more orthodox though astylar Classicism in a composition of vast height and area. Holden wanted the building to last 500 years, and to insure its perdurability, he largely ignored novel building technologies and employed stone load-bearing walls, reserving the steel frame for its tower.

Edwin Lutyens stands out from his generation for first mastering the vernacular mode and then, in middle life, turning toward Classicism as the language of the public realm. Once introduced to values of the high Classicism of the Modern era, Lutyens revelled in the style, mastering its linguistic structure and producing compositions of the highest complexity. While his contemporaries executed backward somersaults trying to avoid the overt use of what they

deemed a dead lexicon, Lutyens exulted in Classicism, which through his inspired efforts was revealed as a living language.

Like Wright, Lutyens had only the sketchiest training in architecture. After a brief term at the South Kensington School of Design, he ended his education at eighteen to work for Ernest George, an architect known in the 1880s for his eclectic designs which often larded half-timbered Tudor designs with picturesque details from various other European vernaculars. In 1889, when he was twenty, Lutyens set up his own office and began a career as a precociously successful country house architect. Under the influence of the Arts and Crafts movement and of Gertrude Jekyll (1843–1932), a talented garden designer and craftswoman, Lutyens deepened his understanding of the vernacular, so that even the works of his first maturity, such as Tigbourne Court, Witley, Surrey (1899), frequently combined the regional vernacular of England with Classical elements and with quirky compositional strategies that made a house seem at once an inevitable expression of its locale, an ingenious response to the roadside site, and a dignified yet playful work of art. In the first few years of the twentieth century, Lutyens developed a highly personal, yet unambiguously traditional approach to design which revealed him as a master stylist. His restoration of Lindisfarne Castle, Holy Island, Northumberland (1903), executed for Edward Hudson, the publisher of *Country Life* magazine, was so deft in its handling of the Gothic that it is near-impossible to tell where the ancient keep leaves off and Lutyens begins. But it was in the Classical tradition that he was happiest — whether in late eighteenth-century Georgian Classicism, as in Crooksbury, Farnham, Surrey (1898), or in restrained Baroque, as in the Hawksmoor-inspired Orangery at Hestercombe House, Somerset (1904). But it was not until 1906, in his design for the suburban villa of Heathcote in Ilkley, Yorkshire, that Lutyens undertook a work of pure Classicism. At Heathcote he brilliantly fused the formal and geometric rigor of Classicism with the spatial intrigue that characterized his best vernacular-inspired domestic architecture. Built of gray stone, roofed in red pantiles, Heathcote reveals a Classicism at full flood, spirited and witty, yet monumental and thoroughly undomestic.

At Heathcote, Lutyens said, he could begin to play the "high game of Palladio." His shift to a full-blooded Classicism was in part a reaction against the free styles of the turn of the century

55　*Heathcote, Ilkley. Sir Edwin Lutyens, 1906.*

— whether the free naturalism of Art Nouveau or the neo- or crypto-Classicism of the Secession, both of which Lutyens had experimented with — and in part a response to the experience of his friend Herbert Baker, who had become the architect for Cecil Rhodes, the de facto ruler of much of southern Africa. Baker, like Lutyens, was untrained in the Classical architecture which Rhodes required to suit his *Imperium Africanus* yet became proficient in it after an extended Mediterranean tour sponsored by Rhodes. By 1910 Baker had completed an inspired Classical design for the Union Houses in Pretoria, South Africa.

In 1912, Lutyens and Baker were given the commission for the new capital buildings in New Delhi. The British Raj had decided to move the capital from Calcutta to a new city, to be built outside Delhi, and required a vast new complex of buildings both to represent the British Empire's might and to give its rule the stamp of legitimacy by occupying the ancient Mughal capital. Baker designed the Secretariats that frame the approach to Lutyens's centerpiece, the Viceroy's House, which was set on a slight

56　*Viceroy's House, New Delhi. Sir Edwin Lutyens, 1912–31.*

rise at the end of a 2-mile (3-kilometer) vista. The 650-foot- (195-meter) wide stone façade is overwhelmingly Classical in its parade of open colonnades, yet there is a subtle admixture of the Mughal detail that Lutyens was forced to include as a gesture of cultural respect. Lutyens found very few local monuments that he considered worthy of consideration, yet his interpretation of the forms of a highly distinctive vernacular tradition give the Viceroy's House a degree of exoticism and abstraction which make it one of the most haunting works of Modern Classicism. The dome, the central feature, is a half sphere supported by a plain drum, which appears to float — an effect achieved by the use of a *chujja*, a simple projecting Mughal-style cornice, which Lutyens set beneath the drum and above a balcony running around the dome to create a deep slot of shadow. Beneath the dome, the attic story runs across in an unbroken line, interrupted only by a few square windows, each capped by a miniature Mughal dome. Lutyens's pragmatic blend of the Classical and vernacular — taking account of the effect of relentless sunlight — extended to the climatic problems of the enormous house. The columned loggias are designed to catch every breath of air; formal life could proceed out-of-doors in courtyards detailed to look like interior rooms, with the conceit of coves that rise, not to a ceiling, but to the sky. The Viceroy's House is a Mughal fantasy, cooled down by Classical discipline and interpreted in glorious rose-colored sandstone, the same stone used by Mughal emperors to build their monuments in the sixteenth and seventeenth centuries.

By the end of the First World War Lutyens had become an undisputed master of Classicism, with a sense of its geometric and mathematical requirements unmatched by that of any other architect since the seventeenth century. In his design for a temporary catafalque for a Victory Parade in London in 1919, Lutyens responded with a proposal for a cenotaph, a type of monument rarely built, but one that struck observers as uniquely capable of expressing the solemn conclusion of the First World War. Built first in wood and plaster and later in stone, the Cenotaph in Whitehall was inscribed simply with the words "The Glorious Dead." It is a work of cosmic geometry, in which the verticals are imperceptibly inclined in order to meet at a point 1,000 feet (305 meters) above, and the horizontals are actually radials of a circle with its center 900 feet (275 meters) below ground. A planar mass, with a subtly stepped profile, the

57　*Cenotaph Memorial, Whitehall, London. Sir Edwin Lutyens, 1919–20.*

Cenotaph, with its combination of elaborate geometry and unornamented surfaces, typifies Lutyens's series of emotionally arresting monuments, which also includes the memorial to the Missing of the Somme, the Thiepval Arch (1925), in France. In this design, Lutyens expanded upon the Roman triumphal arch, piling block upon block and increasing the number of arches to create an awesome display of

58　*Thiepval Memorial, France. Sir Edwin Lutyens, 1925.*

elemental mass and pure geometry. In the Roman prototype there is a great central arch, flanked by smaller openings. The keystones of the smaller arches reach the height of the spring of the great arch. Lutyens reinterpreted this by cutting arches through the side walls, extending the proportional relationships to another plane. Thus the spring of the great arch on the principal axis is aligned with the keystone of the central arch on the side walls, and the spring of the central arch of the minor axis is aligned with the keystones of the side arches of the principal walls to create a new, wholly three-dimensional type, a vast tower and arch upon which are carved the names of the 73,357 battle dead. At Thiepval Lutyens came as close as anyone to realizing the obsessional scale and transcendent sublimity conveyed in the abstract proposals of Ledoux.

The Viennese-trained architect Jože Plečnik serves as a curious parallel to Lutyens. Unlike Loos, who preferred to confront the deracinated modern with his alienation, Plečnik, like Lutyens, seemed to argue that if there are no roots, the architect should create them — an attitude shared by the American architects Bernard Maybeck, Irving Gill, Bertram Goodhue, and, most profoundly, Frank Lloyd Wright. Born and reared in a far corner of the Austrian empire, now part of Yugoslavia, Plečnik began his important architectural training when he entered Otto Wagner's studio in Vienna in 1894. He joined the Secession in 1901 and became the group's secretary in 1905. During this period he designed his most important building in Vienna, the Zacherlhaus (1904–6). Here he succeeded in creating a version of the modern architecture called for by Wagner. The Zacherlhaus is sheathed in gray-black granite, secured to the wall by granite battens set into the masonry, a rationalistic solution that gives the building vertical emphasis. Beyond the most basic compositional organization, the Zacherlhaus is a sample of a new, fairly tough, ahistorical, urban architecture, whose spirit is well symbolized by the row of muscular telamones supporting a double cornice.

At the end of the decade Plečnik left Vienna for Prague, where he began his academic career in 1911. He had been expected to take over Otto Wagner's professorship in Vienna after the great man's retirement, but the specific opposition of the Crown Prince, Archduke Franz Ferdinand (whose anti-Slav prejudice would earn him an assassin's bullet in Sarajevo) and the general rise of pan-German nationalism prevented Plečnik's

appointment. Leaving Vienna spurred Plečnik to rethink his architecture, to go outside the boundaries of the Secession and the Wagner school to explore the architectural heritage of his own Slavic culture and the Classical language he had been exposed to on an extended trip to Italy in 1899 — a trip that defied the teachings of Otto Wagner, who had, in his book *Modern Architecture*, attacked the tradition of an Italian sojourn for architecture students. Wagner wanted a modern architecture, cut off from the inevitable Romanticism of Italian sojourns, yet perhaps it is significant that two of his best pupils, Hoffman and Plečnik, were profoundly influenced by their stays in Italy.

In Plečnik's *oeuvre* the most profound synthesis of architectural styles is to be found in the buildings he produced after returning to his home town, Ljubljana in 1921. There he became head of the architectural school, a position which obliged him to serve as city architect as well; and he set to work interpreting the revivified Slovene national identity in stone.

To justify incorporating Classical themes in this distinctive new architecture Plečnik theorized that the Slavs were descendants of the Etruscans and, as such, legitimate inheritors of Mediterranean culture. His compelling integration of craft vernacular, High Classicism, and modern construction techniques transformed Ljubljana into one of the great Classical cities — one in which not only buildings but also the furniture of the city's streets and parks reflect the architect's grand vision. Among his gifts to Ljubljana are streets lit by columnar lampposts whose Ionic volutes scroll out into lamps, Classical bridges, and picturesque walkways under pergolas. Most importantly, Plečnik gave Ljubljana a succession of brilliantly designed,

59 *Lamp-post, Ljubljana. Jože Plečnik.*

60 *Slovene National and University Library, Ljubljana. Jože Plečnik, 1932–42.*

inventively detailed public buildings, the most monumental of which is the Slovene National and University Library, designed in 1932 and built between 1939 and 1942, a highly personal fusion of Classicism and the local vernacular. The harsh exterior of the library consists of a rusticated granite and limestone base which carries walls of red brick and stone, laid in a random fashion according to the workmen's impromptu decisions. Against this craft vernacular background the Classical features stand out sharply — particularly two stretched Ionic columns topped by bronze volutes, which, rather than framing the four-story windows to create a kind of colossal Order, slit them in two. In the interior, a grand axial staircase traverses two-thirds of the building to a hypostyle hall of thirty-six unfluted black Doric columns. Plečnik showed that for him Classicism was a living language, to which he fearlessly added neologisms, such as the stair railings, in which the balusters supporting the rail are the cut-off tops of columns, with their capitals — including a proto-Classical Aeolic one — and the top segment of their shafts.

61 *Slovene National and University Library, Ljubljana. Jože Plečnik, 1939–42. Interior.*

62 *Proposal for Slovenian Parliament Building Ljubljana. Jože Plečnik, 1947. Section.*

Two other projects represent the summit of Plečnik's genius. One, the Church of the Sacred Heart in Prague (1928–33), was built; the other, the Slovenian Parliament building (1947), intended for Ljubljana, was not. A deeply religious Roman Catholic, Plečnik imbued his church designs with fervent emotion and spirituality. Whereas the minimalistically articulate pedimented concrete temple façade of his first church, the Church of the Holy Spirit in Vienna (1910–13), seems a particularly bleak distillation of Classicism into raw concrete (which would have been softened if the intended ornamentation, such as column capitals, had been executed), the design for Prague was extraordinarily rich. The long rectangular block of the building is divided vertically between a brick base, a stucco clerestory, and a very gently pitched pediment-gable. This division is repeated in the clock tower, which — rather than being square in plan — rises like a stele, 138 feet (42 meters) high and virtually the width of the main building. The detailing is rampantly original, including granite slabs that jut out at right angles from the brick walls (a rationalistic decoration, like the bolts on Wagner's Post Office Savings Bank, since the granite slabs are interspersed with the bricks and used to bond them. The base flares out beneath the clerestory, where the surfaces are

smooth and white and graced by a row of garlands beneath the cornice. The division of the main block between brick lower walls and a stucco clerestory is repeated on a larger scale in the tower, whose shaft of brick and granite is made wonderfully transparent by the two clocks which have huge glazed *oculi* for their faces.

The Slovene Parliament would have been Plečnik's greatest secular monument if it had been built, the architectural embodiment of his Classical-Slavic cultural dream. Combining one of his favourite motifs, the obelisk, with the political-religious tradition of the dome, Plečnik devised a scheme in which the rotunda's columns leaned inward to reinforce the structural and spatial geometry of the cone they supported. After the Second World War, however, Plečnik's vision of Slavic architecture — ''We Slavs have our own original emphasis, yet we still must often search for it in Rome'' — disappeared with the rise of functionalist orthodoxy.[50]

SCANDINAVIA AND FINLAND

The architects of Scandinavia and Finland who belonged, at least roughly, to the generation of 1870, were, like Plečnik and Lutyens, determined to create an architecture that was both Classical and deeply rooted in its place of origin. The first architectural expression of the nationalist Romantic movements pervading their countries drew on the medieval and folk traditions of building and ornament. Yet while these seemed suitable for small-scale buildings, much like those associated with the Arts and Crafts style in England, they were considered less satisfactory for modern, large-scale public commissions — as was demonstrated by the evolution of the design for the Helsinki Railway Station (1904–14), by Eliel Saarinen, Herman Gesellius and Amias Lindgren, from a folkish Romanticism to a free-spirited Classicism.

The reaction against the vernacular and Art Nouveau in Scandinavian and Finnish architecture went further than the crypto-Classicism of Saarinen. As in Austria, and especially Germany, an openly Classical lexicon was reintroduced, often drawing on the Neo-Classical and Revolutionary designs of Ledoux and Boullée. One of the most influential designs was Hack Kampmann's Police Headquarters in Copenhagen (1919–24), a spare, simplified Doric design organized around a colonnaded circular courtyard.

63 *Concert House, Stockholm. Ivar Tengbom, 1920–26.*

In Finland, Johan Sigfrid Sirén (1889–1961) designed the national Parliament Building (1924–30), a rose-colored granite edifice erected as a great national effort after a divisive and impoverishing civil war. Siren used an elemental Classical style that maintained traditional elevational hierarchies even as he altered the Roman- and Egyptian-inspired detailing.

In the work of the Swedish architect Ivar Tengbom (1878–1968) Classicism is toughened by a process that compacts the mass as it eliminates superfluous detail. Tengbom's Stockholm Concert House (1920–26) is a severely cubic mass relieved at the entrance by a shallow porch, lined by ten slim columns which rise in the full height of the building from unarticulated bases to Corinthian capitals. The result, in the interior as well, is a mannered mixture of an elemental trabeated Classical design with instances of rich ornament.

In Sweden, Eric Gunnar Asplund (1885–1940) went further than his Nordic contemporaries in minimalizing the vocabulary, yet maintaining the grammar of Classicism. His Stockholm City Library (1920–27) consists of perfect geometric masses, a cylinder rising from a cube, an essentialized version of Ledoux's Barrière de la Villette. In the development of Classicism as a living language in the twentieth century, Asplund's work on a smaller scale is important for its incorporation of the vernacular. In the Lister County Courthouse, in Solvesborg (1917–21), Asplund strove for Classical monumentality and vernacular character by gathering up the program into the most elemental of forms, a broad, gabled roof, which gave the façade the formality of a pedimented temple front. His Woodland Chapel in the Enskede Cemetery in Stockholm (1918–20) is a limpid realization of the Primitive Hut, comprising primary geometric forms and Classical elements in the vernacular materials of timber, shingles, and stucco.

FRANK LLOYD WRIGHT

No architect has had a more complex relationship with the ideas of modernity, Classicism, and the vernacular than Frank Lloyd Wright, the self-styled architect of the American spirit. Wright's training — to the extent that he was trained in design at all — was in the Gothicizing Arts and Crafts ideals of Viollet-le-Duc and his English counterparts. He made his most definitive statement of his design philosophy in 1901, in his speech on "The Art and Craft of the Machine." In it, he advocated a Modern vernacular based on machine production, yet stayed aloof from any position that could be defined as materialist or functionalist. Like Labrouste and Viollet-le-Duc, Wright was familiar with Victor Hugo's chapter on the death of architecture in *Notre Dame de Paris*, and, also like them, he drew conclusions perhaps never intended by the author. Dismissing William Morris, who had "miscalculated the machine," Wright asserted that "the steel frame has been recognized as a legitimate basis for a simple, sincere clothing of plastic material that idealizes its purpose without structural pretense." He continued: "The Art of old idealized a Structural Necessity — now rendered obsolete and unnatural by the Machine — and accomplished it through man's joy in the labor of his hands. The new will . . . clothe Necessity with the living flesh of virile imagination . . . ."[51]

At the very beginning of the century Wright was already rejecting functionalism: necessity was *not* the mother of invention. What, however, was the source of "virile imagination"? Wright denounced the Renaissance as "the setting sun which we mistake for dawn"; yet in his quest for a modern vernacular that would achieve the naturalness of handicraft

64 *Blossom House, Chicago. Frank Lloyd Wright, 1892.*

while exploiting machine production for the benefit of mass democracy, he repeatedly grappled with the Classical tradition, denying it in his verbal rhetoric while accommodating it in his designs. In essence, Wright followed a path that was becoming well trodden by architects of the time. It began with a definitive break with the past in the form of a reversal of Classical precedent, with asymmetrical composition replacing symmetry for a more "organic" fit between function and form, and proceeded to incorporate geometrically-derived ornamental motifs to represent the repetitive pattern-making of the machine. Wright credited his sensitivity to the appropriate repetitive, abstract geometric forms to his exposure to Friedrich Froebel's (1782–1852) kindergarten learning system of primary forms, which Wright claimed his mother had discovered at the 1876 Centennial Exhibition in Philadelphia. According to Wright, he was well on his way to creating organic, machine-age forms at nineteen:

When I presented myself as a novice to Mr. Sullivan I was already, and naturally, a potential designer with a T-square and a triangle technique on a unit-system; the technique that could grow intimate with and master the rapacious characteristics of the Machine in consistent, straight-line, flat-plane effects natural to machine technology . . . .[52]

For all his vaunted independence in plan and ornament, Wright often — especially in his public buildings — embraced the Classical values of symmetry, axiality, and cubic clarity. His work in this vein might best be called particulate composition, as opposed to the flowing spatial continuities and interwoven asymmetries of his domestic vernacular. In this respect Wright's career paralleled that of some of his arch-rivals among the Academicists, such as McKim, Mead, and White, as they each in turn moved from the asymmetries of suburban domestic designs to symmetrical, Classical — if, in Wright's case, only crypto-Classical — large houses and public buildings.

During a brief period around the end of his association with Louis Sullivan, Wright came near to becoming a Classical architect. The Blossom House (1892) in suburban Chicago is Wright's sole executed Classical design. Although still working full-time for Louis Sullivan, Wright designed the Blossom House independently, and he made a conscious choice to design in a style at odds with Sullivan's

ostensibly anti-Classical manner. Based on the "Colonial" revival, and especially on McKim, Mead, and White's Adamesque H. A. C. Taylor House in Newport, Rhode Island (1885–6), Wright's Blossom House is clad in a tight skin of narrow clapboarding and ornamented with a thin layer of Classical detail. The porches have Ionic columns, the main floor windows are arranged into Palladian motifs, and giant pilasters tie the house's two stories together.

After leaving Sullivan's office in May 1893 Wright continued to work in a Classical vein. In his competition entry for the Milwaukee Library and Museum (1893), he strove for the monumental Classicism of the World's Columbian Exposition, then under construction. Modelling the façade after the east front of the Louvre and Atwood's Palace of Fine Arts at the Chicago fair, Wright placed a long colonnade above a plain base, with a pedimented pavilion in the center. In the same year he moved toward a more abstracted Classicism in his Winslow House, in River Forest, Illinois, following a direction he had already explored when he designed, on Sullivan's behalf, the Charnley House in Chicago (1891). At the Winslow House (1893) the strict tripartite symmetry of the front elevation lacks Classical details, yet the front door opens directly onto a Classical vision, an arcaded screen which is an etiolated tribute to Brunelleschi's Foundling Hospital. In an unbuilt

65 & 66 *Winslow House, River Forest, Illinois. Frank Lloyd Wright, 1893.*

project for Wolf Lake Amusement Park (1895) near Chicago, Wright drew on the Academic tradition of the plan of the 1893 Chicago fair, which it resembled in its biaxial symmetry, its organization around a central basin, and its uniform cornice heights. The Park also has, in Wright's personalized lexicon, triumphal arches, arcades, and colonnades.

It is interesting to speculate on the career that Wright might have had if he had accepted Daniel Burnham's offer in the mid-1890s of a sponsored sojourn in Rome, after which he was expected to return and work on the huge urban projects typical of Burnham's office. Instead, Wright turned his back on Classicism, and in the residential projects that would establish his reputation around 1900, he moved further from Classical composition and detail to "break open the box" in plan and to devise the asymmetrical elevations and new decorative schemes of his famous suburban villas, the so-called "Prairie Houses." But as Wright took on work of a more public kind, where clarity of procession was required in the plan, not to mention dignity and legibility, he chose Classical axiality and frontality, if not the Classical language itself, producing a succession of important designs that show a non-historicizing but distinctly Classical approach.

In his commercial projects, Wright emulated Wagner and Olbrich by combining an original decorative order with a blocky, elemental sort of Classical composition. The Larkin Building, in Buffalo, New York (1904, demolished 1949–50), was a distilled meditation on an Italian *palazzo*.

68   *Larkin Building, Buffalo. Frank Lloyd Wright, 1904. Interior.*

Wright intensified the type's introverted focus by means of a glazed-in *cortile*. The ornament followed a geometrical style that Wright devised as an abstracted and elemental substitute for the naturalistic forms in the Classical tradition of his "Lieber Meister" as Wright called Sullivan. The strongly articulated pier-like pylons supporting spheres were a direct homage to Olbrich's Secession Building of seven years earlier. (When Wright, who came to be regarded in Germany as the American Olbrich, visited Europe in 1909, he went to Darmstadt in search of Olbrich, only to learn that his hero-colleague had just died.)

Nevertheless, in its placement on the capitals and bases of piers, Wright's ornament was thoroughly Classical in spirit. All of his successful public buildings — even including in its own mad way the Guggenheim Museum (1959), which marries the dynamic expressionism of modern technology to the monumental form of the Pantheon — reflected the same command of Classical composition even as they rejected Classical features. After he lost the commission for the Harold McCormick House to Charles Platt (1861–1933) in 1908, Wright's large-scale domestic designs often incorporated Classical composition. His McCormick project, which consisted of a series of episodic, disconnected pavilions, failed to cohere into a larger entity that would convey the essence of the place and the power of the patrons. Despite Wright's bitterness over the loss, one suspects that he understood why Platt's design, an Italian Renaissance style villa, had succeeded where his had failed. Thereafter his large houses were Classically-composed suites of biaxially symmetrical rooms. More importantly, they were condensed and compacted, with hierarchically-scaled masses which convey a singular, coherent image of the project. This idea of compaction and clarity of image was pursued by Wright in his Barnsdall House (1915–21), in Los Angeles, where an explicitly Mayan mass is arranged around the central courtyard, complete with a Classical exedra, recreating the plan of a Spanish colonial hacienda.

The Imperial Hotel in Tokyo (1915–22, demolished 1968), was Wright's most extended dialogue between Classical composition and

67   *Larkin Building, Buffalo. Frank Lloyd Wright, 1904.*

69   *Proposal for McCormick House. Frank Lloyd Wright, 1908. Aerial perspective.*

70 *Imperial Hotel, Tokyo. Frank Lloyd Wright, 1915–22.*

vernacular detail. Its rigorously symmetrical, hierarchical, and sequentially organized plan, complete with traditional *cour d'honneur*, was a masterful essay in academic formalism. Designed for Westerners visiting Japan, the hotel seemed to draw upon Tuscany for inspiration; its low massing and tiled hipped roofs reflected the influence of Wright's recent stay in Fiesole far more than any drive towards technological expressionism or any special sympathy for local Japanese building traditions. The entrance pavilion in particular — in its proportions, its framed setting within a courtyard, and its straightforward use of rhetorical elements to transform a mundane box — faintly echoed the subtle rhythms of Brunelleschi's Pazzi Chapel.

Bernard Maybeck is best known for his daring eclectic mixtures of vernacular and Classical styles, together with a dedication to the much-belabored ideal of structural honesty; yet his most memorable building is a Classical folly on San Francisco's waterfront, the Palace of Fine Arts, constructed for the Panama Pacific International Exposition of 1915.

The son of a German woodcarver, Maybeck grew up in New York City, where he began his working life as an apprentice in his father's profession. He was impatient with the designs of others, however, and was sent to Paris in 1880 to study furniture design. In Paris, he was apprenticed in a shop across the street from the École des Beaux-Arts, and after a few months realized that he was also impatient with designing furniture himself and wanted to become an architect. In 1881 he was enrolled as a student of architecture at the École des Beaux-Arts, and for the next five years studied in the atelier of Louis-Jules André (1819–90), the architect who had taken over Labrouste's practice. André was to inculcate in Maybeck Labrouste's rationalism and respect for new materials and his own "ideal of beauty," which would serve as Maybeck's lodestar.

On his return to New York in 1886 Maybeck began working for the new firm of Carrère and Hastings on the Ponce de Leon Hotel in St. Petersburg, Florida (1886–8). Thomas Hastings had been Maybeck's roommate and fellow student in André's atelier, and the two friends worked together to produce an exuberantly original Hispano-Classical design. However, Maybeck did not relish the idea of a career as the assistant to these two well-connected New Yorkers, and in 1888 he left the firm to set up on his own in Kansas City. Unable to find work, he left the next year for San Francisco, where he would stay for the rest of his long life.

After a few years of working for other architects Maybeck obtained a position as an instructor at the University of California at Berkeley, which provided the financial security he needed to strike out on his own. It was at Berkeley that he met his great patron Phoebe Apperson Hearst, who accepted Maybeck's designs for the campus's new Mining Building she intended to underwrite (the commission eventually went to

another architect) and agreed to his suggestion of an international design competition for a new master plan for the campus. As a starting point Maybeck offered his own plan. It was a sweeping composition, in which semi-circular arcades enclosed a vast central court, cut by an axis through its center that led past a *tempietto* to a domed temple of learning; and when it appeared in the *San Francisco Examiner* on 30 April 1896, it whipped up enthusiasm for a new Berkeley campus and for architecture that would rival that of the 1893 Chicago fair. Three years later, Maybeck was head of the international competition for the new campus, returning in triumph to his old haunts at the École des Beaux-Arts with Mrs. Hearst in tow.

Maybeck succeeded only too well in bringing the standards of the École des Beaux-Arts to Berkeley. John Galen Howard (1864–1931), who radically revised and executed the design by the competition's victor, Emile Henri Bénard — who declined what he feared would be a stultifying career in the New World — became University Architect and founder of the department of architecture. Howard considered Maybeck an outdated crank, and he was offered neither commissions nor a teaching position by the university during Howard's tenure.

Although Maybeck was largely denied the public commissions that would require the exalted rhetoric of High Classicism, he sometimes invoked Classical precedents if he felt that the character of the client deemed it appropriate. In his Lawson House, in Berkeley (1907), Maybeck came as close to Classicism as he would in a house design, choosing the theme of a "Pompeiian" villa, an appropriate one for San Francisco (which had recently suffered its own geological upheaval, the earthquake of 1906) and for his client, A. C. Lawson, a professor of geology at the University of California. On a practical level, the house was conceived as an "earthquake-proof" design in reinforced concrete — a material that also made the house relatively fireproof (it was fire, rather than the earth tremors that had caused the most damage in 1906.) A rectangular, two-story structure with a low-pitched roof above a concrete gable, the Lawson house is horizontal and monumental, with qualities of axiality and symmetry rare in Maybeck's residential work. His vision of Pompeii was filtered through French academicism and Schinkelesque Classicism; and this indifference to archeologically correct design ensured that the house's "Pompeiian" aspect would be more a matter of overall mood than

71 *Palace of Fine Arts, San Francisco. Bernard Maybeck, 1915.*

specific features. The simple, planar, concrete walls, decorated on the upper story with diamond patterns of colored stones, the modern interpretation of Roman *opus reticulatum*, the simple concrete arches and Pompeiian red walls of the sleeping porch; and the surfaces in pink and buff plaster and smooth-cast white concrete are all highly evocative in the Berkeley light, so much like that of Pompeii itself.

At the First Church of Christ, Scientist, in Berkeley (1910), Maybeck veered from the Mediterranean clarity of the Lawson House to a fusion of Gothic and Oriental stylistic details within a clearly defined Classical composition. Constructed mainly of redwood and concrete, the church employs a wide palette of materials, roughly half of them hand-crafted and half machine-made. The Gothic influence is apparent in two great windows, whose tracery is made of cast concrete. The industrial vernacular is represented by the asbestos tiles that clad the exteriors and by the factory sash used for most of the other windows — neither of which seemed incongruous to Maybeck in a church that combined a Greek cross plan and the low-pitched rooflines of a Japanese shrine.

Maybeck's architectural imagination included the ideals of Viollet-le-Duc, but was by no means hobbled by them, since above all he believed in a rather hazy ideal of beauty. This is nowhere better expressed than in his most compelling building, a temporary structure meant to celebrate art for the duration of a world's fair — that of the Panama–Pacific International Exposition of 1915 in San Francisco. The Palace of Fine Arts was so successful that it was kept standing after the fair ended and, after years of decay, was rebuilt in 1965–7 in permanent materials. It is dominated by a huge, orange, octagonal rotunda at the center of the composition, rising from its reflection in a pond and the thick plantings surrounding it like a romantic vision by Poussin, or, more frighteningly, one by Piranesi, or even Boecklin, specifically his Isle of the Dead. The assemblage of architectural features is equally Piranesian in its freedom with the Orders, both in the rotunda and in the two detached peristyles, whose stocky columns are much too short for their Corinthian order and whose entablatures mix Greek and Roman detail and scale. Maybeck perfectly captured the mood he had set out to express: "sadness modified by the feeling that beauty has a soothing influence."[53] Thus the issues of Modern Classicism were resolved by Maybeck not in a stripped-down essentialist style using new materials, as

in the work of Gill, but rather with the freedom of a movie set designer, albeit one who recognizes, as Piranesi did, that the essence of Modernity is invention.

While Maybeck was working out his rich syntheses of the vernacular and Classical in northern California, Irving Gill, sometimes regarded as the American Adolf Loos, realized an elemental synthesis of the Classical and vernacular in contemporary building techniques in southern California. Untrained in architecture, Gill began to work for Louis Sullivan in 1890 and absorbed the master's ideal of an organic, democratic, American architecture. After two years with Sullivan, Gill was obliged by ill health to leave for a more salubrious climate, and he settled in San Diego, California, then a small town of 17,000 which had already passed through a boom and a bust. The Ionic colonnades of his first San Diego building, the Normal School (1895), showed that Gill, like Wright, was susceptible to the Classical grandeur of the Columbian Exposition.

Although Gill never abandoned the grammar of Classicism, in his mature work he did abandon the grand manner and struggled to resolve the Classical-vernacular conflict in a low-key, local way, attempting a synthesis between two seeming irreconcilables: the need to create an architecture rooted in and reflective of the traditional character of the southwestern United States and the desire to realize those traditional values in the most modern technological terms. Gill first resolved this dilemma when he employed a structure of concrete and hollow tile to recreate the planar, vernacular-Classical adobe architecture of the Spanish missions. For house designs, such as the Laughlin House, in Los Angeles (1907), he used Spanish features, including arched openings, pantile roofs and towers. By contrast, his commercial and institutional designs, like the Wilson Acton Hotel and Scripps Building, both in La Jolla (1908), had square windows rather than the arches of the earlier designs, thus lacking any sense of place and reflecting overall an international anti-aesthetic of industrialization.

Not content with the relatively new technique of concrete and hollow-tile building, Gill devised a tilt-slab method of construction which allowed a concrete wall, complete with its window frames and final cement finish, to be raised into place as one element. One of his tilt-slab buildings, the La Jolla Women's Club (1913), is a triumphant synthesis of the vernacular and Classical paradigms. The tilt-slab con-

72 *Women's Club, La Jolla. Irving Gill, 1913.*

crete walls are in the form of arcades, wrapped around a simple wood-frame building which houses the meeting rooms — an effect resembling the adobe mission architecture. On each side of the arcaded entrance porch, pergolas, constructed of simplified Doric columns supporting a redwood trellis, frame lushly planted courtyards.

Despite his technological determinism and the essentialism of his forms, Gill had, as we have seen, an acute sense of place. It was, however, a rather austere one, which did not always agree with that of the public, especially after the Panama-California Exposition in San Diego (1915), where Bertram Grosvenor Goodhue's ornate Baroque California Building offered a more exuberant alternative to the restrained Gill style and set a fashion that would be followed for some years to come.

Goodhue (1869–1924) had made his reputation as a Gothicist, and the California Building marked a turning point in his career. As the range of his commissions grew he was forced to

73 *National Academy of Sciences, Washington DC. Bertram Goodhue, 1919–24. Entrance.*

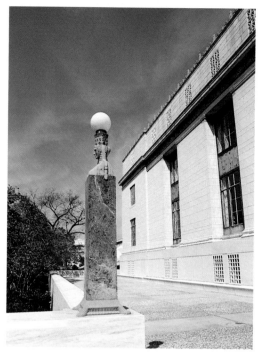

75 *State Capitol, Lincoln. Bertram Goodhue, 1920–32.*

77 & 78 *Pan-American Union Building, Washington DC. Paul Cret, 1907. Front and rear elevations.*

74 *National Academy of Sciences, Washington DC. Bertram Goodhue, 1919–24.*

come to terms not only with a wide variety of local vernaculars, but also with Classicism, which could provide a syntactical foundation for each design. For the National Academy of Sciences, in Washington, DC (1919–24) — the first structure to be built facing the recently finished Lincoln Memorial — Goodhue was expected to provide a Classical design. After considerable soul-searching, he came up with an essentialized Classical scheme, which he proposed be built with bare concrete walls. In the end, the walls were clad in marble, but stripped to a minimum of detail, with no columnar order.

The experience of designing the National Academy of Sciences made Goodhue realize the possibilities of individual expression within Classicism; and in his winning entry in the 1920 competition for the new State Capitol in Lincoln, Nebraska (1920–32) Goodhue produced an even more powerful example of latent, essentialized Classicism. Over a square base he set a massive square tower rising 400 feet (122 meters) above the Nebraska plains. The unprecedented synthesis of the skyscraper and traditional *civitas* made the Nebraska Capitol arguably the most influential American public building of the first half of the twentieth century.

Goodhue's conversion to Classical composition was rapid and thorough. In 1921, for the Liberty Memorial in Kansas City, Missouri, he proposed an acropolis of stoas, grand staircases, and colossal Greek statuary, all centered around an immense pylon. But this design was rejected in favor of one by Harold Van Buren Magonigle (1867–1935), which, ironically, had the diagrammatic clarity of composition and detail of Goodhue's design for the Nebraska State Capitol. Two winged sphinxes frame the approach to the Memorial, which is a three-part composition set on a plinth, composed of a tall shaft at the edge of the promontory, symbolizing the "Flame of Inspiration," flanked by two stripped Classical pavilions.

The leading figure in the trend toward a stripped Classical vocabulary in early twentieth-century America was the French-born architect Paul Cret (1876–1945). Apart from serving with the French forces in the First World War, Cret lived in the United States from 1903, when he arrived fresh from the École des Beaux-Arts to serve as a professor of architecture at the University of Pennsylvania in Philadelphia. While retaining this position, he also became the head of a major architecture firm.

In 1907 Cret won his first important commission through a competition; this was the International Bureau of the American Republics, later known as the Pan-American Union building, in Washington, DC. In realizing his design, in association with Albert Kelsey (1870–1950), Cret gave French Classical forms a Spanish flavor by including arcaded loggias and lush courtyards, with tile details and pantile roofs to create a synthesis that would represent the program of North and South American unity within the context of Washington's monumental Classicism. Cret's subsequent work moved increasingly toward greater purity in the handling of the Orders and simplicity in the detail. His winning entry in the competition for the Indianapolis Public Library (1914–17) has a severe Greek Doric portico.

76 *Proposal for Liberty Memorial, Kansas City. Bertram Goodhue, 1921. Drawing.*

79 *Pennsylvania State War Memorial, Varennes. Paul Cret, 1924.*

Cret went further toward Doric simplicity in the war memorials he designed during the 1920s to commemorate American military participation in France. For the Pennsylvania State War Memorial in Varennes (1924) he simplified the idea of the Classical colonnade by turning the columns into square piers, still with simple capitals, supporting an entablature carved with garlands. At Château Thierry, Cret's American Battle Monument Memorial (1928) abstracted the Doric order with fluted columns that became shafts of stone, without capitals.

Cret responded to technology more positively than any other Classical architect of his generation. His collaboration with the engineer Ralph Modjeski (1861–1940) produced a series of superbly crafted bridge designs in which the lightness of tensile steel was counterbalanced with the compressive weight of masonry — perhaps never more impressively than in the Delaware Bridge, between Philadelphia and Camden, New Jersey (1922), in which the profile of the anchorages restates the curve of the suspension cable grounded beneath cyclopean masonry. In 1928, writing about "The Architect as Collaborator with the Engineer," Cret characterized the marriage of pure aesthetics and functionalism implicit in his work:

In the cold, simple, and intensely practical forms that have been created to meet the clear-cut demands of utility, there are logic and utility . . . . But though the imagination is stirred, it is not satisfied. Logic and clarity and strength, though they are elements of the beautiful, are not all there is to beauty. Until they are emphasized by subtle modifications of lines and structural proportions — until a sense of harmony, of rhythm and accent fuses them into an aesthetic unit, they remain mute; they are seen, but they are not felt.[54]

In his Folger Shakespeare Library (1929), in Washington, Cret brought to the stripped Classical aesthetic the delicacy of detail that had made his Pan-American Union building seem so fresh a decade before. A synthesis of Classical mass and the Modernist ideal of an archtecture of volume, the library is a triumph of representation. Being located near the United States Capitol, the library had to be Classical for contextual reasons, and yet at the same time it had to reflect its contents, the world's greatest collection of Shakespeariana. Cret's Modern Classical exterior, in white marble, resembles his battle monuments in its stripped-down colonnade, in which pilasters are reduced to fluted panels between the windows, and its plain entablature. The simple Classical façades, however, serve as blank pages, inscribed with encomiums to Shakespeare and illustrated with his characters, carved in relief beneath the windows. In the interior, Cret felt no qualms about shifting to an architectural language contemporary with Shakespeare's writings, including an Elizabethan great hall as the main library and an Elizabethan theater. For all his devotion to Classicism, Cret had also made his peace with American aesthetic pragmatism, and he was more than willing to use a traditional vernacular style when the situation warranted it. Similarly,

82 *Federal Reserve Board Building, Washington DC. Paul Cret, 1935.*

he had, a few years earlier, used the Tudor style for a suburban villa, the Geist Residence in Villanova, Pennsylvania (1926).

Cret's Federal Reserve Board Building (1935), in Washington, is as refined and detailed as his Folger Library, yet it also has a powerful, almost aggressive mass appropriate to the bastion of an agency created to regenerate a depressed capitalist economy. The beautiful white marble exterior is a study in compactness, stripped down yet still exhibiting a rich sense of the potential of Classical form. The contrast between the gentle rise of climbable stairs leading up to the entrance portico and the huge steps of the building's plinth is among the most beautiful effects in Washington. In the interior, the stair hall recalls the elegance of Schinkel's Altes Museum in its composition of Classical columns and inventively patterned metal railings.

STRIPPED CLASSICISM
An International Style

Stripped Classicism flourished as an international language of architecture from the 1920s until the end of the Second World War. Frequently characterized as hopelessly reactionary compared to the work of the Modernists and frequently, and unfairly, disparaged on political grounds because it was employed in Nazi Germany and Fascist Italy, Stripped Classicism was as popular among democrats as among fascists. Taken on its own terms, the style can be seen as a robust and inventive movement within the tradition of Modern Classicism.

In 1924, two years after he had assumed power, Benito Mussolini proclaimed his architectural vision for Rome: "We must liberate all of Rome from the mediocre construction which

80 *American Battle Monument Memorial, Château Thierry. Paul Cret, 1928.*

81 *Folger Shakespeare Library, Washington DC. Paul Cret, 1929.*

disfigures it, but side by side with the Rome of antiquity and Christianity we must also create the monumental Rome of the twentieth century."[55] Mussolini's speech was nothing new; ever since Garibaldi had arrived in 1870 and turned a sleepy city of 230,000 inhabitants into the capital of a new Italian republic, Romans had been trying to devise and implement a master plan that would give their city the up-to-date grandeur of Haussmann's Paris. No one had succeeded, however, and Rome was rapidly built up in the greedy way of real estate speculation, a process known as *edilizia febbrile* ("feverish building").

Armando Brasini (1879–1965) may have understood and been able to express Mussolini's lust for monumental architecture better than anyone of his generation. Thoroughly at ease with theatricality and bombast, Brasini was almost entirely self-taught and had worked as a set designer, notably for the epic about ancient Rome, *Quo Vadis* (1913). He exercised a scenographer's liberty with history in adapting Mannerist and Baroque architecture into vast projected set pieces for Rome, such as L'Urbe Massima (1917) and, in 1929, his plan for a new imperial Rome. Brasini's colleagues, conservatives and Modernists alike, were appalled by his untutored taste and suppressed his 1929 plan, keeping it out of an exhibit at the XIIth International Congress on Housing and Urban Planning, held in Rome in September and October 1929. Mussolini, however, saw and admired Brasini's project; and during the next two years Brasini became one of a triumvirate of architects, including Marcello Piacentini (1881–1960) and Gustavo Giovannoni (1893–1947), who were given the responsibility of developing a master plan for Rome.

The thesis of the plan was Mussolini's: the ancient and Christian monuments had to be "liberated." It was reasoned that only bold *sventramenti* ("disembowelings") through existing districts could give the city sufficiently imperial vistas. Examples of liberating evisceration include the clearing of the Via dei Fori Imperiali, from Trajan's Column to the Colosseum, and the razing of the structures around the Mausoleum of Augustus (first century AD), which had been used as a fort, bullring, and concert hall for the past thousand years. The best known *sventramento* is the Via della Conciliazione, named after the Vatican's pact with Mussolini, which cut through the Renaissance neighborhood of the Spina del Borgo, from the Tiber to St. Peter's.[56]

83 *Buon Pastore, Rome. Armando Brasini, 1922–30.*

In addition to tearing down, the architects had to build up. Brasini's vision was too bizarre and individual to merit the status of official architecture, although he did manage to finish the miniature city of the orphanage of Buon Pastore (1922–30) and oversaw the slow evolution of the Cuore Immaculata di Maria Santissima church (1922–55). Here the combination of a plan of Neo-Platonic geometries is expressed in a violently original façade which is surely one of the most extraordinary tributes ever offered by an architect to Michelangelo.

Of the three architects who participated in the design of the master plan, Piacentini became by far the most influential in determining the

84 *Buon Pastore, Rome. Armando Brasini, 1922–30.*

85 *Senate Building, University City, Rome. Marcello Piacentini, 1932–5.*

course of architecture under Mussolini. An architect who had worked earlier in the crypto-Classical vein of the Secession, Piacentini moved on to a pragmatic mix of craft and machine elements, used with a fundamentally Classical grammar, in projects that were often aesthetically compelling, despite their ideological motivation. In Brescia, for example, Piacentini wrapped the Piazza Vittoria (1927–32) with simple arcaded buildings which reflected the synthesis of Classical form and vernacular building techniques characteristic of Italian town building.

Piacentini also led the team of architects responsible for the University City (1932–5), in Rome. He reserved for himself the design of the Senate which he housed in a gaunt, starved Classical building, with an entrance portico of four attenuated, stripped piers rising to a narrow band of Latin inscriptions beneath a thin cornice. The Senate terminates the University City's principal axis, which leads from Arnaldo Foschini's main entrance, the long, parallel lintels of which are supported by square, unmoulded piers, the international signature of the stripped Classicism of the 1930s. Piacentini wrote: "Born of an idea of a basilical and transept plan, [the plan of the University of Rome] draws all its impressiveness from order and fundamental symmetry . . ."[57]

The buildings constructed for the Esposizione Universale di Roma (E.U.R.) constitute one of the most recent examples of Classical urbanism. Planned as a world's fair to be held in 1942, the E.U.R. occupies a vast site 3 miles (4.8 kilometers) south of the center of Rome. The Exposition, first drawn up in 1937 by a group including Piacentini, was to be the site of an "Olympics of Civilization," which would show off Italian mastery of the arts and sciences, celebrate the twentieth anniversary of the regime, and serve as a new center of Rome. The international display was meant to surpass the spectacle of the 1936 Berlin Olympics. Under the direction of Piacentini, appointed supervising architect in

86   *Palace of the Congresses, E.U.R. Adalberto Libera, 1938.*

88   *Casa del Fascio, Como. Giuseppe Terragni, 1932–6.*

1938, the master plan was repeatedly 'Classicized," with functional and topographically imposed irregularities minimized so as to detract as little as possible from the monumental axes of circulation, the hierarchical organization of buildings, and the abstract planarity of the brutally stripped Classical façades. The most memorable architecture actually built includes the Palace of the Congresses by Adalberto Libera, a rectangular block fronted by a row of tall, square columns and topped by a flat dome, and the Palace of Italian Civilization (now the Palace of Civilization and Labor), designed by Giovanni Guerrini, Attilio La Padula, and Mario Romano, which broke with traditional Classical hierarchies to stack six stories of identical arcades on each of the four sides. On the ground floor, traditional statuary in the Classical style appears in the nine archways, serving as an antidote to the fatigue induced by the building's belligerent repetitions.

87   *Palace of Italian Civilization, E.U.R. Giovanni Guerrini, Attilio La Padula, Mario Romano, 1939.*

While the projects supervised by Piacentini defined an extreme of abstraction within the Classical tradition, other Italian architects of the time struggled to forge a different, but equally extreme monumentality by combining traditional forms with Modernism. The Casa del Fascio (now the Casa del Popolo) in Como (1932–6) by Giuseppe Terragni (1904–43) is one of very few to succeed on these terms. Terragni housed the local fascists in a purified Italian Renaissance Palazzo, designed to be "rational" and modern in its clearly articulated, trabeated concrete structure, and lack of cornice, colonnades, and porticoes. Yet Terragni also identified the building as tied to the Mediterranean tradition, and it is patently Classical in its perfect half-cube form, tripartite organization around a covered cortile, and marble cladding. Virtually none of Terragni's Italian contemporaries, and only a few Modernist masters such as Le Corbusier and Mies van der Rohe, ever fused Classicism and Modernism so powerfully.

STRIPPED CLASSICISM IN GERMANY

In Hitler's Germany, a specific architectural aesthetic — defined in part negatively as the opposite of the Weimar Republic's — was prescribed as the representative architecture of the Third Reich. The ahistorical materialism of Modernism was considered thoroughly inadequate to the requirements of a government intent on legitimatizing itself by usurping as many of the traditional symbols of political power as possible. In the official architectural hierarchy, the most important public buildings were to be designed in an austere Classical style that stood for the *Macht* ("power") of the state. Classicism, which might be racially suspect due

to its Mediterranean origins, was justified by the Party's cultural propagandists, who explained that the Greeks were Aryan, too, which made Classical architecture, through an additional feat of mental gymnastics, simply a sub-category of the German building tradition.[58] Public buildings of a more local nature could be executed in the medieval German vernacular, and domestic buildings required pitched roofs and traditional materials to represent the virtues of the German *Volk*. Industrial buildings, at the bottom of the symbolic hierarchy, could follow the functionalist aesthetic no longer permitted for public buildings and housing.

Paul Ludwig Troost (1878–1934) set the Reich's standard of monumental Classicism. His Temples of Honor, in Munich (1934–5, demolished in 1947), commemorating the fallen of the abortive *Putsch* of 1923, resembled Cret's First World War monuments in their stripped Classical solemnity. They consisted of two open pavilions, mounted on plinths, with fluted pillars supporting a decoratively barren yet syntactically correct entablature. Troost's House of German Art, in Munich (1933–7), is a similarly severe Classical composition, the long colonnades of which were no doubt intended to bring some of the Greco-Prussian austerity of Schinkel's Altes Museum to the less rigorous ambiance of the Bavarian capital.

After Troost's death in 1934, the young architect Albert Speer (1905–81), who had been an assistant to Heinrich Tessenow when the Nazis took power, became the most important architect of the Reich. The achievement that brought Speer to the attention of the Führer was the design of settings of spectacular Classical grandeur for the mass meetings essential to the Nazi movement. At the Zeppelinfeld, in Nuremberg (1935, demolished 1967), Speer constructed a grandstand loosely inspired by the Pergamon Altar, a Hellenistic monument from the second century BC which had been reconstructed in a Berlin museum. The shape and details of Speer's monument were far larger and simpler than those of the prototype, and thus able to deliver their message more immediately to thousands of parading Nazis in the field. Speer insisted that the grandstand have a genuine stone structure, rather than a more expeditious steel structure, because he believed that the buildings of the Third Reich should eventually become beautiful ruins like those of the Classical world. It is ironic that Speer's monument was best known at the time as the background for a much more ephemeral, and more spectacular kind of architecture. On 11

89 *Zeppelinfield, Nuremberg. Albert Speer, 1935.*

September, 1937, giant projectors shot pillars of light into the sky to form a square 26,500 feet (8,000 meters) above the field, making a *Licht-Dom* ("Cathedral of Light"). Well aware of the power of the media, Hitler had films of the event distributed throughout Germany.

Hitler, however, still believed in the power of architecture itself, and he wanted permanent architectural monuments to the Reich. Like Mussolini, he desired an imperial city commensurate with the empire he was building, and he commissioned Speer to design it. Speer's model proposed a broad axis through the center of Berlin, from an enormous new railroad station at the south end to a Great Hall for mass meetings at the north. The project, praised by the architect and critic Leon Krier as "the legitimate heir to Haussmann's concept of a metropolis in the age of mass transport,"[59] had a megalomaniac scale exemplified by the Great Hall, designed to accommodate up to 180,000. In attempting to realize this project, however, Speer found himself at odds with his Führer. Speer, the architectural idealist, dreamed of a dome, 720 feet (220

90 *Master plan for Berlin. Albert Speer, 1936–43.*

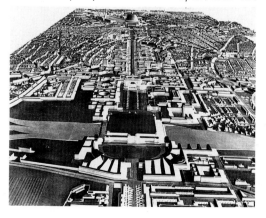

meters) high and 460 feet (140 meters) in diameter, constructed entirely out of masonry; Hitler, the pragmatic scenographer eager for results, ordered that the dome be framed in steel. But even this expedient proved too time-consuming, and the stadium was never begun. There were aesthetic differences, too. Speer's years with Tessenow had made him an essentialist, but as Hitler's power and megalomania grew, he pushed his architect toward his own tastes, for the exuberance of the Paris Opéra and the monuments of Vienna's Ringstrasse which had fuelled his frustrated ambition to become an architect.

Hitler's dream city remained largely unbuilt, except for a few elements, most notably the New Chancellery (1938–40, demolished 1945), a chilling example of intelligence and talent in the service of megalomania. After penetrating a reasonably sedate façade, faced in light-colored stucco and travertine, the official visitor, who was to arrive by chauffeured car, would begin a *promenade architecturale* ("architectural sequence") which led into a court of honor in which pavement, walls, and columns were all built of Dolomite stone. To enter the building itself, the visitor passed through a portico, four scarcely modulated columns *in antis*, which led to a vestibule, then on through 20-foot (6-meter) high doors to the Mosaic Gallery, then up a short staircase, into the domed rotunda, and then, as the axis turned to the right, into the enormous reception hall. To reach Hitler's office, the visitor had to proceed about half the length of the reception hall, which was lined by windows on the left, and then turn to the right. Inside, the office (perhaps most effectively interpreted in Charlie Chaplin's 1940 film *The Great Dictator*) was characterized by its enormous scale and luxurious materials. The walls and moulding were of rose marble, with a broad keystone panel above the five windows, and above was a coffered wooden ceiling.

Speer's most recent apologist, Krier, has argued that the criticisms of the New Chancellery are entirely associational — that its architecture is condemned only because of the regime that built it: "Classical architecture is quite simply incapable of imposing terror by the force of its internal laws . . . . It is certain that the grandeur, elegance, solidity and stability of the monuments of the Nazi regime were in no way intended to frighten or terrify the masses," but rather to seduce them.[60] Several architectural critics disagree with Krier; and Speer himself wrote: "[It] is right to detect Hitler's desire for

91 *New Chancellery, Berlin. Albert Speer, 1938–40. Court of Honor.*

power and the submission of others in my buildings. The main character of my architecture expressed this urge. In those years, I believed in the claim to absolute domination and my architecture represented an intimidating display of power . . ."[61] Colin St. John Wilson, criticizing Krier's evaluation of Speer's work, mocks the *promenade* of the New Chancellery as a "Long March to the Scaffold" and cites Geoffrey Scott's theory of "humanist" architecture in which the viewer empathizes with the building:

In Scott's terms your self-confidence is diminished by the massing of forms that threaten to crush you and by the inflation of dimensions of elements that are familiar (such as doors) so that your sense of body size is disoriented. You are made to feel vulnerable. Awareness of personal identity is drained by a numbing repetition of elements that make it impossible to identify or attribute significance to any one element. Space is manipulated not to shelter and to invite but to expose, to provoke a sense of insecurity. Windows have the blind stare that seems to deny any acknowledgment of your existence. Neither proportion nor detail imply any human presence. All these are the mechanisms of humiliation and intimidation.[62]

Speer also designed less monumental buildings. His design for his own family's house in Berlin (1935) has great charm. The entrance hall, located off-center on the garden façade, projects slightly forward of the block of the house, yet does not break the roof-line. Five plain columns of solid timber flank triple-hung floor-to-ceiling windows and support a simple entablature. Speer's atelier which was situated in Hitler's security zone of Berghof in the Alps interpreted the vernacular chalet type in a strictly symmetrical design.

The most intriguing architecture of the last years of the Reich was not by Speer but by Wilhelm Kreis (1873–1953), who designed a series of *Ehrenmal* ("memorials") beginning in 1941. Before the First World War, Kreis had designed several monuments to Bismark, characterized by a grotesque but compelling sense of massing and a primitivist Classicism. His successful career had continued after the war, and he built the monumental Planetarium and Art Exhibition building in Düsseldorf (1926), that had both a vividly Expressionistic interior in the planetarium and sober, stripped Classical pavilions. Most of Kreis's memorials to the German war dead throughout the countries conquered by the Reich were never completed, but his drawings of them are a catalogue of Classical traditions interpreted by an architect seeking a brutal, somber effect. They are reminiscent of Boullée in their reductiveness of form, yet also tied to place — a pyramid for Africa, an acropolis for Greece, a crenellated cylinder for Poland, as well as less site-specific cones, colonnades, and towers.

THE STYLES TO END ALL STYLES
The Struggle Between Stripped Classicism and International Functionalist Modernism

By the time Kreis was designing his monuments to the Nazi dead, the rivalry between stripped Classicism and Modernism was in full swing. There had already been several decisive confrontations during the previous decade. The first of these occurred in the competition for the design of the 1927 Palace of the League of Nations, when, on a trumped-up technicality, the prize was snatched from the hands of the Modernists Le Corbusier (1887–1966) and his partner and cousin Pierre Jeanneret (1896–1967) and placed in the open palms of a panel of architects who came up with a stripped Classical design. Then, in the competition for the Palace of the Soviets, announced in 1931, Le Corbusier's entry lost to a stripped Classical design by Boris Iofan (1891–1976), which was never built.

In these two incidents, the alternatives of stripped Classicism and Modernism appeared only in drawings and models and words; but visitors to the 1937 International Exposition in Paris could see the constructed evidence of both

92   *Palais de Chaillot, International Exposition, Paris. Jacques Carlu, Louis-Hippolyte Boileau and Léon Azéma, 1937.*

positions. The permanent buildings of the fair, the Palais de Chaillot and the Musée d'Art Moderne, were intended to reconcile modernity with monumentality. The Palais de Chaillot (which encased a 59-year-old building within its new façades) consisted of two wings, curved like the peristyles of a villa by Palladio, which were designed by Jacques Carlu, Louis-Hippolyte Boileau, and Léon Azéma. Instead of a villa at the center, there is a *place*, at the top of a monumental double staircase on axis with the Champ-de-Mars on the opposite bank of the Seine. Many observers found the architecture of the Palais de Chaillot bland. The Musée d'Art Moderne (P. Viard, M. Dastugue, J. C. Dondel, A. Aubert) was more compelling, because despite the conventionality of its plan of colonnades surrounding a court of honor, the usual hierarchy and massing of Classicism was largely abandoned in favor of simple cubic volumes and reductive structural expression. The best show

of stripped Classicism, however, was on the Left Bank of the Seine, where the German and Soviet pavilions faced each other across the entrance to the Pont d'Iéna. Intended specifically as a political confrontation between fascism and communism,[63] the two buildings were remarkably similar in their austerity. The fluted piers and blocky masses were executed in a ham-fisted manner by both Speer and his Soviet counterpart, Boris Iofan. Speer's pavilion was a static design which placed a sharp-edged, massive tower above the entrance. The similarly massive Soviet pavilion featured a stepped-back tower, rising in stages to a platform for the stainless-steel sculpture of a factory worker and a peasant charging forward, hammer and sickle in hand.

Amid the Classical designs of the French, German, and Soviet buildings, Le Corbusier threw down the gauntlet of Modernism with a tented exhibit hall, the Pavillon des Temps Nouveaux ("Pavilion of Modern Times"). Where the Classicists offered a stiff grandeur executed in faked materials for a temporary exhibition, Le Corbusier offered an industrial-age version of the "Primitive Temple" he had illustrated in *Vers une Architecture* ("Toward a New Architecture") fourteen years before, itself an oblique reference to Laugier's primitive hut. A steel latticework formed the columnar order which combined with tensile cables to support a tented canvas roof. Nestled in the trees, it was a virtual non-building, inside which visitors were treated to a dry recitation of Le Corbusier's urban order.

By the time of the Paris Exposition, Modernism — which had been born in the aftermath of the First World War — had reached its first maturity, exemplified by the work of Le Corbusier, Mies van der Rohe (1886–1969), and

93   *German Pavilion, International Exposition, Paris. Albert Speer, 1937.*

94   *Soviet Pavilion, International Exposition, Paris. Boris Iofan, 1937.*

95 *Villa Schwob, La Chaux-de-Fonds. Le Corbusier, 1916.*

Walter Gropius (1883–1969). It is important to emphasize that the members of the generation that initiated Modernism were imbued with the Classical tradition and, at least in the case of Le Corbusier and Mies, who were the greater artists of the three, the evolution of the new architectural language was in virtually every critical detail measured against the standards of Classicism that it sought to supplant. In crucial aspects, the language of Classicism, in particular its compositional ordering system, was fundamental to virtually all the significant work that would be created by the champions of the new, aggressively present-oriented aesthetic.

Born in La Chaux-de-Fonds, Switzerland, and christened Charles-Edouard Jeanneret, Le Corbusier (a family name he first used as a *nom de plume*) established his reputation as the prophet of the new architecture with a series of essays published in *L'Esprit Nouveau* ("The New Spirit"), the magazine he edited with the French artist Amédée Ozenfant, from 1919 to 1923, which were then published in book form as *Vers une Architecture* (1923). In *Vers une Architecture* (later translated under the title *Towards a New Architecture*, 1927) Le Corbusier argued for a new language of form explicitly and exclusively based on the vernacular of machine production. At the same time, he attempted to incorporate synoptically the 250-year old reformist argument of French Classicism that began with Perrault and continued through Laugier, that architecture must literally express its structure. Beneath a photograph of an automobile's frontwheel brake, he wrote as a caption: "This precision, this cleanness in execution go further back than our re-born mechanical sense. Phidias felt

in this way: the entablature of the Parthenon is a witness. . ."[64]

In propounding a structurally rationalist position, Le Corbusier updated Durand's argument of 120 years earlier, repeating as Modernist gospel the watchword of French academic architecture, "the plan is the generator," meaning that every aspect of a design — the volumes, the façade, the details — could be developed from the plan, which fluently embodied the logic of the building program. Le Corbusier was not content with the naked, if structurally innovative crypto-Classicism of his contemporary Auguste Perret. He would not rest until he could evolve an aesthetic even more elemental than that of Boullée or Ledoux; his real goal was to create a system of composition for reinforced concrete and metal as implacable as Durand's was for masonry. He wrote:

Architecture is the masterly, correct and magnificent play of masses brought together in light. Our eyes are made to see forms in light; light and shade reveal these forms; cubes, cones, spheres, cylinders or pyramids are the great primary forms which light reveals to advantage; the image of these is distinct and tangible within us and without ambiguity. It is for that reason that these are *beautiful forms, the most beautiful forms.*[65]

Le Corbusier undermined the seeming clarity of this essentialist approach to technology and geometry by introducing a second set of considerations — ones based on the painterly experiments of Cubism — and this introduced a decidedly anti-Classical dimension of continuous space and freely arranged wall-planes. As arranged in his early houses, these wall-

96 *Villa Stein, Garches. Le Corbusier, 1927.*

97 *Villa Savoye, Poissy. Le Corbusier, 1929–31.*

planes define a functionally determined sequence of movement through the ideal construct of the Classical grid. This impulse toward natural, free-flowing movement through the ideal grid represents an attempt at an additional synthesis between the abstract ordering of Classicism and the naturalism of the vernacular, with its *ad hoc* agglutinative approach to building. Le Corbusier came to this through his extensive reading of John Ruskin's writings on architecture and Owen Jones' *Grammar of Ornament* (1856) to which he was introduced by Charles L'Eplattenier, his teacher and mentor at the school of applied arts in La Chaux-de-Fonds.

Le Corbusier's education began a second stage in 1907 after he left La Chaux-de-Fonds, first for a sojourn in Vienna, where he rejected an apprenticeship with Hoffmann. In the same year in Lyon he met Tony Garnier and was enraptured with the latter's utopian socialist visions of an industrialized society filled with radically simplified, standardized Classical buildings. The next year, 1908, Le Corbusier worked in Paris for Perret, who seems to have convinced him that unfaced reinforced concrete was the material for building the new Classical socialist utopia. In 1910 Le Corbusier went to Germany, to study both concrete construction and the decorative arts. There he came into contact with Tessenow and worked for Behrens for five months. In the years before the outbreak of the First World War, Le Corbusier travelled extensively and taught at the Arts and Crafts School in La Chaux-de-Fonds. He toured the Balkans and Central Asia, the Greek islands, and in Italy, developing a sense of the Mediterranean vernacular that would form a subtext of most of his mature work.

The Villa Schwob (1916), in La Chaux-de-Fonds, is a synthesis of Le Corbusier's education and early professional experience and the last house he designed before settling permanently in Paris. The house has a Classical, Palladian organization in both plan and elevation. The structural innovation of a concrete frame has scarcely altered the exercise, and Le Corbusier has added to the conventionality by piercing the walls of the upper stories with elliptical windows and finishing the top with a simplified cornice. The central feature of the house, however, is an aggressive Mannerist ploy. The eye is drawn, by virtually every means available to the architect, to a blank panel. It is a blunt refutation of the conventionality of bourgeois houses, as well as a successful shock which prefigures the polemical relationships to Classical composition that typify Le Corbusier's later work. As a device it renders sentimental, by contrast, the otherwise similar façade composition of Frank Lloyd Wright's Hardy House in Racine, Wisconsin (1906), which Le Corbusier could have seen in publication.

By the time he completed the Villa Stein (1927) and the Villa Savoye (1929–31), he had developed theories of art, architecture, and urbanism. Together with Amédée Ozenfant he had become the founder of Purism, an art movement whose machine aesthetic advocated pure, geometrical forms, in opposition to the distortions of Cubism and Expressionism. In his architecture, Le Corbusier struggled to reconcile the irreconcilable: to synthesize structural rationalism with the primary forms of Purism, to give to raw, fabricated materials such as reinforced concrete the timelessness of elemental geometry in stone. Colin Rowe's essay "The Mathematics of the Ideal Villa" underscored the Classical elements in Le Corbusier's canonic villas by comparing the siting of the Villa Savoye which, like Le Corbusier's design, is set on a small hill in an arcadian landscape, an icon of idyllic life, with the siting of Palladian villas, especially that of the Villa Rotonda (c. 1550). Beyond noting the striking similarities in Classical mood, Rowe analyzed the parallels between the composition of the Villa Stein at Garches and that of the Villa Foscari, the Malcontenta (1550–60).[66] The Villa Stein exemplifies Le Corbusier's vision of modernity, consisting of a volume encasing a multilevel, free composition of spaces. Le Corbusier's own diagram of the villa analyzes the façade according to the ratios of the Golden Section. Where Palladio's Malcontenta aims for repose, the Villa Stein aims for gyrational shocks. Le Corbusier further rejects Classical symmetry in the plan, in which the Classical order of a columnar grid is played off against an episodic journey past perfect forms, as if the visitor were released within the confines of a

Purist painting, or as if the right-angled geometry of modern city planning overlaid the irregularities of a medieval town.

Around 1930 Le Corbusier appears to have begun to doubt whether the weightless, pure abstractions of his white stucco villas could elicit the full range of emotions he desired from architecture. Rather than abide by his previous strictures of "free plan, free façade, independent frame,"[67] he began to seek an equivalent to the monumentality of Classical masonry construction. To do this he rejected the light metal frame of his Purist work for the reinforced concrete structure of Perret. In projects for Paris, including Porte Maillot (1930) and his "Plans pour les musées de la ville et de l'Etat" in Paris (1935), as well as in the Pavillon Suisse of the Cité Universitaire (1930–32), Le Corbusier introduced a sense of physicality totally opposed to the weightlessness and tectonic insubstantiality of the canonic Modernism of the 1920s: the new Modernism would share the empathetic physicality of Classicism and its fundamental compositional discipline.

Le Corbusier's only equal within the early Modernist movement, the German-born Ludwig Mies van der Rohe (1886–1969), also attempted a convincing equivalent to the Classical tradition, creating a new "order" of steel and glass. Unlike Le Corbusier, who saw architecture with a painter's eye, Mies, the son of a stonemason, saw it mainly in tectonic terms:

Architecture is the will of the epoch translated into space. . . . If we discard all romantic conceptions, we can recognize the stone structures of the Greeks, the brick and concrete construction of the Romans and the medieval cathedrals, all as bold engineering achievements. . . . Our utilitarian buildings can become worthy of the name of architecture only if they truly interpret their time by their perfect functional expression.[68]

Mies's designs, however, abound in references to Classical precedent formalistically arrived at. The latent Classicism of his mature work is explicit in his early projects. To commemorate Bismarck, he proposed a Classical temple set in a Romantic landscape (1910). Long colonnades of stripped masonry piers delimit two sides of a one-acre (half-hectare) festival field. At one end of the field, next to the cliff falling off toward the Rhine, he placed a semicircular screen of heavy piers. He carried the refinement and compression of Classical details

98 *Pavillon Suisse, Cité Universitaire, Paris. Le Corbusier, 1930–32.*

at reduced scale in his unexecuted design for the Kröller-Müller House project (1912) in The Hague and in his early villas, such as the Werner House (1913) in Berlin.

In the disarray of postwar Germany, Mies reacted to a variety of aesthetic movements, including the architecture of Frank Lloyd Wright and the Dutch movement, De Stijl ("The Style"), as well as the functionalism that would be taken up in earnest by Walter Gropius (1883–1969) and Hannes Meyer (1889–1954). Under the sway of these various movements, Mies designed such memorable revolutionary work as two glass skyscrapers (1919 and 1920–21, neither executed) and a monument to Karl Liebknecht and Rosa Luxemburg (1926, later demolished by the Nazis). But by the late 1920s, perhaps under the influence of Le Corbusier, he entered a new stage, fusing his predisposition to Classical stability with a new feeling for space and structure. This could be seen in his German Pavilion, for the Barcelona Exhibition (1929), and his Tugendhat House in Brno, Czechoslovakia (1930).

But it was not until after 1937, when Mies emigrated to the United States, and confronted directly for the first time the realities of a thoroughly industrialized civilization and an everyday architecture of steel and glass, that he began to create a Classical order for the machine age. He settled in Chicago, where the city's grand Classical spaces, as exemplified by the lakefront parks of Burnham, may have influenced him, and where it is likely that such rationally conceived monumental buildings as the Drake Hotel (Marshall & Fox, 1922), which resembled his unrealized Reichsbank proposal of 1933, impressed him.

Mies first revealed the Classicizing formal

99 *Proposed monument to Bismarck. Ludwig Mies van der Rohe, 1910. Drawing.*

drive that animated his architecture of *beinahe gar nichts* ("almost nothing") in his first schemes for the Illinois Institute of Technology (I.I.T., then called Armour Institute), begun in 1939. As realized, the Classical plan gave way to a loose arrangement of interwoven spaces. But the palette of industrial materials does not prevent several of the buildings from resembling Classical temples in their symmetry and adherence to a new order of steel. The design for Crown Hall (1952–6), the Institute's School of Architecture, distills the symmetry and mathematical order of Schinkel's temple of art, the Altes Museum in Berlin into a glazed, steel-framed temple of architecture.

The ultimate Modernist temple archetype, Crown Hall does not fit easily into America's urban typologies, just as most forms of work and study do not fit into its open plan. But Mies's austere steel and glass aesthetic was successfully applied to the consummate American commercial building type, the skyscraper, most notably in his design for New York's Seagram Building (1954–8). Here again, there are echoes of Schinkel; Philip Johnson has pointed out the resemblances of the symmetrical podium arrangement and emphatic corners.[69] More important, perhaps, was Mies's understanding of the Classical, columnar nature of the American skyscraper — in the Seagram Building he came very close to his ideal of a Modernist

101 *German Pavilion, International Exposition, Barcelona. Ludwig Mies van der Rohe, 1929. Interior.*

Classicism that would subsume the facts of structure into the representation of humanistic order.

MODERNIST CLASSICISM
A Contradiction in Terms

Given the origins of Modernism in the ashes of the First World War — which had so thoroughly discredited the old monarchies, with their cynical diplomacy and militaristic ambitions — it is not surprising that its proponents rejected the very idea of monumentality, no matter what the style. Lewis Mumford, for example, embraced the new architecture precisely because it was anti-monumental. In his book *Sticks and Stones* (1924), Mumford mocked "The Imperial Façade" of the American Renaissance, calling Henry Bacon's Lincoln Memorial a "sedulously classic monument" which reflected the "generation that took pleasure in the mean triumph of the Spanish-American exploit. . . ."[70] As an

historian and critic, Mumford dedicated his life to the institution of a new, machine-age vernacular, raising a vigorous, compelling voice against the monumental ideal in architecture. But in time, the desire of Modernist architects and propagandists to impose their way of building (they refused to call it a style) universally, supplanting all that had preceded, naturally led to a call for a Modernist monumentality. One of the fundamental principles of Modernism as it emerged after the First World War was that the old architecture of masonry and mass was to be replaced by a new architecture of light, space-containing volumes. Monumental architecture was built to symbolize; the new architecture was intended to serve and to function. The pursuit of monumentality shook the ideological scaffolding of the entire Modernist enterprise.

The engineer, art historian, and polemicist of Modernism Sigfried Giedion (1893–1968) was the first to acknowledge the need for the new architecture to take on the traditional tasks of monumental architecture. In the essay "Nine Points on Monumentality" (1943), Giedion, writing in association with the painter Fernand Léger (1881–1955) and the architect José Luis Sert (1902–) declared:

102 *Seagram Building, New York. Ludwig Mies van der Rohe, 1954–8.*

100 *Kröller-Müller House, The Hague. Ludwig Mies van der Rohe, 1912.*

Monuments are human landmarks which men have created as symbols for their ideals, for their aims, and for their actions. They are intended to outlive the period which originated them, and constitute a heritage for future generations. As such, they form a link between the past and the future.

Giedion's statement became the main topic of the 1952 meeting of CIAM, Congrès Internationaux d'Architecture Moderne, the polemically-motivated group founded in 1928 by Le Corbusier and Giedion. This was an enormous shift for CIAM, whose Athens Charter of 1933 had been a manifesto of strictly functionalist architecture and urban planning. Although Giedion and his peers hardly advocated traditional monumental styles, they recognized that "the people want the buildings that represent their social and community life to give more than functional fulfilment."[71]

The art historian Vincent Scully has claimed that while post-Second World War Modernists were arguing about the appropriateness of monumentality and its possible progressive forms, Le Corbusier went ahead and built them:

His method became one which made a building not only a container for human beings and their functions — as most buildings are — but also — as most buildings are not — a sculptural unity that itself seems to act, like figural sculpture, and so acting to embody the peculiarly human meaning of the function it contains. In accomplishing this, Le Corbusier has created the monumental architecture of his time, even while his colleagues of the CIAM were debating whether or not monumental architecture was a 'good' thing, or about the need for it, or about how it would come when society was finally 'integrated.' Le Corbusier's is a modern monumentality because, like all monumental art, it deals with the most naked revelation of what the best of our thought believes to be real, which — so most metaphysical philosophy of the mid-twentieth century would indicate — is not the City of God, or the state, or afterlife, or a political dialectic, or material progress (which has never produced a monumental art yet) or even ourselves, but only our acts as we acknowledge them, try to understand them, and if possible, to ennoble them.[72]

For Scully, the government buildings of Chandigarh (1951–65), the capital city of the northern Indian state of the Punjab, embody an ideal of

103   *High Court Building, Chandigarh. Le Corbusier, 1951–6.*

existentially heroic monumental architecture. Their architect, Le Corbusier, had been given the commission of designing the whole city, which was to be more than a mere provincial capital. Since the newly independent republic of India had taken as its capital the city of New Delhi, with the existing government buildings of the British Raj, Chandigarh was nationally significant as the first entirely new architectural expression of the independent Indian government. The buildings of the capitol complex are oriented to the distant mountains, a relationship that Scully has argued is typical of Greek temples and palaces, rather than in relationship to each other, forming coherent spaces between them, which would have been a more Roman approach. The capitol complex itself, isolated from the residential part of the city according to Le Corbusier's urban planning ideals, consists of the Secretariat (1951–7), the High Court Building (1951–6), and the Palace of Assembly (1951–65). The buildings are uncompromisingly avant-garde and assertive sculptures constructed of unfaced concrete. Primordial forms break through roof-lines and stair towers, and irregular fenestration punctuates the façades. The High Court Building has a "columned" entrance of enormous, violently colored piers, with ramps rising behind them. In analyzing this building, Scully favorably concludes:

If we compare the High Court's piers with the columns of the House of German Art in Munich, we can best understand why Le Corbusier has

been able to create a convincingly monumental architecture in modern terms and why the Nazis, and indeed, many other power groups, were not able to do so with their columned façades. The latter are inert, not monumental, because they do not value the individual act; but Le Corbusier's aggrandize the man who stands before them by stretching his own force empathetically upward with them.[73]

Although the buildings of Chandigarh may be more exciting works of art than much of the stripped Classicism built before the Second World War and may "aggrandize" the individual, they fail to represent effectively the larger whole, the government and the nation which the individual must accommodate, or vice versa, and the culture, which necessarily transcends a single moment in time.

The other outstanding example of a grouping of monumental Modernist buildings is the new capital of Brazil. Located away from the traditional urban centers on the Atlantic Coast, on a *tabula rasa* of cleared jungle, Brasilia was planned, beginning in 1956, by Lucio Costa (b. 1902), a leader of Brazilian Modernism. Its buildings are the work of Oscar Niemeyer (b. 1907) who, twenty years earlier had collaborated with Costa and Le Corbusier on the design of the Ministry of Education and Health (1937–42) in Rio de Janeiro. Although the design of Brasilia was infused with Le Corbusier's urbanism, it was far more traditional than Chandigarh in its detailed planning. The cross-axial plan has a central focal point marked by the cleft towers of the Senate and Assembly offices, the Assembly saucer, and the Senate dome, which are sited at the points of an equilateral triangle, on a vast plaza high above the ground plane. Three miles (5 kilometers) away, the glass box of the President's Palace (1956–8) is set behind a cage-like peristyle of decoratively shaped concrete pillars that look like the colonnades of Mussolini's E.U.R. inverted to suit the rhythms of the *bossa nova*.

The Presidential Palace at Brasilia is similar to the hyper-attenuated Classicism of Edward Durell Stone's New Delhi Embassy (1957–60), in which Stone drained the sculptural force of a favorite device of Le Corbusier, the *brise-soleil*, by designing it as a perfectly regular pierced screen. In many respects this building inverts the machine-age aesthetic of Modernism while still being fundamentally ahistorical. Stone, curiously, was proud of the least Modernist aspect of his work — its manual construction. "This thing was literally built by hand," he said in an interview. "There were forges on the site to make the rough hardware. Except for the mechanical equipment, everything has a hand polish. This building was assembled like the Parthenon."[74] For contemporary observers, Stone had succeeded in creating a light Classical style, an architecture for easy viewing. A writer in *Architectural Forum* was enthusiastic:

What Ed Stone sought to do was to design a building that would represent this country's democratic vitality and romance, its pleasures as well as its powers, its strength, all without ponderous weight. Just completed, his graceful, glittering, eye-luring structure . . . fulfills most of the extravagant hopes aroused by first sketches three years ago, which awoke many people to the possibilities of a new government style.[75]

105   *United States Embassy, New Delhi. Edward Durell Stone, 1957–60.*

104   *President's Palace, Brasilia. Lucio Costa and Oscar Niemeyer, 1956–8.*

In the same issue, however, the then United States Ambassador to India, Ellsworth Bunker, pointed out that the style of the building was personal to Stone and had little connection with the larger traditions of the government which it was representing. As a result, Bunker warned, the "resemblance between his headquarters and a subsequent Stone design for a pharmaceutical plant in the U.S. . . . could debase the governmental character of this architectural currency."[76]

Eero Saarinen (1910–61), too, struggled to achieve an appropriate monumentality outside the Classical tradition. His United States Embassy in London (1960) attempts, in its detailing, to maintain the Georgian scale of neighboring buildings if not their hierarchical arrangement of parts. Faced in Portland stone and straw-colored anodized aluminum, the Embassy has a clearly defined, columned base, four relentlessly regular office floors, and a receding roof which resembles the roofs of the surrounding buildings on Grosvenor Square. For the English engineer and art historian Reyner Banham, the embassy is proof positive that a monument cannot be done in a Modernist idiom. In *Architectural Forum* he wrote that "The trouble here appears to be that somewhere inside all this a good architect is fighting to get out. . . . In an age when the authority of government depends on personalities, statistics, and communications, any attempt to build 'representational' buildings for prestige will simply produce empty cenotaphs."[77]

Saarinen's terminal building for the Dulles International Airport at Washington, DC (1964) is more successful in conveying a sense of monumental grandeur, though its columnar order fails to resonate with the symbolic authenticity of Daniel Burnham's Union Station, built more than half a century earlier (1903–8).

106   *United States Embassy, London. Eero Saarinen, 1960.*

The most articulate proponent of a rapprochement between traditional monumentality and Modernism is Philip Johnson (1906–). A protegé of Mies van der Rohe, Johnson had long noted the formal, Classical character of Mies's architecture. Rather than follow Mies's reductivist approach, however, Johnson demanded greater liberty. Analyzing his Glass House of 1949 in terms of its historical sources and precedents, Johnson made public his intentions toward a synthesis, citing influences from Greek temples, buildings by Schinkel and Mies, and twentieth-century art. He was the first to break the Modernist faith, recognizing as early as 1959 that the language of functionalist Modernism was insufficient to realize the goals of a truly monumental program. Yet even he refused to embrace a fully realized Classicism: "My direction is clear: eclectic tradition. This is not academic revival; there are no classic orders in my work, no Gothic finials."[78]

Regarded at the time as heretical retreats from Modernism, buildings such as the Sheldon Memorial Art Gallery in Lincoln, Nebraska (1960–63) and the Dumbarton Oaks (Washington) Art Gallery (1962–4) can be seen only as well-intentioned contradictions. Johnson upheld history as a "background of ideas" and a corpus of forms, and so these buildings are Classical in composition but highly idiosyncratic in their specific forms. He was still committed to the Modernist tenet that the essence of architecture is the will to *new* form, and so he tried to enrich his vocabulary through a peculiar transmigration of forms. Whereas in the traditional interpretation of the Classical temple the Greeks adapted the forms of rude wooden buildings for their temples of stone, Johnson tried to create a new public architecture by a similar kind of structural transposition, applying the forms of poured concrete to travertine. His efforts were far less successful than those of the Greeks,

107 *Dulles International Airport, Washington DC. Eero Saarinen, 1964.*

108 *Glass House, New Canaan, Connecticut. Philip Johnson, 1949.*

perhaps because the primitive struggle against the elements that is at the heart of wood construction offered, in its structures and limitations, an urgent rigor, utterly extrinsic to the permissive continuities of twentieth century reinforced concrete construction.

In New York, Johnson contributed to the plan and design of Lincoln Center for the Performing Arts (1956–68). An attempted fusion of Modernist and Classical languages, Lincoln Center has strikingly clear evocations of Mussolini's E.U.R. buildings. The obsessively repetitive quality of the Italian buildings reappears in the work of Johnson and his collaborators, Wallace K. Harrison (1895–1981), Max Abramovitz (1908–) and others. Johnson proposed that all of the Center's buildings be linked by a continuous colonnade, a gesture against what Colin Rowe has dubbed the "object fixation" of Modernism. In the end, separate, free-standing buildings were built. The New York State Theater, built principally to house George Balanchine's New York City Ballet, went to Johnson, whose characteristic attention to the processional nature of architecture renders it greatly superior to the others. Yet the

109 *Sheldon Memorial Art Gallery, Lincoln. Philip Johnson, 1960–63.*

110 *New York State Theater, Lincoln Center, New York. Philip Johnson, 1964.*

building is ultimately unsatisfactory, perhaps because of Johnson's Modernist disregard for the old forms of "academic revival." The decorative program of the exterior and interior is neither Modernist nor Classical. Instead, it has qualities derided as "ballet school" architecture: the interior's thin and impatient detail is both glitzy and numbingly repetitive.

The Estonian-born American architect Louis Kahn (1901–74) was educated at the University of Pennsylvania under Paul Cret, but later adopted a Modernist approach. Earlier than most Modernists, he called for a grander public architecture, in his article "Monumentality," published in 1944, yet he opposed the "ballet school" of monumentalism that developed in the early 1950s and 60s.[79] Like most of his generation in America, Kahn had rejected the Classical tradition under the initial impact of European Modernism, and it was only after the Second World War that he was able to re-evaluate Classicism while studying at the American Academy in Rome during the 1950–51 academic year. Kahn's search for an appropriate monumental expression was complex and took him back in time to the Romans, yet he never fully rejected the essential anti-historical bias of Modernist form-making, so that, although his achievement can be said to parallel that of the visionary architects of revolutionary France, the preoccupation with new building techniques often denies Kahn's buildings the cultural resonance that their historically derived abstractions possess.

Kahn's earliest move in the direction of Classicism was the Jewish Community Center (1954–9, project) and the Bath Houses (1955–6) in Trenton, New Jersey in which he placed the

111 *Salk Institute, La Jolla. Louis Kahn, 1959–65.*

fundamental, Vitruvian shapes of circle and square into an equally fundamental cross-axial composition, as though determined to begin at the beginning of the Classical tradition. In designs for the Fleisher House (1959) Kahn proposed a series of rounded arches, drawing on both Roman and Mediterranean vernacular precedent, and in elevation, the composition of rounded void with a slot below was drawn from the ruins at Ostia, Rome's ancient port, which Kahn had visited in 1950.

Completed in 1965, the Salk Institute in La Jolla, California (1959–65), goes much further. The programs called for laboratories, a meeting house, and housing, spectacularly sited on a bluff overlooking the Pacific. Kahn responded with designs derived from his studies of Classical, specifically Roman architecture. In the plans for the labs and the meeting house, he used the curvilinear patterns of Hadrian's second-century villa outside Rome, referring to Piranesi's maps of Rome (c. 1762) as well. The meeting house reinterpreted both the plan of Hadrian's

villa, combining lucid axes wih diagonal shifts, circular pieces with orthogonal ones, and also restated specific elements, taking the peristyle court, the "Piazza d'Oro" as a model for a fountain courtyard.

In the National Assembly building in Dacca, Bangladesh (1965–74), Kahn struggled to recover what he considered architecture's "loss of center." The building is one of primary geometries, simple shapes surrounding a circular plane. Its beauty of shape — the wonderful circles, triangles, and diamond cutouts, the utter power and simplicity in which all is composed; its obvious clarity; and its obvious richness triggered a whole new loosening-up of architectural form-making. It is a clear statement of Kahn's method, an illustration of his dependence on the particulate composition of Beaux-Arts design (separate enclosures of space, as opposed to the free-flowing spaces of orthodox Modernist architecture) and his ability to adjust and inflect the rigid shapes of geometry growing from that tradition to the immediate needs of a highly complex program.

112 *National Assembly Complex, Dacca. Louis Kahn, 1965–74.*

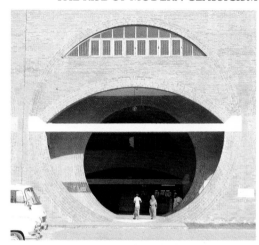

113 *National Assembly Complex, Dacca. Louis Kahn, 1965–74. Hospital.*

This essay has been an attempt to show the continuing validity of the Classical tradition as a way of designing buildings, and in so doing to find at least some explanation for what has been called "the secret of Classical architecture's eternal youth."[80] I have argued that the record of Classicism's adaptability to the changing ideologies and building technologies of the past five hundred years is evidence of the Classical tradition's inherent suppleness and strength. If this is polemical, it is only a polemic against the historians and critics in this century who have written, and continue to write, that Classicism is at best a dying tradition.

The following section of the book, *Current Classicism*, is intended to offer convincing testimony to the continued appeal of Classicism to contemporary architects, an appeal that was deemed virtually unthinkable twenty years ago.

CURRENT CLASSICISM

Previous pages:
City Hall, Mississauga.
Jones & Kirkland, 1982–6.

This book began with the thesis that Modern architecture is a continuum beginning in the fifteenth century, and that the aggressively ahistorical Modernism of the mid-twentieth century, which played fast and loose with this continuum, doomed itself to a short, nasty, brutish, and private sort of life. Although the rhetoric of some zealous Modernists was directed toward a repudiation of the Classical tradition, the most gifted adherents of the movement were still tied to this tradition, if only because it served as a standard of excellence — although not as a source of inspiration. Nonetheless, this bond was not enough to overcome the symbolic chasm that their rejection of the vocabulary of Classicism had opened between them and the very public they sought to address. By the 1950s, Modernism had congealed into an aesthetically reductive, schismatic and remarkably simple-minded approach to design, headed for destruction by its very lack of internal contradictions. Although in this respect of internal consistency, Modernism can be said to have succeeded on its own terms and, in the process, created some beautiful buildings, it is the concepts, not the artifacts, of Modernism that must be questioned.

In the 1960s architects began to question Modernism's premises, advocating a more inclusive philosophical and aesthetic stance, inaugurating a new era of the Modern, which in the late 1970s was designated "Post-Modernism." Although the adjective "Post-Modern" is often misleadingly applied to this movement, the correct term is "Post-Modernist," for what it repudiates is the reductionism of the Modernists — not the continuity of the Modern tradition, which the new movement, in fact, reaffirms. Where the history of Modernist aesthetics is one of philosophic and stylistic battles to establish a single, all-encompassing, uniform point of view — as evidenced by the succession of competing "isms," from Constructivism to Expressionism to Functionalism — the Post-Modernist position accepts as valid and even desirable that there be contradictions within itself, and even acknowledges Modernism as a logical counterpoint within the Modern tradition. In an essay entitled "The Doubles of Post-Modernism" I attempted in 1980 to define the complex, hybridized nature of this phenomenon, pointing out that there are two kinds of Post-Modernism: the schismatic strain, which completely repudiates Modernism, and the traditional strain, which proposes not only to free new building from the rigid constraints of orthodox Modernism but also to reintegrate or subsume Modernism within the broad category of the Modern as a whole.[1]

The concluding section of this book concerns itself with contemporary architects who represent in varying degrees the traditional strain of Post-Modernism, whether they choose to acknowledge it or not. Today's renewed invocation of tradition is not analogous to the rejection of the past led by Le Corbusier or Mies; nor is it comparable to the attitude of the post-War generation of Modernists, including Stone, Johnson, and Kahn, who yearned after Classicism but never seriously challenged the fervent Modernist commitment both to a technological basis for architectural language and to expressing the spirit of the times. The present generation has rejected this kind of "originality," preferring instead to work within a tradition, having realized that without a tradition, architecture, like any other art, cannot communicate — that buildings cannot be understood as unique, self-referential objects that impose themselves on the world, but as participants in a complex culture, relying on the willingness of individuals to accept them on the basis of what they know from the past. As the anti-Modernist Egyptian architect Abdel Wahed El Wakil (b. 1943) has written: "To abandon tradition, to disregard the achievements and models of the past and to be caught up in the trauma of change means to be incapable of handling the new."[2] Lucien Steil (b. 1952), a Luxembourg architect who believes in rebuilding the traditional European city, has written: "Tradition has, on the one hand, a dimension of timelessness and universality, being the 'selective wisdom' of people throughout the ages and, on the other, a character of local and geographical specificity."[3]

Most of the architects discussed in the following pages advocate a new-old architecture, a traditional architecture that can handle the new — that is to say, an architecture that is essentially traditional in its values although distinctly modern in its response to problems. Above all, in place of the aesthetic and environmental brutishness of the 1950s and 1960s, the present generation is committed to an architecture that is refined in its composition and respectful to its context.

In the 1960s, after two generations of combative Modernism, architects and urbanists began to reassess the place of tradition in the production of new work. For the first time since the early 1920s, the cultural hiatus that Modernism presumed to go hand-in-hand with twentieth-century experience began to be challenged on many fronts, most notably those of aesthetics and sociology. Although it was accepted that the twentieth century is qualitatively different from previous ages, the technological determinism and concomitant engineering-derived aesthetics of Modernism were seriously challenged for the first time and the cultural basis of architecture reaffirmed. In the United States the failure to supply a coherent alternative to traditional urbanism triggered a strong popular reaction against the principles of Modernist architecture. Jane Jacobs, a writer who discussed architecture and urbanism from a humanist viewpoint in the tradition of Lewis Mumford, observed with horror the products of America's urban renewal after the Second World War, in which the stale, inherently anti-urban ideals of Le Corbusier's *Ville Radieuse* had been institutionalized by law and realized by design. The message of Jacobs' book *The Death and Life of Great American Cities* (1961) was urgent: from the point of view of the city dweller, the slum districts being razed often had more of the ingredients required for a meaningful, life-sustaining urbanism than the meticulously planned, idealistically conceived housing "projects" built in their place. She argued that in order to survive, a city needed traditional streets, small blocks, old buildings, and most of all, a diversity of residential, commercial, and institutional uses. Vincent Scully, the architectural historian, carried the argument further, identifying in 1967 the "three destructive fallacies" of what had by then become standard American city planning: "the cataclysmic, the automotive, and the suburban." These fallacies, continued Scully, might be "characterized in a few words: the cataclysmic insists upon tearing every-thing down in order to design from an absolutely clean slate; the automotive would plan for the free passage of the automobile at the expense of all other values; the suburban dislikes the city anyway and would just as soon destroy its density and strew it across the countryside."[4]

Gradually such observations grew into a recognition by architects that the universal grids idealized by the Modernists were usually manifested in the debased currency of the housing project and the highway strip, and that the traditional city of streets, façades, squares, and civic buildings, of places hierarchically organized and sequentially arranged, was as valid as it had ever been. Thus it is essential to understand that the principal impetus to the traditional Post-Modernism discussed in this book is not merely a reaction to the prevailing aesthetic taste but a profound affirmation of the continuing validity of traditional patterns of human settlement and traditional hierarchies, even as new technologies and political conditions emerge.

In this opening up of architecture to its wider cultural responsibilities and in the recognition that even the anti-historical styles of Modernism have, in turn, taken on the aspect of a tradition, it seems to many today that only the Classical tradition, as it interacts with the infinitely varied traditional craft- and Modernist machine-driven vernaculars, has within it the capacity to coherently marshall these cultural forces. Because this book is concerned primarily with Classicism, the following discussion will only occasionally touch on another direction within traditional Post-Modernism, the effort to perpetuate pre-industrial craft vernaculars in the face of pressures of mass democracy and machine culture, although three of the movement's leading exponents — Leon Krier and the Basque architects Manuel Manzano-Monís y Lopez-Chicheri and his father Manuel Manzano-Monís — are discussed here in the light of their relation to Classicism.

It goes without saying that to be Modern is to be acutely aware of one's relationship to history, as often as not architects reject stylistic categorization as constraining. The architects discussed here are categorized only as a way to begin to interpret their designs. Within each approach they are presented in an essayistic order, beginning with those who were either first to define the design philosophy, or first to express it most emphatically. Most importantly, this discussion is intended to establish the extent and the profundity of the change that has overcome architecture in the past two decades. The change has given back to architecture its essential, civilizing purpose, which was described by Lewis Mumford, one of the most important twentieth-century critics of achitecture, in these words:

> The future of our civilization depends on our ability to select and control our heritage from the past, to alter our present attitudes and habits, and to project fresh forms into which our energies may be freely poured. On our ability to re-introduce old elements, as the humanists of the late Middle Ages brought back the classic literature and uncovered the Roman monuments, or to introduce new elements, as the inventors and engineers of the last century brought in physical science and the machine-tool technology, our position as creators depends.[5]

In looking at the work of today's Modern Classicists, the role of words, of the countless articles, books, and speeches must be acknowledged. When architects, not historians, began, after the hiatus of Modernism, to write about architecture in historical terms, the groundwork of today's activity was laid. Philip Johnson (b. 1906) made his famous quip, "you cannot not know history," at the end of the 1950s, and the generation that followed believed it. Charles Moore (b. 1925), for instance, took on one of the most provocative architectural designs of ancient Classicism in his essay, "Hadrian's Villa" (1960)[6], Robert Venturi's *Complexity and Contradiction in Architecture* (1966) is saturated with his familiarity with the history of architecture and is, in fact, as powerful a polemic as Le Corbusier's *Vers une architecture* (1923). Le Corbusier wanted to throw out historical precedent, except for the Parthenon and a few other buildings; Venturi wants to keep it all. Once the floodgates were open, architects found history inspiring at the drawing board as well as at the typewriter. The evidence of historical research is not only in essays written by architects, say those by Michael Graves (b. 1934) on Asplund[7] and Allan Greenberg (b. 1938) on Lutyens[8], but also in the buildings and projects that they design. The generation now dominating the international scene has continued the tradition of grounding work in historical precedent, whether from the distant past of the Ancients or from within the Modern period.

With the reacceptance of the idea of a Modern Classicism, architecture, once again, resumes its role as an evolving tradition. In order to better understand how that tradition is now evolving, I have identified five current approaches to Classicism.[9] The earliest approach to emerge was that of Ironic Classicism, whose most important theorist and practitioner is Robert Venturi. In place of the presumably content-free functional and technological determinism of Modernism, Venturi has proposed a semiotically motivated approach which more completely reflects the heterogeneous culture that contemporary architecture is destined to serve. Classical elements may be included in this architecture, yet always with "quotation marks." Historically-based elements ("signs") function as pretense, although useful pretense. The traditional distinctions between architecture and building, high art and the vernacular, are not respected by many of the Ironic Classicists. It should be noted that many of the architects adopting this approach have evolved beyond some of its early premises as they became aware that in the play between high culture and low there is a danger of producing architecture that is elitist in the least defensible form: ostensibly communicating on many levels, while in fact often making a joke at the expense of the proverbial man on the street. The ironic point of view also has similar problems to earlier Mannerist architecture, which its practitioners admire — that is, its efforts to amuse a highly knowledgeable in-group can lead to exaggeration ending in awkward and even ugly shapes. In the hands of many ironists, architecture becomes a matter of built jokes, and nothing goes flat faster than a joke.

Another approach, Latent Classicism, grows out of the historian Colin Rowe's observations that many of the significant Modernist buildings, especially those designed by Le Corbusier in the 1920s, not only were imbued with a desire to re-state the traditional values of Classicism in contemporary terms, but also aimed to compete directly with the masterworks of the Classical tradition. According to this argument, it is possible to marry the technologically driven aesthetic of Modernism to the compositional principles of Classicism, if not to its vocabulary of details. This is best seen in the parallels, drawn by Rowe, between Le Corbusier's villa of Garches and Palladio's Villa Foscari, the Malcontenta. Although Latent Classicists are not content to confine themselves to the rather minimal structural house of cards that held the Modernist masters in thrall, at the same time they are unwilling to play with the full Classical deck. While wishing to embrace Classicism's inherent compositional hierarchies, they are not willing to take on its symbolically charged formal vocabulary. The Latent Classicist is faced with a dilemma: how to convey the supple richness of Classical architecture and urbanism while pursuing a path of linguistic self-denial. Speaking only in serviceable prose, the Latent Classicist runs the risk of discovering that he or she is no Hemingway — and that straightforward syntax alone may result in an art that is not so much simple as simplistic.

Similarly, the third broad approach, Fundamentalist or Essentialist Classicism, carries with it a puritanical streak of self-denial, seeking to reduce buildings to the purest geometrical constructs, in an effort to achieve "natural," essential truths. Refusing to embrace any of the complex elaborations of the language of high Classicism, the Fundamentalists, unlike the Latent Classicists, go all the way in their rejection of Modernism. The Fundamentalist position seeks a Classicism that is timeless; it rejects distinction. To the Fundamental Classicist, the pre-industrial city, in both its Classical and vernacular manifestations, is the essential fact of architecture, and the task of today's architect is the analysis of the post-industrial city in relation to traditional urbanism.

The fourth approach, Canonic Classicism, also rejects the Modernist movement out of hand as an unfortunate spasm in the Modern tradition, but it revels in the high language of Classicism and in the authority of the past. For Canonic Classicists, the art of architecture, though tied to the evolution of culture, does not have any particular obligation to evolve in direct relation to societal changes; architecture, they argue (as do the Fundamentalists) is the tectonic representation of age-old humanist ideals, and not a thermometer to measure social health or a byproduct of technological evolution. In seeking to turn the aesthetic clock back to about 1750–1820 — that is to the period just before industrialization in the West — and to go forward from there, more or less as if all that went between then and now was nothing but a childish indiscretion, Canonic Classicism raises serious questions about history itself. Paradoxically, while revering history, Canonic Classicism cavalierly seeks to reverse it; perhaps this attitude is just as ahistorical as Modernism in its rigid selectivity regarding what is and is not architecture. Equally to the point, it does not follow the time-honored Modern method of refreshing Classicism by a return to the wisdom of the Ancients or an infusion of stimuli from without (the craft or industrial vernacular), but instead confines itself to the state of things at a particular point in Modern time. In so doing, the Canonic Classicists may be missing the essential fact of Modern architecture — that it succeeds in so far as it stretches and enlarges upon the examples of the Ancients, not as it feeds on the achievements of its immediate predecessors.

The final broad approach, Modern Traditionalism, attempts a synthesis, trying to reach a level of architectural discourse in which representation is not necessarily ironic, types and ordering systems do not preclude the picturesque, and styles are seen as evolving dialects within a common language, a language so supple that it can include the "Newspeak" of the Modernist era — such as Russian Constructivism, German and Dutch Expressionism of the early 1900s, the cardboard Cubism of the 1920s International Style, and even the "googie Modern" of the American 1940s and '50s — incorporating them, for example, in the way that English allows neologisms from, say, computer programmers.

In seeking a synthesis, Modern Traditionalism is, in effect, advocating a stylistically eclectic approach, opening itself up to charges of cultural, technological, and aesthetic opportunism, of "bourgeois" surrender to the tastes and production methods of consumer capitalism. Yet, for me at least, Modern Traditionalism offers the most optimistic and accommodating of all the points of view and best renders architecture capable of achieving in our time the integrative role it enjoyed in its most illustrious periods. Even more important than the various approaches to design that these categories represent is the fact that the inclusive, historically integrative base that all five share brings with it a recognition that once again, architecture is conceived of as a collective public entity, built up over time, continuing a dialogue with the past in the present.

1

IRONIC CLASSICISM

The essence of the ironic — which might also be called the semiotic — approach to architecture is that when Classical or other traditional elements or plans are used, they are always set in high relief against the standards of contemporary building techniques and programmatically determined masses. While in the emphasis on startling juxtapositions there is a relationship with the mannerist tradition of Michelangelo, Giulio, Soane and Lutyens, there is also a profound difference. Today's Ironists, unlike traditional mannerists, do not use Classicism as an overall ordering system. Instead, they accept the banalities of modern building technology as an economic necessity, while making very clear that it is hopelessly mute and unsuccessful as the basis for an architectural aesthetic. The elements of Classicism — a column, a pediment — are used as a semiotic overlay and the effect is ironic in its contradiction of Modernist and Classical, because it deprives the Modernist building of its only aesthetic rationale — symbolic form achieved through expression of structure — and deprives Classicism of its *gravitas* by slicing its language as thin as a glossy billboard.

The ironical stance suits those who believe that, while Modernism has been drained of most of its cultural meaning, it continues to perform syntactically. Modernism lost its meaning in the view of the Ironists, because the bond between advanced 'avant garde' technology — avowedly the principal formal generator of Modernist work of the 1920s and 30s — and architecture is no longer believable in a world where the most important technological advances have to do with electronic communications and not construction, the microchip rather than the I-beam. For Ironists the disassociated elements of Classical architecture are one way to give architecture meaning, so, too, are the elements of popular commercial culture. Thus they have tenuously and ironically revalidated the continuity of the Classical tradition.

1   *Henley Regatta Headquarters, Henley-on-Thames. Terry Farrell Partnership, 1986. View of west elevation.*

ROBERT VENTURI

For Robert Venturi (b. 1925), it would seem the survival of architecture and indeed of the very values that constitute culture depend on irony. As he proclaimed in his polemically-charged book, *Complexity and Contradiction in Architecture*[10]:

> The architect who would accept his role as a combiner of significant old clichés — valid banalities — in new contexts as his condition within a society that directs its best efforts, its big money, and its elegant technologies elsewhere, can ironically express in this indirect way a true concern for society's inverted scale of values.

Venturi does not reject the "contemporary" impulse of Modernism — the will to form in relationship to the realities of everyday life and the understandable impulse of an artist to carve out new territory — and his references to the past remain as counterpoint, ironic commentaries and asides, as it were, to the main theme of industrialized building.

In 1972, in collaboration with his design partners, Denise Scott Brown and Steven Izenour, Venturi outlined the semiotic method to his ironic approach in a book entitled *Learning from Las Vegas*. A principal thesis of *Learning from Las Vegas*, like that of *Complexity and Contradiction in Architecture*, was that architects should learn to interpret contemporary culture and building as they are, rather than ignoring them or dismissing them as meaningless. In their book, the authors draw a distinction between buildings that are "ducks" and those that are "decorated sheds":

1 Where the architectural systems of space, structure, and program are submerged and distorted by an overall symbolic form. This kind of building-becoming-sculpture we call the *duck* in honor of the duck-shaped drive-in, 'Long Island Duckling,' illustrated in *God's Own Junkyard* by Peter Blake.
2 Where systems of space and structure are directly at the service of program, and ornamentations applied independently of them. This we call *decorated shed*.[11]

2

3

2 *North Penn Visiting Nurses Association Headquarters, Ambler, Pennsylvania. Venturi and Short, 1960. View of entrance.*

3 *North Penn Visiting Nurses Association Headquarters, Ambler, Pennsylvania. Venturi and Short, 1960. View of entrance and street elevations.*

4 *Design for a country house, based on Mount Vernon, Venturi and Rauch, 1976. Unbuilt project. Rear elevation.*

5 *House in Delaware. Venturi, Rauch & Scott Brown, 1978–83. View of west elevation.*

REAR ELEVATION

4

Venturi is more sympathetic to the decorated shed, and he advocates an architecture of explicitly simple structures upon which ornament is lavished, in order to convey specific meanings that grow out of his interpretation of a building's program and its physical and cultural context. For Venturi, the symbols of architecture must be separated from the facts of building in order for both to succeed, and the symbols must refer to contemporary life. This segregation of symbol and fact and the insistence of contemporaneity is the key to why he has never designed in a straightforward historical style, which Venturi and his associates have frequently disparaged as "too easy." In an extended critique of the Museum of Modern Art's 1975 exhibition on the École des Beaux-Arts, Denise Scott Brown declared that the revival of interest in the French academic tradition was just another version of Modernist elitism, which still refused to "learn from Las Vegas:"

> . . . I fear that current establishment interest in the Beaux-Arts will be a fad and an evasion — a continuation of Modern purism in a new guise. The gains in social insight and social receptivity of the 1960s seem already lost, as architects forge into Post-Modernism, Radical Eclecticism, the New Rationalism, and the Beaux-Arts. These easier concepts, both visually and socially, help architects to avoid the harder task of defining a social architecture for our time.[12]

Despite an almost belligerent modernity, Venturi and his partners nonetheless propose a fundamentally Classical point: architecture's capacity to communicate an idea is not based on structural reality, but on form. In so doing, they have led the way toward an enriched, historically allusive aesthetic which has frequently been inspired by the grand monuments of the Classical tradition.

At the North Penn Visiting Nurse Association Headquarters Building in Ambler, Pennsylvania (Venturi and Short, 1960), Venturi showed the absolute distinction between the building's very simple structure, determined by the practical limitations of economics and function, and its far grander representational aspirations to architecture. The entrance is composed of elements whose form and interrelationship evoke Classical precedent. The wooden arch, cut out of cheap siding and laid over two diagonal braces, is at best a vestigial pediment, yet it gives a very modest building a measure of civic dignity, even monumentality, commensurate with one far grander. In the house built for his mother, in Chestnut Hill, Pennsylvania (Venturi and Short, 1961–5), Venturi used the remarkably modest occasion of a suburban villa to create a work of considerable profundity. Describing it, he has written: "The front, in its conventional combinations of door, windows, chimney and gable, creates an almost symbolic image of a house."[13]

Venturi deliberately rejects any tendency toward a full-bodied return to the Classical language, preferring to use its representative elements as counterpoints to what are, in effect, vernacular buildings. He roots his small buildings in regionally related craft vernaculars — as in his houses in Vail, Colorado (1975) and Tucker's Town, Bermuda (1976) for the Brant family; his bigger buildings, in the industrial vernacular. Subtly changing the scale of these representative elements, and frequently flattening them out to the thinness of cardboard cutouts, Venturi achieves the same disquieting tension that Giulio Romano achieved in his Palazzo del Té, even though Venturi's interpretation is deliberately graphic rather than physical. In his unrealized design for a country house based on Mount Vernon (1976), Venturi came as close as he has in any project to embracing a past mode as a whole. An extremely quirky variation of the Adamesque Georgian of the late eighteenth century, Mount Vernon is a cherished symbol of the American house. Rather than correct the design, as have many Classicists from Stanford White on, Venturi decided to exaggerate its quirkiness, pushing the entrance to one side, increasing the scale of the side buildings, enlarging the cupola, flattening the details, at every turn reminding the viewer that his design was a symbol of Mount Vernon, not the real thing, and that to communicate those associations without commenting upon them would be irresponsible. In contrast to Theodate Pope Riddle's (1868–1944) collaborative effort with Stanford White on the same theme at Hill-Stead in Farmington, Connecticut (1899), where features of Mount Vernon and the Connecticut farmhouse vernacular are skillfully combined in a syncopated composition, Venturi's design seems to confine invention to the forcing of scale and an exaggeration of detail which, though mainly sympathetic, has undertones of parody.

In his Eclectic Houses (1977), Venturi continued to demonstrate his sense of the history of architecture as a collection of symbolic images. Conceived as minimal vacation bungalows, these imaginary little houses are identical in all respects except for the front elevations, which play with traditional architectural elements, including a battered Egyptian temple entrance, a Greek Doric portico, and a Renaissance serliana. At a house in Delaware (1978–83), the basic outline and materials harmonize with its farm country setting: its low-lying profile reflects the area's eighteenth-century barns; its wood shingle roof, multi-paned, double-hung windows, shiplap siding, and masonry base are traditional to the region. To raise this modest vocabulary to the level of "architecture," Venturi introduced the Classical elements in a pair of huge "lunettes," which are vaguely Palladian and Adamesque, and related to the eyebrow dormers on Henry Hobson Richardson's (1838–86) "Shingle Style" houses. On the west side, the screen arches over the porch, which is supported by flat, cutout cartoon columns, a light-hearted irony in which it is the symbolic image of the column that counts, rather than its structural or formal purpose or its empathetic force.

The juxtaposition of pleasant vernacular design with startlingly incorrect Classical details has become a trademark of Venturi's office, including the work of his partner Steven Izenour, whose design for his parents' house in Long Island Sound (1983), blows up the scale of an exceedingly small building at once to celebrate and mock the grandeur of a temple by the sea, a little like those in Selenunte, Sicily, which Venturi so admires. With its four flat, clapboarded columns, and a large fanlight detailed as though it were a pilot's wheel, a "kingpin" becoming an analogue for a keystone, Izenour's design locates his temple in its distinctly American place.

Venturi's design for the Hampton Site Extension to London's National Gallery (the Sainsbury Wing, 1986–) involves critical issues of Classicism, context, hierarchy, and monumentality, as well as the relatively straightforward task of housing one of the National Gallery's most important collections, that of Early Renaissance paintings, and accommodating the "blockbuster" changing exhibitions that have become the mainstay of contemporary museum economics. The background to Venturi's obtaining the commission for the National Gallery extension illustrates vividly the public's increasing disenchantment with Modernism. In 1981 a competition was held for a combination gallery and office building on the site. None of the seventy-nine entries was deemed satisfactory, but it was finally decided that the British firm of Ahrends, Burton & Koralek should develop a more appropriate design. Their original design, a large "U" of double barrel-vaulted galleries around a circular entrance court, whose street façade had the historical stylistic touch of a series of arched windows, with "keystones," and the contextual one of a scale and cornice height that agreed with the main building, was to be modified chiefly to change the gallery spaces. After two years, however, Ahrends, Burton & Koralek did far more, moving from a somewhat contextually sensitive design to a radically Modernist one, replete with a glass tower set at the corner of the site, rising high above the cornice of the main building and vying with its pedimented portico for pride of place as the architectural symbol of the museum. The trustees stood behind the new design, but they met fierce resistance from the local government and abandoned it after Prince Charles, in a much-publicized speech to the Royal Institute of British Architects in 1984, likened the design to "a vast municipal fire station" and a "monstrous carbuncle on the face of a much-loved and elegant friend."[14] In a limited competition held in 1986, Venturi emerged the victor.

Set just to the west of the National Gallery's main building (William Wilkins, 1832–8), the Sainsbury Wing will occupy a key site at one corner of Trafalgar Square where it joins Pall Mall. Venturi's episodic, didactic, and semiotically charged design relates both to the square and main building and to the adjacent office buildings. Venturi took on the monumentality of Wilkins' design, undercutting its right-minded formality by repeating the Corinthian colonnade and at the same time "liberating" it by marrying it to an irregularly curving façade which encloses a sequence of galleries and lobbies, the plans of which owe as much to the Baroque as to the subtle, functionally driven, spatial complexities of the master Finnish Modernist, Alvar Aalto. At the east corner, several of Venturi's Corinthian pilasters are crammed together, as if the architect had run out of room. The rest are placed at intervals along the quirkily angled entrance façade. In the process, they graduate from half-buried pilasters to free-standing columns, after which they abruptly cease, as the façade turns toward Pall Mall. A similar borrowing occurs with the blind second-story windows, which Venturi carries from one building to the next but leaves hanging in all their elemental dignity, much like the engaged column at the turn to Pall Mall.

Despite its asymmetries, the main façade makes an appropriately grand, if fragmented, contextual gesture to the square; and having played a bar or two of architectural pomp and circumstance, Venturi can afford to indulge his taste for humbler forms and less rhetorically charged gestures in the rest of the design. Taken as a whole, this is a building with a vertiginous sense of infinite regress, in which the Modernist and the Classical keep reappearing unexpectedly. Behind the giant Corinthian order, through the porch cut beneath the base, masked by a gridded glass wall, is the entrance. By placing the entrance so low, at street level, Venturi has defied Classical principles of hierarchy. This is a Modernist building with Classical signs hanging on it, a point reiterated in the choice of materials. Along Jubilee Walk, which divides the main building from the new wing, Venturi has placed a glass wall. Yet this symbol of Modernism is only a transparent screen for the interior grand staircase, a traditional feature that rises beside a stone wall — a brilliantly conceived play upon the forced perspective of Bernini's Scala Regia (1663–6) at the Vatican. The most impressive view is at the top landing, where the stairway's path crosses the axis of the bridge joining the main building to the new wing. There are two exaggerated perspectives: one looking down the staircase, which narrows towards the bottom, and one looking toward the galleries, their entrances arranged as a series of receding arches.

6 *House in Delaware. Venturi, Rauch & Scott Brown, 1978–83. North-south section.*

7 *Vanna Venturi House, Chestnut Hill, Pennsylvania. Venturi and Short, 1961–5. View of front elevation.*

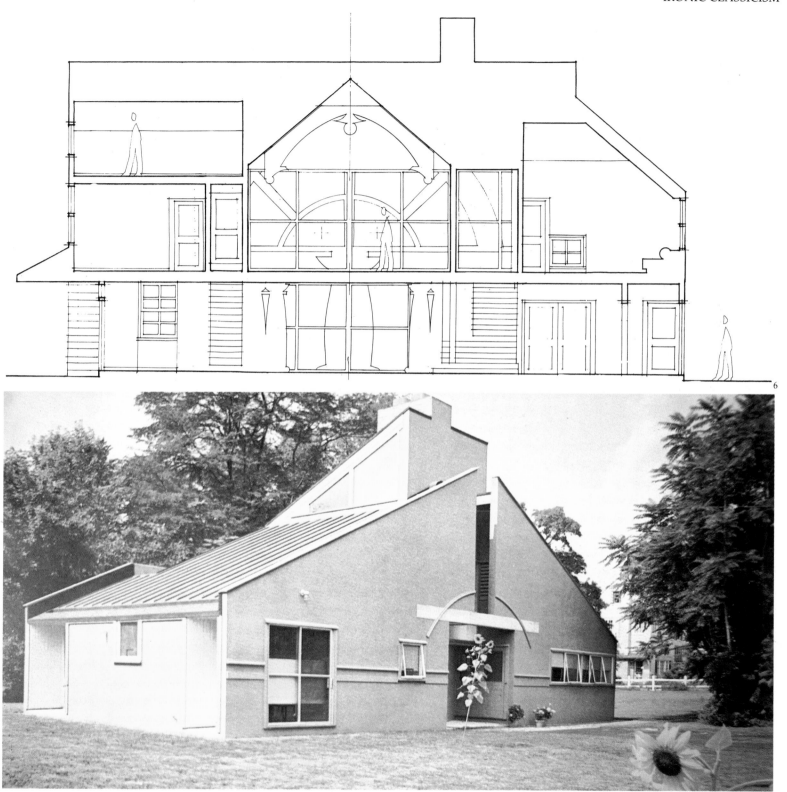

6

7

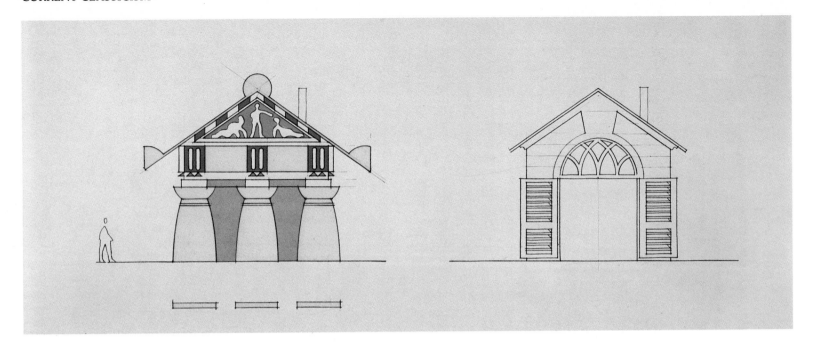

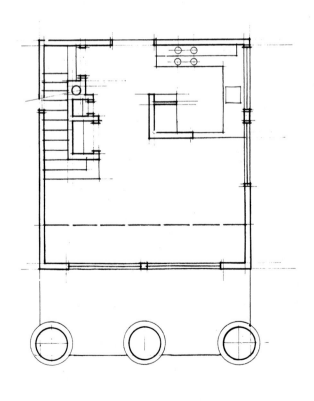

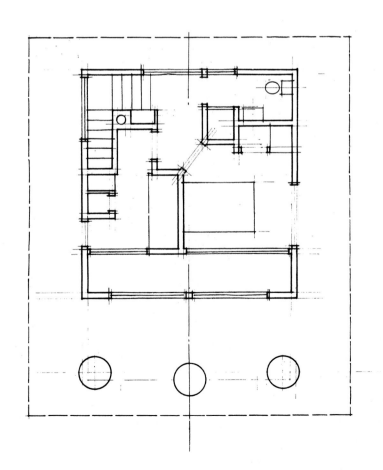

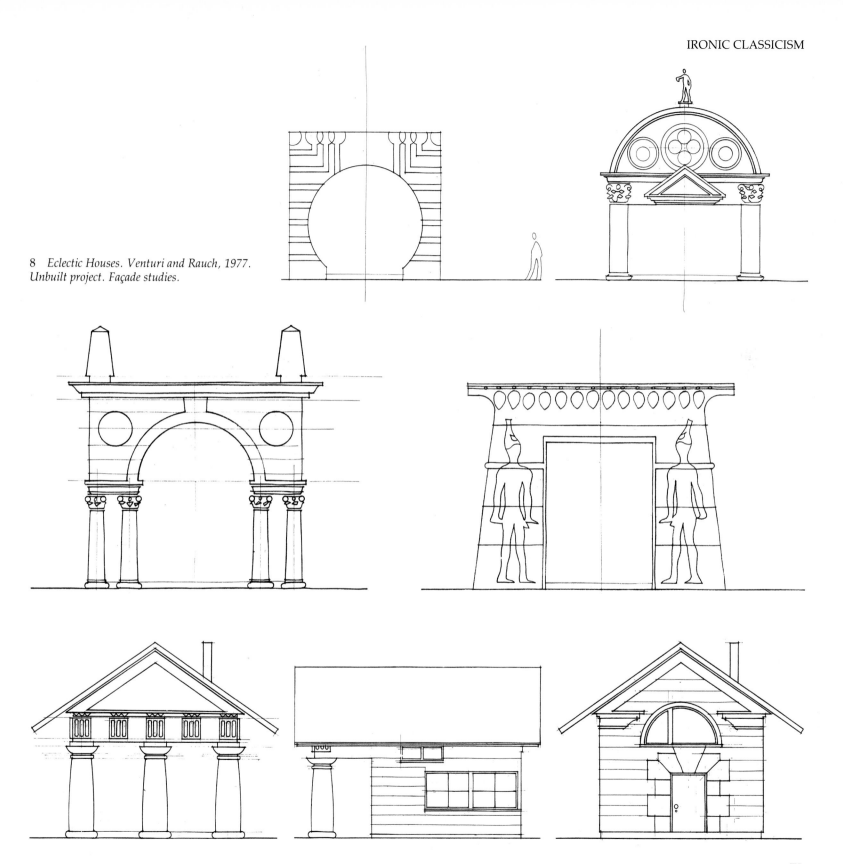

8   *Eclectic Houses. Venturi and Rauch, 1977.*
Unbuilt project. Façade studies.

9

10

12

11

13

9   *House in Delaware. Venturi, Rauch & Scott Brown, 1978–83. View of east elevation.*

10   *House in Delaware. Venturi, Rauch & Scott Brown, 1978–83. View northwest.*

11   *House on Long Island Sound, Connecticut. Venturi, Rauch & Scott Brown; Steven Izenour, designer, 1983. View of entrance.*

13   *House on Long Island Sound, Connecticut. Venturi, Rauch & Scott Brown; Steven Izenour, designer, 1983. View of waterside elevation.*

12   *House on Long Island Sound, Connecticut. Venturi, Rauch & Scott Brown; Steven Izenour, designer, 1983. Interior view.*

14   *Extension to the National Gallery, the Sainsbury Wing, London. Venturi, Rauch & Scott Brown, 1986–. Perspective from Trafalgar Square.*

14

CHARLES MOORE

In the late 1970s, even before Venturi was able to do so, other American architects, influenced by the example of his writings, early small buildings, and widely published unbuilt projects, carried Ironic Classicism into the public realm. Charles Moore's Piazza d'Italia in New Orleans (1977–8) and Michael Graves's Portland Public Service Building in Portland, Oregon (1980–2), reintroduced the values of Classicism into the civic architecture of the American city, reestablishing traditional architectural symbolism as well. Moore, like Venturi, has pretty much remained loyal to the semiotic, ironic approach to Classicism. Graves, on the other hand, has gone on, as we shall see, toward a more holistic approach.

In an essay entitled "You have to Pay for the Public Life" (1965), Charles Moore outlined the direction which he would take nearly a decade later in his first significant public commission, the Piazza d'Italia (with Urban Innovations Group, August Perez Associates, Malcolm Heard, Allen Eskew; colors by Christian Beebe.) Against all prevailing wisdom, Moore viewed Disneyland as an authentic expression of the public realm. He declared it the greatest urban project of the previous two decades, praising its public spaces — which, like the architecture that defined them, represented values that were intellectually accessible to the public. The design of Disneyland's streets and squares, its buildings and transportation systems, even if susceptible to castigation as kitsch, released a flood of associations that the public found woefully absent in conventional Modernist architects' urbanism. It is the creation of such places that Moore considers the ultimate goal of architecture. In his 1967 essay "Plug It in Rameses, and See if It Lights Up: Because We Aren't Going to Keep It Unless It Works," Moore wrote:

> If architects are to continue to do useful work on this planet, then surely their proper concern must be the creation of *place* — the ordered imposition of man's self on specific locations across the face of the earth. To make a place is to make a domain that helps people know where they are, and by extension, know who they are."[15]

At the Piazza d'Italia Moore presented a raucously sophisticated response to a tough, topical challenge: in Francophile New Orleans, he was asked to create a place that would represent the Italian–American community and provide the physical setting for that community's public festivals and celebrations.

Moore's piazza refers explicitly to the collective past of the project's sponsors. At its center, the outline of Sicily rises at the end of an 80-foot (24-meter) pool whose "stepping stones" form a relief map of Italy. Vertically planar Classical temple fronts frame the fountain, their concentric and discontinuous colonnades painted in the earth tones of vernacular Italian architecture. The entablatures have Latin inscriptions, recalling the great public buildings and places of Italy. On the Tuscan colonnade, stainless-steel capitals hide nozzles which spray "shafts" of water. The Doric entablature has delicate sprays mounted in each of the cutout metopes, coyly renamed by Moore "wetopes."[16] Ionic capitals are cut out of steel sheets, the Corinthian columns are topped by steel and plaster, and both Orders are delineated by blue and red neon strips.

15 *Piazza d'Italia, New Orleans, Louisiana. Charles Moore with Urban Innovations Group; August Perez Associates, Malcolm Heard, Allen Eskew; colors by Christine Beebe, 1977–8. Aerial view.*

16 *Piazza d'Italia, New Orleans, Louisiana. Charles Moore with Urban Innovations Group; August Perez Associates, Malcolm Heard, Allen Eskew; colors by Christine Beebe, 1977–8. View northeast.*

17 *Piazza d'Italia, New Orleans, Louisiana. Charles Moore with Urban Innovations Group; August Perez Associates, Malcolm Heard, Allen Eskew; colors by Christine Beebe, 1977–8. View northeast.*

Although Moore seeks to create an urban experience equivalent to Rome's Trevi Fountain (Nicolas Salvi, 1732), he falls short of this goal partly because unlike its inspiration Piazza d'Italia does not include a representational sculptural focal point. In the Classical tradition, architecture depended on other arts, especially painting and sculpture, to communicate effectively, and without these Moore's design is a little too abstract.

The Piazza is at once a staged contest and a volatile marriage of Classical themes and Modernist materials and spatial concepts. It pleased some critics but outraged others, offending Modernists and Classicists alike. Lebbeus Woods, a New York architect-illustrator, condemned the design as "a sequence of one-line jokes . . ."[17] Charles Jencks admired the work's radical eclecticism[18], and Christian Norberg-Schulz, the Norwegian architect and critic, considered the effect of the overlapping colonnades, with their shifting scales and fragmented character, more an embodiment of the principles of Modernist collage than of those of Classical space.

18

At the Rodes House in Los Angeles (with Robert Yudell, 1978), Moore pushed himself toward more explicit, if not necessarily less papery, historicism, with a Baroque villa stripped to its essence. Sheathed in grey stucco, it achieves a compact and rigorous elegance in its curved façade, flanked by two pergolas whose curved metallic pediments are the vertical echoes of the horizontal bow in the house's plan. The Rudolph House, in Williamstown, Massachusetts (Moore, Grover, Harper, with Robert Harper, 1979–81) relies less on semiotics than on traditional Classical composition. It is an inventive, if somewhat heavy-handed, synthesis of Palladian organization and Soanean sense of light.

In several subsequent projects, Moore and his collaborators have endeavored to go further beyond semiotics toward a full-bodied Classicism. One of these, the Extension Center and Alumni House at the University of California at Irvine (with Urban Innovations Group, Bill Hubbard, Michael Bernard, Bart Phelps, and Jerry Radin, 1983–5), gathers together a modest group of "vernacular" buildings to form a public space, defined in boldly scaled Classical porticoes and exaggerated gable ends. In its details as well as its general form, the Center's design not only alludes vaguely to the Spanish Colonial architecture characteristic of California but also adapts the facades of three chapels by Flaminio Ponzio (1560–1613) on the Celian Hill in Rome (1607). In so doing, Moore provides a human-scaled, distinctly defined outdoor public space of a kind almost absent from the rest of the Irvine campus, which was designed by William Pereira at near-megalomaniacal scale in the 1950s and '60s.

19

In the extension to the Beverly Hills City Hall (Urban Innovations Group, Edgardo Contini, James Morton, Stephen Harby, Richard Best, Shinji Isozaki and Renzo Zechetto, with Albert C. Martin and Associates 1982–), Moore seems to have abandoned semiotics. Although the language is at several removes from the stylized Spanish baroque of the existing City Hall (William J. Gage, 1932) — it is more than a little inspired by Art Deco — the design nonetheless sympathizes with the older building and succeeds in creating a commensurate sense of solidity and mass. When completed Moore's project is to include a new fire and police headquarters and a public library.) The proportions and massing of the new buildings are similar to those of the old, and the bay spacing is the same. The earlier building's materials — stucco with cast-stone details and a ceramic tile dome — have been essentially matched by the poured-in-place concrete, pre-cast concrete, and plaster, all painted in two buff colors, and the tiles used for the new structure.

In their design, Moore and his associates wanted to reinforce, rather than detract

20

from, the earlier building's status as the pre-eminent civic symbol of Beverly Hills. Thus they focused the energy of the design not on the perimeter, which they conceived of as faceless, but on the carved-out spaces of three oval courtyards strung along a powerful diagonal axis, an ingenious solution to a site cut by a cross street and also an invocation in plan of the Baroque spirit in the details of the City Hall. The courtyards are ringed by free-standing arcades, whose forms allude not only to the local Spanish traditions but also to the Moorish style favored in many early Hollywood epics and in the city's more permanent architecture as well.

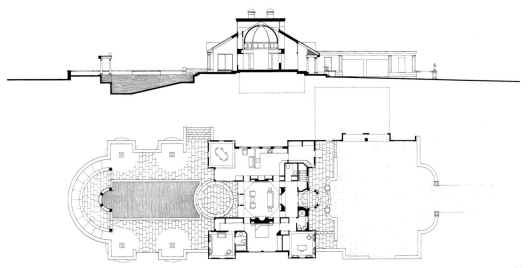

23

21

22

18   *Piazza d'Italia, New Orleans, Louisiana. Charles Moore with Urban Innovations Group; August Perez Associates, Malcolm Heard, Allen Eskew; colors by Christine Beebe, 1977–8. View southwest.*

19   *Rudolph House, Williamstown, Massachusetts. Moore, Grover, Harper with Robert Harper, 1979–81. View southwest.*

20   *Rudolph House, Williamstown, Massachusetts. Moore, Grover, Harper with Robert Harper, 1979–81. Interior view of dome.*

21   *Rudolph House, Williamstown, Massachusetts. Moore, Grover, Harper with Robert Harper, 1979–81. Plan and section.*

22   *Rudolph House, Williamstown, Massachusetts. Moore, Grover, Harper with Robert Harper, 1979–81. View north.*

23   *Extension Center and Alumni House at the University of California at Irvine. Charles Moore with Urban Innovations Group, Bill Hubbard, Michael Bernard, Bart Phelps, and Jerry Rudin, 1983–5. View northwest.*

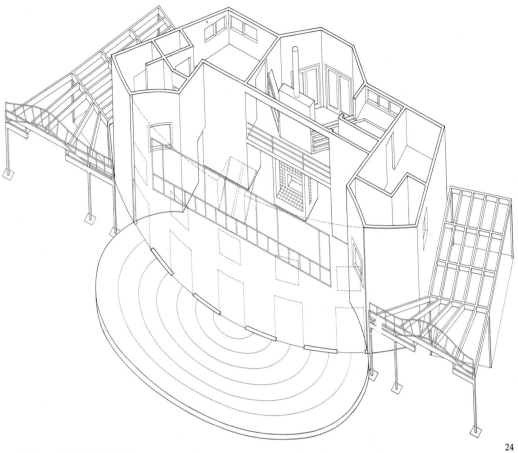

24

25

24   *Rodes House, Los Angeles, California. Charles Moore with Robert Yudell, 1978. Axonometric.*

25   *Rodes House, Los Angeles, California. Charles Moore with Robert Yudell, 1978. View of front elevation.*

26   *Beverly Hills City Hall Extension, California. Charles Moore with Urban Innovations Group, Edgardo Contini, James Morton, Stephen Harby, Richard Best, Shinji Isozaki, Renzo Zechetto; Albert C. Martin and Associates, 1982– . Perspective northeast.*

27   *Beverly Hills City Hall Extension, California. Charles Moore with Urban Innovations Group, Edgardo Contini, James Morton, Stephen Harby, Richard Best, Shinji Isozaki, Renzo Zechetto; Albert C. Martin and Associates, 1982– . View of City Hall from southwest gate.*

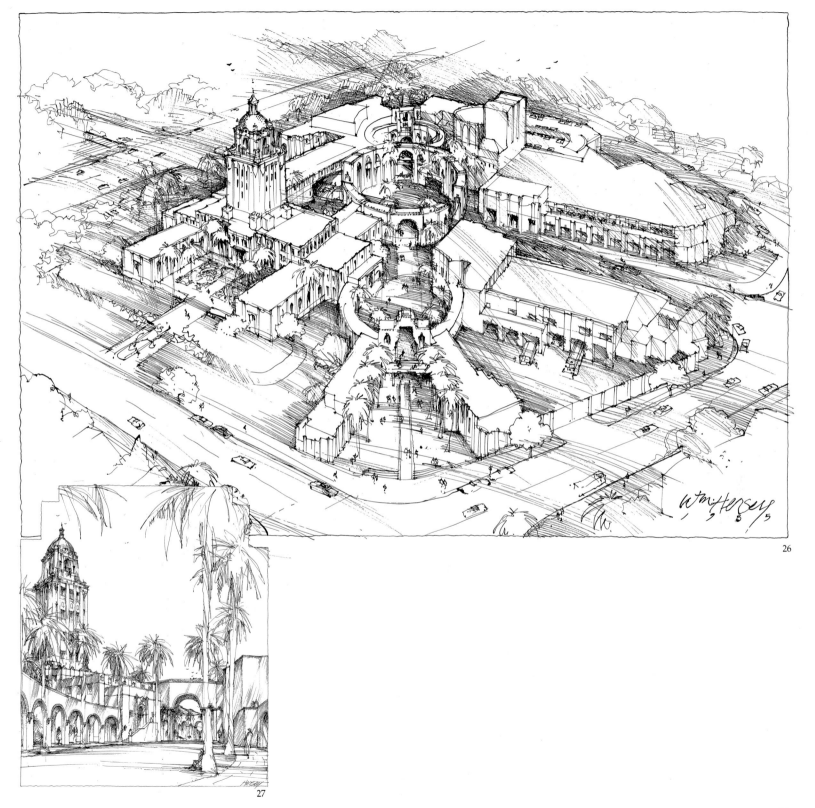

26

27

MICHAEL GRAVES

As no building before it, Michael Graves's Portland Public Service Building, in Portland, Oregon (with Emery Roth & Sons, associated architect; Edward C. Wundram, associated architect, 1980–2) called public attention to the change in architectural sensibilities that the term Post-Modernism represents. Though compromised by the inherent contradictions of its symbolic aspirations to Classical *gravitas* and the seemingly inherent commercialism of the circumstances of its construction, it is nonetheless a work of critical importance. Philip Johnson, who served as the architectural consultant to the Portland Building design competition committee, encouraged the choice of Graves' entry which made startling, if poster-board like and highly personal use of the Classical language. The design committee's choice was as brave as it was wise. An architect from Princeton, New Jersey, Graves was, before the Portland competition, better known for his drawings than for his buildings. He produced a design that transformed what was in effect little more than a low-budget municipal office building into a grand civic symbol.

Graves set out to create a sculpturally modeled composition, but was compromised by budgetary restrictions and a ridiculously hostile reception from a group of local architects who should have known better. As a result, the Portland Building was a flawed work — a Pop Art version of the Classically inspired ideals its architect had offered in the early sketches. Yet enough was realized to show what could have been done. At the base, which is faced in green tiles, Graves placed a loggia of unornamented piers. The cream-colored cube of the main building above is more a polemic against the Modernist window-wall than a wholly resolved composition. The windows are tiny squares, punched through a wall to create a neutral, if inert pattern. The façade's strength lies in the personal version of traditional Classical elements that Graves had been developing since he abandoned Cubist vocabulary and syntax in the mid-1970s. Multistory pilasters are surmounted by 10-foot- (3-meter)-high projecting "capitals," above which tinted strip windows (a Modernist machine-aesthetic device) and earth-red tiled walls form a five-story "keystone," pierced at the center by a romantic belvedere which convincingly reasserts human scale.

In the public debate over the Portland Building, Graves portrayed himself as the dragon-slayer, the dragon being the Modernist bland box. Graves defended the overall design and the superscaled Classical elements as part of the empathetic, anthropomorphic tradition in architecture, echoing the principles advanced by Geoffrey Scott (1885–1929) in *The Architecture of Humanism* (1914): "The tendency to project the image of our functions into concrete forms is the basis, for architecture, of creative design. The tendency to recognize, in concrete forms, the image of those functions is the true basis, in its turn, of critical appreciation."[19] But in reality, the building is more convincing as a billboard for an idea, rather than its embodiment. In his later buildings Graves has presented a more convincing case for an expressly figural architecture, and has progressively reduced the number of Modernist references, fully abandoning the so-called free plan and fully embracing the representational aspirations of Classical architecture.

28 *Portland Public Service Building, Portland, Oregon. Michael Graves; Emery Roth & Sons, associated architects; Edward C. Wundram, associated architect, 1980–82.*

PHILIP JOHNSON

Whereas Venturi, Moore, and Graves belong by chronology as well as conviction to the Post-Modernist generation, Philip Johnson was, until recently, an established Modernist architect. His Saul-Paul conversion to Classicism in the late 1970s was a pivotal event in the changing attitude of the public and the professional rank and file to the nature of architectural form. His support of Graves' design for the Portland Building in the face of local opposition was a critical factor in that building's realization. Some twenty years earlier, Johnson had made several stabs at a Modernist Classical style, reaching the intriguing but ultimately unsuccessful dead ends of the Sheldon Museum in Lincoln, Nebraska, and the New York State Theater discussed earlier. By the late 1960s he appeared to have returned to the orthodox Modernism with which he was so long associated. The Investors Diversified Services Company (IDS) Tower in Minneapolis (Johnson & Burgee, 1973) realized a version of Mies's crystalline skyscraper projects of 1919–21, in its expressionistic outline and sophisticated curtain wall, a feat at last made possible by technological advances in glass.

Having achieved one of Modernism's most elusive goals, an all-glass tower, Johnson seems to have deepened his investigation of the nature of the tall office building by struggling toward a more profound reading of its corporate and civic obligations — a search that led him to the traditions of the Classical skyscraper of the American Renaissance. The AT&T Building in midtown Manhattan (Johnson & Burgee, with Simmons Architects, associated architects 1978–84) is a hybrid which overlays the compressed slab of orthodox Modernism with convincingly proportioned and executed representations of Classicism. From the point of view of polemics, the AT&T Building is an indisputable landmark: no building has done more to defy the nihilism of the unadorned glass box. Like the 1922 competition for the Chicago Tribune Tower, the AT&T Building reawakened corporate America to the representational power of skyscrapers. Although the language of Classicism is generic, AT&T seeks to be, if not site-specific, at least recognizably regionalist. It is, in fact, Johnson's homage to New York City's architectural heritage. One can pick out the references — the arcade from Sant' Andrea in Mantua; the *oculi*, with their deep, chamfered reveals, from the Duomo in Florence; the Carolingian lobby, with its Lutyens-like floor pattern, Roman *opus reticulatum*, and household god — the statue of the AT&T symbol, "Golden Boy." Whereas the Seagram Building, with its luxurious materials and elaborately assembled cladding, can be pictured as a decorated version of the Chicago frame, AT&T can be seen as a Modernist slab exquisitely tailored in the finery of New York's great historicizing skyscrapers.

In contrast to French-trained Classicists of the first skyscraper era, such as Thomas Hastings, who had advocated façades treated as *revêtement*, a taut skin of stone that accentuates the building's volume rather than its structural cage, Johnson follows a more organic approach, with an elaborate, if perhaps disappointingly flat, plaiting of spandrels and mullions which represents the push and pull between structure and accommodation. The treatment of the base is a specifically New York inspiration, modelled on McKim, Mead & White's Municipal Building (1907–13) in which a triumphal arch tunnels through the building and in which grand, vaulted hypostyle halls lift the offices off the ground.

29 *AT&T Building, New York. Johnson & Burgee; Simmons Architects, associated architects, 1978–84. View northeast.*

In an article for *Architecture* magazine, Johnson explained his design's relationship to the *genius loci*:

> . . . it seems to me the most viable history, if there is any in New York City, is McKim, Mead & White. I have tried to reestablish two interesting eras. The '20s, when you had masonry skyscrapers with windows in them, and the '90s, with their Classical cornices, which are no longer allowed.
>
> So, I went a little astray and broke the pediment, which may have its humorous aspects, but you'll know it's our building.[20]

Pushed to the lotline, the entrance loggia is so huge in scale that it appropriates the street itself as a front yard. "Golden Boy," Evelyn Longman's 1917 statue of *The Spirit of Communication*, dominates the lobby, yet can be adequately viewed only from the opposite sidewalk, and even there one must crane one's neck to glimpse the top of the arch that frames it. The hypostyle hall is contained by the sides and corners of the building, where the granite skin is pulled down low to almost domestically scaled openings. Within the hall is the lobby, which, like the cella of a Greek temple, is deliberately misaligned with the bays on either side; one has a sense of being forced to walk around a sacred box in its holy grove of columns.

Johnson's last phrase, "You'll know it's our building," is crucial. Despite the return to the Classical tradition, with its shared language and emphasis on timeless values of composition, Johnson insists on individual, even unique expression — a Romantic notion that colors so much Modernist architecture. The "will to form" of Modernism still prevails in Johnson's approach; the Classicism, though certainly correct in its details and convincing in its physicality, is used semiotically. It is not pursued out of a conviction of Classicism's inherent characteristics, but rather uses Classicism to say something about the state of architecture, about New York, and most importantly, about AT&T.

Like the younger Venturi, who has taught him so much, Johnson maintains his distance from Classicism, although he lacks Venturi's compelling irony. Johnson admires the past, even appropriates it, but fundamentally sees it as something very different from the present, a toybox of forms useful in design, a rulebook for composition, perhaps a coherent set of elements, but not as a supervening set of fundamental principles and values. Nonetheless, Johnson has accomplished a lot with his Classical enthusiasms. For the School of Architecture Building (John Burgee with Philip Johnson, with Morris/Aubry, associated architects, 1982–5) at the University of Houston, Texas, he took as his model Claude Nicolas Ledoux's project for a House of Education (Chaux project, 1773–9), which he altered according to the program and his own aesthetic imperatives. Ledoux had elevated his building on a plinth, a feature Johnson eliminated. He also omitted a first floor loggia, made the proportions of the wings more horizontal, and converted the rooftop temple from a circle to a square. The architecture school is clad in salmon brick, trimmed in cast stone, which is also the material of the rooftop temple. The effect of the scarcely modulated walls and unsegmented windows is that of an architectural drawing, or a Styrofoam model — perhaps a comment, flip or profound, on the architect's bookish inspiration and the abstract flattened dimensions of architectural education.

For all its irony, Johnson's Houston design follows a tradition of architecture school buildings that are heuristic tools, built textbooks detailing the problems and solutions of architectural design. Choosing Ledoux's House of Education as his model underscored Johnson's didactic purpose. Yet the building's full potential as a teaching device must be realized by the faculty and students who use it. In this case, they went a step further: not merely analyzing the building but using it as inspiration for one of their own. Johnson had put a temple on top of the building; Professor Ben Nicholson, together with 120 students, put a temple inside it. Using measured drawings, published in 1843 by P.-M. Letarouilly (1795–1855), along with photographs, Nicholson and his students reconstructed Bramante's Tempietto (San Pietro in Montorio, Rome, 1502) at full scale in lightweight materials inside the building's atrium. The plan and proportions were as exact as possible, although recreated in cheap materials including plywood, cardboard, and two-by-fours. Some elements of the students' tempietto formed a worthy parallel to Johnson's irony. For example, since the Corinthian columns on the Roman Tempietto were "found," quarried from an unidentified ancient monument, it was decided that the columns of the Houston tempietto could also be "found," and they were discovered among the cast-off machine parts of modern industry.

30   *AT&T Building, New York. Johnson & Burgee; Simmons Architects, associated architects, 1978–84. View northwest of entrance.*

30

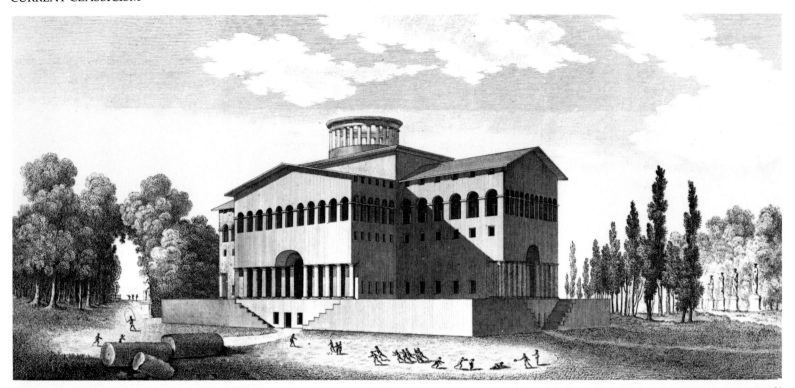

31

32

31 *House of Education, Chaux, France. Claude-Nicolas Ledoux, 1773–9. Unbuilt project. Perspective.*

32 *School of Architecture Building, University of Houston, Texas. John Burgee with Philip Johnson; Morris/Aubry associated architects, 1982–5. View of entrance elevation.*

33 *School of Architecture Building, University of Houston, Texas. John Burgee with Philip Johnson; Morris/Aubry, associated architects, 1982–5. View of atrium.*

34 *School of Architecture Building, University of Houston, Texas, with reconstruction of Bramante's Tempietto San Pietro. Fall semester, 1986.*

33

34

FRANK GEHRY

Frank Gehry (b. 1929) is an anomaly among contemporary architects: one who has moved from successful but conventional commercial practice to the financially risky world of a personally directed, artistically motivated atelier. Best known as an intuitive master of *ad hoc* composition, Gehry revels in the "found" aesthetic of cheap materials. However, his is not a fundamentalist approach, but rather a gentler, childlike collage suggestive of the *Merzbau* (constructions) of Kurt Schwitters. Gehry has found more success in his professional reincarnation than ever before, and as a result the prestigious, large-scale public commissions that would never come to a commercial architect are now coming to him. In these, interestingly, Gehry has begun to explore Classical themes, joining formal and compositional imperatives to his more characteristic free-wheeling aesthetic, an attempted highwire act that he almost pulls off. Gehry has come closest to a true Classicism in his design of Loyola Marymount University's Law School (1984–6). One of the starting points for the design was to find out what might symbolize the study and practice of law to the students and faculty of a Jesuit university. At Loyola, Gehry discovered that they firmly associated the law with the Classical columns and pediments typical of American courthouses and civic buildings. If Gehry wanted to satisfy the expectations of his clients, he had at least to refer to Classical architecture. In addition, he had to create a campus. The obvious model was Jefferson's University of Virginia. Although Gehry's Loyola Law School bears little resemblance to its nineteenth-century precedent, there is a genuine architectural continuity between the two.

35 *Loyola Marymount University Law School, Los Angeles, California. Frank O. Gehry & Associates, 1984–6. Site plan.*

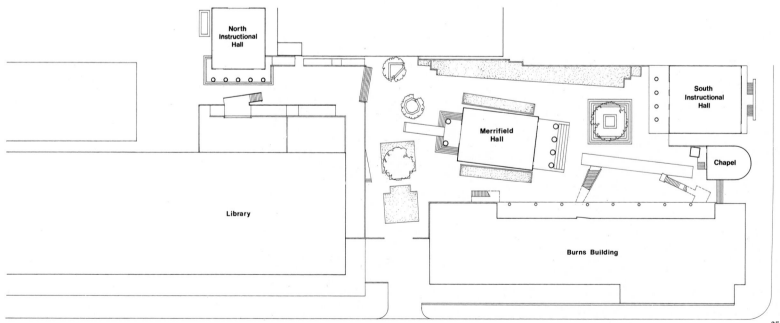

35

36

37

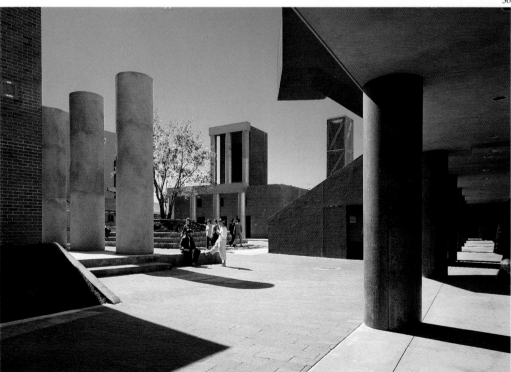

38

36   *Loyola Marymount University Law School, Los Angeles, California. Frank O. Gehry & Associates, 1984–6. View north from Olympic Boulevard.*

37   *Loyola Marymount University Law School, Los Angeles, California. Frank O. Gehry & Associates, 1984–6. View north showing the Burns Building (left) and Merrifield Hall (right).*

38   *Loyola Marymount University Law School, Los Angeles, California. Frank O. Gehry & Associates, 1984–6. View southeast showing South Instructional Hall (center).*

The Loyola Law School's pre-existing campus, at the edge of downtown Los Angeles, could not have been less Classical or campus-like. The low-rise buildings on campus were contextually reponsive, in that they reflected the banality of the surrounding neighborhood, which Gehry has described as "in transition for so long it's not in transition." Gehry felt that a necessary first component was a central focus of activity. His scheme, then, was to house the required facilities in small-scale individual buildings, arranged in a central open area created between the redesigned large classroom/office building and the parking garages to the north. The result, as he describes it, is "a pileup of buildings like an acropolis," which constitutes a miniature campus that simultaneously provides the university with a distinct place of its own and maintains an appropriately low scale and understated street façades that are harmonious with the city outside.

The largest building in Gehry's campus, the Burns Building, has a street façade clad in light gray stucco. The side facing the campus, however, is treated as a bright ochre screen, which serves as a backdrop to the smaller buildings arranged in front of it. The façade "splits open" with a trio of deviantly asymmetrical staircases, the middle one climbing to the building's "pediment" — a glass greenhouse-like structure.

In the center of the campus, Merrifield Hall, a pitch-roofed brick box, is rotated off-axis and fronted by a "porch" of free-standing, squat, 18-foot (5 meter)-high concrete columns. Although stark in their lack of bases and capitals, they evoke a formal language associated with the building's function as a moot court. Symbolically these columns elevate the structure to a temple of justice.

Like Jefferson, Gehry has taken the circumstances of a particular place and time and, using the forms and symbols of the past, raised the real to the ideal. At Loyola, the circumstances included a limited budget, necessitating the use of humble materials, and a rather bleak but visually complex urban context. Whereas Jefferson's campus includes bold acts of architectural synthesis, Gehry's, in its heterogeneous urban setting, is more fragmented. Each structure is isolated, and yet all are closely interrelated, like the elements of a still-life painting or a Cubist collage. In its very heterogeneity and its deference to the city's complexity, the campus has achieved a critical balance: it is at once open to its context and protected as a special domain, reassuring in its associations with the past and provocative in its startling juxtapositions of forms and materials.

The Frances Howard Goldwyn Regional Branch Library in Hollywood, California (1986) avoids the direct civic associations of a colonnade; yet here, too, Gehry explores Classicism, if only in a cryptic way, discernible in the tripartite scheme, trabeated interior, and overall symmetrical rigor. Gehry's design is also clearly indebted to the work of the Japanese architect Arata Isozaki, whose Kitakyushu City Museum of Art (1972–4) has a similar symmetrical massing of discrete cubic forms.

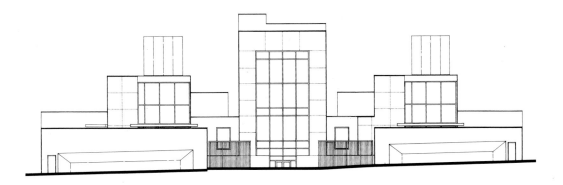

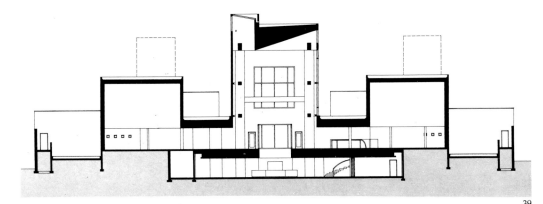

39 *Frances Howard Goldwyn Regional Branch Library, Hollywood, California. Frank O. Gehry & Associates, 1986. East elevation (top); north–south section (bottom).*

40 *Frances Howard Goldwyn Regional Branch Library, Hollywood, California. Frank O. Gehry & Associates, 1986. View southwest.*

39

40

ARATA ISOZAKI

The work of Arata Isozaki (b. 1931), Japan's best-known Post-Modernist architect, offers critical insights into the fundamental relationship between Classicism and the modern experience. Isozaki's approach is necessarily more ambiguous than that of a Westerner: the relationship of Japanese culture to the equally foreign influences of Classicism and Modernism is at best complex. Japan did not emerge from its medieval tradition until well into the nineteenth century, and to this day its national identity is intimately tied to its pre-Modern culture. Whereas the emergence of the Modern in Europe in the fifteenth century was partly a return to an older Western tradition — that of the Classical world — but not a departure from the general continuum of European experience, in Japan, the move to modernize the nation along Western lines in the late 1800s to early 1900s meant adopting a wholly foreign tradition and leaving the continuum of Oriental culture in the uncertain role of a parallel and conflicting value system. Today, Japan, more than any other industrialized nation, is racked by cultural conflict: indigenous and Western culture exist side by side, and most attempts to synthesize them have been ludicrous. Yet during the hegemony of Modernist architecture in Japan which followed the Second World War, even the most passionately internationalist Japanese architects recognized that Modernist design, whether in composition, forms, or details, had to come to terms with their traditional culture — an issue that hardly ever arose in the West. Even so ardent a Modernist as Kenzo Tange (b. 1913) tried to represent traditional forms, as in the corner beams of his Kurashiki City Hall (1958–60).

41   *Civic Center, Tsukuba, Japan. Arata Isozaki, 1979–83. View of entrance to concert hall.*

With Isozaki the need to explore the role of Western tradition in modern Japanese architecture has become a near obsession. He tries to use Western Classicism as a closed condition of established formal meanings, which he introduces into the Japanese context as "quotation" for emphasis. Rather than trying to rediscover the origins of Modernist architecture in the spatial concepts of traditional Japanese building, as Gropius and others did in the 1950s, Isozaki has concentrated on Platonic solids, assembling them as did one of his heroes, Ledoux, disregarding the traditional hierarchies so that each part of a building stands independently in relation to the other elements.

In his early buildings, such as the Fujimi Country Clubhouse (1975), Isozaki used only the primary shapes used by Ledoux, arriving, as he says, somewhat inadvertently at a barrel-vaulted design reminiscent of Ledoux's "House for the Directors of the Loue River." In the Tsukuba Civic Center (1979–83), Isozaki continued with his project of combining Platonic solids, especially cubes, yet added Classical details:

> As it is an urban scheme, rustication is applied to the base wall. As the construction site is located in a stone-quarrying district, the use of stone was naturally required. Moreover, as Tsukuba Civic Center is a complex of this town I decided to introduce architectural motifs of urban context. Since rustication and pure geometric form are also major features of the Barrières it is natural that a remarkable resemblance to Ledoux is seen in my scheme.[21]

42   *Civic Center, Tsukuba, Japan. Arata Isozaki,
1979–83. Aerial view.*

42

Isozaki took on more than Ledoux in his design for Tsukuba, whose program called for a hotel, concert hall, information center, shopping mall and community center. The main plaza is a sunken version of Michelangelo's Campidoglio, which seems an almost desperate attempt to insert some urbanity into Tsukuba, a new town 38 miles (60 kilometers) from Tokyo where the government had succeeded in establishing university and research institutions but failed to get anyone to stay after classes or work.

In an article containing an interview with Isozaki, the Japanese architectural critic and photographer Yukio Futagawa suggested that in the Tsukuba Center "perhaps real modern architecture had been created in Japan for the first time," arguing that Isozaki was the first Japanese architect to resolve his relationship to the history of architecture, both Western and Japanese. As Isozaki puts it: "My generation is the first which has been able to look at, for example, the Parthenon, Chartres and the works of Palladio in the same way as we look at Japanese classics, and from the same distance." The result, according to Isozaki, was benevolently schizoid: "By treating the parts in a schizophrenic way the building as a whole is brought to a resolution."[22] This ambivalent attitude, which Isozaki considers a positive and important design concept, consists of a desire simultaneously to create and destroy images of traditional urban architecture. Surely here is the most extreme manifestation of an ironic view, with Isozaki's use of the Campidoglio as a perfect symbol of the approach. Here the architect has used one of the most famous urban set pieces in Europe, yet has inverted almost every quality of the original: his version is sunken and concave rather than raised and convex, and the black and white paving is reversed. For Isozaki, it is a comment on the current state of Japanese society, in which the traditional hierarchical pyramid with the emperor on the top has been leveled since Japan's defeat in the Second World War. In Michelangelo's Campidoglio, an equestrian statue of the Roman emperor Marcus Aurelius occupies the center; in Tsukuba's plaza, as in Japan itself, there is a void, rather than an emperor, at the center.

Isozaki has been able to explore further his principles of using fundamental Classical shapes in a non-hierarchical way in projects such as the Okanoyama Graphic Art Museum (1986), which has a colossal order of free-standing and engaged concrete columns and an interior staircase invoking that in Michelangelo's Laurentian Library. But his largest-scale project since Tsukuba is in New York: the Brooklyn Museum renovation and extension, a commission he won in collaboration with the New York firm of James Stewart Polshek and Partners (1986–). Designed in 1893 by McKim, Mead & White, the Brooklyn Museum has never fulfilled its promise as both an architectural monument in its own right and an element in the urban composition of Classical public buildings and monuments bordering Prospect Park. McKim Mead & White designed the largest museum in the world, planned as a huge square divided into four quadrangles. Only the main façade block was completed, and its integrity as a monument of the American Renaissance was violated in 1934, when in a fit of Modernist zeal William Lescaze (1896–1964) removed the grand staircase and replaced it with a ground floor entrance deemed more functional.

The program for the extension required a "historically sensitive" restoration of the staircase and rotunda lobby as the principal entrance; but for the new portion there were no restrictions on the architectural vocabulary. Isozaki decided to "complete" McKim, Mead & White's square in a characteristically ironic way, simultaneously reinforcing and breaking away from the nineteenth-century master plan. The new main entrance, on the façade facing the park, sustains the symmetry of the plan,

43

43   *Okanoyama Graphic Art Museum, Nichiwaki Hyogo Prefecture, Japan. Arata Isozaki, 1986. View of entrance.*

while around it everything falls apart. A new quadrangle is skewed to align with a parkway. Another quadrangle is only outlined, partially complete, with a small square gallery cranked off-axis, like the new quadrangle, to align with the diagonal of Washington Avenue. The language is — depending on one's point of view — either a travesty or a deep interpretation of Classicism — for example, the main entrance portico looks like a diagrammatic reduction of a design by Palladio or Ledoux and invokes the latter's designs for Chaux in the tall obelisk atop the great hall rising behind it.

46

44   *Brooklyn Museum renovation and extension, Brooklyn, New York. Arata Isozaki & Associates; James Stewart Polshek and Partners, 1986– . Site plan.*

45   *Brooklyn Museum renovation and extension, Brooklyn, New York. Arata Isozaki & Associates; James Stewart Polshek and Partners, 1986– . Longitudinal section.*

46   *Brooklyn Museum renovation and extension, Brooklyn, New York. Arata Isozaki & Associates; James Stewart Polshek and Partners, 1986– . View south of model showing existing building and proposed addition.*

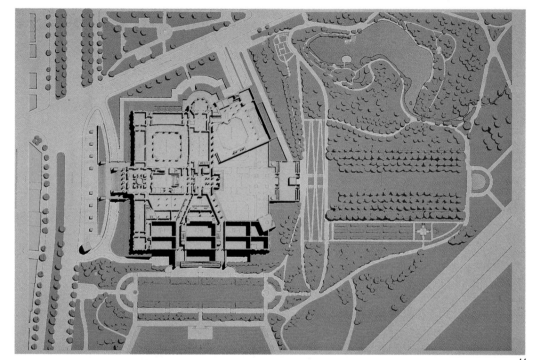

44

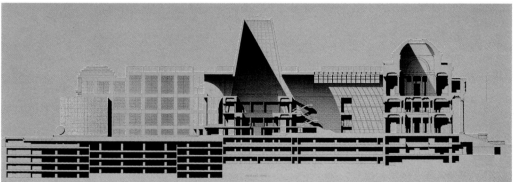

45

TERRY FARRELL

The English architect Terry Farrell (b. 1938) spent his journeyman years designing carefully detailed, reductivist Modernist buildings with his onetime partner Nicholas Grimshaw. Since forming his own firm in 1979, Farrell has become a catalyst for a more aesthetically outspoken architecture, juxtaposing a palette of Modernist materials with Classical motifs which are emblazoned with the billboard sensibility of Pop Art, in a clear link to the work of Venturi. To the extent that his designs have held together, they have done so due to Farrell's approach to the issues of urbanism.

Farrell's first client after he struck out on his own was Clifton Nurseries, which hired him to design two temporary sales spaces in London, one of them in Covent Garden (1979). Farrell's theatrical design for the Covent Garden shop, a pastiche of the "Etruscan" portico on Inigo Jones's St. Paul's Church across the square, was a harbinger of that neighborhood's architectural renaissance. But he first came to international attention as a Classical designer with his design for TV-am Studios (1983) in Camden Town, London, a mainly run-down district rapidly being gentrified. The commission called for the transformation of a 1930s parking garage into studios and offices for what was then a new idea for British television, a morning news and entertainment show. Farrell, who was expected to make a splash, began by dividing the project into three parts: the street façade, a central atrium, and the rear façade facing the Regent's Canal. Throughout, he followed the maxim of his client's medium — to communicate you have to entertain. Most of the front elevation gives little immediate gratification. Set above a plinth of black and gray blocks, the windowless walls of the studios are clad in steel divided into four bands, possibly to give the impression of blown-up, rusticated masonry. At the corners, the "quoins" reveal themselves as the initial letters of the show: "T," "V," "a," and "m." Despite this touch, the effect would have been of a nondescript industrial building, were it not for Farrell's bold stroke — the diadem arch over the center. Made up of hollow aluminum sections, painted blue and anodized in silver, and held by a huge keystone with stainless-steel fins, the arch joins the bipartite façade and frames an entry court.

An axial route takes visitors and employees from the entrance court inside the building to the 100 by 30-foot (9-meter) atrium, which serves as the company's showpiece. Farrell has spoken of the atrium's design as the thematic complement to the television show produced around it, claiming it as an "appropriate story-line: east/west, sunrise/sunset, news from all over the world."[23] The perennially newsworthy Middle East takes center stage, in the form of a staircase rising in vaguely ziggurat fashion, climatologically identified by palm trees. To represent the Far East, Farrell provided a Japanese-style pavilion, for the far West, there is a cactus garden, bordered by a "Dallas"-type wall of steel and reflective glass. Between the Mesopotamian staircase and Dallas, in the midst of a Mediterranean garden, stands a Greek gateway, in correct geographical and chronological sequence. On the canal side, Farrell exaggerated an existing sawtoothed industrial profile by adding steps to the steep slope of each tooth; and at the top step, an egg in an eggcup — the breakfast show's symbol — appears as a finial, a play on the pineapple and acorn finials of Georgian architecture. On the walls below, Farrell cut in arched windows reminiscent of England's nineteenth-century factories. The vigorous outline and brightly-colored details are a welcome relief from the rather somber surrounding buildings.

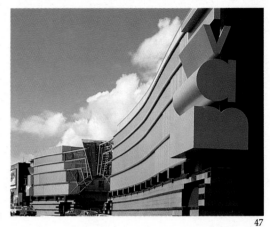

47   *TV-am Studios, Camden Town, London. Terry Farrell Partnership, 1983. View of Hawley Crescent elevation.*

48   *TV-am Studios, Camden Town, London. Terry Farrell Partnership, 1983. View from Regent's Canal.*

The British architecture critic Simon Jenkins, commenting on the studios, worried that the design has an "uneasy aura of transience, of a good joke that could begin to pall."[24] Whatever the validity of an argument against the impermanence of flash and wit (Jenkins also points out that the eggs and their cups are already cracking), Farrell has reached for a more enduring rhetoric in recent projects, including a commission completed for a client far more tradition-bound than TV-am, the Henley Regatta. For the administrators of this world-class rowing event Farrell designed a headquarters (1986) combining a dock, boathouse, meeting rooms, offices, and a two-bedroom apartment for the secretary. Somewhere between a folly and a lock house, the building sits on the Thames, adjacent to an eighteenth-century stone bridge. The base is a handsome brick plinth, the same height as the neighboring bridge and well in keeping with the traditional brick architecture of Henley-on-Thames. On the two floors above, however, Farrell cut loose with a polychromatic free Classical scheme in stucco and wood. The river façade, above the plinth, is conservatively tripartite, pedimented, and temple-like, but boldly articulated by pink stucco wall-pilasters, a red architrave, and a blue cornice. In addition, the temple's center has been hollowed out, and the plinth below it is divided by the entrance to a covered dock. In the section suspended above, a serliana window rises from the floor to burst through the lower cornice line into the pediment's tympanum, which is itself a window with panes radiating from the serliana frame's arch. The result, for the interior, is a dramatically scaled room in a small building, and for the exterior, it is a small-scale example of Farrell's urban-minded balance between contextuality and individual identity.

In his renovation of Comyn Ching Court, near Covent Garden in London (first phase, 1985), Farrell has shown how a modest-scale renovation can make a neo-Georgian silk purse out of an eighteenth-century sow's ear of speculative building. The respectable front elevations were dutifully restored, but the messy triangular back yard has been unified into a court, distinguished by a moulded curb around its perimeter, voluptuous wood benches designed at the turn of the century by Lutyens, and timber and stone entryways notable for their fully articulated and highly mannered Classicism reminiscent of Vanbrugh.

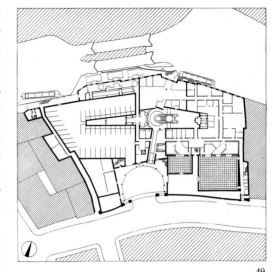

49

49 *TV-am Studios, Camden Town, London. Terry Farrell Partnership, 1983. Ground floor plan.*

50 *TV-am Studios, Camden Town, London. Terry Farrell Partnership, 1983. Axonometric showing entrance and atrium.*

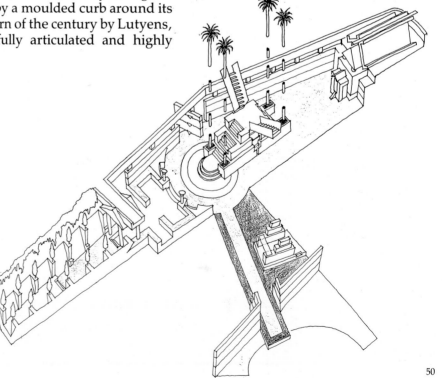

50

51

51 *Clifton Nurseries, Covent Garden, London. Terry Farrell Partnership, 1979. View from Covent Garden Market Building.*

52 *Clifton Nurseries, Covent Garden, London. Terry Farrell Partnership, 1979. View of column detail.*

52

CHARLES JENCKS

Charles Jencks (b. 1939), an American architect and critic now based in London who has done much to stimulate an ironic approach to traditional form, worked with the Terry Farrell partnership in the design of the exterior of his own house in London (1982–5), while reserving for himself the design of the interiors. In a definition first enunciated in 1978 and reissued in an argumentative pamphlet in 1986, Jencks has characterized Post-Modernism as *"double coding: the combination of Modern techniques with something else (usually traditional building) in order for architecture to communicate with the public and a concerned minority, usually other architects"* [Jencks's italics].[25] The situation of double-coding is inevitably ironic, and exemplified by what Jencks defines as "Free-Style Classicism," in which Classicism is seen in its widest sense as the generic language of architecture from the Egyptians through the Greeks and Romans. Jencks sees "Free-Style Classicism" as more symbolic and able to accommodate industrialized building techniques than the Classicism of the five Orders.

Jencks's own house, a renovated early Victorian townhouse built around 1840, is an object lesson in his philosophy. The oval entrance hall contains a mural by William Stok depicting Jencks's heroes, including Hadrian, Erasmus, Thomas Jefferson, and Hannah Arendt, all models of open-mindedness, often skeptical and ironical, and all declared enemies of totalitarianism — an affliction Jencks sees as a fundamental aspect of Modernism (a moralistic and utopian totalitarianism, to be sure, but just as implacable nonetheless). To fit his architecture to his philosophy, Jencks is obliged to undermine any system he creates, to show that the pretense of an overall order is a lie. This places Jencks squarely in the idiosyncratic Anglo-American tradition, which includes the theorists of the picturesque, as well as John Soane and Geoffrey Scott, and at odds with the European rationalist tradition of Laugier, Durand, the Modernists of the 1920s, and many of the Classicists of the current scene.

The first principle of Jencks's Thematic House, as he calls it, is that of Geoffrey Scott's *The Architecture of Humanism* (1914), which argues that we experience architecture empathetically, humanizing inert building matter by imagining it as our own body. So the front door of Jencks's house has a face instead of a fanlight above it, and the rear façade is entirely given over to a facial theme. Inside, the two themes are of cultural and cosmic time. The most articulate expression of the first is the portraits in the mural; the second is conveyed by the "sun stair" spiralling up through the center of the house and by the surrounding rooms representing the five seasons of spring, summer, Indian summer, fall, and winter. The theme of each room is carried out in color, furniture, art, and sometimes words, since Jencks does not think that "a visual form is entirely complete until it is given a caption. . . ."[26]

The spirit of Soane's House at Lincoln's Inn Fields is invoked throughout Jencks's house, not only in the artful embellishment of the façade, so that it is still at ease with its sober neighbors but more architecturally expressive, but also in the general desire to use every corner to make a statement. There is a taxonomic excess, an almost self-defeating pursuit of architectural meaning (sometimes grotesquely satirical, as in the "Cosmic Loo," which parodies the grandiose theme of the adjacent "Cosmic Oval" with a decorative scheme of postcards instead of murals and witty labels instead of a philosophical credo), and an aura of humor — anathema to architects who believe that wit and seriousness are mutually exclusive.

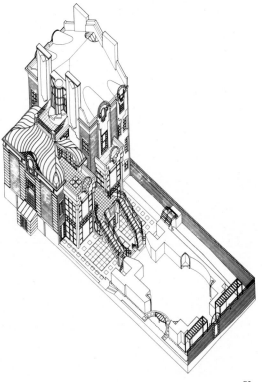

53   *Thematic House, London. Charles Jencks; Terry Farrell Partnership, 1982–5. Axonometric showing garden elevation.*

53

54

54   *Thematic House, London. Charles Jencks;*
Terry Farrell Partnership; interiors, Charles Jencks,
1982–5. Interior view of kitchen.

55   *Thematic House, London. Charles Jencks;*
Terry Farrell Partnership; interiors, Charles Jencks,
1982–5. View of entrance; oval ceiling showing
mural by William Stok.

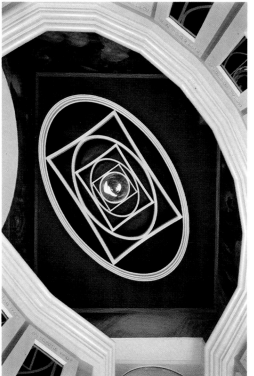

55

FRANK ISRAEL

In his Clark House (1982–), Frank Israel (b. 1945), a Los Angeles architect, mixes an academic knowledge of Classical architecture with the glamor styles of 1920s Hollywood. For a site a block and a half away from Frank Lloyd Wright's Ennis House (1924), Israel proposed a compact, introspective fortress which would provide a counterpoint to Wright's in style and siting. Wright's concrete-block, Mayan temple-like house spreads its long horizontal forms along cliffside terraces, overlooking a panoramic view of downtown Los Angeles. Israel begins with the Villa Farnese, the sixteenth-century pentagonal palace-fortress built in Caprarola at the center of the vast estates of the Farnese family, designed by Antonio de Sangallo the Younger and Baldassare Peruzzi beginning in the 1520s, and finished by Giacomo da Vignola in the second half of the century. The choice of the Villa Farnese is not capricious for the architect and his clients, who visited it together in 1974, when Israel and the art historian Nancy Clark were both fellows at the American Academy in Rome.

The principal parallel between Israel's house and Sangallo's is the plan, a pentagon with a circular courtyard. The other references, like the rusticated base, heavy quoins, and battered walls, are more oblique. The battered walls, for instance, are also inspired by the 1920s Egyptian fad derived from Hollywood film sets. Israel has studied the sets themselves, which he considers the most interesting scenography in the history of American film, and the Los Angeles buildings that incorporated this style. The Egyptian influence can even take over Renaissance elements in Israel's design, as where the serliana window, already blinded in one eye, is battered for an Egyptian look. Although the Classicism is somewhat overwhelmed by the scenography, it re-emerges on the garden side, where the pediment is a simple triangle, set behind a stepped roof of a projecting portico. Instead of having the character of a pediment, it is just another shape on the rooftop terrace which surrounds the cylindrical drum of the central courtyard, like the barrel-vaulted skylight and the totemistic pillar.

56

56 *Clark House, Los Angeles, California. Frank Israel, 1982. Unbuilt project. View of model.*

57   *Clark House, Los Angeles, California. Frank
Israel, 1982. Unbuilt project. Site plan.*

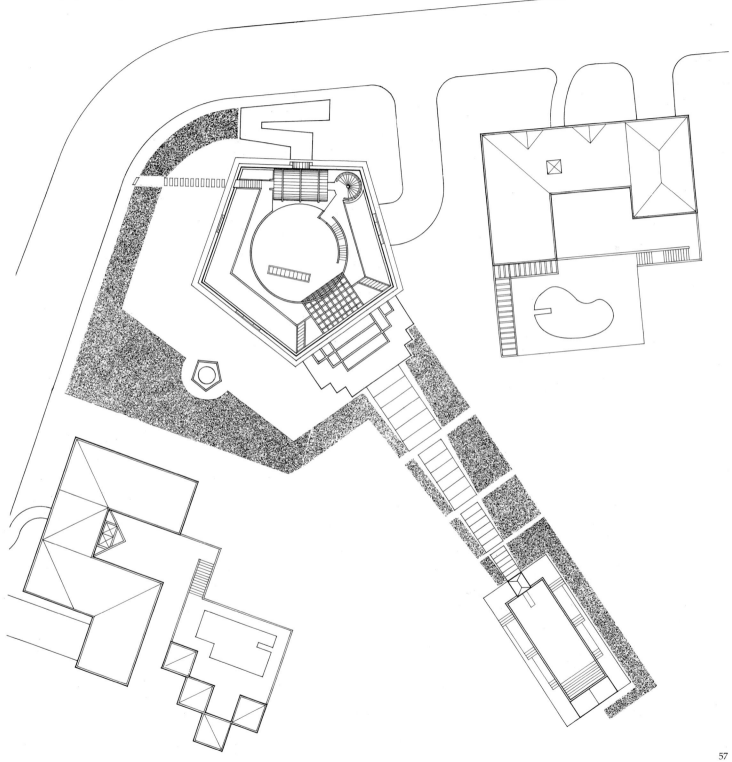

JAMES STIRLING

For the British architect James Stirling (b. 1926), irony is the only plausible response to a world in which no architect can fully believe in either the Classical or the Modernist tradition. In some ways, Stirling is as obsessed with the *Zeitgeist* as Mies was: at every turn he insists on the difference between the "now" and the "then." Refusing to be nostalgic, rejecting true reintegration, he nonetheless is intent on a reconciliation with the past. In his designs for two museums, the Neue Staatsgallerie in Stuttgart (James Stirling Michael Wilford and Associates, 1977–84) and the Clore Gallery, an addition to the Tate Gallery housing the Turner Collection, in London (James Stirling Michael Wilford and Associates, 1980–86), he deftly balances traditional and Modernist compositional elements yet never gives either the upper hand.

Stirling rose to prominence in the 1960s when, after a brief love affair with the primitivism of Le Corbusier's late work, upon which he based his flats at Ham Common, London (with James Gowan, 1956), he turned for inspiration to the early styles of Modernism — in particular to Russian Constructivism, which he revived in his Leicester University Engineering Building (James Stirling and James Gowan, 1959–63), and to the glass and metal architectural technology of the nineteenth century, such as the great train sheds, which inspired his technologically problematical Cambridge University History Faculty (1968). Long after many Modernists had settled into the Classicizing mode of Mies's mature work, Stirling produced at Leicester a design that, although it looked at first glance like an industrial plant, revealed itself on closer inspection as a sophisticated essay on recent history, invoking not only the dynamic assemblage of standardized industrial elements, characteristic of Russian Constructivism but also the massing of the soaring research tower astride the squat office base that Frank Lloyd Wright used for his Johnson Wax Building in Racine, Wisconsin (1936–52). To these, Stirling added a mid-nineteenth-century aptitude for exposing standard industrial parts, picking up, so to speak, where Paxton left off.

At the new gallery in Stuttgart, Stirling did not in any way abandon his love for nineteenth-century technology, yet at the same time he enriched his palette with equal amounts of Classicism, counterbalancing diaphanous, virtually billowing walls of metal and glass with an eroded, fundamentally static mass of travertine masonry. It is a high-wire performance that perilously balances the opposites of Modernism and Classicism. Although Stirling seeks to give the viewer a lesson about history, he goes beyond the semiotic approach to infuse his forms with the physical power of their respective traditions. When the design was ignorantly attacked in the German press as a reactionary, monumental structure, Stirling replied to his critics that a city without monuments would not be a city at all and that he was "sick and tired of boring, meaningless, non-committed, faceless flexibility, and the open endedness of so much present day architecture."[27] The design can probably best be understood as a commentary on, and encyclopedia of, Stirling's own work and as an essay on how to rebuild the European city after the ravages of the Second World War and the automobile, finding an alternative to both the stone-by-stone reconstruction of Warsaw and the glass-and-steel anomie of Düsseldorf, Frankfurt, and Cologne.

The museum is set on what was once a tree-lined avenue but is now a traffic-clogged boulevard. Stirling's "colonnade" of trees along the museum's façade is both

58   *Neue Staatsgalerie, Stuttgart, West Germany. James Stirling Michael Wilford and Associates, 1977–84. View south of gallery entrance.*

a reference to the traditional museum setting exemplified by Schinkel's Altes Museum, and a comment on and response to the reality of the site facing a highway. Behind the trees, Stirling made a gesture toward tradition with a wall banded with travertine and sandstone. Yet he undermines the traditionalism of this entrance façade in two ways: first, by making sure that it is clear that the travertine and sandstone are applied as a veneer, not laid stone upon stone, by refusing to add superfluous mortar to the appliqué, and second, by underplaying the building's entrance as an odd gateway, an aedicule which suggests Abbé Laugier's primitive hut in steel I–beams painted blue and orange — a colorist Stirling is not. From this miniature industrialist temple, the visitor chooses either a Modernist ramp — reminiscent of Le Corbusier — or a stairway. The handrails, overscaled fiberglass sausages painted garish colors, seem deliberately to mock as pretentious the beautiful stone. Stirling's design is no mere self-indulgence of form but a tangible statement of a message: Modernist architecture is in shambles; to express this, Stirling has created a ruin. The brightly painted Modernist fragments — a piano-curve of green steel and glass, a blue-I–beam, a scrap of red trusswork — all possess a decorative, jokey character, revealing the discredited state of their functionalist iconography.

Inside, within the sanctuary of art, tradition obtains, at least in the plan of the exhibition floor. As in Schinkel's Altes Museum, exhibition galleries arranged *en filade* surround three sides of a central rotunda. Yet even within the traditional dimensions of the galleries, Stirling cannot refrain from moments of fragmentation, such as the pieces of moulding projected off the wall as light fittings, augmenting their decorative character with a functional one. Outside, the unsettled, incomplete character of the Modernist elements is applied to the traditional ones, also. An outdoor rotunda evokes the traditional monumental and organizing space of the museum type since the early nineteenth century. Stirling's rotunda contains a Doric portico jammed into the ground. It lends the courtyard an archeological air, looking for all the world like an incomplete excavation given up by an archeologist who no longer saw the point of digging. Stirling's is a picturesque view, a Romantic Classical vision, and perhaps an affirmation that living among the ruins of Western architecture is better than trying to reconstruct an irrecoverable past.

Stirling's design for the Clore Gallery (1982–6) is apparently more sympathetic to its immediate context than the Stuttgart museum despite the billboard flatness of its diagrammatic façades. Adjoining the Classical set piece of the Tate Gallery to the south, the Clore Gallery forms an "L" heading north and then east, stopping just short of the Lodge, a Georgian red brick building facing the Thames. There are zealously contextual elements to the design. The cornice of the Tate is pulled across to the new façade, its contour continuing along the length of the inside of the "L." Stirling approximates (and rationalizes) the orders of the main building by dividing the walls of the new gallery into a grid of Portland stone ribs which wraps around most of the building. The grid is Stirling's way of dealing with the blind walls — so often canvases for Classical exercises — typical of art galleries, and its infill is an opportunity for more contextual gestures. Close to the main building, the panels are painted a buff yellow; close to the Lodge, they are of red brick. Once beyond the elevations facing the garden, Stirling appeals to the twentieth century context of the Tate Gallery's neighbors, as well as to the "functionalist" aspects of the back of an institutional building. Turning the corner adjacent to the Lodge, Stirling gives up the red brick infill and then the grid itself, in favor of unmodulated brick and strip

59

59 *Neue Staatsgalerie, Stuttgart, West Germany. James Stirling Michael Wilford and Associates, 1977–84. View of courtyard entrance detail.*

60 *Neue Staatsgalerie, Stuttgart, West Germany. James Stirling Michael Wilford and Associates, 1977–84. View of wall detail showing vents for parking garage.*

60

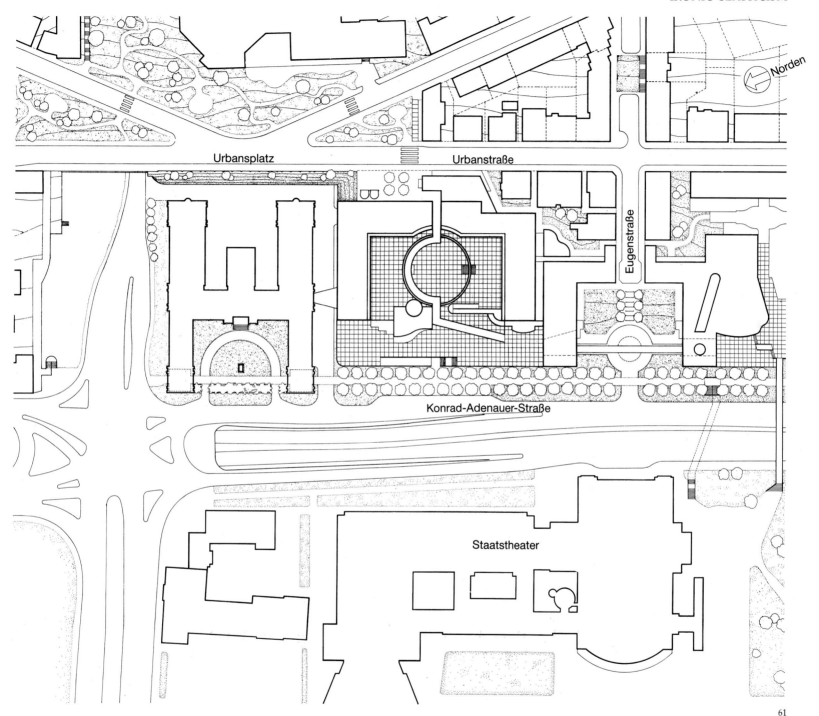

Norden

Urbansplatz   Urbanstraße

Eugenstraße

Konrad-Adenauer-Straße

Staatstheater

61

61 *Neue Staatsgalerie, Stuttgart, West Germany.*
James Stirling Michael Wilford and Associates,
1977–84. Site plan.

windows. The north façade is equally blunt, and on the west, overlooking the parking lot, the wall becomes almost nothing but the grid, with low, semicircular archways cut through the base as though it were a warehouse from the beginning of the Industrial Revolution.

As at the Stuttgart gallery, Stirling is determined to point out that the skin of his building is a cultural pretense, not structural expression, and he shows this by taking out the corner across from the Lodge, cutting a window through what had appeared to be a square concrete frame. He breaks through the fake frame again, three-dimensionally this time, with a window jutting out in a clear reference to Marcel Breuer's Whitney Museum of American Art in New York (1966).

The design is so ironic that it seems to make a mockery out of the principles of contextuality and structural representation, skewering them as just two more of architecture's sacred cows. The main entrance, running east-west, joining the two principal façades and facing the Tate's main building across a terrace garden complete with a long reflecting pool, addresses both these issues. Contextualism is dispatched by inverting the façade of the earlier gallery — in Stirling's design, the lunette window goes on top and the pediment goes below. As for structure, the "pediment" is a void cut into an ashlar wall, which floats improbably above the glazed entrance. Yet for all its built-in commentary, the main entrance façade provides the only moment of architectural peace. A negative temple portico, it also recalls in its form the most ancient sources of Western architecture, the beehive tombs of Mycenae, as if to imply that meaningful architecture is still possible — with the ultimate banal object of contemporary architecture, a revolving door, stuck in the center.

62

62   *The Clore Gallery, Tate Gallery, London. James Stirling Michael Wilford and Associates, 1982–6. Interior view of main stairhall.*

63   *The Clore Gallery, Tate Gallery, London. James Stirling Michael Wilford and Associates, 1982–6. View of model showing, from left to right, the Tate Gallery, the south elevation of the Clore Gallery, and the Lodge.*

64   *The Clore Gallery, Tate Gallery, London. James Stirling Michael Wilford and Associates, 1982–6. View north of main entrance.*

63

LATENT CLASSICISM

Latent Classicism exists in a kind of halfway house between the traditional and the Modernist, without the intent or effect of irony, and without any concern for architectural semiotics. In fact, it can be defined as a movement against the interpretation of architecture as a system of signs, whose adherents have no intention of "learning from Las Vegas." In its handling of form, in looking back to early Modernism, it values less the cataclysmic originality of Le Corbusier than the "banal," structurally rationalist architecture of Auguste Perret, whose buildings often fit discreetly into the Parisian scene. Like Perret, the proponents of Latent Classicism attempt to realize a Modern Classicism with contemporary building techniques, as if one could realize the drawings of Durand directly in reinforced concrete.

Latent Classicism is a kind of erased Classical language, in which the traces, outlines, and impressions of the constructionally based forms remain, but the ornamental detail, whether in the decorative system of an order or in idiosyncratic nuance, is eliminated. There is a key distinction between Latent and Fundamental Classicism. The Latent Classicist seeks to use the full range of forms and types from the Classical tradition, and re-deploy them in industrial-age terms; the Fundamentalist, eschewing advanced technology, seeks to reduce architecture to a few essential shapes and then build up an architecture from there.

65   *Talbot House, Nevis, West Indies. Taft Architects, 1981.*

JAQUELIN ROBERTSON

In the United States, the Latent Classical synthesis enjoys a particularly rich patronage by the corporate sector, combining as it does the authority of traditional form with the presumed economic advantages of a minimalist approach to materials. The Amvest Headquarters in Charlottesville, Virginia (1985–7), designed by Jaquelin Robertson (b. 1933), Dean of the University of Virginia's architecture school, takes as its point of departure the typical Classical, Palladian country house of eighteenth-century Virginia's landed gentry. Unlike Monticello, with its rich stylistic overlays, Amvest is simple and direct to the point of minimalism. It is sited in a valley, straddling a small stream, which now runs through two culverts beneath the building, and the principal façade faces a pond fed by the stream. With its central portico flanked by low-set wings, Amvest has the tripartite division of an eighteenth-century Virginian country house such as Mount Airy, Richmond County (1758–62). The cladding materials are traditional, from the fieldstone lower story to the main story sheathed in brown "Charleston brick" (now painted a light putty color at the insistence of the client), to the copper roof. Stone and brick are the correct "banal," traditional materials for a corporate house, but Robertson's quest for a synthesis between Modernism and Classicism is apparent in the glazed window wall, an icon of Modernism, slipped in behind the diagrammatically Classical central portico.

For Concord Walk, a project including townhouses, shops, and a restaurant in Charleston, South Carolina (1985–), Robertson has designed a version of traditional Charleston townhouses around lushly planted courtyards. He has rationalized the row house by articulating the grid of post and beam and infill panels that compose its regular façade. Although there are traditional decorative details, such as cross-hatched parapets and shutters, structural members are the main ornament, as in the gables with open trusswork. At Concord Walk, as at Amvest, Robertson's fundamentally Modernist preference for the abstract and the tectonic is balanced by a sensitivity to local tradition and taste, without being either literal or ironical.

66   *Amvest Headquarters, Charlottesville, Virginia. Eisenman Robertson Architects; Trott & Bean Architects, 1985–7. Lakeside elevation.*

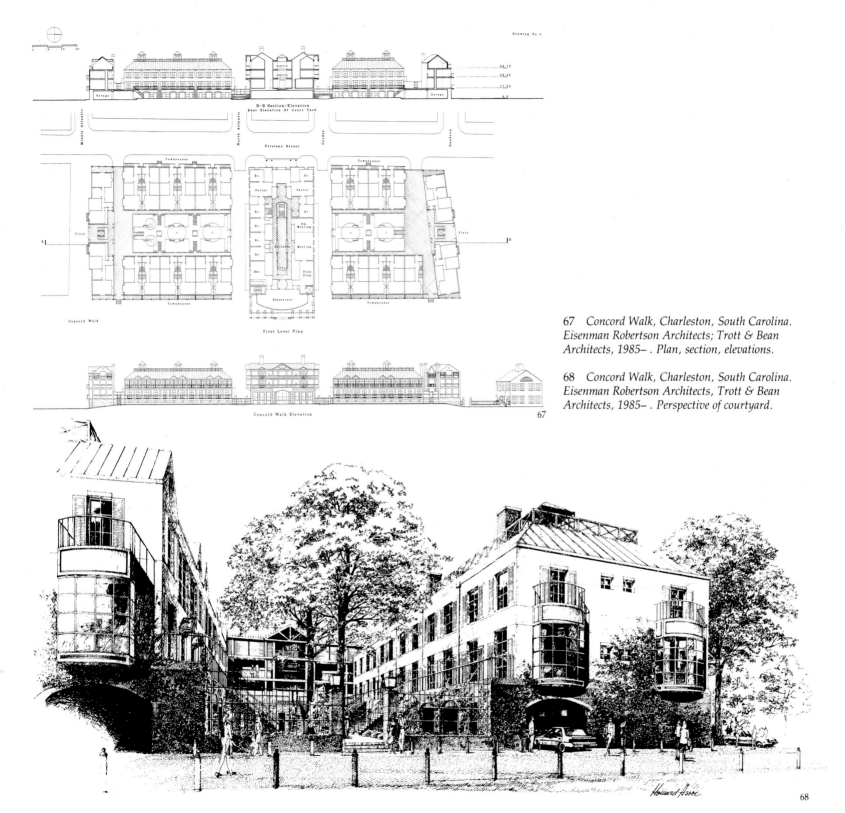

67   Concord Walk, Charleston, South Carolina.
*Eisenman Robertson Architects; Trott & Bean
Architects, 1985– . Plan, section, elevations.*

68   Concord Walk, Charleston, South Carolina.
*Eisenman Robertson Architects, Trott & Bean
Architects, 1985– . Perspective of courtyard.*

TAFT ARCHITECTS

A team of three partners, John J. Casbarian (b. 1946), Danny Samuels (b. 1947), and Robert H. Timme (b. 1945), Taft Architects credit their Bauhaus-derived training at Rice University and the indirect influence of Eero Saarinen as the foundation of their approach, which relies principally on abstract ordering systems rather than semiotics or style to convey meaning. Following this method, they have succeeded in giving original yet appropriate expression to building types ranging from sewage treatment plants to resort villas.

Their Municipal Control Building in Missouri City, Texas (1978), has the modest functional requirement of providing a lunchroom and office space for the employees of the Quail Valley Waste Treatment plant and the ambitious task of elevating a rather mundane facility to the level of a significant public building. The second requirement was crucial because the Municipal Control Building has a prominent site, in the center of the community golf course, and the extra burden of compensating for an aesthetically unpopular, already constructed metal and concrete plant. Taft Architects provided a stucco and tile façade which refers to the Classical utility buildings common at the turn of the century in its tripartite composition of a central entrance arch, beneath a pediment, flanked by two lower wings. From a distance, across the greens, the building has a powerful Classical presence. Up close, it becomes clear that the abstract ordering system, for all its rigor, is not a Classical one, and has generated the façade as well as the internal organization.

For the Talbot House in Nevis, West Indies (1981), Taft Architects were able to apply their modular compositional technique to the tradition of the formal, Classically organized country house. But here the design was enriched because local materials rather than industrial products were appropriate. In addition, Taft made inventive use of traditional decoration to complete their composition. Located on the former site of the main house of the Jessups Plantation, the house is arranged into four pavilions set at the corners of a large central pavilion, reflecting a plan which gathers private functions in the corners and reserves the center for a large room. The house is also designed in response to the specific and general qualities of its tropical site. Every room has windows on four sides, to provide as much ventilation and as many views as possible. The already-cut stone used for the corner pavilions was found on the site and had probably been used for the buildings and garden walls of the Jessups Plantation. The palette is local to the island and includes red-orange and blue-green painted wood and a red roof, whose color is considered friendly in the local vernacular.

In their most complex work to date, the River Crest Country Club in Fort Worth, Texas (1981–4), Taft had a specific precedent to emulate, and without betraying it they were able to incorporate a complicated program within a simple, singular shape. The old club, a 1911 lodge that was vulgarly Georgianized in the 1950s, had burned to the ground, and the architects' brief began with the desire of the club's members for something much the same, which to the collective mind was "Colonial." Taft drew on the American tradition of Classical buildings in brick, with a cross-axial plan reminiscent of Palladio and Jefferson, and — moving into a twentieth-century aspect of that tradition — on the sculptural modelling and the pronounced roof-silhouettes of Lutyens. The architects were able to sustain the Modernist ideal of abstraction, yet

69

69　*Quail Valley Municipal Control Building, Missouri City, Texas. Taft Architects, 1978. View of entrance elevation.*

70　*River Crest Country Club, Fort Worth, Texas. Taft Architects; Geren Architectural Division/CRS Sirrine, Inc., associated architects, 1981–4. View of west elevation.*

116

give walls the depth and level of detail of traditional architecture: the base is "rusticated," with thick concrete bands divided by green tile "joints," and the main story has free-standing brick columns without capitals. The principles, but not the ordered expression, of a Classical building are also evident in the relationship between the building and the landscape, where an *allée* of trees marching across the golf course gave the architects the opportunity to tie the formal axes of their building to those in the landscape. The result is an unembarrassedly grand setting for the social rituals of the Fort Worth establishment.

Taft's design for the Corpus Christi City Hall, Texas (with Kipp, Richter & Associates, 1984–7) draws on the same principles of formal and symbolic clarity as the River Crest Country Club. Once again, a cross-axial plan organizes the building, while the massing is based on a traditional type, in this case the nineteenth-century Texas Country Courthouse.

71

72

74

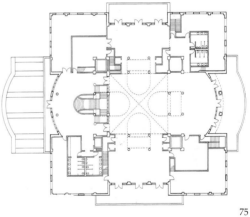

75

73

71   Talbot House, Nevis, West Indies. Taft Architects, 1981. View of rear elevation.

72   Corpus Christi City Hall, Texas. Taft Architects; Kipp, Richter & Associates, associated architects, 1984–7.

73   River Crest Country Club, Forth Worth, Texas. Taft Architects; Geren Architectural Division/CRS Sirrine, Inc., associated architects, 1981–4. Interior view of ballroom.

74   River Crest Country Club, Fort Worth, Texas. View of east elevation detail.

75   River Crest Country Club, Fort Worth, Texas. Ballroom floor plan.

119

FRED KOETTER AND SUSIE KIM

Fred Koetter (b. 1938) has been closely associated with Colin Rowe, with whom he wrote *Collage City* (1978), a devastating critique of the effect of Modernist planning and architecture on the city. As a designer, Koetter, who now works in partnership with Susie Kim (b. 1948), gingerly embraces Classicism, fully aware of its typological and contextual subtleties, yet retains a Modernist's apprehension regarding its specific forms. The Codex Corporation Headquarters in Canton, Massachusetts (1986), is a loft-type office building set in the pastoral landscape of a New England horse farm. Arriving visitors pass the existing carriage house and stable. The Codex headquarters are organized into two buildings: the three-story main building, containing offices, and a two-story "house," containing an auditorium and dining rooms, joined at a 45-degree angle. The materials are traditional to New England — brick, granite trim, slate roof — and the "house" is of the Palladian country house type. This simple parti, or scheme, is elaborated with a series of elements that respond to the site and programmatic details. A dining terrace curves along a rebuilt trotting track on one side, and a rounded tower marks the main employee entrance on another. The intricate perimeter gives way to an inner ring of flexible office space, and at the center of the project is a glazed 40 by 60-foot (12 by 18-meter) courtyard, a reference to the glass-and-iron roofed courts of late nineteenth-century office buildings, particularly those in Chicago, as well as the winter gardens of country houses and hotels. Yet although these various components — pedimented house, terrace, tower, courtyard — are essentially traditional in their materials, organization, and hierarchy, they are rendered in a stripped-down, abstracted vocabulary which seems to undercut the humanistic intent of the whole.

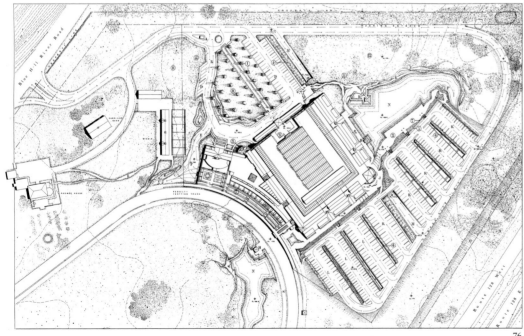

76 *Codex Corporation Headquarters, Canton, Massachusetts. Koetter, Kim & Associates, 1986. Site plan.*

76

77

78

77   *Codex Corporation Headquarters, Canton, Massachusetts. Koetter, Kim & Associates, 1986. View of north elevation.*

78   *Codex Corporation Headquarters, Canton, Massachusetts. Koetter, Kim & Associates, 1986. View of atrium.*

LAURENCE BOOTH

Laurence Booth (b. 1936), the principal designer of the Chicago firm of Booth/Hansen & Associates, has somewhat more cunningly combined Modernist abstraction and Classical form in several projects, especially in the Casa della Luce, a Chicago townhouse (1985), and an addition to the Krannert Art Museum, the Kinkead Pavilion, at the University of Illinois at Urbana-Champaign (1985–8). At the Casa della Luce, a specifically Palladian façade of stone over brick shows Classical elements reduced to their minimum: columns become embedded cylinders; capitals, splayed stone blocks; arched entryways, a pattern of window panes; window surrounds, a single jutting sill, yet the tripartite division, both horizontal and vertical, is still there.

The Kinkead Pavilion by Booth/Hansen adds office space and both indoor and outdoor exhibition space to an existing 1960s museum. Seeking to reorient the museum to the campus's principal east-west axis, Booth/Hansen's addition is equal in length and parallel to the existing one-story marble box, yet shifted toward the new axis. Two pavilions flank a long, bowed middle section. One pavilion is enclosed; the second is the entrance portico, with Egyptoid columns around the perimeter of a glazed cella, an effect similar to the portico at Robertson's Amvest Headquarters. Like the Casa della Luce, the Krannert Museum addition is essentially abstract, yet it is the work of a firm open to changing aesthetic trends, willing to accommodate the more subtle grammar and figural vocabulary of Classicism when it seems appropriate.

79 *Kinkead Pavilion, Krannert Art Museum, University of Illinois at Urbana-Champaigne. Booth/Hansen & Associates, 1985–8. View of model.*

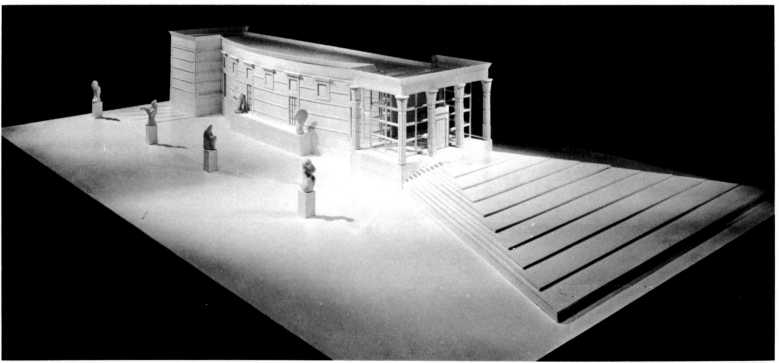

79

80

80   *Casa della Luce, Chicago, Illinois. Booth/Han-sen & Associates, 1985. View of street elevation.*

MARIO CAMPI

In the Italian-speaking canton of Ticino, Switzerland, Mario Campi (b. 1936) has made occasional forays in the direction of Classicism. Although he has declared that "the Modern Movement is still alive [and] . . . is not just a part of history like other styles,"[28] Campi's Casa Maggi, in Arosio, Switzerland (1980), presents a strong image of the elemental house-temple worthy of Heinrich Tessenow's Art Colony at Hellerau. Its principal façade is that of a temple with two white cylinder-like columns *in antis*, rising from a fieldstone base and flanked by fieldstone piers. Although a powerful representation of the tense relationship between Modernism and Classicism (and a possible inspiration for Robertson's Amvest Headquarters), the abstraction of the forms has a flat quality, which makes it more convincing as a graphical sign than as architecture.

81 *Casa Maggi, Arosio, Switzerland, Mario Campi, 1980. View of west elevation.*

82 *Casa Maggi, Arosio, Switzerland. Mario Campi, 1980. View southwest.*

81

MARIO BOTTA

Another architect of Ticino, also fundamentally Modernist in the reductionism and abstraction of his approach, Mario Botta (b. 1943) credits Carlos Scarpa, his design critic during his schooling in Venice, as his foremost influence. He is also strongly influenced by Louis Kahn, for whom he worked in the 1960s, learning his vocabulary of distilled Classically-inspired, technologically rationalized forms. Although in the past decade Botta has increasingly accepted existing forms and types as the starting point of design, he still adheres to Modernism's thesis of historical determinism, which claims that architecture is a mirror of its times:

> There is a very beautiful definition which I enjoy recalling every now and then, namely that architecture is the formal expression of history. Today we live in an epoch where there are materials which by themselves are not noble. It is our duty, our work as architects, to make these materials speak, to make them become the highest expression possible for our time.[29]

Despite the fact that Botta has been characterized as a regionalist — largely because his work thus far has been mostly in Ticino — his overpowering geometry and love of unitized concrete masonry militate against this, and Botta admits that all but his clients and a few friends consider his buildings out of place and ugly. Since the second half of the 1970s, his houses have become more and more Classical in plan and elevation and have assumed the form of belvedere. The Casa Unifamiliare, in Viganello (1980–81) has a tripartite composition which Botta has used before consisting of two solid cubic masses flanking a glazed spine running through the building's center, realizing the roof as a barrel vault whose great arch completes a simplified serliana. The result is an almost Loosian combination of straightforward building and the language of Classicism, albeit in a very reduced, emblematized way. Also in the tradition of Loos, or more recently, Kahn, the house at Viganello, like Botta's other designs, uses ordinary materials finished at an extremely high level of craftsmanship.

83   *Casa Unifamiliare, Viganello, Switzerland. Mario Botta, 1980–81. View of west elevation.*

KEVIN ROCHE

Kevin Roche (b. 1922), an American architect who is Irish by birth and early education, has had an important career as a staunch advocate of Modernism in the service of corporate clients before refocusing his work toward more overtly historical forms. Roche's early training in architecture in Dublin was in the Beaux-Arts system, but he threw aside its lessons, first in London and then when he began his American career in 1948, studying in Chicago at Mies van der Rohe's architecture school, the Illinois Institute of Technology. After a short time there and a brief stint working for the committee of United Nations architects in 1949, Roche went to work for Eero Saarinen in 1950. By 1954 when he had reached the position of Saarinen's chief design assistant, Roche had collaborated with Saarinen in the designs for the TWA Terminal at Kennedy Airport and for Dulles Airport. Inheriting the firm after Saarinen's death in 1961, Roche established his own firm, Kevin Roche John Dinkeloo and Associates, in 1966. On his own, Roche became known for buildings, such as the Ford Foundation Headquarters in New York (1963–8), that combined the aggressive overscaled forms and sculptural qualities of the late work of Le Corbusier with the smooth finishes and severe geometries then characteristic of American corporate practice. The Ford Foundation building disdains traditional urban scale. Enormous stone-clad piers rise from the street to the roof-line, supporting a 6 by 6-foot (1.8 by 1.8-meter) steel-and-glass grid. The offices are arranged around a glazed central court, planted with a lush garden, so that everyone has a view of the garden and of each other. According to Roche, this was to provide a sense of community: "We're building a house for them. . . . The fact that it is composed to a large extent of office space has nothing to do with its character."[30]

Fourteen years after beginning the design of the Ford Foundation, Roche set about designing another corporate house, a headquarters for the General Foods Corporation in Rye, New York (1977–83). Continuing with the ideas of the Ford Foundation, Roche said about General Foods: "I am very interested in the idea of the corporate headquarters as a house. The house analogy really has to do with the family — the idea being that any group of people who work together becomes a family . . ."[31] This time, however, Roche chose to express the house's "character" (a word from the tradition of his Beaux-Arts training) in a Classical form. Rising on its wooded hillock in suburban Westchester County, the General Foods Headquarters is clad in vinyl-coated aluminum to look like an overscaled, slicked-up, blindingly white Palladian villa. To appropriate the country house type for an office building is not so surprising: in Italy, as in Britain, the country house in the past usually served as the administrative and social center of a district; it was as much a public building as a private house. In its basic form of a central dome flanked by two wings ending in pavilions, General Foods carries the analogy quite a bit further, taking on the public symbolism of state and national capitols and continuing an American tradition of business arrogating to itself connotations of civic importance.

Despite the strong Classicism of the composition, Roche holds on to many of his Modernist principles in the specific details of the design. The aluminum cladding forms a thin skin which in no way articulates critical compositional intersections such as corners. The rotunda is undercut by a driveway into the parking garage; the corporate temple's plinth and the horizontal strip windows undo any fleeting

84 *General Foods Corporation Headquarters, Rye, New York. Kevin Roche John Dinkeloo and Associates, 1977–83. View of south elevation detail.*

impression of traditional structure. Around the back, on the other side of the grand entrance, the elevation looks considerably more industrial than Classical. Furthermore, Roche wanted nothing to do with Classical detail:

> My interest . . . was in the principles of classical composition. I did not want to get into mimicking any of the other aspects of classical architecture, not attempting column capitals, cornices, swags, base course, dadoes, or anything else. And I did it all from memory. I didn't research classical plans or buildings because I don't like to work that way."[32]

Roche applied much the same philosophy to his design for the Bouygues headquarters outside Paris (1983–), where the deliberate references to Classical planning — including the overall axiality, the arms curving out from a central block, as in a Palladian design, and the formal French gardens laid out next to the building — are innocent of even the vestige of a column or entablature.

85 *General Foods Corporation Headquarters, Rye, New York. Kevin Roche John Dinkeloo and Associates, 1977–83. View northeast.*

85

FUNDAMENTALIST CLASSICISM

To the Fundamentalist Classicist, the study and practice of architecture must begin with an understanding of the traditional, pre-industrial city, and the primary task of the contemporary architect is the critical reintegration of architecture into the urban tradition. Rather than designing in the historic styles, however, the Fundamentalist seeks to distill architecture to its essential geometries and then apply them to contemporary circumstances. In its search for essentials, Fundamentalist Classicism belongs to a tradition of reform in architecture, of periodical calls to order, whether by Vitruvius, Alberti, Laugier or Loos, demanding a return to origins in which architectural expression is "timeless," transcending current banalities. Aldo Rossi, who is unquestionably the most important theorist and practitioner of contemporary Fundamentalism, has distilled the particular shapes of buildings in the traditional city into pure geometries of cone, cylinder, cube and triangle. The approach is almost opposite to that of the Ironists, who use Classical forms in a consciously contemporary way, and also embrace today's commercial culture. Rossi and other Fundamentalists try to sweep away the clutter of commercialism and search for timeless cultural resonances, to communicate on a basic and profound level they believe still possible.

Leon Krier, also a prominent Fundamentalist yet one who often uses more specific traditional language, has gone even further in his advocacy of an urban culture cleansed of the excessive commercialism of a Times Square, Ginza or Las Vegas strip. His most important contribution has been to the vision of the city as a whole, developing many of Rossi's ideas of organizing an institution to the level of an entire district, and his work is discussed in the later section on the Modern Classical City.

86   *Galen Medical Building, Boca Raton, Florida. Duany and Plater-Zyberk, 1981–3. View southwest.*

ALDO ROSSI

In *The Architecture of the City* (1966), Aldo Rossi (b. 1931) argued that buildings had to be analyzed as "urban artifacts," according to a formal typology rather than to their functional purpose, because function had little to do with the "principal questions that arise in relation to an urban artifact—among them; individuality, *locus*, memory, design itself."[33] Rossi was proposing a profoundly anti-Modernist method of design: to begin with the constructed fact of the city, and work backward to elemental forms, rather than beginning with the materials of industrialized building technology and working forward to satisfy the "functions" of life. Rossi was interested in the forms which had transcended "history" — their original functional purpose — and persisted as part of the collective "memory" of the city. Thus Rossi's primary interest is neither a synthesis between the aesthetics of industrialized building techniques and traditional form, as it is for Latent Classicists, nor the utopian urbanism advocated by Modernists, which has had such disastrous effects on the European city. For Rossi, who was the first to establish the fundamentalist point of view, architecture is a continuum across time, and the exigencies of politics and an evolving technology are incidental to the architect's principal responsibility: to understand the fundamental forms of architecture and bring them to bear on contemporary problems in an intelligent way.

Rossi regards the existing architecture of the city as referential data, and he marries the traditional methods of architectural composition and design to the techniques of urban planning: cartography, topography, and typology. His approach is part of an ongoing search — extending from Claude Perrault, through Durand, and the Italian Modernists of the 1920s and '30s such as Giuseppe Terragni — for an architecture more concerned with formal essences than with issues of technology or functional accommodation. Rossi and his followers aspire to an architecture of objectivity, a pursuit implicitly bound to tradition, in which, as the Spanish architect and critic, Ignasi de Solà Moràles says, "architecture does not invent since its repertoire has always existed."[34] Rossi recognizes that the typologies of Durand are insufficiently articulate to connect buildings to particular cultural situations.

He admits that the objective analysis of architecture does not preclude a subjective element. The title of his book *A Scientific Autobiography* (1981)[35] encapsulates these two elements: analysis is the science, artistic expression the autobiography. Whereas in his early projects Rossi adopted an extremely reductivist procedure, breaking architecture into a limited vocabulary of parts which he then reassembled, in his mature work he has increasingly both recognized the subjective nature of his preferred forms and lost interest in them as pure, Platonic abstractions: "Ever since my first projects, where I was interested in purism, I have loved contaminations, slight changes, self-commentaries, and repetitions."[36]

The "memory" of the city which is the basis of his architecture is both personal and collective, naive and educated. Childhood memories of a hotel near the beach and learned knowledge of architectural monuments are equally valued in Rossi's process of creation, which juxtaposes grand visions and ordinary details to create surreal urban visions similar to the paintings of Giorgio de Chirico (1888–1978), which have had an enormous influence on Rossi's designs.

87

87   *Cemetery, Modena, Italy. Aldo Rossi with Gianni Braghieri, 1971, revised 1976. View of arcade.*

88   *Cemetery, Modena, Italy. Aldo Rossi with Gianni Braghieri, 1971, revised 1976. View of cemetery and shrine.*

132

88

A cemetery in the north Italian city of Modena (Aldo Rossi with Gianni Braghieri, 1971, revised 1976) was Rossi's first opportunity to articulate fully his conception of urbanism, albeit in a grim translation of the city of the living to the city of the dead. Constructed of the most basic geometric forms and building types, Rossi's Modena cemetery is surrounded by a wall consisting of long, narrow columbaria beneath a pitched roof. In the center, close to the entrance, is an eight-story cube whose voided windows convey its role as an apartment house of the dead. Behind that, there is an ossuary of parallelepipeds organized into a triangle that points to a great cone which dominates the common graves and rises high above the cemetery. This monument holds a social meaning for Rossi: "the common graves contain the remains of the abandoned — the dead who lost touch with the world, often people from hostels, hospitals, prisons, leading a desperate existence or forgotten altogether. To these oppressed people, the city builds the highest monument."[37] Unlike the traditional Anglo-American idea of a cemetery, where the dead are planted in a pastoral scene suitable for family picnics and private contemplation, Rossi's cemetery, which builds upon Italian precedent, is a frighteningly rationalized image of a city without life. In a sense, it is the *reductio ad absurdum* of the typological approach to architecture, taking the existing, archetypal forms of a given building type — in this case the Italian cemetery — and then reducing them to their simplest recognizable form. It is also a commentary on the dilemma of purely abstract architecture, since architecture's forms can be truly pure only when they are uncompromised by human activity — when their only inhabitants are the dead.

Rossi's designs for the living are free of such puristic ideals. For the reconstruction, renovation, and additions to Carlo Barabino's Carlo Felice Theater in Genoa (1825–8), he provocatively combines historic preservation, reconstruction, and new work to produce a wholly integrated Classical composition which is essentially timeless (with Ignazio Gardella, Fabio Reinhart, and Angelo Sibilla, 1982). Before it was bombed during the Second World War, the theater had been the prime symbol of the city. In the new design, Rossi followed the lead of the first architect hired to reconstruct the theater, Carlo Scarpa, deciding that the exterior should be essentially a reconstruction of Barabino's building, that the auditorium should be reconstructed in the traditional form of a *cavea*, and that the stage tower should be enlarged. For the interior, Rossi proposed several of the forms and materials characteristic of his vocabulary, including a conical opening over the entrance foyer, a great chimney bringing light down through several stories, and the steel stairs and bridges (also used at the Modena cemetery) of the stage tower.

In Buenos Aires, Rossi tested his philosophy with a characteristic twentieth-century building type: an office building (with Gianni Braghieri, Miguel Oks, Gianmarco Ciocca, and Massimo Scheurer, 1984). The program called for a slab-like office tower as one element in a building related to the existing church and convent of Santa Catalina, a severe example of Spanish Colonial architecture which is to be converted into a museum. Although the office slab is a Modernist rather than a traditional type, Rossi approached it with characteristic respect. However, he abandoned its usual neutrality of composition and expression for a design with two principal elevations (slab sides, slab ends). The stepped pyramid that crowns the central portion is a reference both to the Pre-Columbian architecture of Latin America and to the headiness of 1920s New York skyscrapers, particularly the New York Life Insurance Company Tower by Cass Gilbert (1928), which fascinates Rossi on his frequent visits to New York.

The office slab is clearly not a sympathetic type for Rossi — its potential as object and space definer is too ambivalent, and in an attempt to rationalize its form, he is propelled toward an affirmation of the universal solutions which Modernism endorsed. There is an unintentionally ironic quality of righteousness in the architect's own statement that the project seeks to unite the private and public spaces of the block ''into a series of architectural elements (formal and functional) that attain unity in an image which is or should become typical of Buenos Aires.''[38] In the notion that types are made rather than interpreted by architects, one may discern the long shadow of Le Corbusier (to whom Rossi has never been sympathetic) with his ardent belief in a standardized world in which architects set the standards.

89

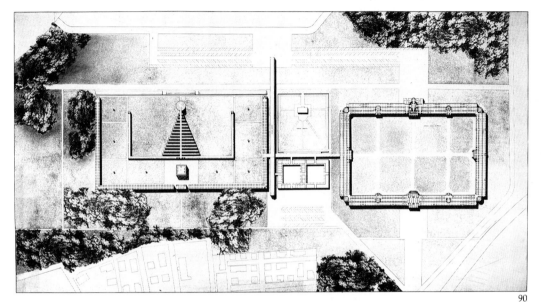

90

91

89   *Cemetery, Modena, Italy. Aldo Rossi with Gianna Braghieri, 1971, revised 1976. View through graveyard towards columbarium.*

90   *Cemetery, Modena, Italy. Aldo Rossi with Gianni Braghieri, 1971, revised 1976. Plan.*

91   *Cemetery, Modena, Italy. Aldo Rossi with Gianni Braghieri, 1971, revised 1976. View of shrine.*

92

93   94

92   *Reconstruction, renovation, and additions to Carlo Felice Theater, Genoa, Italy. Aldo Rossi with Ignazio Gardella, Fabio Reinhart, and Angelo Sibilla, 1982. Unbuilt project. Perspective of main entrance.*

93   *Reconstruction, renovation, and additions to Carlo Felice Theater, Genoa, Italy. Aldo Rossi with Ignazio Gardella, Fabio Reinhart, and Angelo Sibilla, 1982. Unbuilt project. Perspective and section sketches by Aldo Rossi.*

94   *Office Building, Buenos Aires, Argentina. Aldo Rossi and Gianni Braghieri with Miguel Oks, Gianmarco Ciocca, and Massimo Scheurer, 1984. Unbuilt project. Perspective by Aldo Rossi. Perspectival sketch by Aldo Rossi.*

95   *Office Building, Buenos Aires, Argentina. Aldo Rossi and Gianni Braghieri with Miguel Oks, Gianmarco Ciocca, and Massimo Scheurer, 1984. Unbuilt project. Plan.*

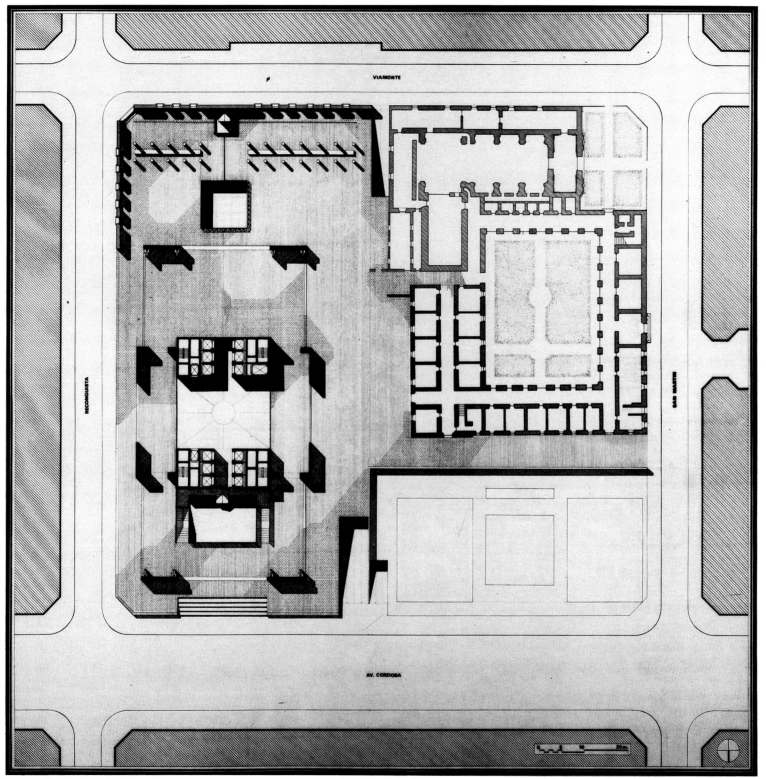

RAFAEL MONEO

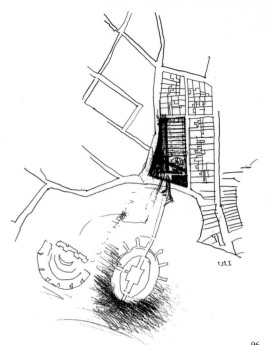

Although Rossi's production has been limited, his approach has been highly influential, particularly in places where the machine culture has had small effect on building and where the vernacular building tradition has remained essentially Classical in its composition and logic. Nowhere has Rossi's influence been more profound and positive than in Spain, where Rafael Moneo (b. 1937), Miguel Garay (b. 1936), and José-Ignacio Linazasoro (b. 1937) have emerged as dominant figures in the post-Franco era.

Rafael Moneo's National Museum of Roman Art in Mérida (1985) is built over the ruins of the most important Roman city in Spain and linked by tunnels to two of the major remaining monuments, an amphitheater and theater. Founded by Augustus Caesar in 25 BC, Mérida was almost destroyed during the Arab invasion of the eighth century and has never recovered its past glory. Its citizens began to appreciate its former greatness only with the excavation of its rich Roman remains.

Moneo's design is a paradigm of the complex rationality proposed by Rossi. Its materials and shapes manifest Mérida's historical drama. Rather than attempting to build a pavilion with a clear span over the excavated streets and buildings, Moneo proposed an architectural palimpsest, not as an ancient or medieval designer might have, melding old and new together into a continuous and virtually seamless web, but as a Modern, acutely holding inviolate the artifact of the past. Nonetheless, Moneo engages the ruin directly, threading his regular grid of loadbearing piers and walls through the more random ancient pattern, yet taking care to avoid the most important sites, a Roman house and a basilica. And rather than opening up the ruins to the main galleries, he has re-buried them in a sepulchral basement. Rational though the museum is, it is also a romantic work employing historical associations, with exposed brick Roman arches and a basilical plan; in essence it is the inner skeleton of Roman building awaiting its stucco and marble. As Moneo himself has said: "I would like people visiting the museum to have the feeling that not only the crypt but also the new walls were 'found' by excavating, that the walls have been there since the third century after Christ and were uncovered in the process of building another building some centuries later."[39]

Moneo's walls, divided into a series of arches, consist of unreinforced concrete surfaced by long, narrow Roman bricks. The walls relate to the structure but not to the expression of Classical architecture. It is as if the marble facing of a Roman monument has been carted away, along with the rhetoric of a columnar order, to reveal the underlying tectonic realities.

Where Rossi argues for a pure architecture to justify his design, Moneo, in his museum, offers a structural rationale, pointing out that in addition to housing ruins and a collection of antiquities, the museum had to serve as a retaining wall for the crumbling Roman road leading to the ancient theaters. Solving this problem produced the highly evocative series of parallel walls hollowed out into arches which compose the almost 50-foot (15-meter) high nave of the main exhibition space. And he is willing to undermine the aura of antiquity achieved in the space, where light comes from skylights and high-placed "clerestory" windows, by revealing the thin concrete slabs of the mezzanine-level side galleries' floors and linking the side galleries with skinny pipe-railings.

96 *National Museum of Roman Art, Mérida, Spain. Rafael Moneo, 1985. Sketch of site plan.*

97 *National Museum of Roman Art, Mérida, Spain. Rafael Moneo, 1985. Interior view of main floor.*

The exterior of the building articulates the ambiguities of structure, urban typology and historical associations. On the south façade, the gallery's heavy, buttressed walls seem ancient. On the north side, the gallery looks like a tough, nineteenth-century industrial building, with plain brick walls rising to a roof-line of ten small, identical gables, inset with glass roofs. The entrance block, to the east, is at the same scale as the gallery but has a much more domestic character, relating to the scale of neighboring buildings. The ground floor is bare, the second has the large windows of a *piano nobile*, and the third has slightly smaller ones; the windows on both of these floors have shutters. Dormers break through the pitched pantile roof. Only on the entrance façade does Moneo feel compelled to acknowledge that the building is not an ancient artifact but an interpretation. The sheer brick wall, smoothed by the apparent absence of mortar — one of Moneo's favorite techniques — rises the full height of the building to screen the pitched roof behind. A blind, round-headed arch frames the entrance. The infill, recessed the thickness of a brick, contains a niche, occupied by a decapitated Roman statue of a woman. She rests on the one piece of marble in Moneo's building: a heavy lintel above the one-story entrance doors, inscribed with a sign that describes the building as type: "MVSEO."

98   *National Museum of Roman Art, Mérida, Spain. Rafael Moneo, 1985. Ground floor plan showing Roman ruins and road.*

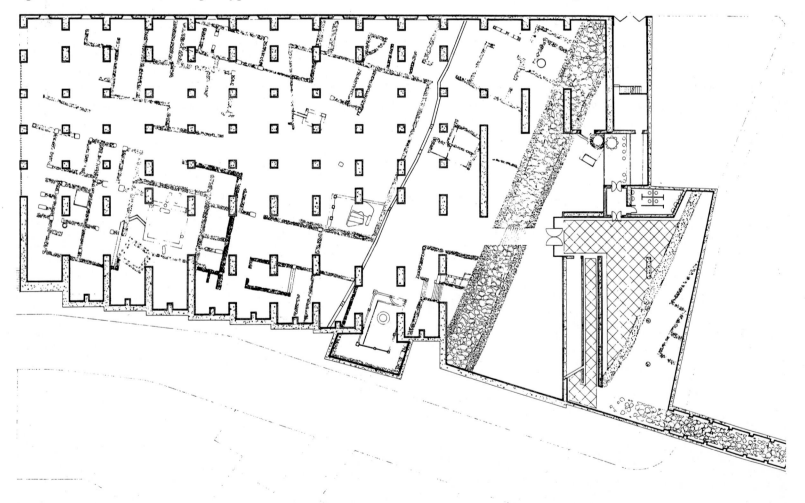

98

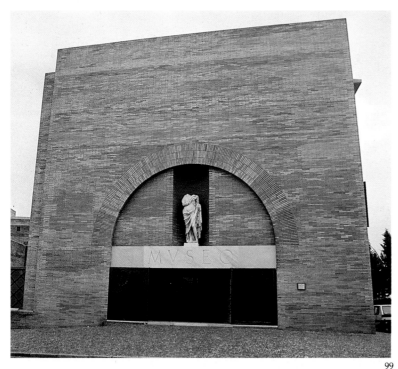

99

99   *National Museum of Roman Art, Mérida, Spain. Rafael Moneo, 1985. View of entrance.*

101   *National Museum of Roman Art, Mérida, Spain. Rafael Moneo, 1985.*

101

100

100   *National Museum of Roman Art, Mérida, Spain. Rafael Moneo, 1985.*

102   *National Museum of Roman Art, Mérida, Spain. Rafael Moneo, 1985. Interior view of ground floor showing Roman ruins.*

102

MIGUEL GARAY AND JOSÉ-IGNACIO LINAZASORO

The philosophy of both Miguel Garay and José-Ignacio Linazasoro, who have collaborated on several projects, relies in part on the same engine of contempt that ran the architectural avant-garde in the early twentieth century — contempt for "styles" — but it does not extend to a contempt for tradition. Linazasoro believes in the "essentialization" of architectural forms, a process which does not preclude ornament or historical precedent but does not exactly embrace it either. Positioning himself in a tradition of twentieth-century Classicists, he has written:

> With Tessenow and the Scandinavians we witness a phenomenon that had a distant precedent in Palladio: Classical forms are mixed with others of a rural character. This is not a case of mere combination; instead, Classical forms recover their essential, immediate character and are thereby freed of all stylistic niceties. In Tessenow's Hellerau Institute the rural pediment combines with the slender order of the pillars: vernacular and Classical architecture are no longer separated by stylistic barriers.[40]

In their first important work, the School (*Ikastola*) in Fuenterrabia, northern Spain (1974–8), Garay and Linazasoro registered their disapproval of the recent development of the surrounding area — where, as they wrote, they were "confronted with a site which lacked a coherent urban fabric due to the disruption and fragmentation effected, on the one hand by the economic strategy of parcellization of land, and on the other by the process of individualization of culture as exemplified by the countless miniature chalets implanted by land developers."[41] Behind this remark lay complex political issues involving Basque separatism and the rapid "modernization" of post-Franco Spain. The Ikastola is a Basque school, where instruction is for the most part in the Basque language. The derided "chalets," however, are occupied mainly by Spanish-speaking newcomers to the region. Basque aspirations to nationhood and an autonomous culture are threatened and rapidly eroding in the face of pressure from the Spanish majority. For the architects, their school, conceived in opposition to this centralizing force, though aggressively urban, was also intended to be typological, and — however improbably, given the depth of their aesthetic debt to Aldo Rossi's early work — quintessentially Basque. They strove to develop an urban fabric in the Basque countryside by combining the courtyard of a traditional Basque villa with an axial city street. The Ikastola is organized as a single-story square around a large courtyard, which is split down the center by the "street," composed of two long, narrow entrance courts at opposite ends of a four-story central block. Yet there are no overt gestures to traditional Basque architecture. All is abstract, emulating the architects' hero, Rossi, with a severe geometry of nearly barren, rectilinear walls, and colonnades of unmodulated piers.

In a collaboration five years later, Garay and Linazasoro allowed themselves a slightly richer palette, which was also closer to the vernacular side of Tessenow's essentializing philosophy. For an apartment block in Mendigorria (1979–80), they took the U-shaped plan of the typical Navarre house as their starting point, and

103

103   *Apartment block, Mendigorria, Spain. Miguel Garay and José-Ignacio Linazasoro, 1979–80. View toward courtyard.*

142

104

104   *Casa Mendiola, Andoian, Spain. Miguel Garay, 1977–8. View of entrance.*

proceeded to give a Classical order to a basically vernacular design. The principal façade, facing the street, is organized into a cement block base, brick façade, and pantile roof. It is biaxially symmetrical, with a central entranceway consisting of a semicircular arch springing above an opening in the cement block base. The fenestration makes the Classical distinction between the ground floor *piano nobile*, and upper story, and has the vernacular addition of wooden shutters. The entrance frames a view of the courtyard and the open country beyond. The courtyard is bracingly minimal: square brick piers, without a base or top, uniform in size from the first story to the third, line three sides of the courtyard, supporting the balconies' exposed concrete slabs.

The rear façade as a whole, divided between the two legs of the ''U'' and the courtyard between them, more casually restates the more complicated themes of the street façade. The fenestration is no longer Classically composed, yet the two gables are made to resemble pediments by their pitch and by the presence of the side walls' cornices slipping around the edge to the rear to form the vestigial architraves of a ghostly entablature.

In their independent projects, outside their *ad hoc* and occasional partnership, Garay and Linazasoro have each moved toward a more representational use of vernacular and Classical elements. Garay's Casa Mendiola in Andoian, also in the Basque country (1977–8), is a villa set on a hill above a valley near San Sebastián. On the side overlooking the slope, the house, which is sheathed in yellow-gold stucco, has the general layout of a Palladian villa, with a large central block flanked by arcades, except that here the arcades have become a squared-off gallery. The entrance portico has also been rationalized — the columns are simple cylinders supporting a glass and steel canopy. On the opposite side, the house appears as a much smaller pavilion, without wings, set on a lawn traversed by winding, picturesque paths.

In a project for a railway station square, the Plaza de Atocha in San Sebastián (with Enrique Muga, 1983), Garay employed the more obvious Classical forms of a public square — stoa, pavilion and pergola — for a site adjacent to the railway station and beside a late nineteenth-century tobacco factory. Here the prejudice for tectonic expression is still strong, but the choice of less abstract, more identifiable forms shows a more literal sense of urbanism than at the school in Fuenterrabia.

In a cultural center in Ormazabal, Pasaia Antxo (1983), Garay has abandoned the astringent puritanism of his earlier designs. The small building is rich in detail, symbolism, and figural space. The façade, with an entrance arch similar to that of the apartment building in Mendigorria, is faced in yellow stone and detailed in white marble, and flanking the portal there are panels ornamented with stylized depictions of branches, the sun, and the moon, all in blue and white. Inside, the visitor moves through an elliptical lobby into an auditorium which has a circular stage. Throughout, there is a new attention to the possibilities of less rigid geometries and the use of decorative details, such as a star pattern on the ceiling of the stairwell.

In his design for a medical center in Segura, a small town in the hills above San Sebastián (1983–5), Linazasoro has also revealed a taste for more articulated designs. Located on the site of the former town hall, the medical center is meant to be contextual to its chiefly residential neighborhood and at the same time to maintain a civic character. Although the scale is modest and the materials ordinary, Linazasoro has imbued the building with Classical *gravitas*. The stucco-clad cement block base has a rigid order of simplified pilasters, with a high window set in each bay. A frieze between the first and second floors, set off by concrete mouldings above and below it, ·

105

105   *Cultural Center, Ormazabal, Pasaia Antxo, Spain. Miguel Garay, 1983. View of street elevation.*

is inscribed with a Greek key pattern. The stucco wall above is largely blank, except for two bisymmetrically placed windows at its edges. In the top center there is a narrow band of clerestory windows. This formality is carried into the interior, where the lobby, though entered from off center, is a symmetrical, stripped-down Classical room. There are simplified pilasters and sconces on the walls and a coffered ceiling.

In another project in Segura, a pavilion and garden (1983–5), Linazasoro tried to provide an impressive urban place for a town rich in historical architecture but poor in public spaces. The basic design of the pavilion looks like an archetypal form that could have been reproduced in Durand's *Précis des leçons d'architecture données à l'Ecole Polytechnique*, yet Linazasoro also identifies his sources as the rural and the picturesque. Facing the street and acting as the focus of the town's most important square, the pavilion consists of a wide, gently pitched gable, banded with brick and painted stucco. A semicircular arch framing a fountain is at its center. Although the materials may be picturesque, the plan has a Classical formality. Two arcaded pergolas flank the pavilion and run forward to the street, forming an entry court.

106 *Railway station square, Plaza de Atocha, San Sebastian, Spain. Miguel Garay with Enrique Muga, 1983. Unbuilt project. Perspective.*

106

145

107

108

107   *Medical Center, Segura, Spain. José-Ignacio Linazasoro, 1983–5. View.*

108   *Medical Center, Segura, Spain. José-Ignacio Linazasoro, 1983–5. View of elevation detail.*

109   *Medical Center, Segura, Spain. José-Ignacio Linazasoro, 1983–5. Interior view of entrance hall.*

109

110

111

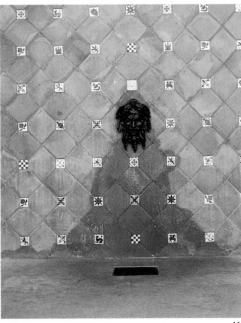

112

110   *Pavilion and garden, Segura, Spain. José-Ignacio Linazasoro, 1985. View of entrance elevation.*

111 & 112   *Pavilion and garden, Segura, Spain. José-Ignacio Linazasoro, 1983–5. View of entrance elevation details showing fountain.*

BATEY AND MACK

In a series of houses built in the Napa Valley north of San Francisco, as well as elsewhere in California and in Texas, the partnership of Andrew Batey (b. 1944) and Mark Mack (b. 1949), which has now broken up, carried Rossi's Fundamentalism and rationalism further than any other American firm. Speaking at a meeting of New York City's Architectural League in 1982, the Austrian-born-and-educated Mark Mack drew on Abbé Laugier's primitive hut and the work of Schinkel, Loos and others to support his claim that "all meaning in architecture is derived from structure and construction."[42]

Despite the appealing tectonic rigor of Batey and Mack's Napa Valley houses, the attempted alchemy of turning base materials such as cinderblock into "noble" matter did not at first succeed.

The breakthrough came with their Holt Residence, on the bay in Corpus Christi, Texas (1984), which, because it bent the house rules, in both plan and materials, achieved a remarkable balance of rigor and grace. The plan of the Holt Residence begins with a model more advanced than Laugier's primitive hut, the Roman villa suburbana. Like its Classical prototype, the Holt Residence has a formal, almost windowless wall facing the street — a four-lane highway — and a more open, verandah-like façade overlooking the Gulf of Mexico. The house has an open-air atrium, porticoes, pergolas, and the genuinely noble materials of marble and granite. There is no mistaking it for the picturesque, however. The design is a disciplined geometrical construct, with a 4 by 4-foot (1.3 meter-square) module used to determine the proportions of the rooms, floors, walls, windows, and ceiling. The house is also emphatically axial, with an 8-foot- (2.5-meter)- wide *marche* from the atrium through the center of the house straight into the Gulf of Mexico. The pillars lining the stairway to the shore continue into the water, in a surreal commentary on the villa's sense of place and history.

113   *Holt Residence, Corpus Christi, Texas. Batey & Mack, 1984. View from the Gulf of Mexico.*

DUANY AND PLATER-ZYBERK

The Florida partnership of Andres Duany (b. 1949) and Elizabeth Plater-Zyberk (b. 1950) tends to use a gently understated Classical vocabulary which owes as much to the compositional purities of Durand as to the Mediterranean styles of south Florida. Duany and Plater-Zyberk first came to international attention for their master plan for Seaside, a new community in Florida's Panhandle (1983), where they reasserted the primacy of places, streets, and traditional vernacular wood-framed architecture. As architects, Duany and Plater-Zyberk avoid the cosy informalities that characterize the Victorian-inspired wooden houses which proliferate at Seaside. Charleston Place, a 110-unit townhouse development in Boca Raton (1984), is more typical of their work. Here they disciplined a picturesque palette of tiled gabled roofs, a variety of pastel-painted stucco walls, and brick walkways beneath arbors of wisteria, to a regular linear grid.

In their private houses, Duany and Plater-Zyberk manage to convey the aura of Classical design with a minimum of Classical detail. In the De La Cruz House in Key Biscayne, Miami (1983), they remodelled a suburban ranch-style house into the Classical type of the Pompeian house. A blank one-story wall seals the house from the street and forms one side of a courtyard for automobiles. The house wall is equally hermetic, pierced only by the tiny atrium entrance. On the garden side the house opens up to the view, with a loggia on the ground floor and a narrow balcony above. The loggia is lined by fat square piers, whose severe detailing is limited to a strip of moulding to indicate a capital. The Classical nature of the house comes from the inclusion of open spaces such as the loggia, the vestigial details, and the overall compositional rigor of parts fitting into a Classical whole.

In the Vilanova House, also in Key Biscayne (1984), Duany and Plater-Zyberk used the Erechtheum (421–405 BC) as their model, as well as the highly stylized work of the mid-nineteenth century Scottish architect, Alexander "Greek" Thompson, assembling temple porticoes and more banal side walls in the seemingly *ad hoc* way of the Athenian monument, massing its elements with a specific oblique view in mind. Yet like many contemporary architects, they seem uncomfortable with a purely visual approach and seek to establish their credentials as purifying reformers, insisting that they do not need details and that massing, proportion, and sound building are enough: "The architecture . . . does not depend on craftsmanly ornament. Elaboration is confined to the clarification of constructional data."[43] To prove their point, the architects decided that the construction of their Galen Medical Building in Boca Raton, Florida (1981–3), a massive cube, should be masonry (concrete block) rather than the steel or wood frame typical of the stuccoed Miami Beach hotels of the 1930s which served as their inspiration. Duany and Plater-Zyberk have applied a credo of structural integrity to their design in order to recreate the "look" of a much less rationalized and highly nostalgic architectural precedent. Like the designers working half a century earlier, they realized that a building with a bold geometric shape, strong symmetries, deep, shaded reveals, and a minimum of detail would look good in the Florida sun.

In one of Duany and Plater-Zyberk's recent projects, constructional data really seem to be all there is. The Williams, an apartment complex in Hialeah, Florida (1986–7), has four-story façades of stuccoed concrete block pierced by an infinitely

114 *Charleston Place, Boca Raton, Florida. Duany and Plater-Zyberk, 1984. Site plan.*

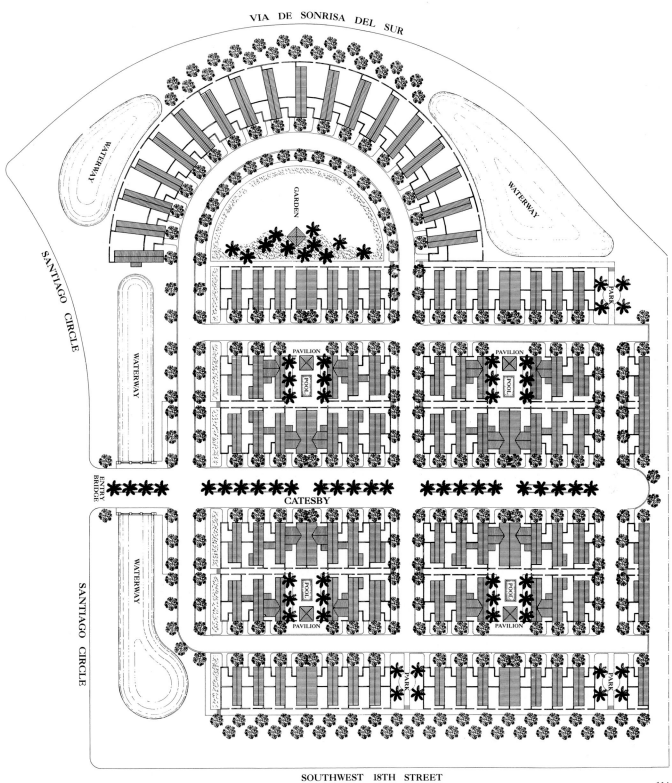

VIA DE SONRISA DEL SUR

WATERWAY

WATERWAY

GARDEN

SANTIAGO CIRCLE

WATERWAY

PARK

PAVILION

POOL

PAVILION

POOL

ENTRY BRIDGE

CATESBY

SANTIAGO CIRCLE

WATERWAY

POOL

PAVILION

POOL

PAVILION

PARK

PARK

SOUTHWEST 18TH STREET

repeatable pattern of regular windows. Suggesting projects by Loos (and, at a few entrance archways, Wright), The Williams combines an extremist anti-ornamental position (perhaps partly determined by budget) with a profoundly conservative sense of urbanism. The apartments are organized into three L-shaped buildings around courtyards, really parking lots, softened by a perimeter of pergolas and trees.

115

115 *Charleston Place, Boca Raton, Florida. Duany and Plater-Zyberk, 1984. View of typical street.*

116 *The Williams, Hialeah, Florida. Duany and Plater-Zyberk, 1986–7. Construction view of courtyard.*

116

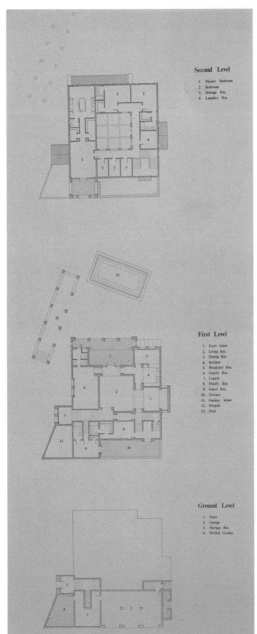

118

117   *Vilanova House, Key Biscayne, Florida.*
Duany and Plater-Zyberk, 1984. Plans.

118   *Vilanova House, Key Biscayne, Florida.*
Duany and Plater-Zyberk, 1984. View of north
elevation.

117

ALEXANDER TZANNES

The Australian architect Alexander Tzannes has reacted against both the formal peregrinations of the typical brutalist Modernism of post-war Australian design and the picturesque architecture typical of British-inspired vernacular styles by adopting many of the principles of the Fundamentalist primitive hut. Tzannes's Henwood House in Paddington Sydney (1982–5) has an erased Classical façade shockingly at odds with its picturesque neighbors. Between highly ornamented Victorian row houses, which have distinctive cast-iron verandahs rich in filigree, Tzannes has offered up the ghost of a triple-bayed Georgian townhouse. In his design for the Federation Pavilion housing the symbol of Australia's government, the Foundation Stone, in Sydney's Centennial Park (1985–7), Tzannes followed a more overtly Classical course. Tzannes's building, replacing one that lasted only a few years before it was demolished in 1903, is a circular temple design with a shallow dome floating above it. Although the exterior is static and true to type, the interior is relatively kinetic, animated by a floor that slopes to the stone in the center and by a soffit above decorated with vitreous enamel panels.

119 *Federation Pavilion, Centennial Park, Sydney Australia. Alexander Tzannes, 1985–7. Section.*

119

120

121

122

120 *Henwood House, Paddington, Sydney, Australia. Alexander Tzannes, 1985. View of street elevation.*

121 & 122 *Henwood House, Paddington, Sydney, Australia. Alexander Tzannes, 1985. Views of rear elevation.*

ROBIN ESPIE DODS

For the Ashton House in Woollahra, Sydney (1982), another Australian architect, Robin Espie Dods designed a severe gray brick façade, windowless on the ground floor, but softened somewhat by the green ground cover and iron railing of the shallow yard. The squat entrance portico is both mannerist and blunt. The rusticated brick columns support a thick, solid architrave, which also suggests vestigial capitals in the two little curves cut out on its sides. The frieze and pediment are undetailed gray brick. It is as an architecture of contrasts, rather than of detail that Dods's house succeeds, with the massive, windowless façade of the entrance serving as a prelude to an entrance hall brilliantly lit from above by a large skylight, and the closed, masonry face of the public side of the house shielding the open, "natural," private side with its indoor pools, loggias, and balconies.

123 *Ashton House, Woollahra, Sydney, Australia. Robin Espie Dods, 1982. View of entrance.*

On a magnificent site in Bowral, New South Wales, overlooking rolling hills, forests and fields, Dods has realized a fuller Classical vision. The plan of the Grey House (1987) is very traditional and hierarchical, with a central entrance portico on axis with a rectangular courtyard enclosed by the house on three sides and delineated by columns on the fourth, which add to the feeling of an outdoor room and also provide a powerful Classical frame to the view of the open country. Less traditional and less hierarchical, however, is the decision to give all the pediment-gables the same scale, so that the house, despite its overall tripartite symmetry, looks like an assemblage of equally privileged parts.

124 *Grey House, Bowral, New South Wales, Australia. Robin Espie Dods, 1987. View of side and rear elevations.*

125 *Grey House, Bowral, New South Wales, Australia. Robin Espie Dods, 1987. View of courtyard.*

125

DEMETRI PORPHYRIOS

The underlying Classical bias of Fundamentalism — which like virtually every Modern Classicist movement before it, is fired by a moral conviction that contemporary architecture has been corrupted and must return to its origins in ancient experience — is perhaps more explicit in the work of Demetri Porphyrios (b, 1949), a Greek-born architect and critic who works principally in London. The evolution of Porphyrios's style offers an interesting commentary on Fundamentalism: as he develops from a polemicist to a practitioner he seems to be moving toward a more conventional Classicism, yet he continues to define himself as a Fundamentalist. Positioning himself as a vigorous opponent of pluralism, which accepts a multitude of stylistic and theoretical approaches, he has written that "the lessons to be learned today from Classicism . . . are not to be found in Classicism's stylistic wrinkles but in Classicism's rationality."[44] Thus he rejects Venturi's irony and theory of architecture as a "decorated shed" as well as the playful approach of other semiotically-minded Classicists in whose designs, as Porphyrios sees it:

> . . . figurative and syntactic sensuality takes on the quality of nightmare: weightless pediments, 'neon'-Classical cornices, emasculated orders, metopes enfeebled by the arrogance of architects in search of fame, engrossed voussoirs, drooping garlands, frenzied volumetric articulations and androgynously historicist plans, in short all sorts of upholstered coteries degenerate into a mere "style-heap"; without essential meaning other than the cult of "irony" and the illusion of a make-believe culture.[45]

Given the vituperativeness and the high-minded moralism of his polemic, in his own work Porphyrios has a great deal to answer for, and he has wisely limited himself to modest proposals which, to some degree, support his conviction that "All classic architecture — that is, all architecture we speak of as enduring — has derived its forms by means of imitating its building techniques."[46] His Classical pavilions at Highgate, London (1981), on the grounds of a mock-Tudor mansion, are a built essay on the vernacular origins of Classical architecture, including a gazebo, storehouse, garage, and other outbuildings. The gazebo consists of a row of four brick columns, without bases but with capitals and a minimal entablature in Portland stone, supporting a timber roof that is a lesson in trilithic construction, with all the functional wooden pieces which the Greeks were to translate into decorative stone. The other buildings are subtler, without columns, yet with gables on the verge of becoming pediments, and mouldings about to turn into pieces of an entablature, as if the observer were privileged to be present at the birth of Classicism. In a modest way, one is reminded of the moment Louis Kahn used to describe, when the walls parted and the column became.

Porphyrios's design for a propylon in Virginia Water, Surrey (1985), repeats the tectonic lessons of the gazebo at Highgate. On the side, the ends of the roof's timber beams look like triglyphs on a Doric entablature, and the top-heavy roof with the deep overhangs resembles an early Roman temple. When called upon to design something more pragmatically demanding than a folly, Porphyrios has pretty much held on to his principles.

126

126 *Propylon, Virginia Water, Surrey. Demetri Porphyrios, 1985. Unbuilt project. View of model.*

127 *Pavilions in Highgate, London. Demetri Porphyrios, 1981. View of gazebo at the edge of the lawn court.*

128 *House in Greece. Demetri Porphyrios, 1981. Unbuilt project. Street elevation.*

127

128

159

In a project for a house in Athens (1981), Porphyrios combined his absolutes of structural representation and formal ordering systems with an essentially picturesque vision of the Classicized vernacular. The projecting central block of the house is nearly blank, except for a small entrance cut through the base and the articulated Classical pediment, and the long, slightly lower block of the main house runs behind. The potential tripartite symmetry is violated, however, by a cylindrical tower wedged into the joint of the two main pieces of the house and by the pergola strung to the right of the entrance. All the pieces fit into the plan's square module, yet the effect is nonetheless picturesque, evocative of a building constructed over time, half-Classical and half-medieval, and is reminiscent of the similar combination of geometric order and happenstance, Classical and vernacular, in Schinkel's Schloss Charlottenhof (1825), and the Greek Villa Kerylos at Beaulieu, France, which E. Pontremeli designed for Professor Theodore Reinach in 1903.

In the Fitzwilliam Museum Extension in Cambridge, England (1986), Porphyrios had to deal with the context of an historically important, compositionally robust essay in Classicism. The Founder's Building of the Fitzwilliam (1837–47), by George Basevi (1794–1845) and C. R. Cockerell (1788–1863), is a serious work of fully articulated Roman Classicism, whose street façade consists of a Corinthian temple front flanked by two pavilions. Porphyrios's proposed new building runs diagonally to the street, establishing a long axis from the side of one of the pavilions to the central entrance of the new building. It defers to the existing building in several other ways, especially in its minimal ornament and its central gable, which echoes the pediment of the Founder's Building and is even crowned by an acroterion, though it is a blank pediment, without an entablature to distinguish it from the stone wall below. In spite of such acknowledgments to the existing museum, Porphyrios's design is strikingly different from Basevi and Cockerell's. Porphyrios is emphatically didactic, notably showing in the obvious relating of the vernacular blank gable to a Classical pediment. For Basevi and Cockerell, making this kind of point was obvious or irrelevant, left behind as they went on to imaginatively employ a rich language. If Porphyrios really believes in what Basevi and Cockerell did, as he says when he writes that "the new extension to the Fitzwilliam Museum should be a testimony to the enduring values of the Founder's Building,"[47] it seems odd that he has resisted using the Classical language in its fullest form.

129 *Fitzwilliam Museum Extension, Cambridge, England. Demetri Porphyrios, 1986. Unbuilt project. Perspective from Trumpington Street showing the proposed extension (left) and the existing Founder's Building.*

130 *Fitzwilliam Museum Extension, Cambridge, England. Demetri Porphyrios, 1986. Unbuilt project. Trumpington Street elevation showing the proposed extension (left) and the existing Founder's Building.*

129

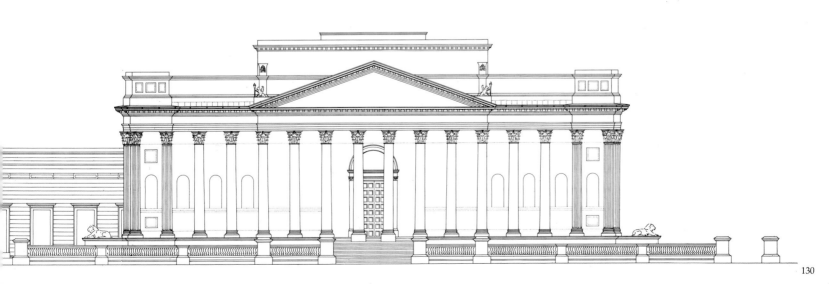

130

CANONIC
CLASSICISM

In a conscious act of aesthetic revisionism, Canonic Classicists argue that Classicism is *the* language of Western architecture, and they propose to ignore virtually everything else, especially Modernism. The key text for the canonic approach to Classicism is Geoffrey Scott's *The Architecture of Humanism*, first published in 1914, but widely read in England and America in the 1950s after it was released in paperback. Scott began by reasserting Vitruvius's trinity of commodity, firmness, and delight, arguing that the most important element of architecture was the last. Considering the aesthetic aspect of architecture to be paramount, Scott knocked down the "fallacies" of the "Romantic," "Mechanical," "Ethical," and "Biological" interpretations of architecture, proposing instead a humanistic one of "empathy" between people and buildings.

In the United States Henry Hope Reed has been the principal champion of a Classical revival, tirelessly campaigning to re-establish orthodox high-style Classicism as the basis of urban architecture. As early as 1953, together with Christopher Tunnard, Reed mounted an exhibition supporting his views at the Yale University Art Gallery. Entitled "Ars in Urbe," it revealed, to a generation immersed in the tenets of Modernism, the achievement of Classical art in embellishing the American city. In his polemical book, *The Golden City* (1959), Reed, who sees in the moralizing Gothic revival the seeds of the Modernism he abhors, illustrated his preference for Classical over Modernist architecture in the first chapter, "The City of Contrasts," which contrasted the rich Classical tradition of late nineteenth- and early twentieth-century architecture in New York with the artistic paucity of New York's Modernist buildings of the 1950s. Reed's arguments were highly topical, a counterblast to the period's shocking, ignorant, and arrogant neglect of monuments epitomized by the treatment of McKim, Mead & White's Pennsylvania Station (1902–11), which was degradingly remodeled in the mid-1950s, when a vast, jarring canopy was installed over the ticket booths (the building finally succumbed to the wrecker's ball in 1963), and Grand Central Terminal (Warren & Wetmore, Reed & Stem, 1903–13), which weathered a threat of destruction in 1954 only to see its main concourse filled with glitzy advertisements. Scores of distinguished buildings had already been demolished for banal modern replacements, such as the Romanesque-style Produce Exchange (George B. Post, 1884, destroyed 1957) and the cast-iron Wanamaker store, originally A. T. Stewart (John W. Kellum 1859, destroyed 1956). While remodelling and demolition of these and similar monuments alarmed the public, the architectural profession was slow to acknowledge that not only were irreplaceable monuments being lost, but also that Modernism was incapable of the formal and symbolic achievements of the Classical styles of the past.

To a handful of architects, most notably John Barrington Bayley (1914–81) in the United States and Raymond Erith (1904–73) in England, the Modernist point of view came to be anathema, but they were largely ignored, and only recently has Erith been re-evaluated as a skilled artist rather than a reactionary crank. Bayley, who studied at

131 *Temple of Venus, West Wycombe, Buckinghamshire. Erith & Terry, 1980. View through park.*

Harvard under Walter Gropius and Marcel Breuer at the same time as Philip Johnson, was never comfortable with the Modernist point of view, and a tour of duty in Paris during the Second World War, followed by a four-year stay in Rome, turned him into a convinced Classicist. In 1957 and 1958, Bayley showed his Classical projects for New York in two exhibitions, "New York Improved," and "Lincoln Center Reconsidered." Bayley's proposal that the projected Lincoln Center be put at Columbus Circle, the logical site for a monumental complex on the West Side, was as much a strong reproach to the incoherent mess of traffic and architectural banality that characterize this long-neglected yet critical site as it was to the inherent contradiction of Modernist monumentality exemplified in the center's buildings. Bayley imagined Columbus Circle ringed by a continuous Classical façade, with vehicular and pedestrian traffic passing through the arches of a colossal base. Cars entered tunnels cut through the base, with pedestrian space lifted above — a solution of questionable practicality. In a proposal for a public housing project for Harlem, in which low-income apartments were placed behind a palace façade and organized around courtyards entered through grand arches, Bayley anticipated Ricardo Bofill's urban projects by twenty-five years. How much more intelligent Bayley's scheme is than the banal project of brutally finished slabs that was built on the site. Bayley was able to build only occasionally, and it was not until the 1970s that he realized a significant project, an addition to the Frick Collection in New York (1977), which added a garden court pavilion in the manner of a French eighteenth-century orangerie to one side of the original building by Carrère & Hastings (1914).

Raymond Erith's quiet pursuit of the Classical ideal amid the post-war Brutalism of the English architectural scene has made him a hero among today's traditionally oriented English architects. Erith deemed himself a progressive Classicist, a description considered self-contradictory in the 1950s when he applied it to John Soane and, by extension, himself: "Soane's aim was to make classical architecture progress and absorb in itself the new needs of a new age. He thought it could be made to absorb the expanding means of construction."[48] From Erith's point of view Soane failed, and afterward the "essential" quality in architecture — "delight" or "beauty" in the words of Vitruvius — was lost. Like Reed and Bayley, Erith conveys a belief that with the demise of Classicism, architecture endured a terrible, inexplicable loss. "Although I think there may be some deep seated cause for its disappearance [that of the essential quality in architecture] I have never been able to find an explanation which really holds water. . . . In the end, I have had to fall back on the idea that in the enthusiasm generated by war, discovery, invention and industrialization the means of producing real architecture was forgotten."[49]

In 1947, in an unrealized proposal, Erith called for a factory-warehouse with a brick base derived from Soane and largely glazed upper stories resembling a sophisticated version of eighteenth-century cast-iron loft buildings. But he was not able to build much until the late 1950s, when he was commissioned to design Lady Margaret Hall at Oxford (1957–66) and to renovate No. 10 Downing Street (1959–63). In 1963 Erith finally had the opportunity to build a large country house, Wivenhoe New Park, Essex, where he could display his Palladian skill at combining Classical grandeur with the modest vernacular appropriate to a farm. But Erith, who died in 1973, realized very few buildings from scratch — having been blocked, as the polemicist author and architect Leon Krier has somewhat melodramatically claimed, by the "Modernist establishment," which "would not cede an inch of their gray empire for fear of an unequal and superior competition."[50]

132 *Wivenhoe New Park, Essex. Raymond Erith, 1963. View of south elevation.*

132

133   *Proposal for Lincoln Center at Columbus Circle, New York. John Barrington Bayley, 1958. Unbuilt project. Aerial perspective southwest.*

134   *Addition to the Frick Collection, New York. John Barrington Bayley, 1977. View of west elevation.*

133

134

QUINLAN TERRY

Erith's protégé and eventual partner, Quinlan Terry (b. 1937), claims not to have begun his serious architectural training until after his schooling at the Architectural Association, when, in 1962, he commenced his voluntary isolation from the main current of architecture by becoming an apprentice to Erith. Terry soon became Erith's principal design assistant, and he took over the firm after his partner's death. Although Erith had enjoyed some belated success in the 1950s and '60s, the market for traditional architecture was scarce in the early 1970s, and all that kept the office afloat was the design for a vast Bahai temple on the outskirts of Teheran. In the late 1970s, however, Terry emerged as the leader of Britain's Classical revival, a movement which has gone beyond housing the nostalgic well-to-do of Thatcher's Britain to large-scale institutional and commercial projects.

Terry's faith in the eventual reappraisal of Classicism is highly personal and closely related to his fundamentalist Christian beliefs, which he acquired while a student. In particular, he believes that the three Greek orders constitute an architectural language given to man by God; and he has written on their hypothetical divine origins: "Indeed, the orders have so many humanly inexplicable characteristics that it is hard to imagine that they came about as a result of human ingenuity or accident of time. Everything about them points to the work of the same mind 'who created the heavens and earth and all that in them is.'" Terry then turns exegete: "It is in the book of Exodus that [Moses] records in detail his commission from God to erect the Tabernacle in the Wilderness. . . . To my mind, the first time the three orders appeared in a recognizable form was in this tabernacle."[51] He goes on to synthesize his two adamantine beliefs — in the Judeo-Christian tradition and in Classical architecture. Whatever the merits of his argument, Terry practices Classical architecture not with the *ad hoc* approach of a pasticheur or ironist, or with the archeological mania of a strict revivalist, but with the confidence of a scholar and the inventiveness of an artist. Nonetheless, like all Canonic Classicists, he resolutely refuses to recognize the role of Modernism in the evolution of architecture.

Much of Terry's command of a range of styles within the Classical tradition was gleaned during his long apprenticeship with Erith. With typical bluntness, Erith once wrote: "I do any style to order, and sometimes the result is a bit ordinary. But I make a point of doing what my clients want, so far as I can, and let them be responsible."[52] When a client wanted a "French house," Erith provided it, as at mansard-roofed Joscelyns, Little Horkesley, Essex (1967–70). Terry, like Erith, is willing to go out and research a certain style: "How does one Frenchify one's detailing?" Terry asks rhetorically; "It is very simple, we go to France with measuring tape and sketch book. This is how to practice in the Classical tradition."[53]

Terry's first public recognition came in the late 1970s, after his designs for a series of small houses, Frog Meadow (1966–80) and a country house, Waverton (1979) were executed and widely published. Frog Meadow is a row of seven houses, some attached and some free-standing, close to the entrance of the village of Dedham, Essex, where the offices of Erith and Terry are located. The first three houses by Erith and Terry and the last four by Terry alone were intended to look like the work of an intelligent country builder. The simple, symmetrical houses have traditional materials and details: brick and stucco, pantile and flat tile roofs, sash and casement

135 *No. 4, Frog Meadow, Dedham, Essex. Erith & Terry, 1977. View of street elevation.*

136 *No. 6, Frog Meadow, Dedham, Essex. Erith & Terry, 1979. View of street elevation.*

windows, and a light touch of frankly Classical detail such as window surrounds, or, in the later houses, with the addition of a trompe-l'œil urn in a niche above the entrance.

In London, Terry picked up the thread of Modern Classical small-scale commercial building design that Lutyens and Reginald Bloomfield made a speciality of between the world wars and just after the Second. Terry's Dufours Place (1981–3) is a seven-story building which contains offices as well as twenty-five residential apartments. Constructed of the most traditional London material, load-bearing brick, it uses a Georgian vocabulary, including stone quoins, mouldings, and lintels, and some ornate Classical features at doorways and roofline, such as a wonderful Baroque gable and a cupola.

Dufours Place is actually more playful and looser in its use of Classical details than most of Terry's country houses. His penchant for the picturesque has come to the fore in a larger project, the Richmond Riverside Development (1983–8). Asked to design a group of commercial offices in a traditional village setting, Terry retained most of the site's existing buildings from the eighteenth and nineteenth centuries, and added to them a series of attached but separate houses with party walls. At Richmond, Terry offers a kind of instant history, with Classical designs whose origins range from the late sixteenth to the early nineteenth centuries. For many, the eclectic series of designs intermixed with actual historical buildings is disingenuous and artificial, yet Terry's biographer, the English architecture critic Clive Aslet, considers the design appropriate to the program and context: "Richmond Riverside is not a stage set — the buildings are real, with load-bearing walls — and, given that the buildings will be occupied by different owners, it is absolutely reasonable to treat them in different styles."[54]

Terry's skill with the picturesque is even more evident in the garden folly he designed for West Wycombe, an eighteenth-century house in Buckinghamshire (1980). Having previously designed a primitive temple with rough-hewn tree trunk columns for a cricket pavilion, Terry created a more formal version of this model, reinterpreting a garden pavilion, a "Temple of Venus," which had been on the estate in the late eighteenth century and was known from paintings of the era. Terry's elliptical temple, with a peristyle of Ionic columns supporting a shallow dome, is built mainly on the foundations of the original eighteenth-century folly, and yet is without a direct, ancient Classical precedent, being more of a mannerist distortion of the round temples of the ancient world and Bramante's Tempietto in Rome.

At Downing College, Cambridge, for which he designed the new Howard Building (1983–7), Terry had to respond to the specific context of nineteenth- and twentieth-century Classical buildings and the wider traditions of English academic architecture. The Howard Building stands at the north end of the West Lodge garden, bordered on the east by the back of the earliest college building, the West Range, designed by William Wilkins (1807–21). Although Wilkins' chaste Greek Doric design dominates the college, Edward Barry (1830–80) completed much of the earlier design (1873), generally adhering to its letter and spirit; and Sir Herbert Baker (1862–1945) contributed the North Range (1930) in a much freer, more mannerist style. In its plan and four-square massing, the Howard Building is Neo-Classical, and Terry also retains the Doric in much of the detailing. The new building, however, breaks into more vivid, sculptural expression in its use of a giant order of Corinthian columns and pilasters and in details ranging from an ornate cartouche over the doorway to voluptuous urns, set astride the pediment and placed in niches at the corners.

137

137   *Waverton, near Moreton-in-Marsh, Gloucestershire, England. Erith & Terry, 1977–9. View of north elevation.*

138   *Dufours Place, London. Erith & Terry, 1981–3. View east of Dufours Place elevation.*

139   *Dufours Place, London. Erith & Terry, 1981–3. View of cupola.*

140   *Dufours Place, London. Erith & Terry, 1981–3. View of door detail.*

168

138

139

140

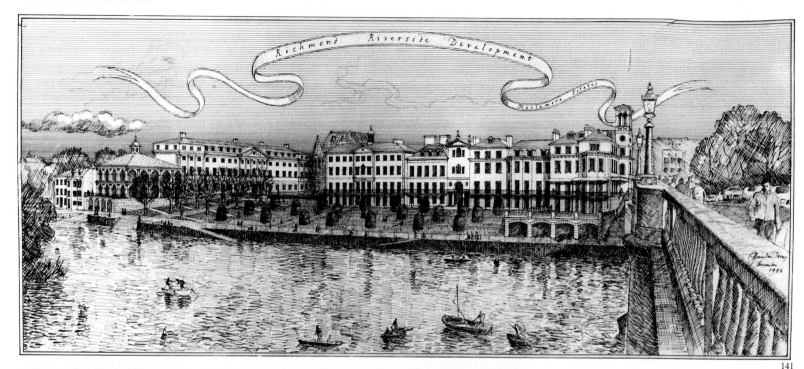

141

142

141 *Richmond Riverside Development, Erith & Terry, 1983–8. Perspective from across the Thames.*

142 *Richmond Riverside Development. Erith & Terry, 1983–8. View of model.*

143 *Howard Building, Downing College, Cambridge. Erith & Terry, 1983–7. North elevation.*

144 *The Origin of the Orders. Quinlan Terry, 1981. Sketches.*

143

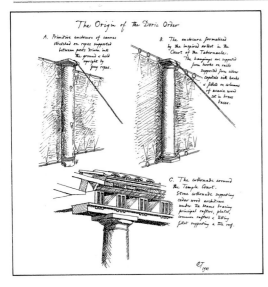

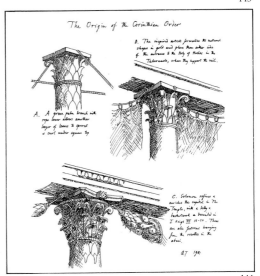

144

JOHN BLATTEAU

John Blatteau's (b. 1943) design for the Roberson Pavilion addition and general renovation of Bayonne Hospital in Bayonne, New Jersey (Ewing Cole Cherry Parsky Architects, 1979), was a landmark for traditionalist designers in the United States. For the first time in decades, a large, institutional commission had been executed in an articulately Classical way. The fact that the building was a hospital, rather than a major governmental building, suggested that the Classical approach could be realized within severe budgeting constraints and establish a hospital as a civilized edifice. At Bayonne, the Classicism is anything but reticent. Two glazed pavilions, composed of four heavily rusticated arches beneath a simplified entablature, serve as porte-cochères for the public and emergency room entrances. At the peaks of their steel and glass canopies, Blatteau placed acroteria, as if to imply that non-traditional materials did not necessarily preclude traditional details. Throughout the design, the details are scholarly, and there is little apparent skimping. The building's mixture of red brick utility and Classical ornament identifies it as a dignified public edifice in a tradition of American architecture that extends back to the eighteenth century.

Recently Blatteau has been able to undertake independent commissions that show an extraordinary command of traditional detail and craftsmanship. In undertaking the redesign of the Benjamin Franklin Dining Room for the U.S. State Department, Blatteau had to fit a Classical interior into a bland 1950s office building. Here indeed was the dilemma of modern architecture that Venturi and his colleagues had identified in their analysis of Las Vegas: the creation of monumental interiors within the low ceilings and long-span structures of the twentieth-century steel-frame vernacular. The Franklin Dining Room, however, unlike the other refurbished Classical rooms in the State Department, had a generously scaled ceiling height of 21 feet (7 meters). Blatteau believed that without violating the room's structural envelope he could make it appropriately grand. He emphasized the height by lining the room with free-standing Corinthian columns, supporting a full Corinthian entablature beneath a coffered cove. His design was inspired by the great colonnaded halls of the eighteenth century, and is strongly reminiscent of the marble hall at James Paine (c. 1716–89) and Robert Adam's (1728–92) Kedleston Hall, in Derbyshire (1760–70), which is lined with fluted, red-veined marble columns topped by gilded Corinthian capitals. The great success of the Franklin Dining Room lies also in the thoroughness of the architect's approach. Virtually every detail — the carefully proportioned door surrounds; the fireplace, with its full Doric order; and the carpet, with its border of acanthus leaves and trophies of wheat and tobacco — brings the eighteenth-century Classical vocabulary to life.

Blatteau has shown the same faith in detail in his recent series of renovations for the Riggs Bank, in Washington DC (1983–5). No building type better exemplified the Classical spirit of the American Renaissance than the bank; and there were hundreds of beautiful Classical banks built near the beginning of this century by firms such as York and Sawyer; McKim, Mead & White; Alfred Bossom; and Daniel Burnham. By the 1950s, Modernism had transformed the bank's traditional image of architectural solidity and immortality into structural derring-do and fragility. The Manufacturers Trust Company building on Fifth Avenue by Gordon Bunshaft of Skidmore, Owings and Merrill (1954) became the model: a glass box with a vault right behind the

145   Roberson Pavilion addition, and general renovation of Bayonne Hospital, Bayonne, New Jersey. Ewing Cole Cherry Parsky Architects, John Blatteau, designer, 1979. View of entrance.

146   Roberson Pavilion addition, and general renovation of Bayonne Hospital, Bayonne, New Jersey. Ewing Cole Cherry Parsky Architects, John Blatteau, designer, 1979. View of porte-cochère detail.

173

window, theoretically so visible to the public that no robber would dare. . . .

For the Riggs management, the image of the bank as a supermarket with the goodies on display behind the plate glass window was no longer appropriate, and their assignment to Blatteau was to insert within existing Modernist premises a traditional bank. Blatteau's semicircular banking hall in the Lincoln Branch office, at 17th and H streets, is characterized by the same thoroughness as in the Franklin Dining Room. The principal feature is a long, curving counter which separates tellers from patrons. The podium has a marble base and marble counters. But the exercise in Classical literacy really begins above the counter, where Blatteau has divided the teller bays with engaged Doric columns. The teller windows are aedicules, with fluted Doric pilasters, and the rest of the bay is filled in with a Roman-patterned lattice screen below and clear glass above. The main doorway is framed by a Corinthian entablature and pilasters. The ceiling, as in the Franklin Dining Room, makes good use of a cove to raise its apparent height. The check desks are modelled on Louis XVI desks that Jefferson might have brought back from France to Monticello.

The aura of high seriousness which Blatteau's literacy and skill give to the Riggs Bank is exhilarating, yet the absence of irony disturbs some observers, who are made uncomfortable by the architect's indifference to the Modernist exterior and to critical problems raised by the existing nature of the interior, such as the column grid that marches through the Classical symmetries of the semicircular banking hall. Some also question the appropriateness of Classical architecture for a bank after the demoralizing experience of the Crash of 1929 and the financial shenanigans of our own times. As the historian Richard J. Betts writes:

> Alberti argued that beauty would inspire the faithful to worship, and also that it would prevent the destruction of buildings in the event of public riots or invasion by barbarians. Surely that is an appropriate and necessary purpose for the ornament of a bank, especially in these times when any customer who can read a newspaper must wonder whether his bankers have sinned too much by making foolish loans to assorted real estate speculators, wildcatters, banana republics, and Texas billlionaires. Blatteau has obliged his clients by giving them a dignified hall whose forms are redolent of religion, including even the tellers' windows, which, being tabernacles, invite the customers to worship mammon while they transact business. If Alberti was right, the architecture should dissuade them from making a run on the bank when they discover what the bankers have done to them."[55]

147

148

147 *Riggs Bank, Lincoln Branch office, Washington DC. John Blatteau, 1983–5. Interior view.*

148 *Riggs Bank, Lincoln Branch office, Washington DC. John Blatteau, 1983–5. Interior view of tellers' windows.*

149

150

151

149   *Franklin Dining Room, State Department, Washington DC. John Blatteau, 1983–5. Interior view.*

150   *Franklin Dining Room, State Department, Washington DC. John Blatteau, 1983–5. Interior view showing detail.*

151   *Franklin Dining Room, State Department, Washington DC. John Blatteau, 1983–5. Interior view showing ceiling detail.*

175

HENRY COBB

In the second round of the competition for the design of the Hampton Site Extension to the National Gallery in London, which was won by Robert Venturi, one of the strongest entries was prepared by Henry Cobb (b. 1926), a partner of I. M. Pei. Cobb's proposal (1986) is an extreme example of the degree to which the forms and ideals of traditional Classicism have insinuated themselves into the mainstream of architectural theory and practice. The proposal itself, and the way Cobb has chosen to explain it, constitute a nigh-Jesuitical attempt to be *in* the traditional Classical world, but not *of* it.

For Cobb, the problem of designing the new wing's main façade was to acknowledge the existing museum to the east, Trafalgar Square to the south-east, and the beginning of Pall Mall to the west. To do so, he proposed a semicircular screen wall closely based on John Nash's semicircular portico at All Souls Church, London (1822–4). In accord with his conviction that the extension had to be sympathetic to the main building and also a powerful independent statement, Cobb adopted, as he put it, a "design strategy that shows appropriate deference to the Main Building by acknowledging its best features while at the same time compensating for some of its salient weaknesses."[56] The best feature, in his view, was the giant Corinthian order of the porticoes, which did much to hide the worst, which was the inconsistency between the façade and the internal spatial hierarchy. In his design, Cobb used a colossal Corinthian order to ally the buildings, yet applied pilasters rather than columns to avoid competing with the columned porticoes of the main building. The result is a dialogue between Cobb's curved screen and the major and minor porticoes of the main building, facilitated by the removal of a raised lawn and creation of a broad pavement between them.

Perhaps the most remarkable quality of Cobb's design is not its sensitive contextuality, but rather the willingness of an architect hitherto preoccupied by the problems of abstract minimalism to produce a full-blown, traditional Classical design. In his controversial design for the Portland Museum of Art (1978–83), Cobb had used the red brick traditional to New England town building, but refused to emulate the local vernacular and based his forms instead on the abstract modernity of Louis Kahn's work in India and Pakistan. But for the Hampton Site Extension Cobb was willing to go beyond hazy acknowledgments of context to the literal business of using a Corinthian capital. It would have been impossible ten years ago for a prominent Modernist architect to think his way through a façade as a Classical exercise, as Cobb did when he decided to add a smaller, Tuscan order to frame the entrances between the Corinthian pilasters, a solution for which he cited the façade of Michelangelo's Conservators' palace on the Capitoline Hill in Rome. Like many architects of his generation, Cobb has been enormously influenced by Louis Kahn, but in this design, if in no other of his projects, he has moved well beyond the essentialized modular forms of his mentor to an openly Classical system of compositon and ornament. The "plain channeled walling" is identified as a Soanean "device," and the galleries' lighting is in the "domed clerestory configuration," which forsakes Kahn for the lessons of the Dulwich Picture Gallery.

152   *Extension to the National Gallery, London. Henry Cobb, 1986. Unbuilt competition project. Plan of entrance levels.*

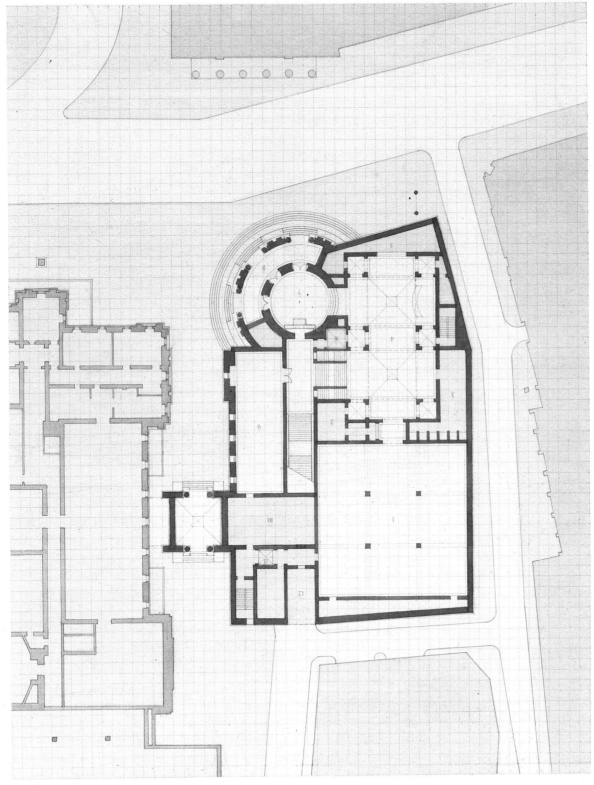

152

153

153   *Extension to the National Gallery, London.*
Henry Cobb, 1986. Unbuilt competition project.
Perspective from Trafalgar Square showing
proposed extension (center) and existing National
Gallery (right).

154

154   *Extension to the National Gallery, London.*
Henry Cobb, 1986, unbuilt competition project.
Elevation detail of porch with corresponding
sections and plan.

TONY ATKIN

Tony Atkin (b. 1950), of Atkin, Voith & Associates, faced problems similar to Cobb's in his entry for a limited competition for the master plan and addition to the Brooklyn Museum (1986). Atkin's explicitly Classical proposal, like Cobb's for the National Gallery, lost to a less literal, more ironic design — in this case one submitted by Arata Isozaki and James Polshek (1986–). Atkin respected the existing building, as well as the spirit, if not the letter, of the original master plan. Since a museum as big as the one originally proposed by McKim, Mead & White could never be realized, Atkin pulled back the façade facing the park, yet marked the outline of the original plan by laying out a vast terrace with a gallery-pavilion at each of the corners.

The design's monumental axiality draws the visitor past McKim, Mead & White's rotunda, through a new glazed, barrel-vaulted hall, into another rotunda and a terrace that opens out to a garden. The decision to enhance rather than jar the symmetry of the earlier design seems equally effective in relating the building to its trapezoidal site. Where Isozaki cranked the façade to face the diagonal of Washington Avenue on the east side, Atkin simply uses a semicircular bay, acknowledging the site, yet letting the building hold to its four-square symmetries. He also uses the bay as a turning point for the giant order of McKim, Mead & White's design, which continues around the bay to re-emerge at the same scale but with its details altered and framing a modified fenestration.

Perhaps the most successful parts of the design are the pavilions. An effective way of marking the transition from building to garden and positioned at the edge of the park, they have the light spirit of garden follies, foils for the monumental façade behind them. Both have serliana windows in the center of their stone façades, a Renaissance detail which contrasts with the Neo-Classical rigor of the main building. The north pavilion, which is domed, was intended to house a Rodin collection; the south pavilion, which has a conical roof, Amerindian totem poles. In Atkin's rendering, the totem poles rise to a corbelled ceiling, against the background of the serliana. The cultural mix is rich, if improbable: icons of native American culture in front of sixteenth-century Italian windows under the ceiling of a Mycenean tomb.

155   *Brooklyn Museum, renovation and extension, Brooklyn, New York. Atkin, Voith & Associates, 1986. Unbuilt competition project. View north of model.*

155

THE
BROOKLYN MUSEUM
MASTER PLAN

ATKIN VOITH & ASSOCIATES ARCHITECTS
ROTHZEID KAISERMAN THOMSON & BEE · GOLDMAN SOKOLOW AND COPELAND
JOHN MILNER ASSOCIATES · JOSEPH M CHAPMAN · KEAST AND HOOD COMPANY
ARENA AND COMPANY · WALMSLEY AND COMPANY · GEORGE IZENOUR

156

156 *Brooklyn Museum, renovation and
extension, Brooklyn, New York. Atkin, Voith &
Associates, 1986. Unbuilt competition project.
Plan and interior perspective.*

CHRISTIAN LANGLOIS

Like Terry in England and Blatteau in America, Christian Langlois (b. 1924) practiced Canonic Classical architecture before it was acceptable to most members of the profession. For the addition to the Senate building on the Rue de Vaugirard in Paris (1975), Langlois designed a massive sandstone façade which incorporates an existing stone porch by Boffrand (1667–1754) and the re-composed elements of an eighteenth-century townhouse. Langlois's four-story office building has an open arcade at street level, sparely detailed stone walls up to the cornice, and slate-covered mansard roofs. The success of this design has helped Langlois win other government commissions, such as the sunken Patio Boulingrins at the Palais de Luxembourg in Paris (1986) and the Regional Council in Orléans, where the context of the cathedral, town hall, and art museum suggested that a traditional building would be appropriate. The result is a vernacular version of Classical rigor, due to the irregular massing and minimal Classical detail. When he wishes, however, Langlois can be adept at handling ornament, as he has shown in the gilded window railings of the Hôtel de la Préfecture in Nancy.

157 *Palais de Luxembourg, Patio des Boulingrins, Paris. Christian Langlois, 1986.*

158 *Addition to the Senate Building, Rue de Vaugirard, Paris. Christian Langlois, 1975. View along Rue de Vaugirard.*

157

MANUEL MANZANO-MONÍS

For the Spanish architects Manuel Manzano-Monís y López-Chicheri (b. 1948) and his father, Manuel Manzano-Monís, the task of architecture is to "intervene." Practicing in an established urban tradition, the younger Manzano-Monís uses an approach that includes archeology, restoration, reconstruction, and new design, a convincing demonstration that the split between historical preservation and design is a false one imposed on architecture by the ideology of Modernism. He undertakes a traditionalist approach not simply for the sake of scholarship or aesthetics, but out of a belief that architecture must not be an imposition on the existing context. His conviction that architecture should also include an ornamental and decorative element separates him from an architect like Moneo, who, in the Museum of Roman Art in Mérida, encountered many of the issues of archeology and contextualism typical of Manzano-Monís's work.

Since 1981 Manzano-Monís and his father have been designing the city museum of Segovia at the Casa del Sol, a former slaughterhouse built up over the centuries, occupying a spur in the outer walls of the historic city. The museum is a fine example of Manzano-Monís's way of incorporating the specific and general history of a city into its architecture. Beginning with the precedent of plans for the slaughterhouse by the nineteenth-century architect D. Joaquin Odriozola, who designed and built the western pavilion and intended to renovate the rest of the Casa del Sol as well, Manzano-Monís (who had to preserve the western pavilion and the rest of the complex) decided to use Odriozola's idea of a trapezoidal central courtyard to organize the group of buildings but to leave aside the rest of Odriozola's plans, which would have demolished much of the older building. The Casa del Sol's courtyard combines a Classical arcade and vernacular materials of stucco, pantile, and hand-chipped and laid mosaics, which depict the twelve signs of the zodiac in a manner influenced as much by Ruskin and Morris as by ancient Rome. The columns around the courtyard are perhaps the clearest declaration of Manzano-Monís's independence of both rationalism and historicism. Unlike the perfectly cylindrical pillars favored by rationalists, his columns, with their exaggerated entasis and flared capitals, are designed to express a more complex message: that architecture is a living language which allows both tradition and change.

159 *City Museum, Casa del Sol, Segovia, Spain. Manuel Manzano-Monis y Lopez-Chicheri and Manuel Manzano-Monis, 1981– . View of courtyard.*

159

MODERN TRADITIONALISM

The most pluralistic of the approaches of Modern Classicism, Modern Traditionalism is imbued with a conviction that although the Classical remains an enduring ideal, by interacting with the vernacular it acquires a sense of circumstantial reality, of place and its relation to ever-evolving technologies and programs, and of timeliness as well. In other words, a traditional building can look as though it was always part of a greater whole, while at the same time conveying, by virtue of its particular design and technology, a particular aesthetic identity and moment in history. In Modern Traditionalism the craft-generated and industrial vernaculars are neither idealized nor disparaged but simply embraced for what they are, and the moral issues of architecture are left to the political or ideological, rather than the structural, realm. The result is that — although many architects would be loath to admit it — Modern Traditionalism has many of the qualities of the eclecticism that enlivened nineteenth- and early twentieth-century architecture. On a case-by-case basis, a Modern Traditionalist decides which architectural language to apply. Architects' renewed interest in using the styles — whether modified to accord with a Romantic ideal of individualistic art or to accommodate new building techniques or programs, or in relatively pure, authentic form — demonstrates the triumph over one of the greatest fallacies of Modernism: the notion that the technology, culture and politics of the twentieth century constitute a mandate to evolve a unique, universal mode of artistic expression, a single international style unlike any that preceded it.

160 *Country house, Sussex. John Outram, 1978– 85. View east of courtyard incorporating a ruined Victorian orangery.*

THOMAS BEEBY

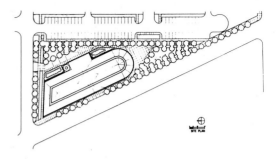

161

The Conrad Sulzer Regional Library in the Ravenswood neighborhood of Chicago (1985), designed by Thomas Beeby (b. 1941) of the Chicago firm of Hammond Beeby and Babka, is a representative work of Modern Traditionalism. Fulfilling the twin ambitions of making a civic gesture and relating to the local context, the library celebrates modern building techniques as much as traditional craftsmanship and scholarly Classical detail. Given a difficult triangular site, Hammond Beeby and Babka did not try to play it up with weird geometries (as did, for example, I. M. Pei in his East Building for the National Gallery in Washington DC) but, rather, responded directly to the conditions, pushing one façade up to the diagonal street, rounding the acute corner with a semicircular hall, and articulating the main façade, which is diagonal to the parking lot, with a portico and a clock tower.

161   Conrad Sulzer Regional Library, Chicago, Illinois. Hammond Beeby and Babka, 1985. Site plan.

The building's steel frame is expressed on the exterior, although it is detailed in a Classical manner, reminiscent of Schinkel's Bauakademie in Berlin (1831–6), with brick used as infill. There is a rusticated base, a pilastered *piano nobile*, and a steel beam emulating a frieze to cap the building. On the interior, figural Classical spaces are combined with lofty, open volumes. The oval entrance lobby is rimmed by smooth Greek Doric columns, beneath a steel-framed skylight. Upstairs, in the high-ceilinged reading room, Beeby has introduced a Doric order of ventilation shafts, beneath the roof's open steel trusswork. In honour of Conrad Sulzer, the Swiss apothecary who was the first permanent settler in what became Ravenswood, the design introduces Swiss folk elements, specifically the fancifully painted and shaped chairs (designed by Tannys Langdon), which are further localized with paintings of Midwestern plant and animal life — a stylistic juxtaposition analogous to the medieval clocktower attached to the Classical façade.

In the American Academy of Pediatrics in Elk Grove, Illinois (1984), a national headquarters building with facilities for conferences and day-to-day administration on a site clearly visible from the highway, Thomas Beeby (b. 1941) and his partners designed a steel-frame structure clad in limestone and brick which is rich in Classical grammar and vocabulary and structurally articulate. The yellow brick base is "rusticated" by a single band of darker brick, a division which is repeated in the thick alternating bands of brick sheathing the *piano nobile*. A giant order, expressed by columns and pilasters, unites the main floors of the building, and suggests the steel structure underneath. The entrance is defined by a portico with two columns *in antis*, and a glass barrel vault rises above the cornice. At the rear, overlooking the lake, the building is opened up by a large, half-conical skylight above a semicircular hall. A colonnaded loggia running the length of the hall recalls Viollet-le-Duc's principles in its simple articulation of steel posts and its literal articulation of a steel beam as an entablature.

In the Formica Showroom which he installed at the Merchandise Mart in Chicago (1984), Beeby flew in the face of the general agreement that one couldn't combine a distinctly contemporary material such as plastic surface laminates with a fully articulate Classical architecture. Conceived as a Greek Doric temple, the showroom features a bold polychromy inspired by the brilliantly-colored archeological renderings of Greek temples by nineteenth-century French architects. As the visitor moves from the public corridor into the showroom, he or she is actually moving from the

162   Conrad Sulzer Regional Library, Chicago, Illinois. Hammond Beeby and Babka, 1985. View north.

163   Conrad Sulzer Regional Library, Chicago, Illinois. Hammond Beeby and Babka, 1985. Interior view of lobby.

164   Conrad Sulzer Regional Library, Chicago, Illinois. Hammond Beeby and Babka, 1985. Interior view of second floor.

165   Conrad Sulzer Regional Library, Chicago, Illinois. Hammond Beeby and Babka, 1985. Interior view of ground floor showing furniture designed by Tannys Langdon.

162

163

164

165

189

temple's imagined cella into the loggia and on to a brightly-lit terrace overlooking an imaginary sea, also rendered in plastic laminates. Frank Lloyd Wright's concern for the "nature of materials" — that is, using them so as to exploit, not negate, their essential character — seems very distant; it is as though the chief characteristic of Formica were its protean variety.

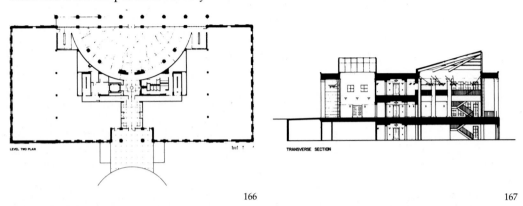

166

167

168

169

166 *American Academy of Pediatrics, Elk Grove, Illinois. Hammond Beeby and Babka, 1984. Entrance level plan.*

167 *American Academy of Pediatrics, Elk Grove, Illinois. Hammond Beeby and Babka, 1984. East–west section.*

168 *American Academy of Pediatrics, Elk Grove, Illinois. Hammond Beeby and Babka, 1984. View of east elevation entrance.*

169 *American Academy of Pediatrics, Elk Grove, Illinois. Hammond Beeby and Babka, 1984. View of west elevation.*

170 *American Academy of Pediatrics, Elk Grove, Illinois. Hammond Beeby and Babka, 1984. View of west elevation detail.*

171 *Formica Showroom, Merchandise Mart, Chicago, Illinois. Hammond Beeby and Babka, 1984. Entablature details.*

172 *Formica Showroom, Merchandise Mart, Chicago, Illinois. Hammond Beeby and Babka, 1984. Interior view towards loggia.*

173 *Formica Showroom, Merchandise Mart, Chicago, Illinois. Hammond Beeby and Babka, 1984. Interior view of loggia.*

170

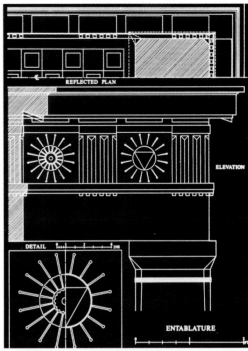

171

172

173

HARTMAN-COX

The evolution of the Washington DC partnership of George Hartman (b. 1936) and Warren Cox (b. 1935) is a case study of the change in architectural sensibilities over the past decade. In their early practice the firm's partners preferred startling, hard-edged geometries, but — perhaps in response to pressure from the public and from Washington's Fine Arts Commission — they have now come to terms with the capital's Classical context. Whereas their National Permanent Building (1977) inflected toward Washington's traditional architecture only in scale and material, their addition to the Folger Shakespeare Library (1975–82) went much further in its acceptance of Classicism as a living language. Paul Cret's design for the original building (1932) was stripped Classical for the exterior and Elizabethan for the interior, which seemed the best way to reconcile the building's program with the Classical style of Washington's public buildings. Tucked into the "U" of Cret's building, Hartman-Cox's addition is faced in the same white marble as the original, and scrupulously maintains its horizontal division of base, main floors, and entablature. The pillars are sheathed in flat shafts of fluted marble (recalling the fluted pilasters of Cret's design), yet in a gesture toward structural realism, they rise to a steel beam — part of the structure from which the building is hung.

The interior of the new reading room is a long rectangle ending with apsidal rooms at either end. Light pours in through a slot down the center of a hung barrel vault, slipping along the sides as well. Hartman-Cox credit Boullée's colossal National Library project as their inspiration. The vault's arches are detailed in false stone, a rebuttal to anyone suspecting them of purely Modernist sympathies, and are modelled on the lobbies of Cret's library. In the smaller-scale items, the new reading room faintly echoes the old, which was based on the Tudor banqueting hall at Hampton Court; the table legs are miniature Tuscan columns, emulating the fashion, in the early English Renaissance for throwing Classical elements into a medieval design.

In recent projects, Hartman-Cox have gone further toward recognizing the full implications of Classicism in the increasingly tradition-oriented Washington architectural climate. Their Georgetown University Law School Library project is faced in precast concrete which emulates limestone. In their proposal for Market Square, the last major undeveloped tract on Pennsylvania Avenue, they have embraced the Classical architecture that confronts them — John Russell Pope's National Archives and its neighbors in the Federal Triangle — with a limestone and brick complex of twin thirteen-story buildings. The sides facing each other form a giant semicircular colonnade, intended to ring a proposed Navy memorial.

174

175

174 *Addition to the Folger Shakespeare Library, Washington DC. Hartman-Cox, 1975–82. Interior view of reading room.*

175 *Addition to the Folger Shakespeare Library, Washington DC. Hartman-Cox, 1975– 82. Interior view of door and column detail.*

176 *Addition to the Folger Shakespeare Library, Washington DC. Hartman-Cox, 1975–82. View northwest.*

176

KOHN PEDERSEN FOX

The New York firm of Kohn Pedersen Fox Associates has achieved its rise to the pinnacle of success as corporate architects mainly by exploring the possibilities of marrying Classical themes to anonymous, loft-like office space and repetitious curtain walls, which are all that is affordable in this building type. Although the firm's principal designer, William Pedersen (b. 1938), has remained noncommittal as to the relative virtues of the Modernist and Classical approaches, his design for a 55-story commercial tower, 1201 Third Avenue, in Seattle, Washington (with The McKinley Architects, 1985–8), promises to strike a blow for the sculptural solidity and bold form of traditional skyscrapers — it also relates, in some measure, to Seattle's earliest skyscraper, the L. C. Smith Building, better known as the Smith Tower (Gaggin and Gaggin, 1914). Pedersen's design is based on the superimposition of two ideal forms beloved by Neo-Platonists, a circle over a square, in which the diameter of the circle is greater than the width of the square, so that in elevation there are four broad bow windows of the circle, between the granite-clad corners of the square. Above the 44th floor, Pedersen cuts into the shaft to give the building an impressive crown, eliminating the bay, chamfering the corners, and terminating the upward thrust with great arches and a pyramidal top. The lucid geometries of the tower's shaft break down slightly at the base, where the architect had to accommodate a steep site, an existing nineteenth-century building, and the scale of the surrounding buildings.

In New York, another of Kohn Pedersen Fox's design partners, Arthur May (b. 1940), has designed a 33-story apartment tower at 180 East 70th Street (1984–6), which is an outright attempt to recreate at super-scale the urbane Classicism of the redbrick, limestone-trimmed "Georgian" apartment buildings of the 1920s and '30s. The design is motivated in part by the developer's express desire to convince prospective residents that a Third Avenue building can have the same aura of history, permanence, and wealth as older buildings on Park and Fifth avenues, and it is also an antidote to the banality of the scores of neighboring post-war highrises which have patently failed to create any sense of place.

In Boston, May was confronted by a much more direct contextual problem. An office tower not only had to fit an irregular, L-shaped lot but also had to preserve the façades of several existing five-story nineteenth-century buildings. The obvious solution would have been something blandly contextual and self-effacing; but May has chosen a bolder approach. The shaft, sheathed in buff-colored granite and limestone-colored pre-cast concrete, is highly modulated in massing and detail, with multistory bow windows, courses and cornices, rising to four pedimented towers at the top. Rather than trying to represent anonymous, loft office spaces, 125 Summer Street (1985–8) fully expresses the aesthetic complexity of its position in the city, resembling the Classically-detailed but almost inadvertently picturesque massing of an office building that has been added to over time.[57]

Although representation of contemporary technology may be an essential responsibility of an architect undertaking a building at the giant scale of Kohn Pedersen Fox's projects — if only because it involves building types in which technological expression is integral to cultural expression, at the generally much smaller scale of civic or "cultural" institutions, the issue of the representation of technology becomes moot. In designing an art museum or a city hall the architect is

177

177   *180 East 70th Street, New York. Kohn Pedersen Fox Associates, 1984–6. View of 70th Street entrance.*

178   *180 East 70th Street, New York. Kohn Pedersen Fox Associates, 1984–6. View northwest.*

194

under no imperative to wrap floors of anonymous loft-like office space in a curtain wall. Neither by tradition nor — many would argue — by present circumstances are such buildings about contemporary technology. Beyond satisfying programmatic requirements, they are concerned with the representation of cultural or political ideals. To me, the representation of enduring ideals often requires that we build traditional architecture.

179   *125 Summer Street, Boston, Massachusetts. Kohn Pedersen Fox Associates, 1985–8. Ground floor plan.*

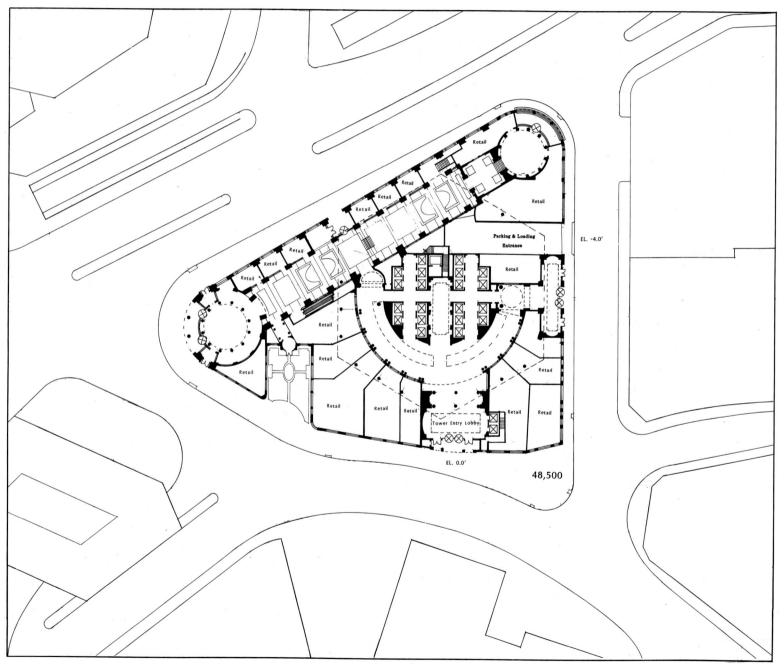

179

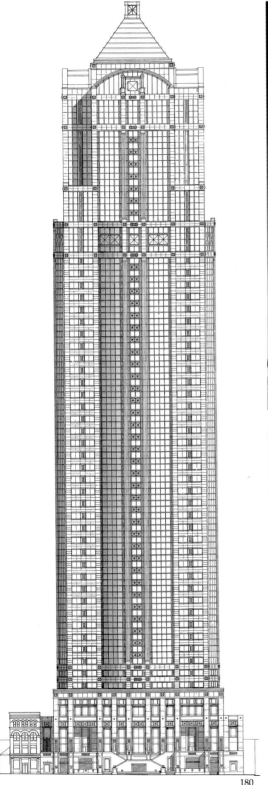

180

181

182

180 *1201, Third Avenue, Seattle, Washington. Kohn Pedersen Fox Associates; The McKinley Architects, associated architects, 1985–8. Second Avenue elevation.*

181 *125 Summer Street, Boston, Massachusetts. Kohn Pedersen Fox Associates, 1985–8. View west of model showing South Street elevation.*

182 *125 Summer Street, Boston, Massachusetts. Kohn Pedersen Fox Associates, 1985–8. View northwest of model.*

197

MICHAEL GRAVES

Although Michael Graves has remained committed to a uniquely personal, even at times ironic, vision of Classicism — he is not only unwilling to take on the full repertoire of the Orders, but even insists on inventing personal versions of its detail — his buildings have become Classical in their mass and Classical in their essential order.

The first signs of Graves's evolution appear in projects at a smaller scale than the tall office building, and also show how deeply he has been influenced by the Fundamentalists in developing an architectural language that is both personal and grounded in tradition. This influence is clearly reflected in his Environmental Education Center (1983), in the New Jersey Meadowlands, across a narrow harbor channel from the Statue of Liberty. The Center consists of a series of wood-framed pavilions, in which exhibits on the natural and historical aspects of the area are mounted. With its series of outbuildings, the Center powerfully explores the relationship of buildings and landscape. The materials are simple and traditional: gray horizontal cedar siding, yellow stucco, reddish-brown timber, and copper roofs. The Classical elements are limited: an "arch," modilions, pilasters and piers with capital-keystones. Yet Graves compacts a genial Classical formality into the plan and elevations. The main building, set on a paved square, is tripartite, with a vestigially basilical arrangement of high central nave, lit by clerestory windows and flanked by four side pavilions. The axiality of the composition and the simple trabeated construction are continued outside, across the square, in a pergola whose straight path leads to the winding trails through Liberty State Park. The progression is a clearly read metaphorical journey from the rational to the organic, from architecture to nature — a journey involving the participation of man, as expressed by anthropomorphic elements: timber columns with trusses like arms, pairs of stucco piers supporting small pitched roofs like three guards lined up along the exhibition space, clerestory windows like eyes, and a dovecote like a face.

In 1985 Michael Graves and the artist Edward Schmidt won a competition for the design of the Domaine Clos Pegase (1985–7), a winery, sculpture court, and private residence set on a hill in Calistoga, California. Given a more varied program than that for the Environmental Center, and a more genial landscape as a site, Graves abandoned the tectonic fundamentalism of the Environmental Center for Ledoux-inspired pure geometry. From the tripartite entrance block beneath an eyelid arch — out of which a sculpted Pegasus emerges — to the wide, low-gabled, fat-columned primitive temple porch and the stepped cylinder of the "Mountain of Pegasus," which looks like a Roman mausoleum, the design included a profusion of figural spaces and anthropomorphic forms, as well as literal puns, like the barrel vaults over the buildings where the wine barrels are stored. Schmidt's murals were to have provided the complement to Graves's communicative designs in his representational, programmatic art, exemplified by the frieze depicting the wine-making cycle that was to be painted around the interior of the "Mountain of Pegasus."

In the original design, a visitor could take a diagonal route from the drum of the "Mountain of Pegasus" to the long, rectangular sculpture court, carved out of the side of the hill, and to an amphitheater beyond it. From there, a path zigzagged up, passing an Egyptoid propylon on the way to the "Grotto of Pegasus," planned as the

183 *Environmental Education Center, Liberty State Park, Jersey City, New Jersey. Michael Graves, 1983. View west.*

184 *Environmental Education Center, Liberty State Park, Jersey City, New Jersey. Michael Graves, 1983. View west.*

183

184

source of a stream which flows down the hill to the winery. Located on the brow of the hill, in front of the owners' house, the Grotto marks the boundary between public and private areas — a necessary function, since the architectural language of the house is virtually identical to that of the winery below. Clos Pegase was completed in 1987 to a modified design of which the significant changes were the deletion of the "Mountain of Pegasus", the sculpture court, the grotto and the stream.

At the Humana Tower in Louisville, Kentucky (1986), Graves has achieved his most fully resolved building to date. Faced with a typical modern anomaly, the corporate office tower in which a mundane private program of offices must be elevated to a symbolic level comparable to that reserved for the institutions of state and religion in earlier, traditional societies, Graves invoked the powerful physicality and underlying Classicism of skyscrapers of the 1920s. Whereas the Portland Building was necessarily little more than a commercial box dressed up with the trappings of civicism, the Humana Corporation was to be an office building that in every detail would represent the corporation and the city of which it was part. Humana wanted a building that would express its dedication to the public good — an understandable goal for a corporation controlling hospitals across the country. Graves responded with a design that conveyed his client's program in a fully articulated, gestural composition.

The Humana Tower stands in downtown Louisville, Kentucky, between a row of cast-iron commercial buildings and a massive but enervated black glass and steel office highrise, and across the street from a performing arts center that suffers from an acute case of "diagonalysis," a compositionally fatal architectural disease of the 1970s. Twenty-five stories high, clad in rose granite detailed to suggest the conflicting nature of the cladded wall as both weighty mass and space-enclosing curtain, the Humana building is divided between the main tower shaft and a four-story, 120-foot (37-meter)-high base, which confronts South 5th Street with a grand portico of massive square piers. The somber mood of the arcade somewhat mitigates the gilded flutings that rise above the green and black stone bases to create an aura of stylized luxury. The lobby's entrance is flanked by a concave arrangement of six fountains whose sheets of water drop 50 feet (15 meters), between bronze bowls, suitable for eternal flames but occupied by jets of water — perhaps a more appropriate metaphor for the company and its location in a riverfront city.

The twenty-fifth floor terrace, whose granite wall bows out 25 feet (8 meters) into space above a spindly trusswork, is a *tour-de-force*. The terrace reasserts the thrill of skyscraper heights and celebrates the view of downtown and the Ohio River that it overlooks. It is also a comment on the relationship of Classicism and technology, a quintessentially romantic belvedere, a temple on a cliff, a marriage of metal and stone and engineering, and stereotomy of which Viollet-le-Duc might well have approved.

In his proposal for Aventine, University Center, La Jolla, California (1985–), Graves has been inspired by the free juxtapositions of Roman imperial villas like the one Hadrian built at Tivoli, and by the city planning of Ledoux. Aventine is a miniature city: the project includes a hotel fronted by an impressive loggia, linked by pergolas to a "Fitness Rotunda," a cylinder with a temple portico attached and an office block, in a fearlessly overscaled show of vernacular Classical elements.

Graves's most traditional, orthodox Classical work to date is his Sunar Furniture Showroom in London (1986), the ninth such facility he has designed for this furniture and fabrics company. Acknowledging the English Classical tradition, Graves not surprisingly (given his own penchant for the idiosyncratic) took Soane, rather than Chambers or Adam, as his model. A renovation of a floor of an old leatherworks, the constraints of the existing building prevented Graves from following a conventional axial plan. Instead, taking lessons from Soane's interior at the Bank of England, Graves created a picturesque Classical route, leading from a rusticated lobby, through a long corridor, bordered on one side by the semicircular textile room, into a rotunda that cranks the route into an octagonal furniture display room, and straight into the main exhibit through a pair of Doric columns. The principal showroom is modelled after John Soane's Dulwich Picture Gallery (1811), with its arrangement of blind alcoves beneath a series of lantern lights.

185   *Clos Pegase Winery, Calistoga, California. Michael Graves, 1985–7. Site plan.*

186   *Clos Pegase Winery, Calistoga, California. Michael Graves, 1985–7. South elevation.*

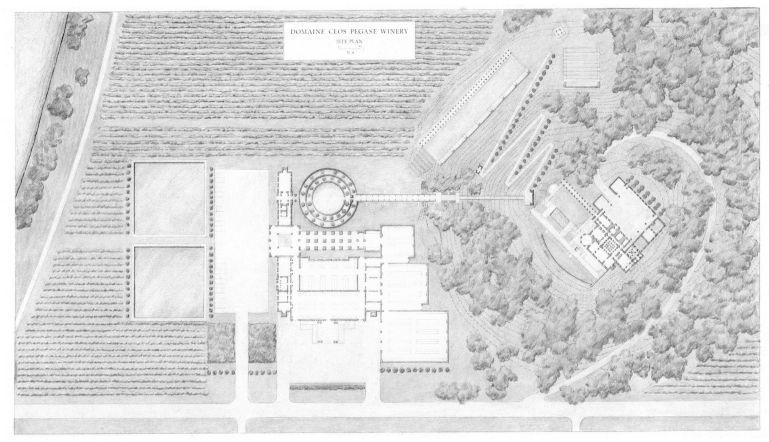

185

186

187

188

189

187   *Humana Tower, Louisville, Kentucky. Michael Graves, 1986. View south across the Ohio River.*

188   *Humana Tower, Louisville, Kentucky. Michael Graves, 1986. View southwest of entrance loggia and tower.*

189   *Humana Tower, Louisville, Kentucky. Michael Graves, 1986. View of entrance.*

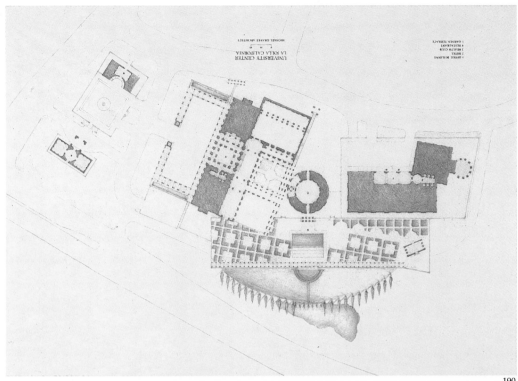

190

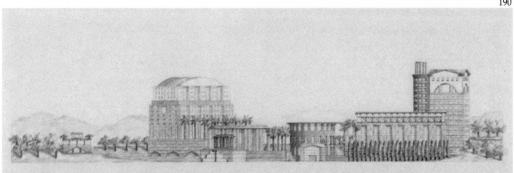

191

190 *Aventine, University Center, La Jolla, California. Michael Graves, 1985– . Site plan.*

191 *Aventine, University Center, La Jolla, California. Michael Graves, 1985– . North elevation.*

192 *Sunar Furniture Showroom, London. Michael Graves, 1986. Plan.*

193 *Sunar Furniture Showroom, London. Michael Graves, 1986. Interior view of office systems showroom.*

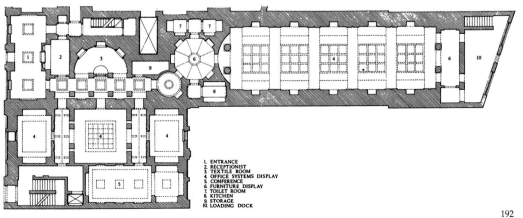

1. ENTRANCE
2. RECEPTIONIST
3. TEXTILE ROOM
4. OFFICE SYSTEMS DISPLAY
5. CONFERENCE
6. FURNITURE DISPLAY
7. TOILET ROOM
8. KITCHEN
9. STORAGE
10. LOADING DOCK

192

193

203

KEVIN ROCHE

Kevin Roche, who as a Latent Classicist firmly rejected all but the most general outlines of Classical design, has recently moved toward a fuller Classical expression, designing the column capitals and cornices he once dismissed. He began in a small, contextually sensitive project, the renovation of the Central Park Zoo (1980–88), for which Roche was asked to design new facilities that would harmonize with the context of a formal plaza surrounded by simple arcaded brick buildings bordered on one side by the castellated Gothic Arsenal (Martin E. Thompson, 1848). He responded with a pergola consisting of brick columns supporting a wooden trellis, running around the central plaza and linking four new buildings for animals. Roche developed a "zoo order" of octagonal columns — a reference to the towers of the Arsenal — with distinct bases and capitals whose blocky geometries are Roche's own invention.

These columns reappear at a huge scale in the Morgan Bank Headquarters (1983–7) on Wall Street, a 48-story skyscraper that boasts a 70-foot (21-meter)-high entrance loggia of paired granite columns. Proportionally they have scant resemblance to any of the five Orders, but they do have pedestals, bases, shafts, and capitals, and they are employed at varying scales to create an order for the entire composition. Above the four-story base, the columnar shaft of the office building itself rises forty-two stories. In this section, two "super-pilasters" are articulated as shallow bays. At the top, an eight-story "capital" has four sets of bay windows to evoke the coupled columns at the base and create a sense of a temple lifted skyward on a gigantic colonnade. Above the entablature, Roche has placed a 40-foot (12-meter) copper mansard roof, an overtly historical gesture to such near neighbors on the Wall Street skyline as Trowbridge and Livingston's Bankers Trust (1912) and Craig Severance & Yasuo Matsui's Bank of the Manhattan Company (1929).

Roche's tower is clad mainly in glass, its use of the traditional materials of granite and copper reserved for the base and crown; yet the overall design, in regard to mass, if not to detail, is — even more than the AT&T Building — a return to the heroic Classicism of the early American skyscraper. Not merely a slab clothed in Classical language, it is a columnar form, with the anthropomorphism implicit in this form.

The Morgan Bank Headquarters has been the fullest expression to date of Roche's rethinking of Modernist principles. When Roche described his goals in 1985, he expressed an intensified desire to serve the public good:

> . . . what we are trying to do now . . . is to find an aesthetic which is more understandable on a more common, more normal level, something that people will understand . . . I have a feeling that people, to a large extent, don't really see much of modern architecture in a positive way, because the aesthetic is too remote for them, too specialized.[58]

194 *Renovation of Central Park Zoo, New York. Kevin Roche John Dinkeloo and Associates, 1980–88. Perspective of pergola.*

194

195   *Morgan Bank Headquarters, New York.*
Kevin Roche John Dinkeloo and Associates, 1983–
7. Perspective northeast.

196   *Morgan Bank Headquarters, New York.*
Kevin Roche John Dinkeloo and Associates, 1983–
7. Collage; view east on Wall Street.

197   *Morgan Bank Headquarters, New York.*
Kevin Roche John Dinkeloo and Associates, 1983–
7. View of model showing entrance.

197

196

KLIMENT & HALSBAND

The New York architectural partnership of Robert Kliment (b. 1933) & Frances Halsband (b. 1943) approaches the Classical language through the back door of context rather than through any conviction of its superior expressive capacity. The architects' non-judgmental, ambivalent point of view works to advantage in the detailing of their Computer Science Building at Columbia University (1981–3). Here they have convincingly mediated between the sophisticated red brick and limestone of McKim, Mead & White's campus of the 1890s, the banalities of the University's 1950s engineering school, and the highly abstract curtain wall of Romaldo Giurgola's Fairchild Center for the Life Sciences Building (1977).

The same approach proved less engaging in the firm's somewhat stiff and tentative Life Sciences Building at the University of Virginia with Wank Adams Slavin, associated architects, (1982–6). Although less constricted then the Columbia site, the Virginia site offered a difficult context of banal Modernist classroom and laboratory buildings from the early 1960s at the end of an axis formed by coldly, sparsely detailed Georgian dormitories from the early 1950s. Kliment & Halsband attempted a design that would organize the site, stand out as a foreground building, and relate to the university's architectural traditions. They did this by designing a red brick building composed of a rectangular box, containing the loft-like laboratory floors, and a half-cylinder containing the library and lecture hall. An entrance tower (level with the roof) is placed to one side of the semicircle, facing the center of the campus. The half-cylinder containing the library refers to the domed rotunda of Jefferson's Pantheon-like library on the Lawn and is given the highest level of detail. Both the tower and the half cylinder have limestone trim for the windows, and each has one principal window, a self-consciously flat and untraditional serliana.

In 1986 Kliment & Halsband were commissioned to design a town hall for Salisbury, Connecticut (1985–8), to replace one that had burned down in the summer of 1985. The architects soon realized that the chief desire of the citizens of Salisbury was to have the old one back, and that failing an exact reproduction, they expected the new town hall to include a columned portico, white clapboard siding, and traditional fenestration. Kliment & Halsband provided the traditional portico; but the columns, far-removed from any identifiable order, support a pediment which is dematerialized, cut out into a fan shape. The procession through the building is perhaps the most Classical and the most inspired part of the design, with the public functions elevated to a *piano nobile*. A broad flight of stairs leads to a generous landing, where a large arched window — the architectural linchpin of the design — overlooks a cemetery dating from the eighteenth century. Although the window provides it with a formal center, the rear façade is actually much less Classical than the front, giving the building an entirely traditional distinction between a symbolic, civic front and a more *ad hoc*, vernacular back.

198   *Computer Science Building, Columbia
University, New York. Kliment & Halsband,
1981–3. View south of courtyard.*

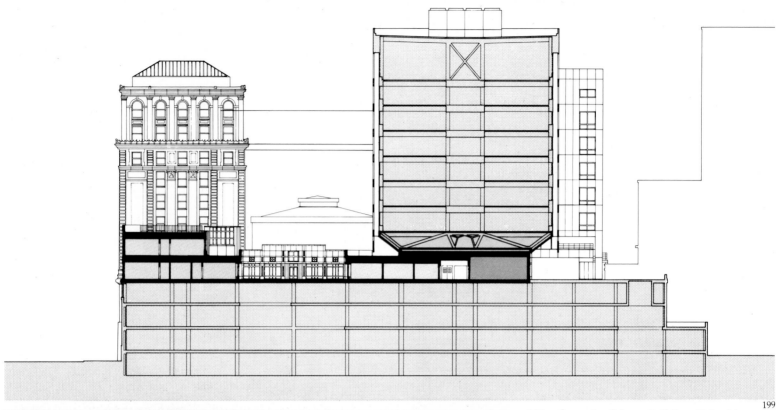

199 *Computer Science Building, Columbia University, New York. Kliment & Halsband, 1981–3. East–west section.*

200 *Computer Science Building, Columbia University, New York. Kliment & Halsband, 1981–3. View southeast.*

201

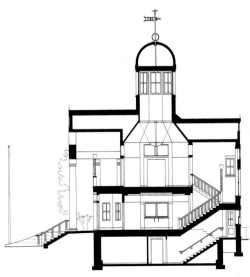

202

201   *Life Sciences Building, University of Virginia, Charlottesville. Kliment & Halsband; Wank Adams Slavin, associated architects, 1982–6. View south.*

202   *Town Hall, Salisbury, Connecticut. Kliment & Halsband, 1985–8. East–west section.*

203   *Town Hall, Salisbury, Connecticut. Kliment & Halsband, 1985–8. Perspective southeast showing rear elevation.*

204   *Town Hall, Salisbury, Connecticut. Kliment & Halsband, 1985–8. Perspective northwest showing front elevation.*

203

204

PETER ROSE

Like Hartman-Cox's addition to the Folger Library, Peter Rose's (b. 1943) Canadian Centre for Architecture (Peter Rose, architect; Erol Argun, associate architect; Phyllis Lambert, consulting architect, 1985–9) reinterprets the traditional elements of a Classical civic building in the light of an ambiguous sense of modernity, retaining the principal materials and compositional strategies, yet simplifying and altering the vocabulary and adjusting the composition to programmatic needs. The center was established in Montreal in 1979 by Phyllis Lambert, the architect and preservationist, to house a collection including architectural drawings, prints, photographs, and a 150,000-volume library, as well as an auditorium. The first challenge for the architects was to accommodate an existing building, the Shaughnessy House, which actually consists of two attached houses designed by William T. Thomas in 1874, standing in un-splendid isolation along a major artery between two freeway ramps.

Rose decided to encompass the nineteenth-century house in a traditional composition, treating it as a pavilion and flanking it with two new pavilions, with a long rectangular block stretching behind them. He also employed Montreal's traditional material for townhouses and civic buildings, greystone, a locally-quarried limestone, and rather than using a thin veneer, as current practice permits, he chose to lay up $4\frac{1}{2}$ to 6-inch (11- to 15-centimeter)-thick slabs to enhance further the impression of massive load-bearing construction.

The traditionalism of the design is contradicted, however, by detailing that includes exposed bolts and a metal cornice, specifically evoking Otto Wagner's Post Office Savings Bank in Vienna. The compromised Classicism of the design, imposed by the Shaughnessy House's duality and reinforced by Rose's treatment of the stone, is also reflected in the handling of the front façade, where the entrance is placed off-center. It is balanced, somewhat, by the bay of the library court; yet the decision to leave a blank panel between them reveals Rose's ambiguity about designing a Classical façade. Like much of the detailing, the blank panel refers to proto-Modernist design — in this case specifically to Le Corbusier's Villa Schwob at La Chaux-de-Fonds (1916), which has the same mannerist ploy and bespeaks the same balance, poised between Palladian composition, traditional materials, and the expression of Modernist design principles and building technologies.

205 *Canadian Centre for Architecture, Montreal. Peter Rose, architect; Erol Argun, associated architect; Phyllis Lambert, consulting architect, 1985–8. View of study model of corner bay.*

205

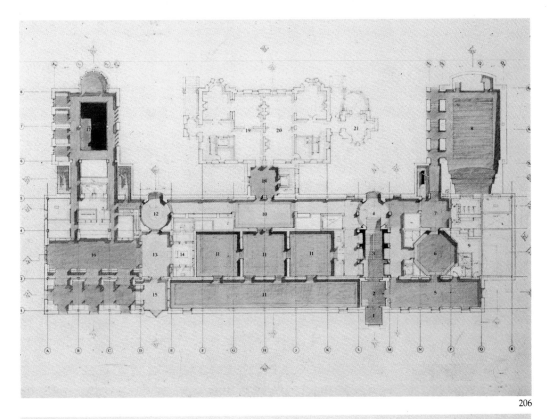

206

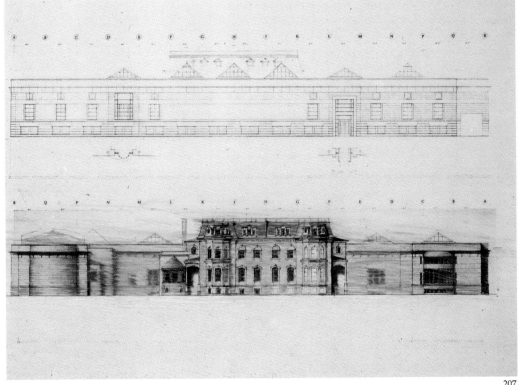

207

206   *Canadian Centre for Architecture, Montreal.
Peter Rose, architect; Erol Argun, associated
architect; Phyllis Lambert, consulting architect,
1985–8. Plan of gallery level.*

207   *Canadian Centre for Architecture, Montreal.
Peter Rose, architect; Erol Argun, associated
architect; Phyllis Lambert, consulting architect,
1985–8. South elevation showing the existing
Shaugnessy House.*

213

ROBERT ADAM

An English architect trained in the late 1960s, Robert Adam is often grouped with Canonic Classicists, yet he is too enthusiastic about contemporary technology and its capacity for influencing untraditional form to fit into that group. Adam, whose clients include computer companies, insists that his buildings are exemplars of the contemporary scene:

> I get very annoyed when I'm told I'm doing it right or wrong according to how close I am to Georgian architecture, as if that is all that the great Classical tradition comes to. . . . Classical architecture has always tackled new technology admirably . . . steel frames made the flights of fancy of Edwardian Baroque possible. High-Tech has just turned the slave into the master; it's an architecture which claims purity but is based on false symbols. There is no visual equivalent of the real high technology, the micro-chip. It's no use claiming that the beams were designed by computer. If I use a computer to calculate the entasis on a column does that make me a high-tech architect?[59]

For Adam, Classicism is a broad language, incorporating the Egyptian and the Romanesque, and is essentially a matter of proportion, central to which is the Vitruvian/Renaissance criterion that every part should relate to every other part. Thus he ranges from Romanesque and Gothic to Georgian without doubting his Classical integrity, and is willing to alter traditional design for the sake of economy or a new material. At Dogmersfield Park, Hampshire (with Gebler Associates, 1986), a three-story Georgian house renovated and expanded to serve as the headquarters of a computer company, the new two-story wings designed by Adam (with Gebler Associates) are more articulately Classical than the main building and consist of chunky little pavilions in brick and plaster with Tuscan entrances and aedicules. While raising the level of Classical detail, however, Adam shocked revivalists by giving the windows no glazing bars, prompting a "glazing bar debate" which he dismisses as absurd. He reasons that because the new building is thoroughly climate-controlled, a sash window is a meaningless gesture. Despite the possible validity of his reasoning, Adam's argument that Georgian revivalists are just reactionaries does not hold. Traditional windowpanes are scale-givers, which relate to the overall proportional system of a building, and to eliminate them is like replacing standard English bricks with cinder blocks.

208 *Dogmersfield Park, Hampshire. Robert Adam, with Gebler Associates, 1986. View of addition (left) and existing Georgian house (right).*

STANLEY TIGERMAN

When neither the technological imperative nor the virtues of aesthetic literalism are sufficient to drive the engine of a truly Modern Classicism, it is the inevitably ambiguous ideal of "appropriateness," the balance between technique and linguistic correctness, that defines it. Thus it is those architects who may at first glance seem the most "expedient," or at least "permissive," that in reality see the issues of design not as built ideology but as complex representations, as works of art and criticism. Stanley Tigerman (b. 1930), a Chicago architect who first became widely known in the 1960s for visionary Modernist projects such as Instant City (1966), has steadily transformed his approach to design, so that he is now a leading advocate of architecture as a complex cultural as well as technological response. Recently Tigerman's work has become increasingly Classical, even though his programs are often trivial. At the Hard Rock Café in Chicago (1985), Tigerman and his firm, Tigerman, Fugman, McCurry, appropriated the kind of Classical garden pavilion that might be found in a European park for the purposes of an introspective, artificially lit, high-class hamburger joint. At first glance, it seems a strange choice for a restaurant affiliated with the original Hard Rock Café in London, a legendary watering hole of the 1970s rock scene, but the Classical vocabulary not only enhances the client's institutional self-conception, but also creates a building that seems particular rather than anonymous, welcoming rather than inhospitable, which would have been the case had the requirements of a "black box" inward-looking restaurant been honored literally. Tigerman adopted Classical architecture for contextual reasons also, responding to a Classically-enveloped electric substation (1986–) located next door. After Tigerman had designed the restaurant, however, but before it was built, the electric company, Commonwealth Edison, decided that the substation had to be replaced. The old one was demolished, and Tigerman was asked to design a new one, which, in turn, was to relate to the context of the restaurant, closing the circle of influence. Tigerman came up with an eighteenth-century Palladian villa, a piece of humanist architecture for a machine which requires almost no human supervision.

In other projects, such as the "One Lane Pool House," in a suburb of Chicago (1987) Tigerman has carried his exploration of Classical themes further, reinterpreting the eighteenth-century Classical *orangerie*, with a panoply of historical references, including Edwin Lutyens's Orangery at Hestercombe, Somerset (1905), most evident in the rusticated pilasters. Tigerman also acknowledges the repetitive, mass-produced nature of building elements since the industrial revolution in the south elevation, which, despite its simplified Doric entablature and pilasters, consists of seventeen indistinguishable bays. For a house in Palm Beach, Florida, he has adopted the courtyards, pantile roofs, arcades and loggias of the Mediterranean Classical style, at least in its Floridian version, referring openly to the Florida villas designed in the 1920s by Addison Mizner. In such work Tigerman is tacitly arguing that the traditional architecture of the early twentieth century can be viewed not merely as a curiosity but as a source.

209

210

209 *Hard Rock Café, Chicago, Illinois. Tigerman, Fugman, McCurry, 1985–6. View south showing entrance.*

210 *Hard Rock Café, Chicago, Illinois. Tigerman, Fugman, McCurry, 1985–6. View east.*

217

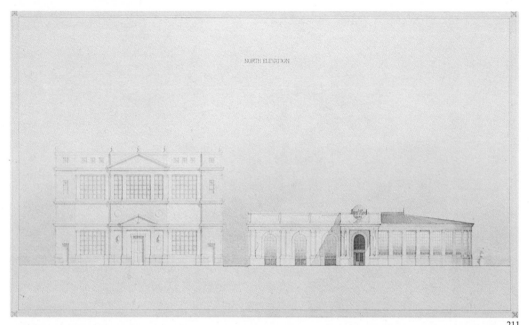

211

212

213

211   *Commonwealth Edison Substation (left) and Hard Rock Café (right), Chicago, Illinois. Tigerman, Fugman, McCurry, 1986– (substation), 1985–6 (café). North elevation.*

212   *One Lane Pool House, suburb of Chicago. Tigerman, Fugman, McCurry, 1987. View of west elevation.*

213   *One Lane Pool House, suburb of Chicago. Tigerman, Fugman, McCurry, 1987. Interior view.*

214   *Private residence, Palm Beach, Florida. Tigerman, Fugman, McCurry, 1987. Site plan.*

215   *Private residence, Palm Beach, Florida. Tigerman, Fugman, McCurry, 1987. West elevation.*

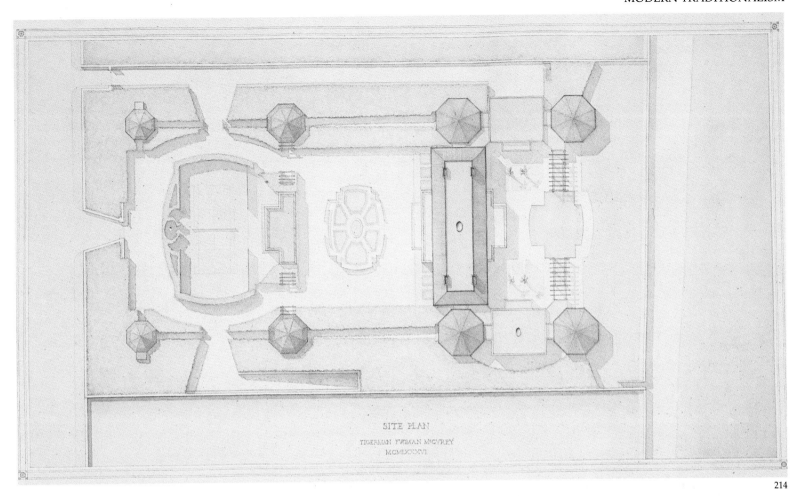

SITE PLAN
TIGERMAN FUGMAN McCVRRY
MCMLXXXVI

214

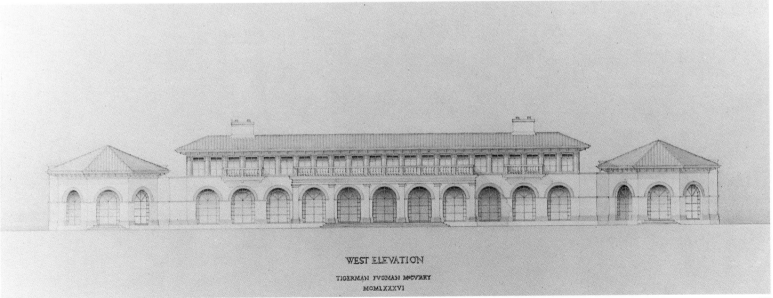

WEST ELEVATION
TIGERMAN FUGMAN McCVRRY
MCMLXXXVI

215

ORR & TAYLOR

American architects have led the way in their willingness to use the "styles" without aggressive distortion. In their unbuilt design for Riverfront Plaza in Fort Lauderdale, Florida (1982), the New Haven architecture firm of Robert Orr (b. 1947) and Melanie Taylor (b. 1952)proposed that the offices, restaurant, bar, "bazaar," and lecture hall be housed in the "Spanish," and "Mediterranean" mode, typical of early twentieth-century Florida architecture, joined by arcades and pergolas running around court-yards filled with fountains and greenery. The design was to have the historical associations as well as the tangible comfort of life in a subtropical climate. Orr & Taylor also sustained the predominant Spanish Colonial architectural style of Santa Barbara, California, in their competition entry for the University of California at Santa Barbara Art Museum (1983), bringing the architectural style of the town onto the undistinguished, blandly Modernist campus. A dome, rising above the entrance rotunda, was to stand as the symbol of the new museum, whose wings, lined with arcades, were to be built around a trapezoidal lawn. Orr & Taylor's design would have given a figural, representative public space to the campus and linked it by association to California's architectural tradition.

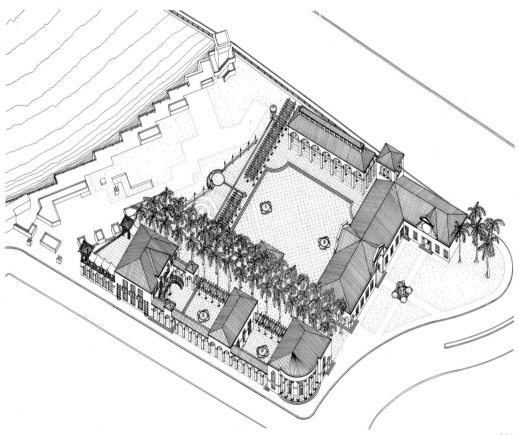

216 Riverfront Plaza, Fort Lauderdale, Florida. Orr & Taylor, 1982. Unbuilt project. Axonometric.

217 Riverfront Plaza, Fort Lauderdale, Florida. Orr & Taylor, 1982. Unbuilt project. Perspective sketch of courtyard.

216

217

218

219

218   *Art Museum, University of Southern California at Santa Barbara. Orr & Taylor, 1983. Unbuilt project. Aerial perspective.*

219   *Art Museum, University of Southern California at Santa Barbara. Orr & Taylor, 1983. Unbuilt project. View along arcade of courtyard.*

ROBERT A. M. STERN

Eero Saarinen used to speak of the "right style for the job," a plea for contextually driven design which horrified his Modernist colleagues, but which has increasingly impressed me since I first heard it as a student in the early 1960s. I have included four projects from my practice to represent my sense of what is possible by way of a Modern Traditional approach that stresses the importance of cultural and physical context.

At the Observatory Hill Dining Hall at the University of Virginia in Charlottesville (associated architects, Marcellus Wright, Cox & Smith 1982–4), the composition of abutting pavilions is a direct response to the University's tradition of Jeffersonian Classicism. For the previous twenty-five years, the University's building program had been committed to Modernism. My decision to "wrap" the existing Modernist dining hall in Classical architecture was influenced in part by Louis Kahn's suggestion that buildings could be wrapped in ruins to elevate the ordinary to the heights of architecture. At Observatory Hill, I tried to wrap what I think of as a ruin of architecture in an exaltation of Classical order and light; to put back what the previous architect had apparently chosen to leave out.

Whereas the University of Virginia provides a specific architectural tradition to accommodate, at Point West Place in Framingham, Massachusetts (with Drummey Rosane Anderson, Inc., associated architects, 1983–5), there was only the quintessential non-place of the American roadside strip. The site and the program, an office building, bring into sharp focus the dilemma that confronts any architect who wishes to be both modern and traditional, to deal with everyday circumstances and yet suggest monumentality. Most people cannot spend much time in such distinguished places as the Piazza San Marco in Venice or the Lawn at the University of Virginia, or even the Rockefeller Center. We are obliged to live our lives on the outer edges, on the highways, in the messy, dehumanizing, sometimes frightening non-places that we have made in the name of material progress. At times it seems we have turned our whole world into parking lots, highways, signs, junk.

Point West Place is adjacent to a toll plaza on the Massachusetts Turnpike, on the site of a former truck depot. For an Ironic Classicist, the setting would be perfect, a place to display the roadside speculative office building as a "decorated shed." In undertaking the commission I hoped to demonstrate that although the situation was laden with irony, one could also go beyond to create something with its own dignity — that it could be a palace of work, set in a garden through which cars move amid the trees as though in a French *parterre*. The developers had hoped to counteract the trivialities of the setting with a building in stone, because stone signifies quality and permanence. Sadly, it was not economically possible in this suburban location to clad the building in a reasonably well-detailed wall of stone. Rather than applying stone thinly, wrapping it around the frame like a curtain wall of glass, I chose to concentrate its use at the entrance and at the base, where its inherent solidity counterpoints the lightness of metal and glass. Yet even the glass can correspond to the ideals of a traditional stone building, for we created glass forms that emulate the age-old techniques evolved in stone. When the building is seen in its totality, the glass takes on many qualities in the different light, the stone remains what it is, a permanent, enduring, unchanging symbol, a hyper-reality, something dignified that must be put

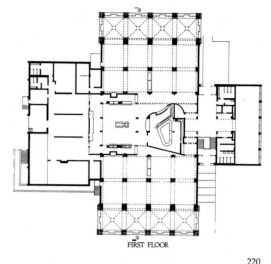

FIRST FLOOR

220

221

220 *Observatory Hill Dining Hall, University of Virginia, Charlottesville. Robert A. M. Stern; Marcellus Wright, Cox & Smith, associated architects, 1982–4. Plans.*

221 *Observatory Hill Dining Hall, University of Virginia, Charlottesville. Robert A. M. Stern; Marcellus Wright, Cox & Smith, associated architects, 1982–4. View north.*

222 *Observatory Hill Dining Hall, University of Virginia, Charlottesville. Robert A. M. Stern; Marcellus Wright, Cox & Smith, associated architects, 1982–4. View northeast.*

together with care, something that exalts each person who sees it and uses it.

The challenge posed by 222 Berkeley Street, an office building in Boston's Back Bay (with Jung Brannen Associates, associated architect, 1986–), was opposite to that of Point West Place. This building will be constructed on an urban site, surrounded by a rich, essentially traditional architectural context which has been dramatically altered by several large office buildings including Hancock Plaza, designed by Henry Cobb in 1975, and Philip Johnson's Classicizing 500 Boylston Street, now under construction.

In response to strong community requests for a design with a distinctly Bostonian and Back Bay character, 222 Berkeley is clad in stone and red brick in an adaptation of the Georgian vocabulary of late eighteenth- and early nineteenth-century Boston architecture, as well as highly regarded twentieth-century revivals such as the Ritz-Carlton Hotel (Strickland, Blodget & Law, 1927). Bay windows at street level and on the floors above refer to the typical late nineteenth-century townhouses of the Back Bay and the small-scale retailers of nearby Newbury Street, as well as to the Coulton Building (1905), which formerly stood on the site. The Boylston Street entrance, which leads to the shopping arcade and glazed winter garden, is lavishly Classicized: paired columns carrying urns flank a revolving door which is housed in a *tempietto*. There is a less exuberant, though equally defined, entrance to the office building on Berkeley Street. A variation on eighteenth-century orangeries, and on Boston's widely admired Horticultural Hall (Wheelwright & Haven, 1901), crowns the office tower, offering a distinct skyline silhouette which places the building firmly in the American tradition of Classical skyscrapers.

A villa in New Jersey (1983–8) was designed for a town in which turn-of-the-century Italianate villas abound. A large house with tightly integrated landscaping and architecture, it draws on various sources: not only the villas of the Italian Renaissance itself but also the *fin de siècle* Anglo-American Italianate villas designed by such architects as Charles Platt, Thomas Hastings, and Frank Lloyd Wright. The house is presented not as an object set against nature, but as a player in a series of scenographic gardens. Inside and outside are linked in a complex relationship, with extensive glazing, framed to maintain the sense of continuous walls. The arcaded lower story (an allusion to Giulio's Palazzo del Tè) contains an indoor pool which has its analogue in the sunken court immediately outside. Apsidal grottoes at both ends of the court offer a mannered commentary on the transitional quality of the space, between the world and the underground and between civilization and nature — a commentary that continues in the forced perspective of the court as it rises to the south.

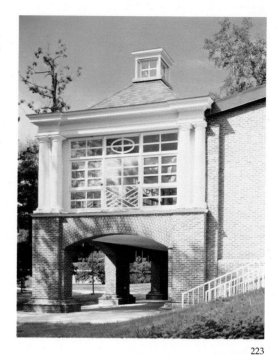

223

223　*Observatory Hill Dining Hall, University of Virginia, Charlottesville. Robert A. M. Stern; Marcellus Wright, Cox & Smith, associated architects, 1982–4. Pavilion detail.*

224　*Observatory Hill Dining Hall, University of Virginia, Charlottesville. Robert A. M. Stern; Marcellus Wright, Cox & Smith, associated architects, 1982–4. Elevation details, sections.*

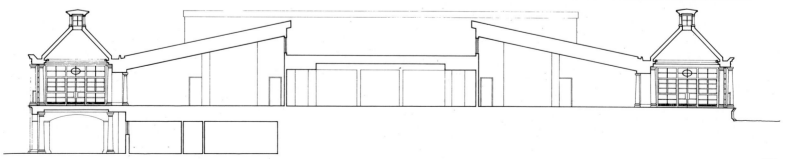

224

225

226

225 *Point West Place, Framingham, Massachusetts. Robert A. M. Stern; Drummey Rosane Anderson, Inc., associated architects, 1983–5. View of east elevation.*

226 *Point West Place, Framingham, Massachusetts. Robert A. M. Stern; Drummey Rosane Anderson, Inc., associated architects, 1983–5. View northwest.*

225

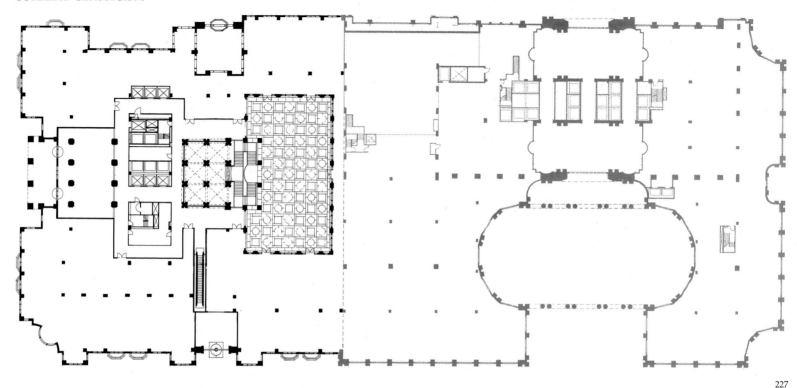

227

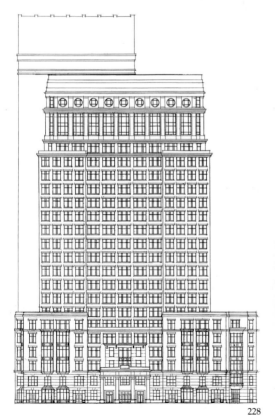

228

229

227 *222 Berkeley Street, Boston, Massachusetts. Robert A. M. Stern; Jung Brannen Associates, associated architects, 1986– . Plan showing 222 Berkeley (left) and 500 Boylston Street.*

228 *222 Berkeley Street, Boston, Massachusetts. Robert A. M. Stern; Jung Brannen Associates, associated architects, 1986– . Berkeley Street elevation.*

229 *222 Berkeley Street, Boston, Massachusetts. Robert A. M. Stern; Jung Brannen Associates, associated architects, 1986– . Perspective southwest.*

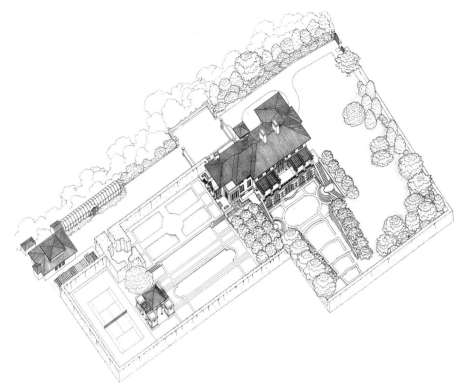

230

231

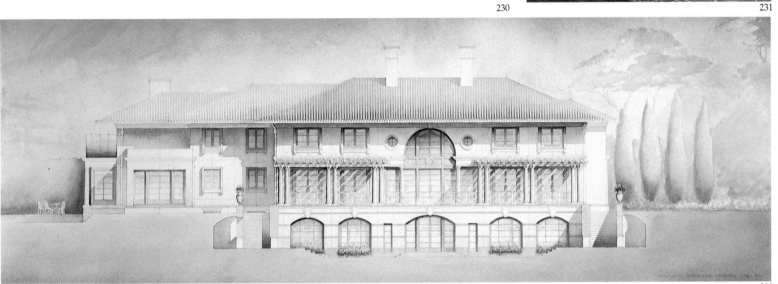

232

230 *Villa in New Jersey. Robert A. M. Stern, 1983–8. Axonometric.*

231 *Villa in New Jersey. Robert A. M. Stern, 1983–8. Façade detail.*

231 *Villa in New Jersey. Robert A. M. Stern, 1983–8. South elevation.*

JOHN OUTRAM

The aspiration of Modern Traditionalism is to create a contemporary architectural culture that coexists within the Classical tradition, yet is not choked by it. If this is possible, it is essential that both the high and the vernacular languages of architecture be used both correctly and in entirely new ways. For John Outram, a British architect trained in Modernism, the Classical tradition is thoroughly open to his own remaking of the language. Outram believes that the task of an architect in an urban culture is, first, that of "seeing man primarily as a biological entity who needs to be reconciled to nature."[60] He abandoned the technological model of the International Style about 1960, largely because he considered it an urban catastrophe. Ambitious as a boy to become an aircraft designer, Outram decided in his maturity that his ardor for technology was misplaced:

> My own 'inside knowledge' of aircraft design showed me, back in 1960, that it was ridiculous to treat buildings as vehicles. It was not only silly technology but, what was worse, the iconography of high-tech proclaimed the supremacy of the vehicle, as symbol, an illogical position to take if one was interested in cities and urban culture.[61]

Returning to nature as a symbol, Outram observes:

> In the 19th century we felt that Nature and Culture were suited by divine ordinance to work together to create progress. One thinks of those great works of engineering in which visions of Nature and Culture managed to come together into a harmonious whole: the railway stations, the pumping houses, the bridges. Machines grew metal leaves. In the early 20th century we felt a deep and total conflict between Nature and Culture such that progress seemed possible only on condition that Nature was radically denied. Culture was proposed as an a-priori rationality that floated above Nature on gleaming metal supports. Culture did not "touch the ground." Whiteness, hygiene, polish were the ornamental modes, the aircraft the cult object.
>
> In the late 20th century we have, through the development of atomic engineering, and now biological engineering, tied Culture and Nature together in a bond that can now never be broken again. We have already irrevocably entered a historical period diametrically opposed to the basic idea of Modernism, that Culture could be successfully separated from Nature. The two are tending more and more towards identity. There is a beautiful side to this as well as a nightmarish one. Also, we are no longer sure, as was the 19th century, that Nature is "on our side."[62]

Despite the ambiguities of the relationship, Outram sees culture and nature as inextricably bound, and his quest to "reconnect architecture to its natural roots"[63] is really a way of re-connecting architecture to culture itself. For Outram, the Classical language is the best way of achieving this.

233

233 *Country house, Sussex. John Outram, 1978–85. View of courtyard entablature detail.*

234 *Country house, Sussex. John Outram, 1978–85. View northwest along south elevation.*

The exigencies of professional practice have led Outram to test this rather grand vision of architecture on several seemingly banal building projects, from workshops to warehouses, most impressively in the renovation of a bland 1960s box into a headquarters for Harp Heating in Swanley, Kent (1983–5). Set at the end of a suburban street, the project hardly seems the place for the rejuvenation of urban culture, but Outram's fat-columned, anthropomorphic headquarters-temple frankly proclaims his ideals and stylistic preferences. Palladio encased Vicenza's vernacular town hall in a Classical shell to give it the status of public architecture; Outram did much the same to Harp Heating's nondescript example of utilitarianism. Having reduced the original building to its frame and floors, he then wrapped it in a hypostyle of semicylindrical brick columns. The columns are hollow and contain vertical ducts and space for boilers and other equipment, but they are, in themselves, of no structural consequence (although most of them enclose the steel I-beam of the original frame); thus their purpose appears to be iconographical: their form communicating Classical ideals; their main material, brick, suggesting the "earth"; and their capitals, wood acanthus leaves turned into flames, symbolizing the client's business. The symbolism of the front and rear elevations is more difficult to comprehend: the rear offers a literal and metaphorical departure from iconography in the form of a fire escape (a spiralling brick staircase), and each façade has a solar disc (ventilation fan) in the center of its pediment.

Outram has designed another industrial temple, a pumping station on the Isle of Dogs in London (1984–8), which reaches back to Egypt for the forms of its battered walls and fat columns. Outram's belief that Classicism is a useful storehouse of symbols and a way of achieving meaning, but not a determiner of forms is obvious in a large single-story country house in Sussex (1978–85). The assemblage of barrel-vaulted pavilions is in the industrial vernacular: steel frame with brick, block, and pre-cast concrete cladding. To Outram, the industrial language does not preclude a rich layering of meaning: the brown base of the pavilions' "columns" represents the primeval ooze; the crushed brick in the shafts, civilization. In the entrance hall, by contrast, a Classical allusion is placed underfoot: the marble pattern on the floor depicts the section of a huge fluted column. In the shell of a Victorian conservatory attached to the new house, Outram reaches a Las Vegas pitch in the profusion of signs, creating an indoor-outdoor room ringed by fat brick half-columns supporting an overscaled entablature. Yet it is a genuine attempt to sustain the "myth of Arcadia," which Outram believes is a necessary creative stimulus in a modern pluralistic democracy.

235   *Country house, Sussex. John Outram, 1978–85. Interior view of entrance hall showing marble floor pattern derived from the column section.*

HARP HEATING

(read sequence of operations upwards from the bottom of the page).

4.0. The "CLASSICAL" building:

The hard-wearing OUTER SHELL encloses the structure and services:

4.1. The big brick columns act as **vertical** service-ducts.

4.2. The brick and precast stone spandrels act as **horizontal** service ducts.

4.3. The pitched roof as a **horizontal** "service-attic" that connects together the tops of all the vertical brick columns.

4.4. Automatic motorised awning blinds with photoelectric and anemometer control prevent solar glare and overheating.

3.0. The "HIGH-TECH" building.

The "SERVICES" are all hung outside the lettable space.

3.1. Main supply and effluent services are taken up from the external underground ducts and drains and rise up outside the existing structural frame and over the top of the existing roof slab.

3.2. Fixed equipment: boilers, electricity distribution boards, are all installed outside the perimeter of lettable space.

2.0. The "EXISTING" building.

The "STRUCTURE".

2.1. The existing building is stripped down to the frame, floors and roof.

2.2. It looks like the typical 'modern' building.

1.0. The "LETTABLE" building.

The ENCLOSED SPACE.

1.1. The Interior space is has. smooth walls, floors and ceilings free of all projections.

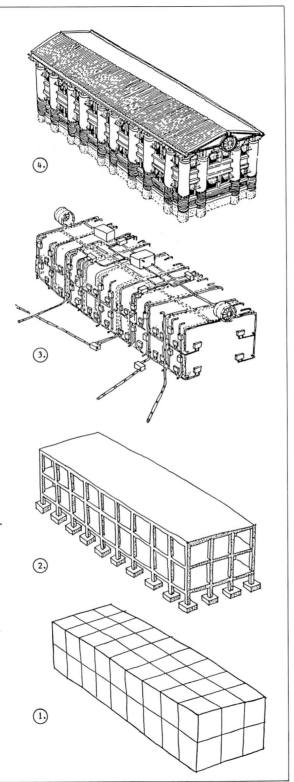

236

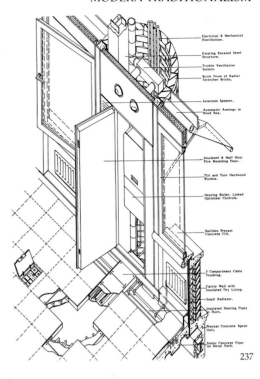

237

236 *Harp Heating Headquarters, Swanley, Kent. John Outram, 1983–5. Analytic axonometrics.*

237 *Harp Heating Headquarters, Swanley, Kent. John Outram, 1983–5. Cutaway axonometric showing structural and mechanical systems.*

238

238 *Harp Heating Headquarters, Swanley, Kent. John Outram, 1983–5. View northwest before renovation.*

239 *Harp Heating Headquarters, Swanley, Kent. John Outram, 1983–5. View northwest after renovation.*

239

240

240 *Harp Heating Headquarters, Swanley, Kent. John Outram, 1983–5. View of free standing column.*

241 *Pumping Station, Isle of Dogs. John Outram, 1984–8. Elevation.*

241

THOMAS GORDON SMITH

Thomas Gordon Smith (b. 1948) has combined Outram's sense of freedom and symbolic plenitude with a passion for Classicism's specific forms and representational systems. A native of Berkeley, California, Smith designs buildings imbued with the Mediterranean-Classical sensibility of Bernard Maybeck in their eclecticism and imaginative use of ordinary materials. Smith's pair of adjoining houses in Livermore, California (1979) — dubbed Tuscan House and Laurentian House after two villas described in Pliny's letters — are two small, wood-framed structures covered in stucco, occupying 40- by 100-foot (12- by 30-meter) lots. Pliny's letters are a purely literary source whose specific architectural interpretation has been a subject of debate that has endured for centuries, and is irresoluble given the uncertain definition of many of the terms he uses and Pliny's greater interest in mood and experience than architectural detail. The letters are only a starting point for Smith, who is also inspired by the archeological evidence of Hadrian's villa and other, roughly contemporary villas, in Pompeii. Yet the entire Classical tradition is called into play, as for example in the Laurentian House's entrance arch, taken from the Italian Renaissance and, perhaps more importantly to the tradition of the suburban house, from the nineteenth-century Italianate villa. Smith's polychromatic surfaces and free-wheeling plans suggest a lighthearted approach, yet like Outram, he sincerely believes in the iconographic possibilities of the Classical tradition.

In the design of his own house in Richmond, California (1982–3), Smith, an accomplished painter, draws upon the tradition of Roman wall painting to create what he calls "Literate Classicism." His villa's centerpiece is the living room on the second floor, which in plan is a large square rotated to a diagonal axis by a pair of ovals. Smith decorated the walls with frescoes in three rings radiating from the painted oculus on the ceiling, depicting, in descending order, the stages of life; four scenes from the myth of Persephone, symbolizing the seasons; and gas stations, representing technological progress as well as vernacular architecture.

Smith's Monroe House in Lafayette, California (1986–), with its asymmetrical plan, laid out with regard to the view out and the view back toward the house, intimate projecting porches, and colorful ornament, relates to the long line of picturesque Classical villas. The architectural historian Richard J. Betts has suggested that Smith is tryng to develop a theory of "decorum," applicable to the small American house, in which the different orders are identified with particular activities: "[Smith] seems to me to be a radical idealist who has chosen to ignore two hundred years of American experience in usage of the orders and seek a new, functional theory of decorum. Each wing of his house has a different purpose in the life of the family, and to each Smith assigns a different order." While noting that Smith does not fully explain himself, Betts goes on to develop his theory that Smith is in the tradition of Classical reformers who have called for a return to origins. "In the eighteenth century Laugier upheld the primacy of the Greeks. Smith, I think, wants to go back to the Mycenaeans, who were the ultimate progenitors of Classical civilization." He finds evidence for this in the resemblance of the Doric living room to a megaron, in a cluster of smaller structures, "not unlike the citadel at Tiryns."[63] Despite this, the evidence of the designs themselves is that Smith's architecture would be unthinkable without the experience of twentieth-century art and architecture.

242

242 Richmond Hill House, Richmond, California. Thomas Gordon Smith, 1982–3. Interior view of living room.

243 Richmond Hill House, Richmond, California. Thomas Gordon Smith, 1982–3. View of front elevation.

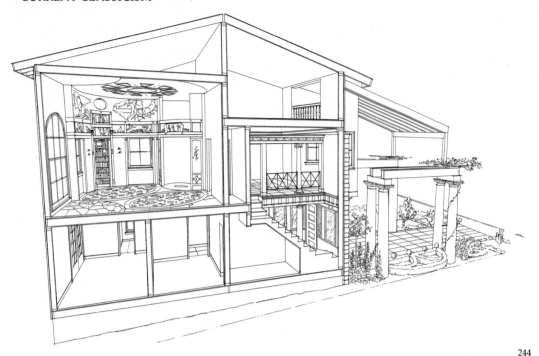

245

244   *Richmond Hill House, Richmond, California. Thomas Gordon Smith, 1982–3. Cutaway perspective east.*

245   *Laurentian House (foreground) and Tuscan House (background), Livermore, California. Thomas Gordon Smith, 1979. View north.*

246   *Laurentian House (above) and Tuscan House (below), Livermore, California. Thomas Gordon Smith, 1979. Plans.*

Key

1 Garage	2 Foyer
3 Kitchen	4 Dining Room
5 Living Room	6 Hall
7 Court	8 Bedroom

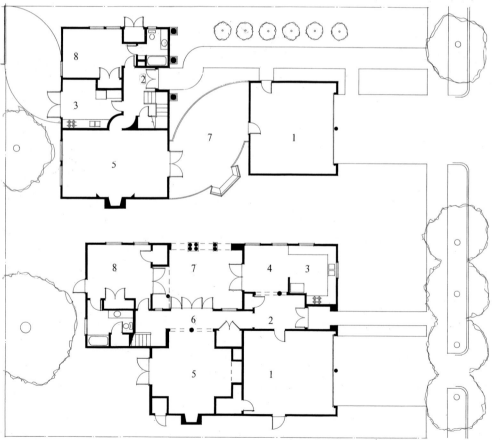

246

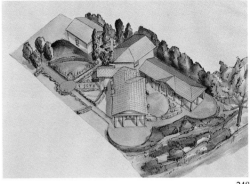

247 *Laurentian House (right) and Tuscan House (left), Livermore, California. Thomas Gordon Smith, 1979. View southeast along street.*

248 *Monroe House, Lafayette, California. Thomas Gordon Smith, 1986– . Aerial perspective.*

249 *Monroe House, Lafayette, California. Thomas Gordon Smith, 1986– . Perspective north.*

250 *1992 Chicago World's Fair. Skidmore, Owings & Merrill, Chicago/William E. Brazley & Associates, with Thomas Beeby, Charles Moore, Jaquelin Robertson, Robert A. M. Stern, Stanley Tigerman, 1984–85. Unbuilt project. Perspective view.*

250

THE MODERN CLASSICAL CITY

Nowhere is the Modern Classical point of view more clearly expressed than in the design of the city. During the Renaissance, the art of planning cities, like that of Classical architecture, was revived. The understanding of the individual monument in relation to the city was an integral part of Vitruvius's text, and his interpreters, from Alberti onward, were greatly concerned both with creating ideal, new cities and with rationalizing — that is to say, Classicizing — existing ones. Although Modernists professed similar utopian and rational urban ideals, they regarded Classical ordering systems and specific Classical cities as respected, but no less defunct, ancestors. In this Le Corbusier was the worst offender, attacking the traditional cities such as Paris and New York, in the belief that the automobile had rendered them meaningless, and proposing in their place a new, gridded, sunlight-drenched townscape in which the traditional relationship of street-hugging, space-defining buildings was reversed in favor of isolated towers rising from green parks — vertical garden cities, to use his term. While rank-and-file architects and planners struggled to come to terms with this idealistic but fundamentally destructive vision, the real city of the automobile age turned out to be a sprawling, low-density conurbation, reaching its most intense level in the linear development of the American West, most notably in sprawling "non-places" like Las Vegas, Nevada, which Robert Venturi, Denise Scott Brown, and Steven Izenour examined as part of their influential collection of essays, *Learning from Las Vegas*, (1972). Venturi had already outlined his ideas about city planning in his earlier book *Complexity and Contradiction in Architecture* (1966), in which he praised the vitality of the contradictory juxtapositions of both the city center and the strip: Trinity Church dwarfed by the towers of Wall Street; the glaring signs of Times Square overpowering the buildings from which they projected; small houses pressed up against an expressway; the sprawling and spasmodic roadside attractions of Route 66. Rather than bemoan the death of traditional urbanism in the wake of the automobile, Venturi showed how the contemporary city could be understood in historical terms, seeing Times Square as analogous to the Piazza San Marco. He tried to find the American equivalent of the Italian urban façades in the sleaziness of strip architecture, incorporating the anti-idealism of Pop Art into his urban theory:

> Some of the vivid lessons of Pop Art, involving contradictions of scale and context, should have awakened architects from prim dreams of pure order, which, unfortunately, are imposed in the easy Gestalt unities of the urban renewal projects of establishment Modern architecture and yet, fortunately are really impossible to achieve at any great scope. And it is perhaps from the everyday landscape, vulgar and disdained, that we can draw the complex and contradictory order that is valid and vital for our architecture as an urbanistic whole.[64]

Vincent Scully, in his introduction to *Complexity and Contradiction in Architecture*, summed up the difference between Le Corbusier's urbanism and Venturi's:

> Le Corbusier's great teacher was the Greek temple, with its isolated body white and free in the landscape. . . . Venturi's primary inspiration would seem to have come from the Greek temple's historical and archetypal opposite, the urban façades of Italy, with their endless adjustments to the counter-requirements of inside and outside and their inflection with all the business of everyday life: not primary sculptural actors in vast landscapes but complex spatial containers and definers of streets and squares.[65]

Venturi's pioneering observations were further developed in Colin Rowe (b. 1920) and Fred Koetter's *Collage City* (1978). In their analysis of the failure of twentieth-century urban utopias, Rowe and Koetter concluded, like the physicist-political philosopher Karl Popper in *The Open Society and its Enemies* (1945), that however useful the determinist theories of the past two centuries are in analyzing history, they are very bad tools for making it. Popper suggested "piecemeal social engineering" as an alternative to Marxist revolution. Rowe and Koetter, who are at pains to point out the weaknesses as well as the strengths of Popper's argument, nonetheless offer up a piecemeal "collage" as the solution to the ongoing "rape of the great cities of the world." The tolerance of this position is immense:

> It is suggested that a collage approach, an approach in which objects are conscripted or seduced from out of their context, is — at the present day — the only way of dealing with the ultimate problems of, either or both, utopia and tradition; and the provenance of the architectural objects introduced into the social collage need not be of great consequence. The objects can be aristocratic or they can be "folkish," academic or popular. Whether they originate in Pergamum or Dahomey, in Detroit or Dubrovnik, whether their implications are of the twentieth or the fifteenth century, is no great matter. Societies and persons assemble themselves according to their own interpretations of absolute reference and traditional value; and, up to a point, collage accommodates both hybrid display and the requirements of self-determination.[66]

It is important to understand that Venturi, Rowe and Koetter begin with the *reality* of the modern city, not an ideal. In *Complexity and Contradiction*, Venturi pointed out that the actual plans for Palladio's urban palazzi are much more complicated than the perfect plans displayed in *I Quattro Libri d'Architettura*; and for Venturi that reality is preferable to the plan. For the modern architect, there is no false vision of the urbanism of the ancient world as a perfectly ordered realm, but instead a grateful recognition that great cities are those that are most complex: that the inherent contradictions of Haussmann's boulevards imposed on the medieval streets of Paris are infinitely preferable to the rational aridities of Lucio Costa's Brasilia.

Although few contemporary Classical architects expect or even desire a purely Classical city to be realized, some reasonably argue that enclaves of Classical order and harmony — modern interpretations of the *temenos*, the walled sacred enclosure around a Greek temple or altar — can be created. In *Classical Architecture: The Poetics of Order*, Alexander Tzonis and Liane Lefaivre explain the failure of efforts to Classicize cities over the past four centuries: "Whatever the intentions behind such classicizing undertakings, from the formal point of view they were self-defeating. Cities were cut up, and alien tissue was grafted onto them in the name of formal consistency. Conflicts did not disappear; they just changed locus." Tzonis and Lefaivre are not, however, gratified by Classical architecture's inability to resolve urban conflicts; furthermore, they lament that in the attempt to apply Classical ideals at the urban scale, a smaller vision of harmony was lost: "In the effort to spread classical realm, urban refurbishings lost the most fundamental achievement of the early classical thinking, the temenos, the conception of a contained totality as a world free of contradiction."[67] Whereas Rowe and Venturi imply that ironic complexity, at every scale from that of a single building to that of the city, is the only possible approach, Tzonis and Lefaivre remind us that the ideal of more straightforward urban order still exists. If this ideal is still valid, can the ideal of the grand design be far behind?

The architecture critic, theorist and teacher Colin Rowe has given design expression to the ideas of *Collage City* in a series of projects for Rome. In 1978 he contributed to Roma Interotta, an exhibition in which fourteen architects prepared projects that examined changes in the urban fabric of Rome, imagining what might have happened had the city been spared disruptive nineteenth- and twentieth-century notions of architecture and planning and continued to evolve as it had until the late eighteenth century. The plan of Rome drawn by Giambattista Nolli in 1748 was taken as the starting point. Among the participants were Robert Venturi, Michael Graves, James Stirling, and Aldo Rossi. Rowe, with Peter Carl, Judith di Maio, and Steven Peterson, took the opportunity to offer a demonstration against the spatial homogeneity and absence of "place" characteristic of Modernist city planning. Using the "figure-ground" analysis, in which the spaces around buildings and the "public" spaces within buildings — the piazzi, streets, courtyards, and rotundas — rather than the buildings themselves become the "figure," they invented a collage of city grids which, while fictional except for the elements of Nolli's map, attempted plausible solutions to current problems in the urban design of Rome. The introduction of the plan of Rockefeller Center below the Circus Maximus was humorous, but it was also meant to work in formal and experiential terms, linking the edge of the Aventino to the north-south axis of the Corso. Their text and drawings have qualities of collage, inventing not only a nineteenth-century Rome that never was, introducing new "discrete set pieces," but also a nineteenth-century Jesuit scholar, Father Vincent Mulcahy, as the chief guide to it.

For the 1987 Triennale in Milan, Rowe and his students in the Urban Design studio at Cornell, Matthew Bell, Robert Goodill, Kevin Hinders, Brian Kelly and Cheryl O'Neill, proposed to rebuild Rome's Piazza Augusto Imperatore, a formidably desolate site created when Mussolini razed a hodge-podge of medieval buildings and the architectural accretions that surrounded the Mausoleum of Augustus, a ruin from the first century AD. The Mausoleum, which had also served as a fort, garden, bullring, and, most recently, a concert hall, was not enhanced by Mussolini's urban purgation, or by the heavy-handed quasi-Modernist buildings (1936–40) by Vittorio Ballio Morpurgo which precluded a sensible approach or pleasing vista. Rowe proposes to reintegrate the Mausoleum with the general texture of Roman urbanism and to create a distinctive place that would gather adjacent monuments and street patterns into a coherent whole, without, however, imposing a simplistic unity. Taking their cue from the Baroque Church of San Carlo al Corso (1668–72), by Pietro da Cortona (1596–1669), which they incorporated into their scheme, they positioned their new buildings to mediate between the Via di Ripetta and the Via del Corso.

Using elements including grand staircases, terraces, and fountains, the solution does not rely on clearing space, but rather on making it sensible.

The Norwegian architect and critic Christian Norberg-Schulz (b.1926) has also helped to stimulate renewed appreciation of traditional urbanism, stressing that the essential issue in city planning is not traffic or social engineering but the establishment, or the maintenance, of a sense of place. Norberg-Schulz wrote in his essay of 1980, "Towards an Authentic Architecture": "Monotony and chaos are apparently contradictory phenomena, but at a closer scrutiny reveal themselves as interrelated aspects of a more general crisis, which may be called the 'loss of place.' "[68] Norberg-Schulz calls for a phenomenology of place, recognizing concrete experience as well as Euclidian geometries to arrive at "the structure of the place," which defines the "genius loci."

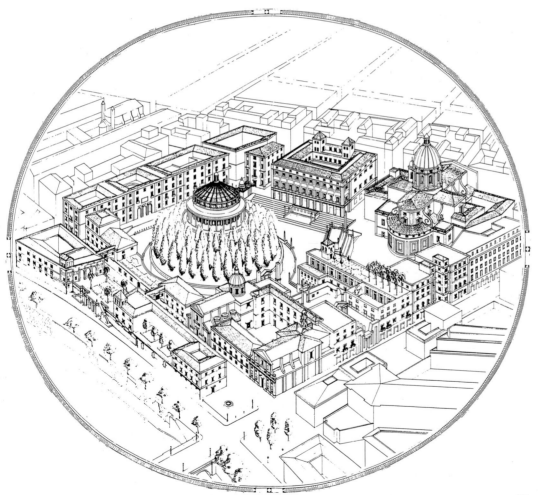

251   *Proposal for reconstruction of Piazza Augusto Imperatore, Rome, Triennale, Milan. Colin Rowe with the students of the Urban Design Studio at Cornell, 1987. Perspective northeast.*

252   *Section VII, Urban Design Intervention, Roma Interrota. Colin Rowe, Steven Peterson, Peter Carl and Judith di Maio, 1978. Site plan.*

251

242

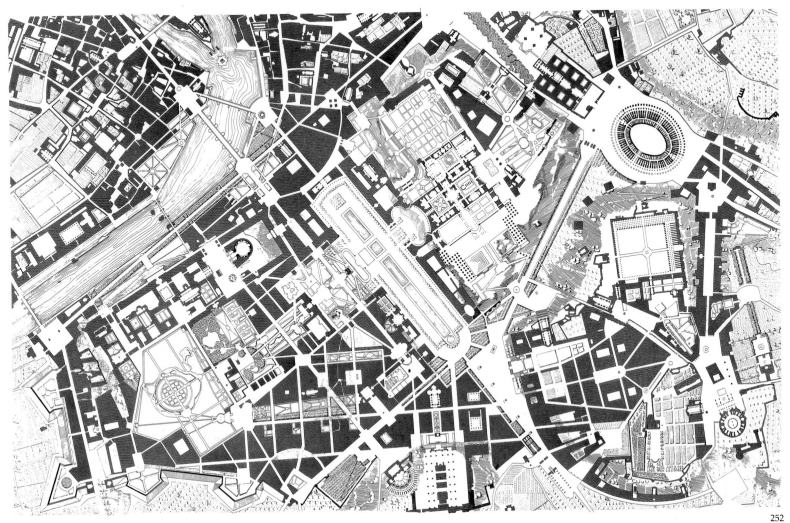

252

PAOLO PORTOGHESI

Norberg-Schulz praises Paolo Portoghesi for his attempt to respect the "structure of place" and for his theory of space as a "system of places." Portoghesi (b. 1931), an Italian architect who successfully balances a professional practice with writing architectural history and criticism, has, since the late 1950s, tried to infuse his ambiguously Modernist designs with a sense of history and place. In his earliest significant work, the Casa Baldi in Rome (with Vittorio Gigliotti, 1959–61), Portoghesi combined Baroque massing with a pseudo-brutalist yet vernacular wall treatment of tufa stone, which mirrored Le Corbusier's late efforts to root architecture in the peasant vernacular of the Mediterranean. Portoghesi contributed to the Roma Interrota exhibition, working with Vittorio Gigliotti to produce a series of games and dreams, such as a remarkable comparison of the "spaces in between" of a natural ravine and those of Roman streets and piazzas. More recently, Portoghesi and Pierluigi Eroli have completed a book entitled *Dopo l'Amnesía Restitutio et Renovatio Urbis Romae* ("After the Amnesia; Restoration and Renovation of the City of Rome" 1986), in which sections of the city are remade and renovated, filled in with fanciful yet fundamentally rational pieces of architecture.

In a residential complex in Tarquinia (1981–), now under construction, Portoghesi offers a tangible example of the synthesis of vernacular and Classical hinted at in his urban projects. The façade is screened by a giant three-story arcade, which endows the building — derived from multi-story housing for Italian tenant farmers — the scale and character of the socialist workers' housing at the Karl Marx Hof in Vienna (Karl Ehn, 1927). In the Piazza for the New City of Sibari (1986), Portoghesi takes the elements of the Classical-vernacular Italian tradition, including simplified columns, gables, square windows, barrel vaults, and courtyard fountains, and ties them together in a composition of colonnaded crescents linked to rigid axial plans. Yet the result is curiously cut off from the tradition of the city, perhaps through the absence of historical detail, or through the overemphatic shifts of scale and hierarchy. Portoghesi more naturally embraces Classicism in a recent project for an open-air theater in Ascea, a town in southern Italy. Portoghesi drew directly on ancient Roman precedent for the design, including a background of stacked, syncopated aedicules, like the façade of the Library of Celsus, Ephesus (117–120 AD).

253

253   *Residential complex, Tarquinia, Italy. Paolo Portoghesi, 1981– . View of model.*

254 *Theater, Ascea, Italy. Paolo Portoghesi, 1987.*
View of model.

"THE PRESENCE OF THE PAST" VENICE 1980

In 1980 Portoghesi organized the First International Exhibition of Architecture at the Venice Biennale, which was a turning point in the contemporary interpretation of the city. The theme of the exhibition was based on the idea that the temporary cities of world's fairs and exhibitions have often proved fertile testing grounds for new conceptions of the city. In a deliberate assault on Modernist architecture and planning, which had devalued both the street and the façade, Portoghesi asked twenty architects to design façades for an imaginary street, the Strada Novíssima, which would be created between two rows of columns inside the Cordería (a former rope factory) at the Arsenale in Venice. The architecture section of the Biennale was provocatively dedicated to the theme "The Presence of the Past," and the façades of the Strada Novíssima were commissioned to proclaim that architecture was free again to employ Classical language on a civic scale.

For the exhibition Robert Venturi provided a variation on his Eclectic House projects of 1978, a cartoon Classical temple façade painted yellow, blue and red, suspended 6 feet (2 meters) above the floor. The fat, truncated columns supported a Doric entablature of bloated triglyphs surmounted by a tympanum decorated with Le Corbusier-like human figures. Charles Moore's entry manipulated a complicated collage of arches and half-arches; Allan Greenberg presented an arch in the form of a fully articulated, correct serliana; Thomas Gordon Smith put the spiralling columns of Bernini's St. Peter's Baldacchino (1624–33) into a Doric frame. The Spanish architect, Ricardo Bofill offered a Ledoux-like drawing of a detail from his Espaces d'Abraxas housing project in Marne-la-Vallée outside Paris. In a gesture at once fundamentalist and ironic, the Austrian architect Hans Hollein rejected the idea of façade as wall, proposing instead four Doric columns: the first, a stripped tree trunk, recalling Laugier's primitive hut; the second, Adolf Loos's entry in the Chicago Tribune Competition, a tribute to the Viennese tradition and the continuity of the Orders; the third, of marble, severed and jagged, presumably in an admonitory message about the dangers of historicism; and the fourth, of grass, reiterating Laugier's point in a surrealistic way.

255 *Strada Novíssima, Venice Biennale, 1980. View of "New Street' showing façades, from left to right, by Venturi, Rauch & Scott Brown, Leon Krier, Josef P. Kleiheus, and Hans Hollein.*

255

256

257

258

259

260

256   *Strada Novíssima, Venice Biennale, 1980. View through a façade by Allan Greenberg to a façade by Thomas Gordon Smith.*

257   *Strada Novíssima, Venice Biennale, 1980. View of façade by Thomas Gordon Smith.*

258   *Strada Novíssima, Venice Biennale, 1980. View of façade by Ricardo Bofill/Taller de Arquitectura.*

259   *Strada Novíssima, Venice Biennale, 1980. View of façade by Hans Hollein.*

260   *Strada Novíssima, Venice Biennale, 1980. General view.*

261 *Strada Novíssima, Venice Biennale, 1980.
View of façade by Charles Moore.*

261

"LIFE IN THE INNER CITY" BERLIN 1979–87

Initiated in Berlin in 1979, the International Building Exhibition (IBA) was undertaken as a practical demonstration of contemporary architecture's ability to recreate the orderly housing districts one associates with traditional cities. The exhibition took as its theme "Life in the Inner City" and was deliberately opposed to the Modernist planning of the post-war International Building Exhibition held in 1957 (Interbau), which had the theme "The Reconstruction of the City" and took as its compositional manifesto the total rejection of traditional urban patterns. Intended as a symbol of democratic, pluralistic society which would contrast with the "totalitarian" axiality and monumentality of the Stalin Allee nearby in East Berlin, the 1957 Interbau's reconstruction of the Hansa quarter was defined by isolated monuments and free-standing apartment blocks such as Le Corbusier's 17-story Berlin Type Apartment House, closely modelled after his Unité d'Habitation in Marseilles.

The IBA exhibition was placed under the direction of Josef Paul Kleiheus, who invited an international roster of architects to participate, with designs that would eventually occupy several different quarters of the city. Among those who made notable contributions to the project — not only by virtue of individual designs, but by their ability to convey a sense of the overall orderliness essential to the Classical city — no one has done more than the Luxembourger Rob Krier (b. 1938), who undertook a number of large projects for the IBA including the master plan and "gatehouse" of the Rauchstrasse apartment development.

262   *Gateway Building, Rauchstrasse, South Tiergarten area, Berlin. Rob Krier, 1980–84.*

262

ROB KRIER

Along with his younger brother Leon (b. 1946), Rob Krier has been instrumental in developing an anti-Modernist ideology of public spaces and monuments. The opportunities to build have come to him rather than to his brother because his more pragmatic philosophy of building allows for the creation of traditional urban spaces and monuments without the use of traditional building technologies. For IBA's Rauchstrasse site, in the Tiergarten, a neighborhood, an area originally reserved for exclusive private residences and foreign embassies, Rob Krier created a master plan that called for five-story apartment houses set along a long formal court like super-scaled villas (1980–84). Krier also created the gateway building, with its memorable arch and figural sculpture. Other architects invited to design the individual apartment buildings included Hans Hollein and Aldo Rossi, who succeeded in designing strikingly different buildings while working within the typological constraints of the master plan.

On another IBA site, Ritterstrasse Nord, in the Friedrichstadt district, Krier literally reconstructed the Feilner House (1828–9) by Karl Friedrich Schinkel. The house is set on the projected Schinkel Platz, which Krier envisions as a "public" and commercial square bordered by arcades (and, in Krier's early studies, statues set on pedestals), in the center of a two-block project of four residential quadrangles north of Ritterstrasse. Given its central position in the master plan, also designed by Krier, the Feilner House is both an act of homage to nineteenth-century Germany's greatest architect and a built manifesto declaring the crucial link between the past and the present. From the "historic" realm of Schinkel Platz one passes to the "contemporary" realm of the surrounding quadrangles (one passageway is cut through the base of the Feilner House), which were designed by six other teams of architects in a synthesis of Modernist and traditional elements and materials, including flat roofs, planar white stucco walls, fenestration governed by rationalist grids, as well as brick façades articulated into a version of the Classical tripartite scheme.

263   *No. 6, Rauchstrasse, South Tiergarten area, Berlin, Rob Krier, 1908–84. View of south elevation detail.*

264

264   *Gateway Building, Rauchstrasse, South Tiergarten area, Berlin. Rob Krier, 1980–84. View northwest showing street elevation.*

265   *Rauchstrasse, South Tiergarten area, Berlin. Rob Krier (master plan), 1980–84. Axonometric.*

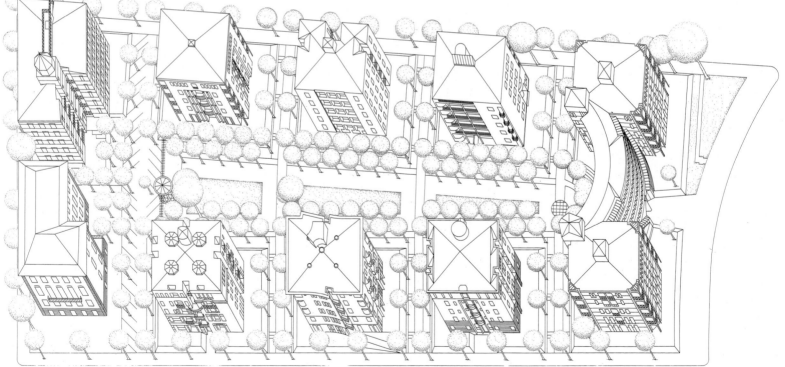

265

266   *Schinkelplatz, South Friedrichstadt, Berlin.*
Rob Krier, 1982– . View south of model showing
(center left) reconstructed Feilner House.

LEON KRIER

In contrast to his more pragmatic brother, Leon Krier has refused until recently to compromise his vision of the Modern Classical city by building anything. Claiming that a thinking architect cannot build in a world where the rules of zoning and construction were made by short-sighted Modernists, he has said that he "cannot build because [he is] an architect. . . . Nobody who builds nowadays can be called an architect."[69] Krier has led an international crusade for the revitalization of both the vernacular and the high language of Classicism, although he has been reluctant, in his own designs, to embrace the Classical language in the manner of a Lutyens or a Terry. The drawings that first brought Krier to international attention in the 1970s, in fact, revealed a taste for stripped-down, rational architecture, devoid of ornament — an architecture of nearly pure composition. Although Krier's early designs struggled to achieve a kind of timeless essentiality of form, they seemed in fact to be Loos-inspired abstractions, poised at the beginning of Modernism. Krier also paid indirect homage to the enemy, Le Corbusier, depicting antique airplanes overhead and antique cars on the streets below, a reference to Le Corbusier's projects for Paris of the 1920s which contained these images. Krier's rhetoric, always a little ahead of his designs, grew into a straightforward equation: "vernacular building + monumental architecture = a city." Krier's vernacular building is based on the craft tradition, not on the industrial paradigm, which he considers incompatible with architecture or urban life; and his monumental architecture is based on the Classical tradition (but not necessarily on its language). Classicism, in his view, is fundamentally at odds with industrial-age building technology: "Classical architecture and modernist 'architecture' are counter-pointed as contradictory, antagonistic, and incompatible propositions — the former based on artisanal, artistic production; the latter on industrial modes of production."[70]

In his plan for a school at St. Quentin-en-Yvelines (1977–9), a Parisian suburb, Krier applied his theory of the Classical-vernacular town to an institution. Calling the average urban schools of today "factories of education, these prisons of the developing human intelligence, these Auschwitzes of the collective consciousness,"[71] Krier decided to break the school type down into its constituent functions, the opposite tactic to the typical Modernist one of designing a non-specific building meant to contain virtually every activity under one roof. In Krier's scheme, classrooms, dining halls, gymnasiums, and buildings devoted to other functions are tightly organized along streets, alleys, and public squares. To give them symbolic value, Krier used the language of Classical forms — propylae, pediments, and colonnades.

> The symbolic value which buildings must attain cannot be seen as the architect's personal and artistic problem. This value is always created by society, by the *act of inhabiting*, by *custom*, and by the mental activity of associating certain buildings with specific social activities. The architect can neither force not dictate these associations, nor can he invent them as he wishes. He can only help them to take place, encourage them, make them apparent through appropriate iconography and above all, through typological proposals which have proved their appropriateness.[72]

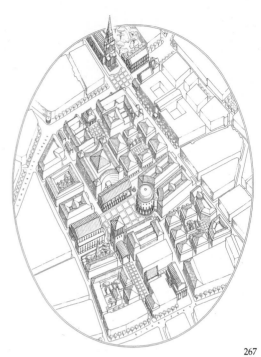

267

267 *Redevelopment of Spitalfields Market, London. Leon Krier, 1986– . Axonometric.*

268 *Redevelopment of Spitalfields Market, London. Leon Krier, 1986– . Site plan.*

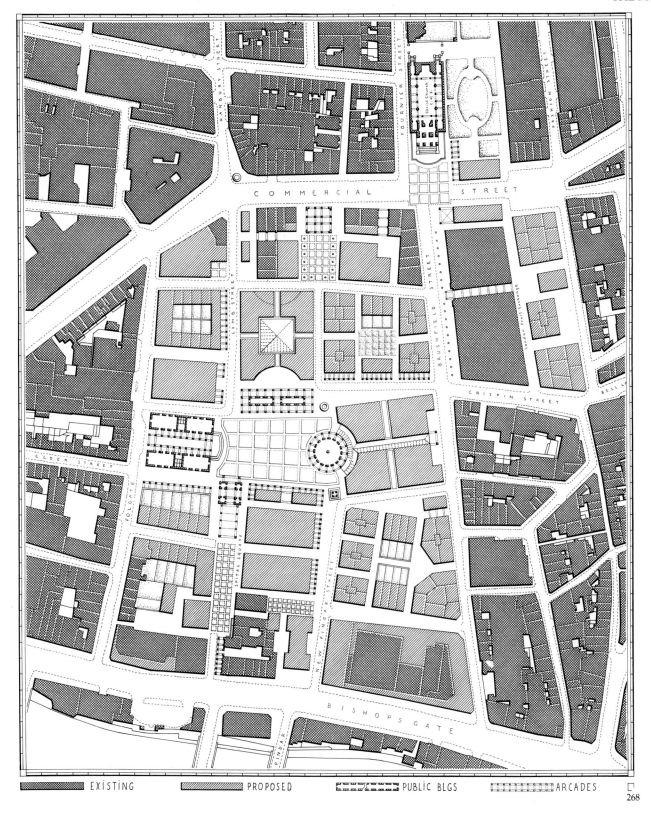

EXISTING   PROPOSED   PUBLIC BLGS   ARCADES

268

257

Krier's designs have become more and more explicitly Classical over the past decade, as can be seen in his reconstruction of Pliny's Villa Laurentium (1981), which, in addition to the belvedere-capped towers which are Krier's signature, has Tuscan columns and pediments topped by acroteria. Yet here, as in his other recent projects, Krier reveals himself as a Romantic Classicist, proposing asymmetrical villas, narrow streets and broad avenues, vernacular and Classical buildings — in short the complexity of ancient Rome, where formal axes were cut through a maze of streets formed by accident and greed, rather than the perfect rectilinearity of the provincial cities laid out by Rome's conquering armies. In his proposal for a 12-acre (5-hectare) site in Spitalfields, London (1986–), Krier went so far as to devise a new medieval street pattern in response to the context. Krier's plan is densely packed, calling for modest buildings facing unexpected courts, often at the end of an alley and with a view of a hypothetical new local monument, a domed cylinder or a tower.

In his master plan for Washington DC (1984–5), a proposal for the city's bicentennial in the year 2000, Krier goes in the opposite direction, to a full-blooded, if highly Romantic Classicism, entailing a radical transformation of America's alabaster city, more ambitious than the proposals of the McMillan Commission of 1902 and coming close, in fact, to Chicago's World's Columbian Exposition of 1893. For example, Krier would improve the Capitol by dividing it into its parts — Senate, Rotunda, and House of Representatives — with a screen of trees hiding the connections; a vast staircase would flow down from the west front of the Capitol to a new plaza, which would overlook a huge basin, created by flooding the Mall. As at the Chicago fair, the basin would be plied by gondolas.

269 *Redevelopment of Spitalfields Market, London. Leon Krier, 1986– . Perspective of Artillery Square.*

270 *Redevelopment of Spitalfields Market, London. Leon Krier, 1986– . Perspective from portico of Assembly Hall to Dealing Hall.*

271 *Redevelopment of Spitalfields Market, London. Leon Krier, 1986– . Perspective up Elder Street towards Artillery Square.*

272 *Redevelopment of Spitalfields Market, London. Leon Krier, 1986– . Perspective of garden court on Crispin Street.*

269

271

270

272

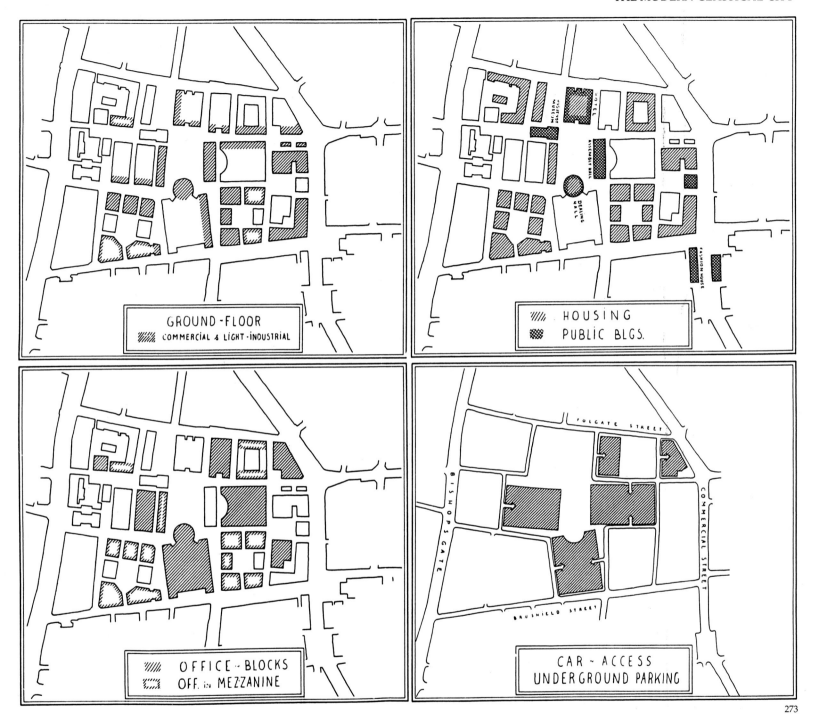

273 *Redevelopment of Spitalfields Market, London.*
Leon Krier, 1986– . Analytical site plan.

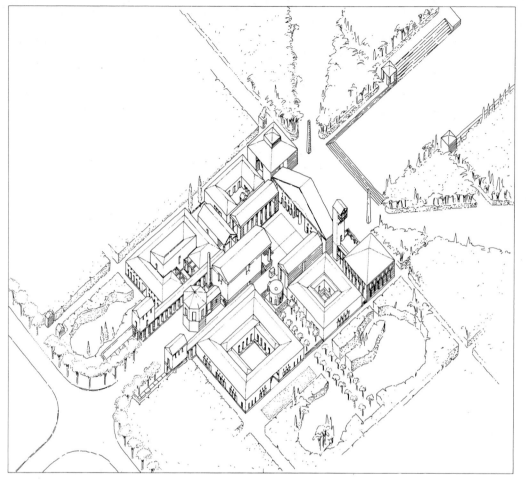

274

275

274   *School at St-Quentin-en-Yvelines, France.*
Leon Krier, 1977–9. Unbuilt project. Axonometic.

275   *School at St-Quentin-en-Yvelines, France.*
Leon Krier, 1977–9. Unbuilt project. Lakefront
elevation.

276   *School at St-Quentin-en-Yvelines, France.*
Leon Krier, 1977–9. Unbuilt project. Perspective of
Place de l'Assemblée.

276

277 *Villa Laurentium. Leon Krier, 1981. Unbuilt project. Perspective south.*

278 *Villa Laurentium. Leon Krier, 1981. Unbuilt project. View of model showing west elevation.*

277

278

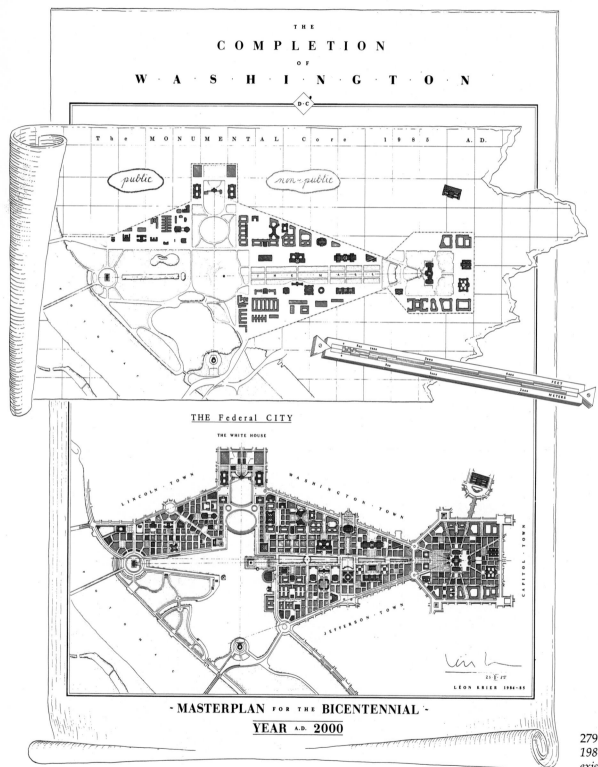

THE
COMPLETION
OF
WASHINGTON
D·C

The MONUMENTAL Core 1985 A.D.

public

non-public

THE Federal CITY

THE WHITE HOUSE

LINCOLN·TOWN

WASHINGTON·TOWN

CAPITOL·TOWN

JEFFERSON·TOWN

LÉON KRIER 1984–85

- MASTERPLAN FOR THE BICENTENNIAL -
YEAR A.D. 2000

279 *Masterplan for Washington DC. Leon Krier,
1984–5. Unbuilt project. Site plan showing
existing city (above) and Krier's proposal (below).*

279

280   *Masterplan for Washington DC. Leon Krier, 1984–5. Unbuilt project. Perspective of the Grand Canal on the Mall.*

281   *House at Seaside, Florida. Leon Krier, 1985– . View northwest of model.*

280

281

263

SEASIDE, FLORIDA

Recently Krier acted as a consultant to Andres Duany and Elizabeth Plater-Zyberk, the architects who devised the plan for Seaside, a new town in Florida's Panhandle. Here, where only traditional wood construction prevails, Krier feels comfortable enough to realize actual buildings: he has designed a belvedere and market stoa for the main square (1987) and a summer house for himself (1985–), to be built on a site given to him as a fee for his work on the master plan. This design combines the American vernacular wood house tradition — a light balloon frame structure, clad in clapboard siding — with a rich array of rationalized Classical details and a Classical composition. The overall effect is of a squat tower with Classical porticoes tacked on as though the house were a frontier Erectheum. On the first story at the entrance is the porch-like aedicula; above this is an open loggia whose construction is an object lesson in the often-asserted correlation between wooden construction and the elements of Classical architecture, with posts joined to the roof by nascent Ionic volutes. The roof pavilion follows the plan and elevation of a Greek temple, with cella and porch, yet once again with rationalized detailing that avoids direct Classical quotation.

Seaside exists because an enlightened developer, Robert Davis, decided that his 80-acre (32-hectare) parcel should be planned as a small town rather than as a typical cluster of developmental units. To prepare the master plan and zoning code (1978–83), Duany and Plater-Zyberk combined their knowledge of small Southern towns with that of the more established urbanism of the Mediterranean Classical-vernacular tradition, to devise a plan for a village of individual houses focused on two connected public squares. The squares, which slope down to the water, are defined by buildings lined by continuous arcades. Streets, ranging from wide, tree-lined avenues to narrow alleys, are laid out in a modified grid which incorporates diagonals and curves while maintaining spatial clarity. The main street, lined with large lots and extending out from the town center, is zoned for private houses, small apartment buildings, and inns. These buildings incorporate a continuous porch on the street façade based on the prototype of the Greek Revival mansion of the antebellum South. Six other streets terminate at the bluff overlooking the beach, where pavilions serve as beach-side changing rooms and as small social centers.

Duany and Plater-Zyberk believed that an authentic town character could not be established by a single architect, so they strove to write a building design code to guide any architect who might work there. Participating architects are required to incorporate certain features of the chosen vernacular, such as front porches, wood picket fences, painted wood siding, and roofs covered with wood shingles or metal and sloped at a specified low angle. In an obvious gesture to Leon Krier's most evocative drawings, the design code encouraged the inclusion of free-standing observation towers.

282　*Seaside, Florida. View of Tupelo Beach Pavilion (Ernesto Buch, 1982).*

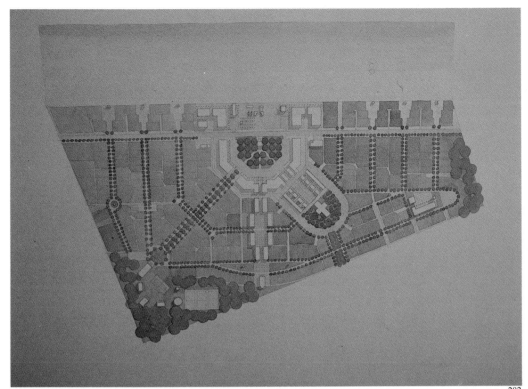

283

284

283   *Master plan for Seaside, Florida. Duany and Plater-Zyberk, 1978–83. Site plan.*

284   *Seaside, Florida. View east of market pavilions.*

285   *Seaside, Florida. General view.*

285

MISSISSAUGA CITY HALL COMPLEX, TORONTO

Perhaps the greatest challenge for the next generation will not be the re-urbanization of traditional cities — a task that is now well under way — but the creation of rational focal points in the placeless sprawl of automobile-dominated suburbia. Seaside is an example of this trend at the scale of a small town in a resort area; there is less cause for optimism in the suburbs. In undertaking the design of a city hall complex for Mississauga (1982–6), a former rural township which became a suburb of Toronto in the 1960s and '70s, Edward Jones (b. 1939) and J. Michael Kirkland (b. 1943) set out to do more than design a handful of buildings on one large lot; as they saw it, and as their clients mandated, their job was to provide an urban focus amid the suburban sprawl, to create something that would help define Mississauga as a place in its region, as a transition point between town and country.

To give the sense of urban character Jones & Kirkland drew on the asymmetrical composition and clock tower of Toronto's late nineteenth-century Romanesque-style Old City Hall, and the "château-style" crowns of early twentieth-century railway hotels and office buildings. They also looked at the composition of Ontario's farms, where barn, silo, water tower, windmill, and main house are often arranged in a tight but asymmetrical plan. Yet, in the final analysis, the greatest influence on the design appears to have come from the work of other architects who have tried to synthesize the Classical and the vernacular, especially Leon Krier, Gunnar Asplund, and ultimately, Claude-Nicolas Ledoux.

The plan resembles the layout of a farm which has had a grand entrance added to the barnyard. At the end of a reflecting pool between an allée of trees, the great wide sloping gable of the administration building identifies it as more a huge barn than a temple — a barn that resembles both Asplund's Lister County Courthouse (Sölvesborg, Sweden, 1917–21), which artfully combined the Classical and vernacular and also stood at the end of an avenue of trees, and Leon Krier's design for the dining hall at the school of St. Quentin-en-Yvelines. The clear formality of the front yard collapses behind the administration building, which turns out to be more of a screen than a barn in its dimensions. Behind it is the cylindrical drum of the Council chambers, an echo of Asplund's Stockholm Public Library (1926), which incorporates both the civic connotations of the rotunda and the rural ones of a silo.

Jones & Kirkland's design was hailed by the architect and critic Trevor Boddy as an inspiring example of "New Regionalism," for its sincere examination and articulation of the theme of how a city might exist in the Canadian suburbs.[74] Yet for all its references to history and place, Mississauga City Hall is really an architect's game: poetry about other poets, architecture about other architects, and incomprehensible compared to a more traditional building.

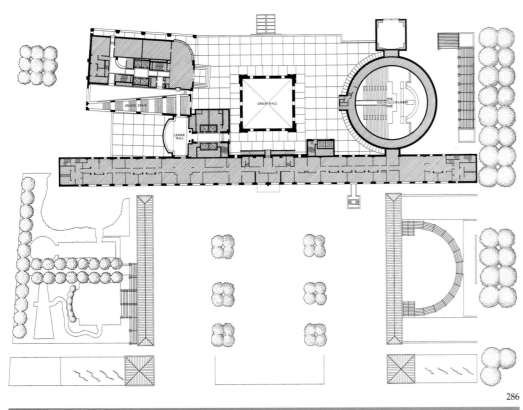

286 *City Hall, Mississauga, Canada. Jones & Kirkland, 1982–6. Fourth floor plan.*

287 *City Hall, Mississauga, Canada. Jones & Kirkland, 1982–6. Aerial view northwest.*

HORS-CHÂTEAU, LIÈGE

The urban planning ideas of Leon Krier have thus far had their most direct European realization in the work of the Belgian architect Charles Vandenhove (b. 1927). Like many cities in Europe, Liège, Belgium, underwent two destructive experiences in recent history: the bombardments of the Second World War and the devastations of urban renewal. By the 1970s the middle class had fled the city, leaving the character-less new apartment buildings and the remaining corners of the old city to those who were too poor to go anywhere else. Awakening to this newest form of urban destruction, the city leaders of Liège decided to try to revitalize the old center. In the Hors-Château quarter, a mixed-use development of apartments, offices, restaurants and shops (1978) was planned as the catalyst. The project included the restoration of twelve former single-family dwellings, dating from the sixteenth to the nineteenth century, and the construction of a new thirty-unit apartment building. Although trained as a Modernist, Vandenhove had become more and more attentive to traditional design, including the vernacular of his native Meuse Valley. In Hors-Château, he gave careful consideration to the overall plan and individual elements that would create a distinctive place in the city as the Liègois remembered it. To make a place out of the back alley between his new and restored buildings, Vandenhove first decided that the entrance should be an *arvos* — a portico cut through the street wall to give access to the closed alleyways or *impasses* typical of the old city. Taking great care with the design of this gateway, Vandenhove ornamented it with cylindrical columns capped by gigantic "Ionic" volutes. In his scheme, what had been an *impasse* became the Place Tikal, defined along its sides by the three- to five-story restored houses and the new mixed-use building, and at the ends by two low, simple red-brick buildings. At one end of the cobbled court there is a small fountain whose run-off is channelled through a straight narrow cut or rill leading to a pool at the base of "Tikal," a tall slab stepped back like a Pre-Columbian pyramid designed by Anne and Patrick Poirier. For the existing buildings, Vandenhove proved a sensitive restorer, replacing missing windows with bronze casements which, though not quite historically correct, are nonetheless traditional. For the new buildings, Vandenhove filtered traditional elements through his own powerful aesthetic. The thirty-unit apartment building is designed according to a modular system, with a strong rational expression of concrete post and beam, yet manages to evoke typical vernacular buildings. The wealth of finishes and details, such as highly polished concrete, marble trim, natural slate roof tiles, and cast-iron window boxes, combined with the familiar shapes including rounded stoops and stepped gables, all help to tie the new architecture to an older tradition.

For Vandenhove, it is traditional space and craft, and not necessarily historical forms, which are the most important factors in creating a place in the city. In stating his belief in memory and craft, Vandenhove often sounds like an earlier generation of architectural moralists, that of Ruskin and Morris:

> The danger is to make large, unified projects . . . . it is necessary first of all that those who make the houses of others take pleasure in doing it. Thus, it is necessary to restore the knowledge of the artisans and their colleagues who construct a house . . . that is where our society is derailed — Charlie Chaplin

already understood that when he showed, in his films, people overwhelmed by the assembly line — everyone must claim the pleasure in doing if one wants to change society.[75]

Ultimately, for Vandenhove, as for Leon Krier or Colin Rowe, it is the aesthetic of the assembly line, of the endlessly repeatable language of the machine, which is the enemy of architecture and of the city alike.

288

288 *Reconstruction, renovation, and additions to Hors-Château, Liège, Belgium. Charles Vandenhove, 1978. Column detail, showing passageway to Place Tikal.*

289

289 *Reconstruction, renovation, and additions to Hors-Château, Liège, Belgium. Charles Vandenhove, 1978. View of Place Tikal.*

LES HALLES, PARIS

In America, the New York partnership of Steven Peterson (b. 1940) — who collaborated with Colin Rowe on his 1978 entry to Roma Interotta — and Barbara Littenberg (b. 1949) has taken Latent Classicism into the realms of active design, attempting to achieve the solidity of nineteenth-century urbanism without sacrificing the structurally inspired simplicity of mid-twentieth century Modernism. Their entry (1979) for the Les Halles competition to fill the gaping hole in the heart of Paris left by the senseless destruction of the market buildings in the 1960s demonstrated their skill in this respect. Although it modified the Classical vocabulary almost beyond recognition, what they proposed had otherwise virtually all the ingredients of traditional urban architecture. The design included long loggias with simplified Doric colonnades, vestigial pediments held up by skinny cylindrical pillars, and elevations which had a clearly delineated base, middle and top. But the overall plan included long vistas and formal axes, including cross-axial paths atop vaguely Moorish arcades crossing sunken gardens and providing access to the subway and to the lower level of shops, which were required of each entry in the competition.

In 1986 Peterson, Littenberg Architects contributed a design, for the Miller Park Offices, for the redevelopment of several blocks in downtown Chattanooga, Tennessee, a mid-size southern city. The design guidelines, devised by Koetter, Kim & Associates, were strict, specifying open loggias, setbacks, cornices and brick or stone façades — in essence, traditional urban buildings. Peterson and Littenberg responded with a consciously American design, recalling Henry Hobson Richardson's 1880s version of Romanesque, but without the heavy massing and sculptural force of a Richardson design. The center of the building is cut through by a glazed arcade that recalls the open shopping streets of the nineteenth century and sustains the impression by its proportion and detail. In this, as in their other projects, Peterson and Littenberg reveal the strengths as well as the limitations of Latent Classicism in a large-scale urban scheme. Although the thin, planar quality of the façades is an apt reference to the thin-skinned Modernism of the 1920s, its marriage to the robust masonry forms of pre-Modernist urban architecture veers skittishly in the direction of parody.

John Blatteau's much more explicitly Classical entry for the Les Halles competition (1979) proposed a clearly defined central square, delimited by the colonnaded façades of stone-faced Classical buildings. Semicircular courtyards relieved the overall plan from being a stiff exercise while acknowledging the oblique placement of the church of Saint-Eustache and the round stock exchange building, La Bourse du Commerce (Paul Blondel, 1885).

290 *Urban design for Les Halles, Paris. Peterson, Littenberg, 1979. Unbuilt competition project. Aerial view of model.*

291 *Urban design for Les Halles, Paris. Peterson, Littenberg, 1979. Unbuilt competition project. Perspective east toward the Church of Saint-Eustache.*

292 *Urban design for Les Halles, Paris. Peterson, Littenberg, 1979. Unbuilt competition project. Perspective.*

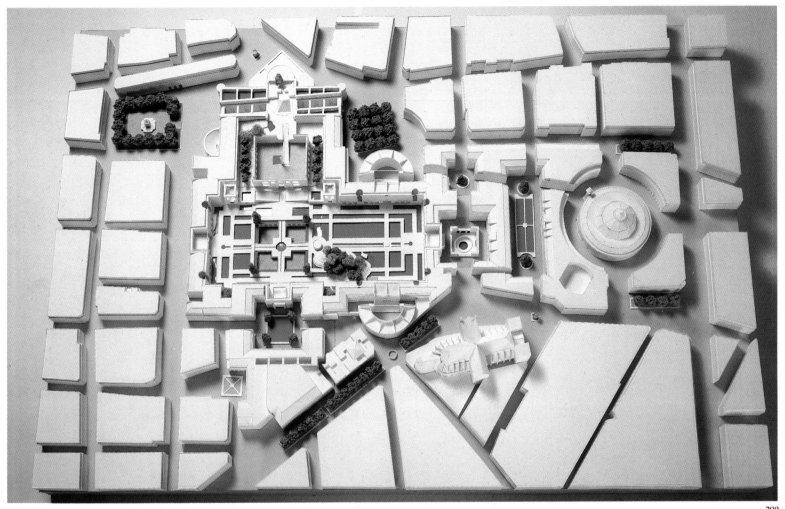

290

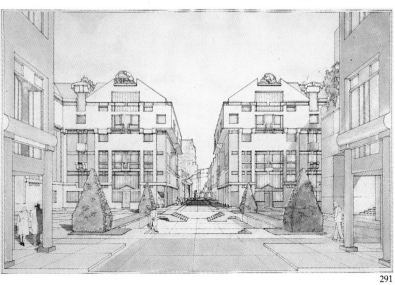

291

292

293 *Miller Park Offices, Chattanooga, Tennessee. Peterson, Littenberg, 1986. Unbuilt project. View of model.*

294 *Urban design for Les Halles, Paris. John Blatteau, 1979. Unbuilt competition project. Site plan.*

293

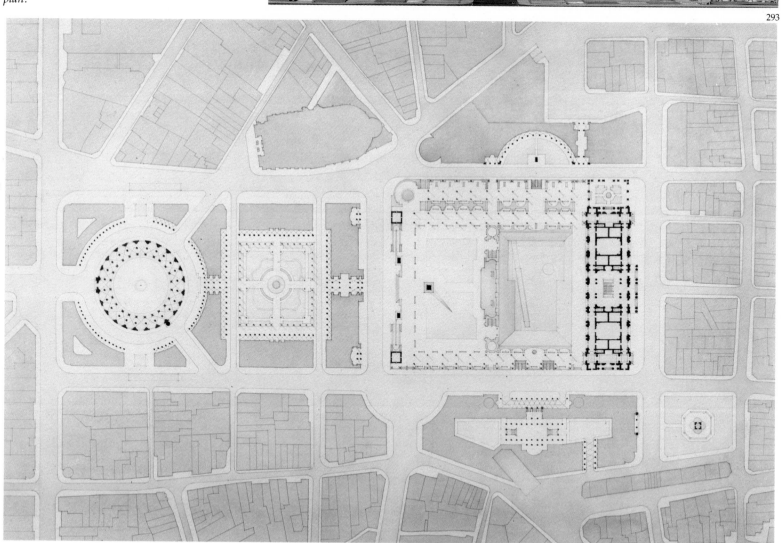

294

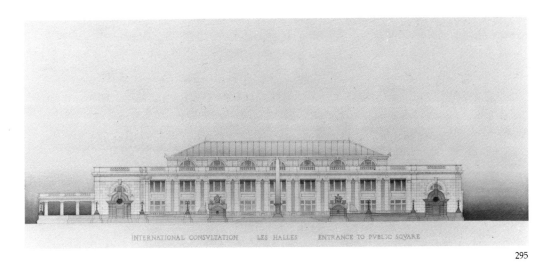

295

295 *Urban design for Les Halles, Paris. John Blatteau, 1979. Unbuilt competition project. Elevation of entrance to Public Hall.*

296 *Urban design for Les Halles, Paris. Ricardo Bofill/Taller de Arquitectura, 1974–9. Unbuilt project. Plan and sketches.*

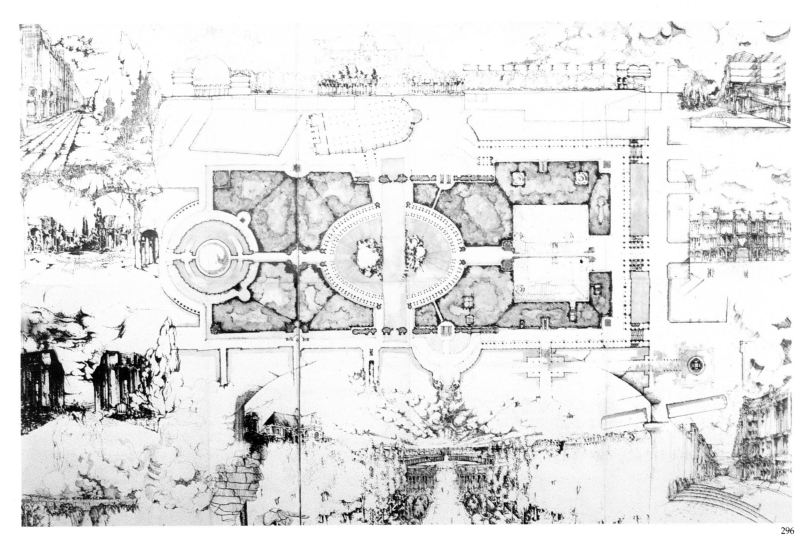

296

RICARDO BOFILL

Peterson and Littenberg's and Blatteau's proposals for Les Halles were entered in the competition which followed the debacle of an earlier design (1974–7) by Ricardo Bofill (b. 1939). In his *Plan Voisin* of 1925, Le Corbusier had proposed to rip out the heart of Paris and replace it with towers set on the intersections of a grid. At Les Halles, also in the heart of Paris, the site was already razed, and Bofill's goal, contrary to Le Corbusier's, was to give it a traditional urban configuration. For Bofill, only the living language of French Classicism was appropriate for this quintessentially urban site. He proposed a formal French garden, defined by Classically detailed buildings. In the center was an elliptical arena, surrounded by a peristyle. Somewhat modified, Bofill's design for Les Halles began construction, only to be stopped after the erection of the first few columns and razed to the ground on the orders of the Mayor of Paris, Jacques Chirac, who was engaged in a very public power struggle with the then-President Valéry Giscard d'Estaing. As a result, Paris lost a great scheme and got instead a cheap-looking version of an American shopping mall.

Bofill and his firm, Taller de Arquitectura, have gone further in our time than any others toward realizing the Classical sense of urbanism. Bofill's urbanism is simple: the buildings, usually accommodating stacks of repetitive apartments, create continuous walls which define and clearly articulate public open space — outdoor rooms reserved for pedestrians to use as parks, plazas, and playgrounds. The buildings themselves are Classical, not only in compositon but also in detail. Bofill's Classicism not only organizes the façades into the time-honored compositional triad of base, shaft, and cornice/capital, but ingeniously modulates the components of the housing type, including balconies, elevator and stair towers, and mechanical shafts, to create Classical effects such as those of colossal columnar orders and fluting. In addition, he organizes his façades according to strict principles of geometry and figuration and employs traditional Classical devices, notably the pilaster, to great effect. Moreover he achieves, down to the smallest details of windows and waterproofing, a convincing Classical composition in that most obdurate of modern materials, reinforced concrete. After decades of de-urbanization, Bofill has demonstrated that it is possible once again to endow commonplace building types with dignity and eloquence.

Bofill first came to international attention in the 1960s with two projects in Spain: the Barrio Gaudí (1964–8), a public housing project in Reus, Tarragona; and Xanadu (1966), an apartment-hotel in the holiday village of La Manzanera in Calpe on the Costa del Sol. Reus is the hometown of Antonio Gaudí (1852–1926), the Spanish Gothic-inspired architect whose dream-like fabulism has inspired Bofill's projects. At the Barrio Gaudí, Bofill and the Taller decided not to instruct the poor in how to live, but rather to ask them how they wanted to. The answers revealed that the prospective inhabitants of the Barrio wanted the intricate pattern and familiar features of the old city: squares, streets, alleys, and buildings with pitched pantile roofs. Bofill's highly disciplined tectonic puzzle included these elements — although some of the narrow walkways and plazas were pushed up to the roof. At Xanadu the Taller had the lighter task of designing resort architecture, and they produced a building closer in spirit to Gaudí's than the Barrio bearing his name, with the swooping curves and figural shapes of Gaudí, and pantiled roofs and rows of arched windows that court comparison with the regional vernacular.

297 *Les Echelles du Baroque, Paris. Ricardo Bofill Taller de Arquitectura, 1979–86. View of courtyard elevation.*

297

Bofill's great success as an architect and town-planner, however, has been in France. In the 1971 plan for La Petite Cathédrale at Cergy-Pontoise, Bofill seemed to go back to a more fundamental structuralism, embracing Gaudí's spiritual mentor, Viollet-le-Duc. Bofill turned to Viollet-le-Duc not for his Gothicism, but for the structural and geometric discipline that lay behind it, in order to create a design which was both structurally articulate and representative of history. At Cergy-Pontoise, the structure and, to a considerable extent, the mass of the housing block — if not the internal plan or the exterior decorative detail — strongly evoked a Gothic cathedral.

It was in the project for Les Halles that Bofill fully came to grips with the discipline of architectural urbanism as rationalized place-making by adopting Classicism as a language. Since Les Halles, Bofill has completed several projects in France, and he has gone even further in his use of the plans and elements of Classical architecture. In his project for a middle-class apartment complex in Marne-la-Vallée outside Paris, Bofill realized some of the promises of his Les Halles scheme. Allusion no longer overlays the geometry, as it did in the early Spanish projects. Instead there emerges a more profound synthesis, in which the Classical order and Classical space determine the form and atmosphere of the building and of the place. Bofill named the project Les Espaces d'Abraxas (1978–83) — *abraxas*, the word for the Mesopotamian symbol of good and evil, translates roughly as "magic." The spaces and the buildings that surround them compress a dense, theatrical, Classical urbanism into a comparatively small site in a typically anti-urban "new town," staging the drama of city life in a condensed version at the end of a commuter train line. The main building is the "Palace," a nineteen-story "U" opening onto the "Theater," another apartment building, nine stories high and wrapped around a semicircular amphitheater. Between the two, celebrating the axis from the entrance straight on through to the "window" cut out of the "Theater," is the triumphal "Arch," which also has apartment units in it.

Bofill and the designers of the Taller mocked the technological determinism of Modernism by using reinforced concrete structure and prefabricated concrete panels to build in the Classical style. At the same time, they refuted the notion of presumed Classical rigidity, violently stretching and inverting the Classical language to accommodate a new scale of habitation and new means of construction. The interior façade of the Theater has a seven-story colonnade with half-columns whose shafts are formed of panes of glass. Rather than supporting anything, the column is topped by a balcony. To complete the inversion, above the cornice one can see that the roof is planted with grass and trees. At the corners, and on the Theater's exterior façade, there is an even larger order of columns, this time "solid" concrete stairwells pushed out of the main block into fluted Doric columns.

As Paolo Portoghesi has observed, for Bofill, as for any serious Classicist today:

> The classicism . . . is not . . . the classicism of the academic tradition, nor that reinvented (and so very much impoverished) by post-illuminist, academic culture, emptied of its contradictions and entirely oriented towards analysis. Bofill confronts historical classicism, considering it as a fundamental reference for any operation of enrichment and development. This is a classicism to be rediscovered and redefined in order to assure its *continuity*, to augment its infinite history of dialectical variation and change.[76]

Although one may question some of Bofill's uses of the language, especially the inflation of scale required to suit mass-housing programs and to achieve maximum efficiency from the use of pre-casting techniques in reinforced concrete, it is clear, nonetheless, that he has restored the dialogue between place and form, symbol and program that existed before the hegemony of Modernism. Bofill does not seek to turn the technological clock back, as does Leon Krier. Instead, he carries further the Modern tradition, picking up, in part, where the American architect Louis Kahn left off. Kahn saw the potential of pre-cast concrete to become the "stone" of a revitalized twentieth-century monumentality. Bofill also continues the discourse between Classical form and the technology of reinforced concrete that preoccupied the French architect Auguste Perret. But Perret was too much involved in the skin-and-bones minimalism of Modernism, too competitive with Le Corbusier, to risk attempting a synthesis between the new building techniques and traditional symbolic language. Perret's buildings have the composition of Classical buildings, but their expression is inert, too direct a revelation of the structural frame. Bofill has none of the old hang-ups:

> I treat concrete like a noble material. . . . Many architects feel modern technology prevents them from reinterpreting the past. But I have found that precast concrete's repetitive nature has helped me to perfect a consistent logic for a new classical language.[77]

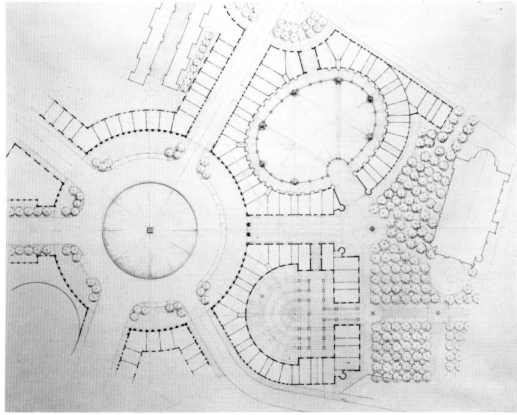

298 *Les Echelles du Baroque, Paris. Ricardo Bofill/Taller de Arquitectura, 1979–86. Site plan.*

299 *Les Echelles du Baroque, Paris. Ricardo Bofill/Taller de Arquitectura, 1979–86. Perspective of courtyard.*

298

299

277

In Paris, where the private realm of housing has traditionally created the places of the public realm, Bofill has designed housing that vies for position in the typological urban hierarchy. Les Echelles du Baroque (1979–86), a 274-unit housing project near the Montparnasse train station in Paris's 14th *arrondissement*, uses a combination of Classical spaces and pre-cast concrete Classical details similar to those used at Les Espaces d'Abraxas. The courtyard apartments are built around interlocking *places* — a half-circle theater, an ellipse, and a circle. Two colossal Doric column-stairtowers frame the entrance to the elliptical *place*, a glittering outdoor room enclosed by glass walls, including a glass colonnade capped by concrete capitals beneath a giant entablature of 6-foot (2-meter) triglyphs, positioned to hide the joints in the frieze, and window-metopes. The exterior façades appear more conventional, often with a clear distinction of rusticated base, *piano nobile* with segmental and triangular pediments over the windows, and an attic story of square windows.

The Antigone complex, in Montpellier (scheduled for completion in 1989, but already substantially realized), takes on the broader challenge of creating a new district and revitalizing the core of an existing city. Set at the edge of downtown, Bofill's vast residential and commercial project is also in line with the seventeenth-century aqueduct and eighteenth-century fountain of the Peyrou Gardens, which unite the center of the city with the distant countryside. The main plaza is La Place du Nombre d'Or (1978–84), paved in baked-earth stones and landscaped with a peristyle of palm trees, has a plan of ideal ratios and forms — the golden section, the square, the circle ultimately derived from the Renaissance, especially Michelangelo's St. Peter's. Although the façades on the exterior of the *place* are articulated into townhouse-scaled elevations, the interior has monumental façades. The shops and services of the ground floor are framed by the pedestals of the single and paired five-story-high pilasters which rise to a phantom dome, implied by three progressively projecting cornices, springing to the vault of the sky. The projecting cornices frame the heavenly dome and bring to human scale the vastness not only of nature, but of this housing complex built by man.

There are many ambiguities in Bofill's success. Although he has learned to manipulate his colossal orders with skill, the giantism of his projects is disturbing. Given a similar program to Bofill's in Montpellier — a commercial ground floor and six stories of apartments above — nineteenth- and early twentieth-century architects used the Classical language with considerable aesthetic success and functional deftness without the stridency of much of the Taller's work. In 1981 Portoghesi described the development of Bofill's design as a "progressive shedding of inhibitions."[78] The Post-Modernists' recent battle with the Modernist concepts of *Zeitgeist* and socio-technological "will to form" seems still too much on Bofill's mind. Lacking as well is the sensitivity to natural forms that is also a part of the Classical tradition.

300 *Espaces d'Abraxas, Marne–la–Vallée. Ricardo Bofill/Taller de Arquitectura, 1978–83.*

300

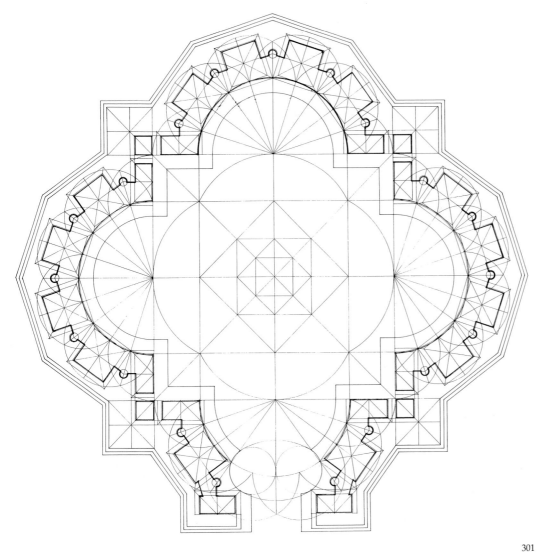

301

302

301   *Place du Nombre d'Or, Antigone complex, Montpellier, France. Ricardo Bofill/Taller de Arquitectura, 1978–84. Plan.*

302   *Place du Nombre d'Or, Antigone complex, Montpellier, France. Ricardo Bofill/Taller de Arquitectura, 1978–84. View of exterior elevations.*

303   *Place du Nombre d'Or, Antigone complex, Montpellier, France. Ricardo Bofill/Taller de Arquitectura, 1978–84. Exterior elevation.*

303

279

WHAT MIGHT HAVE BEEN: CHICAGO 1992

In 1984, Bruce Graham (b. 1925) of Skidmore, Owings, and Merrill, Chicago, together with William E. Brazley & Associates, led a team of architects including myself, Thomas Beeby, Charles Moore, Jaquelin Robertson, and Stanley Tigerman, in developing a master plan for the then-projected and now-abandoned 1992 Chicago World's Fair, which was intended to celebrate the 500th anniversary of Columbus's discovery of the New World. The plan dealt with two major concerns: first, the fair had to be a once-in-a-lifetime event which demanded to be experienced in person rather than through the media; second, it had to leave lasting, beneficial "residuals" for the city of Chicago in the form of parks, cultural facilities, and renewed urban infrastructure.

Like Chicago's 1893 World's Columbian Exposition, the 1992 fair was to take place on the lakefront. The site extended along the city's south side, using some of the land created for the 1933 Century of Progress Fair, including an island, as well as waterways and basins which formed the organizing fabric of the design. A new waterway running parallel to Nineteenth Street would be excavated to connect Lake Michigan and the fair site with the south branch of the Chicago River, providing a permanent amenity intended to stimulate redevelopment on the south side of Chicago.

The World's Fair plan called for a central entrance at Nineteenth Street opening to a circular court, from which a curved grid of pedestrian streets led to various national pavilions. To the north, the Court of Honor was in many ways an homage to the designers of the fair held in Chicago almost a century earlier, an aggressive declaration that representative, scenographic — and Classical — architecture had returned in strength. Colonnades lined the curved sides of the court, colossal temple fronts projected at regular intervals, and at the head of the lagoon, a glass-stepped pyramid evoked Hunt's Administration Building.

The fair would also have been a microcosm of the world's urbanism and a survey of its architecture. Not only were there the representative spaces of the academic tradition of the École des Beaux-Arts; there was also the tightly knit street pattern of a medieval city. Open country lay to the south, where a working farm was planned. At the head of the Court of Honor, a pyramid was to exemplify the foremost trend in current architecture: an age-old architectural theme — one that traces its origins back to both Egypt and the Pre-Columbian civilizations of the New World, would be restated in contemporary terms and realized in the most advanced materials. It was a Romantic vision — perhaps nowhere more so than in the suspended walkways that cut through the pedestals of huge glass columns, four on each side, as they led into the pyramid, brightly illuminated at night.

In June 1985, the Illinois General Assembly voted not to renew the fair's funding, and the project, which had begun in 1978, was dead. Politics killed it. Bruce Graham publicly protested: "We put public health in the hands of physicians, so why isn't the health of the city in the hands of the architects? Architects are the guardians of culture; they know how to project images and visions of cities."[79] Mayor Harold Washington and neighborhood activists were less sanguine, however; they feared that the fair would be an expensive and wasteful project whose parks and exhibition spaces were not the kind of lasting benefits that Chicago's South Side needed. The end result, however, is that the people of Chicago got only an embarrassing example of a failure of nerve. As the architecture critic Catherine T. Ingraham put it: "The old guard didn't have sufficient authority to erect a crystal palace, and the new guard didn't have sufficient authority to offer an alternative."[80]

304 *1992 Chicago World's Fair. Skidmore, Owings & Merrill, Chicago/William E. Brazley & Associates, with Thomas Beeby, Charles Moore, Jaquelin Robertson, Robert A. M. Stern, Stanley Tigerman, 1984–5. Perspective of Court of Honor.*

304

AFTERWORD

This book was written with the full knowledge that Classicism itself presents a provocation to those who cannot set it apart from the good guys (progressive and Modernist) versus bad guys (regressive and Classicist) dichotomy, which has characterized architectural debate for most of this century. While rejecting this view as simpleminded, I do not believe that Classicism, any more than any artistic movement, exists in a vacuum of pure aesthetics. Classicism is not absolute. It evolves in relation to internally generated artistic impulses, and to the external stimuli of programs and technology. In our time, Classicism has developed in response to the challenge brought to bear on it by competing, anti-Classical points of view, and then by the subsequent failure of virtually all of those viewpoints to satisfy the very critical social, environmental and cultural demands from which they claimed to derive. The anti-Classicism of this century has been as much the result of an hermetic aestheticism as the Classicism it so derided. Looking back from the end point of the century at the great artistic battles of its adolescence and early maturity, I am struck by how much of the debate was forced and illogical. What was largely a matter of taste was pursued as an issue of moral essence.

Where Modernism consisted of a number of movements such as Constructivism in Russia, Functionalism in Germany, and Purism in France, these were largely aesthetic, not cultural in their origins. On the other hand, one need only consider the varying Classicisms of Scandinavia, Italy, Germany and the United States in the 1920s and 30s to lay to rest any notions of a monolithic Classical aesthetic or culturally alienated architecture.

Built in large part upon negative impulses to reject the past and to overthrow tradition, Modernist movements were self-ordained to function brilliantly as catalysts to reform, but doomed to survive as enduring art. What was propounded as architectural liberation—the ahistorical impulse of stylistic modernism—now seems more like a brutalizing of the art, a reduction of vocabulary so severe as to prune architectural diction to the barest levels of communication. The counterpoint to Classicism today, in keeping with the retrospective quality of Post-Modernism, is once again an impulse toward anti-traditional reform; indeed we see about us a revival of Constructivism, Functionalism, Purism and other Modernist movements. Now, however, whatever socio-cultural meaning these styles might have had at their points of origin is no longer valid and they are being pursued for almost purely aesthetic reasons, advocated for their formal logic rather than as catalysts for societal revolution.

Architecture is an art of imagination and memory; it lives in the present and depends on the past for its meanings and ideals. How an architect approaches Classicism varies as much as the tradition itself but the intrinsic struggle is shared by all, to recall and to invent, to participate in a continuum yet contribute to its evolution, to be fresh and inventive without casting aside the time-honored values and the fundamental discourse that make it all intelligible. For so long the target of Modernist contempt, Classicism has been made to serve as a symbol of social and political dysfunction and of a troubled status quo. But in fact, cannot such an argument be made for the stale rhetoric of reductivist Modernism at this time? Is not the pleasure of the Classical canon, the discipline of its methods and the richness of its vocabulary an optimistic undertaking for architects operating in a culture that in other aspects values equally measure and bravura, computers and rock and roll? Classicism offers the architect a canon as a guide, but what a liberal and tolerant canon it is. It proposes models of excellence in composition and detail. It does not set out on a singular route but points out various ways. With its deep cultural ties, its innate hierarchy of form and detail and its capacity for purity and hybridization, Classicism still seems, after nearly a century's struggle to overthrow it, perhaps not inevitable and certainly not God-given, but surely much more than merely viable. Taken in its broad sense it seems to be a last best hope to recapture the act of building as a reconciliation of individuality and community, of the innovations demanded by a fluid culture and the sense of continuity and even of "traditional value" that such fluidity seems to make even more important. Classicism has flexibility and built-in tolerance, but do our architects have the skill and scholarship, the art and the wisdom to work within its great canon? Isn't it just easier to fling a pot of paint in the public's face?

BIBLIOGRAPHICAL ESSAY

At the heart of this project lie the many scholarly works which not only illuminate the careers of individual architects but also the various trends within Modern Classicism. Equally important are numerous recent books and essays which have influenced current theory and practice, and inevitably have helped to shape my approach. Wherever the specific words or ideas of another author are used, I have noted the source, but many other authors have helped guide my understanding of past and present Classicism, and of the Modernism which has challenged it in the recent past.

The principal thrust of *Modern Classicism* is the study of history as the key for understanding the essential and the evolving nature of Classicism within the Modern period. In this respect a number of texts are particularly useful. Geoffrey Scott's *The Architecture of Humanism: A Study in the History of Taste* (London: Constable and Co., 1914; second revised edition, 1924; with an introduction by David Watkin, The Architectural Press, 1980) is as brilliant today as it was at the beginning of the century in its rebuttal of the romantic, ethical, and mechanical bases of what then was becoming Modernist theory, and in its call for an empathetic, Humanist architectural tradition. John Summerson's *The Classical Language of Architecture* (London, British Broadcasting Corporation, 1963; revised and enlarged edition, London and New York: Thames & Hudson, 1980, 1987) remains the most lucid account of Classicism and its styles, placed in the historical framework; and a recent work by Alexander Tzonis and Liane Lefaivre, *Classical Architecture: The Poetics of Order* (Cambridge, Massachusetts and London, England: The MIT Press, 1986), offers a more theoretical interpretation of Classicism, presenting it as both a generative system and an ideal.

No discussion of Modern Classicism is possible without an understanding of the architectural history of the Modern period as a whole, and of the early, seminal figures of Modernism. Henry-Russell Hitchcock's provocative and pioneering overview, *Modern Architecture: Romanticism and Reintegration* (London: Payson & Clarke, Ltd., 1929; reprinted, New York: Hacker Art Books, 1970), is in many ways still the best guide to the complex issues that constitute the Modern condition in architecture. His more encyclopedic *Architecture, Nineteenth and Twentieth Centuries* (Baltimore: Penguin Books, 1958) also provides a good insight into the relationship of the Modern to Modernism. Vincent Scully's contribution, with its emphasis on the American condition, has been vital to the writing of *Modern Classicism*, both for his analysis of individual architects, as in *Frank Lloyd Wright* (New York: Braziller, 1960) and *Louis I. Kahn* (New York: Braziller, 1962), and for his more synoptic, interpretive texts, *Modern Architecture: The Architecture of Democracy* (first published as *Modern Architecture*, New York: Braziller, 1961; revised edition 1974) and *American Architecture and Urbanism* (New York: Praeger, 1969).

Kenneth Frampton, a tireless advocate of Modernism's perpetual relevance, has sympathetically interpreted the relationship of Classicism to Modernism, particularly in his discussions of Loos, Perret and Mies. His essays include: "Adolf Loos and the Crisis of Culture," in *The Architecture of Adolf Loos*, edited by Yehuda Safran and Wilfried Wang (London: Arts Council of Great Britain, 1985; second, amended edition, 1987) and "In Spite of the Void: A Note on Adolf Loos," (unpublished essay, 1987), or "Notes on Classical and Modern Themes in the Architecture of Mies van der Rohe and Auguste Perret," in *Classical Tradition and the Modern Movement: The Second*

International Alvar Aalto Symposium (Jyvaskyla, Finland: Finnish Association of Architects, symposium 1982, publication, 1985). Stuart Wrede's essay, "Asplund's Villa Snellman; the Classical, the Vernacular, and Modernism" appears in the same volume.

The thesis of *Modern Classicism,* however, depends on more than an assessment of its enduring power in relationship to an "inevitable" Modernism. Modern Classicism, as I and others have endeavored to see it, has to be reassessed as a powerful force in its own right with a genuine potential for contributing toward future architecture. The groundwork for this reassessment was initially laid by historians and critics who revealed Classicism's hold on the Modernist sensibility. Colin Rowe's essays, cited in the text, as well as others such as Philip Johnson's "Schinkel and Mies," speech of March, 1961, also cited, are key efforts in this regard. More importantly, there has emerged a growing recognition of the validity of Classicism in the twentieth century despite the inroads of Modernism. Major trends, figures, and styles considered as anti-Classical have been discussed in a broader cultural context than was frequently the case in the pro-Modernist historiography of the mid-century, revealing further unacknowledged connections to Classicism. Useful texts include David S. Andrew, *Louis Sullivan and the Polemics of Modern Architecture: The Present Against the Past* (Urbana and Chicago, Illinois: University of Illinois Press, 1985); Carl E. Schorske *Fin-de-Siècle Vienna: Politics and Culture* (New York: Vintage, 1981), for his discussion of Otto Wagner; Jonathan Barnett, *The Elusive City* (New York: Harper and Row, 1986), especially for his chapter on "The Monumental City"; Franco Borsi, *The Monumental Era: European Architecture and Design 1929–1939* (New York: Rizzoli International Publications, Inc., 1987); and Giorgio Ciucci, "Italian Architecture During the Fascist Period: Classicism between Neoclassicism and Rationalism: The many Souls of the Classical," *Perspecta: The Yale Architectural Journal*, 23 (1987). The recent re-evaluation of the architecture of the last century has led to a related reassessment of late eighteenth and nineteenth century architecture in works including Robin Middleton and David Watkin, *Neoclassical and 19th Century Architecture* (New York: Harry N. Abrams, 1976) and David Watkin and Tilman Mellinghoff, *German Architecture and the Classical Ideal* (Cambridge, Massachusetts: MIT Press; London: Thames & Hudson 1987). The critical re-examination of architecture associated with the École des Beaux-Arts has been crucial in understanding Classicism as a contemporary force. Two collections of essays should be noted: *The Beaux-Arts and Nineteenth-Century French Architecture*, edited by Robin Middleton (Cambridge, Massachusetts: MIT Press; London: Thames & Hudson 1982) and *The Architecture of the École des Beaux-Arts*, edited by Arthur Drexler, especially the essays by Arthur Drexler, "Engineer's Architecture: Truth and its Consequences," David Van Zanten, "Architectural Composition at the École des Beaux-Arts from Charles Percier to Charler Garnier," and Neil Levine, "The Romantic Idea of Architectural Legibility: Henri Labrouste and the Néo-Grec," (New York: The Museum of Modern Art, 1977).

Leon Krier has become a leading revisionist of twentieth-century architectural history by taking on controversial subjects: *Albert Speer: Architecture 1932–42*, edited by Leon Krier, foreword by Albert Speer, essays by Lars Olof Larsson, "Classicism in the Architecture of the XXth Century," and Leon Krier, "An Architecture of Desire" (Brussels: Archives d'Architecture Moderne, 1985). David Watkin has placed his revision of the twentieth century in the context of the Modern period as a whole, in *A History of Western Architecture* (New York: Thames and Hudson; London: Barrie and Jenkins, 1986). For a somewhat parallel position, developed in philosophical terms, see Roger Scruton, *The Aesthetics of Architecture* (Princeton, New Jersey: Princeton University Press, 1979). For a diametrically opposed argument, stating that Classicism and the Classical ideal are finished, see Peter Eisenman, "The End of the Classical: the End of the Beginning, the End of the End," *Perspecta 21* (1986).

While some of these arguments against the failings of Modernism may seem as over-zealous as the Modernist diatribes against tradition of a previous era, it should be remembered that without the Post-Modernist challenge, architects and historians might not have been propelled to once again interpret traditional architecture—to understand Classicism. Most importantly, it has often been polemicists and not scholars who have published forgotten or neglected Classical work, making it available to students, architects, and the general public, whether in books such as Krier's on Speer or reprints such as those in the Classical America series, including William R. Ware's *An American Vignola* (New York: W. W. Norton & Co., 1977), which was spearheaded by Henry Hope Reed.

To me, the central issue arising in any consideration of Modern Classicism is its continuing validity, and indeed vitality, as an architectural language. No author has done more to address this question—calling attention to the renewal of Classicism as part of a general Post-Modernist condition—than Charles Jencks, whose recent *Post-Modernism: The New Classicism in Art and Architecture* (New York: Rizzoli; London: Academy Editions, 1987) is a summation of the cultural and philosphical stance which has characterized his prolific production as a writer and editor. While Jencks takes an encyclopedic approach, several other authors have tried to establish a somewhat narrower position within the revival of Classicism, especially Krier and Demetri Porphyrios, both cited in the text, who have argued strongly for a pure Classicism grounded in the tectonics of building. The American Classicists John Blatteau and Allan Greenberg also have taken a hard line regarding the appropriateness of Classicism.

While I do not underestimate the opposing argument that the Post-Modernist condition precludes the continuity of the Classical, I maintain that Classicism is a living language and idea. I prefer the argument offered by Mark Girouard, in "Creation or Pastiche?—The Uses and Abuses of Classicism," *The Royal Society for the Encouragement of Arts, Manufactures and Commerce Journal* 134 (January 1986), that the evidence of the last two centuries shows that Classicism has accommodated any number of new building technologies and programs, and will continue to evolve.

In reviewing my own writings on the topics of Classicism and continuity, I have found that the most critical are: "The Doubles of Post-Modern," *Via: The Harvard Architectural Review*, 1 (Spring 1980); "Classicism in Context," *Post-Modern Classicism: The New Synthesis*, edited by Charles Jencks, Profile 28, Architectural Design 50 (May–June 1980); and "On Style, Classicism, and Pedagogy," *Précis: The Journal of the Graduate School of Architecture and Planning, Columbia University in the City of New York* 5 (Fall 1984).

In conclusion, the most important sources, the essential texts, are the buildings themselves.

286

NOTES

THE RISE OF MODERN CLASSICISM

1 T. S. Eliot, "Tradition and the Individual Talent," *The Sacred Wood: Essays on Poetry and Criticism* (London: Methuen, 1920): 49

2 Reyner Banham, *Theory and Design in the First Machine Age* (London: The Architectural Press, 1960; second edition, Cambridge, Massachusetts: MIT Press, 1980): 327

3 Colin Rowe, "Neo-'Classicism' and Modern Architecture II" (written 1956-7), *Oppositions* 1 (1973); reprinted in *The Mathematics of the Ideal Villa and Other Essays* (Cambridge, Massachusetts and London: MIT Press, 1976): 140

4 Leon Battista Alberti, *On Painting*, revised edition, translated with introduction and notes by John R. Spencer (New Haven: Yale University Press, and London: Routledge & Kegan Paul Ltd, 1970): 39–40

5 Leon Battista Alberti, *De re aedificatoria* ("Ten Books on Architecture"), James Leoni Edition: London, 1726; reprinted, Joseph Rykwert, editor (London: Tiranti, 1955): Preface, IX

6 Henry Wotton, *Elements of Architecture* (London, 1624)

7 Vitruvius, *The Ten Books of Architecture*, translated by Morris Hicky Morgan (Cambridge: Harvard University Press, 1914): Book III, Chapter 1, 72–5

8 John Summerson, *The Classical Language of Architecture* (London: British Broadcasting Corporation, 1963): 18

9 Leon Battista Alberti, *De re aedificatoria, op. cit.*: Book VI, Chapter II, 113

10 Andrea Palladio, *The Four Books of Architecture*, translated by James Leoni with notes by Inigo Jones (London, 1742; New York: Da Capo, 1965)

11 James S. Ackerman, *Palladio* (Middlesex, England, and New York: Penguin, 1966): 21

12 Andrea Palladio, *The Four Books of Architecture, op. cit.*: Book II, Chapter XVI, 65

13 Peter Murray, *The Architecture of the Italian Renaissance* (New York: Schocken Books, 1963): 247–8 (London: Thames & Hudson, 1969): 232

14 For an argument against the attribution to Perrault, *see* Christian Norberg-Schulz, *Baroque Architecture* (New York: Harry N. Abrams, 1971): 321–2, 367 n.19. Robin Middleton and David Watkin write that "those who saw the relevant documents and drawings before they were destroyed in the fire at the Hôtel de Ville in 1870 found no evidence to dispute his claim to authorship." Middleton and Watkin, *Neoclassical and 19th Century Architecture* (London: Thames & Hudson, New York: Harry N. Abrams, 1976): 9

15 Claude Perrault, *A Treatise on the Five Orders of Columns in Architecture*, translated by John James (London: Sturt, 1708)

16 Marc-Antoine Laugier, *An Essay on Architecture*, translated by Wolfgang and Anni Herrman (Los Angeles: Hennessey & Ingalls, 1977)

17 Jean-Louis de Cordemoy, *Nouveau Traité de toute l'architecture: ou l'art 'de bastir: utile aux entrepreneurs et aux ouvriers* (1706)

18 Marc-Antoine Laugier, *An Essay on Architecture, op. cit.*: 40

19 Helen Rosenau, *Boullée's Treatise on Architecture* (London: Alec Tiranti, 1953, in French): 35–6 "[*Les autres avantages du corps sphérique*] *sont de développer à nos yeux la plus grande surface, ce qui le rend majestueux. D'avoir la forme la plus simple: beauté qui provient de ce que sa surface est sans interruption aucune; et de joindre à toutes ces qualités celle de la grâce, car le contour qui dessine ce corps est aussi doux aussi coulant qu'il soit possible.*")

20 Helen Rosenau, *Boullée's Treatise on Architecture, op. cit.*: 27
("*La* [architecture] *définerai-je avec Vitruve, l'art de bâtir? Non. Il y a, dans cette définition, une erreur grossière. Vitruve prend l'effet pour la cause.*)

21 *Ibid.*: 51 ("*C'est la lumière qui produit les effets.*")

22 Claude-Nicolas Ledoux, prospectus of *Architecture Considered in Relation to Art, Mores and Legislation*, translated by Anthony Vidler and Kevin C. Lippert, with the assistance of Marie-Christine Sosthé, in *Architecture de C. N. Ledoux* (Paris: 1818; Princeton, New Jersey: Princeton Architectural Press, 1983): xv

23 Portions of the following discussion of Jefferson's architecture appeared previously in Robert A. M. Stern, *Pride of Place: Building the American Dream* (Boston: Houghton-Mifflin; New York: American Heritage, 1986)

24 Jefferson to Latrobe, Monticello, 12 June, 1817, reprinted in Fiske Kimball, *Thomas Jefferson, Architect* (Boston: 1916; New York: Da Capo Press, 1968): 187–8

25 *Collection of Architectural Designs by Karl Friedrich Schinkel*, edited by Kenneth S. Hazlett, Stephen O'Malley and Christopher Rudolph (Chicago: Exedra Books, 1981) reprint, with notes and translation, of *Sammlung Architektonischer Entwürfe von Carl Friedrich Schinkel* (Berlin: Ernst & Korn, 1866): 48

26 J. N. L. Durand, *Précis des Leçons d'Architecture Données à l'École Royale Polytechnique* (Paris: Firmin Didot, 1819; reprint, Nordlingen, West Germany: Uhl, 1981)

27 J. N. L. Durand, *Recueil et Parallèle des Edifices de tout Genre* (Paris: École Polytechnique, 1800; Princeton: Princeton Architectural Press, 1981)

28 J. N. L. Durand, *Précis des Leçons d'Architecture Donnée à l'École Royale Polytechnique, op. cit.*: 18 ("*Soit que l'on consulte la raison, soit que l'on examine les monuments, il est evident que plaire n'a jamais pu être le but de l'architecture, ni la décoration architectonique être son objet. L'utilité publique et particulière, le bonheur et la conservation des individus et de la société, tel est, comme nous l'avons vu d'abord, le but de l'architecture.*")

29 *Ibid.*: 21 (". . . *qu'en architecture l'économie, loin d'être, ainsi qu'on le croit généralement, un obstacle à la beauté, en est au contraire la source la plus féconde.*")

30 *See* Robert Mark, *Experiments in Gothic Structure* (Cambridge, Massachusetts and London: MIT Press, 1982). Using the analytical techniques of structural mechanics, Mark, who began his analysis in 1967, discovered that while flying buttresses were indeed structural, the finials crowning them, like the vault ribs in the interior, were not. An early critic of Viollet-le-Duc's structural analysis was Pol Abraham (1891–1966), who wrote *Viollet-le-Duc et le Rationalisme Mediéval* (Paris: Vincent, Fréal & Cie, 1934)

31 Viollet-le-Duc, *Discourses on Architecture* (Paris: A. Morel, 1872), translated by Benjamin Bucknall (New York: Grove Press, 1959)

32 Emile Zola, *Le Ventre de Paris* (1874; Paris: Livre de Poche, Fasquelle, 1964): 338–9. This was pointed out in Neil Levine's essay, "The Book and the Building: Hugo's Theory of Architecture and Labrouste's Bibliothèque Ste.-Geneviève," in *The Beaux-Arts and Nineteenth-Century French Architecture*, edited by Robin Middleton (London: Thames & Hudson and Cambridge, Massachusetts: MIT Press, 1982): 141–2

33 Geoffrey Scott, *The Architecture of Humanism* (first edition, Boston: Houghton and London: Constable, 1914; edition cited is London: The Architectural Press, 1980): 110

34 Robin Middleton and David Watkin, *Neoclassical and 19th Century Architecture, op. cit.*: 359

35 The connection between Hugo and Labrouste has been examined at length by Neil Levine in "The Book and the Building," *op. cit.*

36 From notes for a biography of Charles Garnier by Mme. Garnier (1903), cited in *Charles Garnier et L'Opéra*, exhibition catalogue (Paris: L'Académie d'Architecture, 1961): 11

37 Louis Sullivan, *The Autobiography of an Idea* (New York: Press of the American Institute of Architects, 1924): 325

38 Louis Sullivan, "The Tall Office Building Artistically Considered", first published in *Lippincott's* 57 (March, 1896): 403, reprinted in Sullivan, *Kindergarten Chats and Other Writings* (New York: George Wittenborn, 1947): 202

39 Montgomery Schuyler, "The 'Skyscraper' up To Date," *Architectural Review* 8 (January–March 1889): 257

40 Frank Lloyd Wright, "The Art and Craft of the Machine," an address to the Chicago Arts and Crafts Society, at Hull House, 6 March 1901, in Edgar Kaufmann, Ben Raeburn, editors, *Frank Lloyd Wright: Writings and Buildings* (New York: Meridian Books, 1960)

41 Otto Wagner, *Moderne Architektur* (Vienna, 1895), cited and translated in Carl E. Schorske, *Fin-de-Siècle Vienna: Politics and Culture* (New York: Vintage, 1981): 74

42 Otto Wagner, *Die Baukunst unserer Zeit. Dem Baukunstjünger ein Führer auf diesem Kunstgebiet* (Vienna, 1914, 4th edition)

43 Adolf Loos, "Ornament and Crime," translated in *Programs and Manifestoes on 20th-Century Architecture*, edited by Ulrich Conrads, translated by Michael Bullock (Cambridge, Massachusetts: MIT Press, 1970): 20

44 Adolf Loos, "Ornament and Crime," *op. cit.*: 24

45 Adolf Loos, "Architecture," translated in *The Architecture of Adolf Loos*, edited by Yehuda Safran and Wilfried Wang (London: British Arts Council exhibition catalogue, 2nd edition, 1987): 108

46 *Ibid.*: 104

47 *Ibid.*: 109

48 *The Chicago Tribune Competition*, Volume I (New York: Rizzoli, 1980); reprint of "The International Competition for a New Administration Building for the Chicago Tribune, 1922.": 3

49 Charles Holden (unsigned), "Thoughts for the Strong," *Architectural Review*, 18 (July 1905): 27

50 Jože Plečnik, in *Jože Plečnik, Architecte 1872–1957*, edited by François Burckhardt (Paris: Centre de Creation Industrielle, exhibition catalogue, 1986: back cover

51 Frank Lloyd Wright, "The Art and Craft of the Machine," *op. cit.*: 55–73

52 Frank Lloyd Wright, *A Testament* (New York: Horizon Press, 1957): 20

53 Bernard R. Maybeck, quoted in William H. Jordy, "Progressive and Academic Ideals at the Turn of the Twentieth Century," *American Buildings and their Architects*, volume 3 (Garden City, New York: Doubleday & Col., 1972): 300. From Maybeck's own brochure, *Palace of the Fine Arts and Lagoon: Panama-Pacific International Exposition, 1915* (San Francisco: Paul Elder, 1915)

54 Paul Philippe Cret, "The Architect as Collaborator of the Engineer," *Architectural Forum*, 49 (July 1928): 100

55 Benito Mussolini, speech at the Campadoglio to commemorate the 2,677th anniversary of the founding of Rome, quoted in *Armando Brasini: Roma Imperiale*, essay by Donald Clinton and Karen Wilkin (Edmonton, Alberta: exhibition catalogue, 1978): 21

56 *See* Spiro Kostoff, *The Third Rome, 1870–1950, Traffic and Glory* (exhibition catalogue, University Art Museum, Berkeley, California, and Cabinetto Fotografico Nazionale, Rome, 1973)

57 Marcello Piacentini, quoted in Arnold Whittick, *European Architecture in the Twentieth Century* (New York: Abelard-Schuman, Intext Publisher, 1974): 472

58 This is discussed in Lars Olof Larsson, *Albert Speer: Le Plan de Berlin 1937–1943*, translated into French by Beatrice Loyer (Brussels: Archives d'Architecture Moderne, 1983): 223

59 Léon Krier, editor, "Albert Speer: Architecture 1932–42", in *Classicism in the Architecture of the XXth Century*, Lars Olof Larsson (Brussels: Archives d'Architecture Moderne, 1985): 50

60 Léon Krier, "Krier on Speer", *Architectural Review* 173 (February 1983): 35

61 Albert Speer, foreword, "An Architecture of Desire", in *Classicism in the Architecture of the XXth Century*, Lars Olof Larsson (Brussels: Archives d'Architecture Moderne, 1985): 213

62 Colin St. John Wilson, "Speer and the Fear of Freedom," *Architectural Review* (June 1983): 25

63 Albert Speer, *Erinnerungen* (Berlin, 1969): 94f., in Lars Olof Larsson, "Classicism in the Architecture of the 20th Century": 238

64 Le Corbusier, *Towards a New Architecture*, translated by Frederick Etchells (London: The Architectural Press 1927; New York; Praeger, 1946): 121

65 Le Corbusier, *Towards a New Architecture, op. cit.*: 31

66 Colin Rowe, "The Mathematics of the Ideal Villa," *The Architectural Review*, 1947, reprinted in *The Mathematics of the Ideal Villa and Other Essays* (Cambridge, Massachusetts and London: MIT Press, 1976)

67 Le Corbusier, *Précisions sur un état présent de l'architecture et de l'urbanisme* (Paris, 1930): 136–8 (*Plan libre, façade libre, ossature indépendant*)

68 Mies van der Rohe, "Architecture and the Times" (1924), in Philip Johnson, *Mies van der Rohe* (New York: Museum of Modern Art, 1947): 191–2, originally published in German as *Baukunst und Zeitwille, Der Querschnitt* 4, 1924: 31–2

69 Philip Johnson, "Schinkel and Mies," speech of 13 March, 1961, reprinted in *Philip Johnson, Writings* (New York: Oxford University Press, 1979): 167, 171

70 Lewis Mumford, *Sticks and Stones: A Study of American Architecture and Civilization* (New York: Boni & Liveright, 1924): 141–2

71 Sigfried Giedion, in collaboration with Fernand Léger and José Luis Sert, "Nine Points on Monumentality", (1943), quoted in Kenneth Frampton, *Modern Architecture: A Critical History* (New York and Toronto: Oxford University Press, 1980): 223

72 Vincent Scully, *Modern Architecture: The Architecture of Democracy* (New York: Braziller, 1961): 40

73 Vincent Scully, *Modern Architecture: The Architecture of Democracy, op. cit.*: 48

74 Edward Durrell Stone, quoted in "A New Public Architecture" (unsigned), *Architectural Forum* 110 (January 1959): 88

75 "A New Public Architecture", *op. cit.*: 84

76 Paraphrase of Ellsworth Bunker's comments in "A New Public Architecture", *op. cit.*: 86

77 Reyner Banham, quoted in "New Office Building in London", *Architectural Forum* 114 (March 1961): 84

78 Philip Johnson, "Whither Away—Non-Miesian Directions," speech, Yale University, 5 Febuary 1959, first published in *Philip Johnson: Writings, op. cit.*: 227

79 Louis Kahn, "Monumentality" in *New Architecture and City Planning, A Symposium*, edited by Paul Zucker (New York: 1944)

80 Alexander Tzonis and Liane Lefaivre, *Classical Architecture: The Poetics of Order* (Cambridge, Massachusetts and London: MIT Press, 1986): ix

CURRENT CLASSICISM

1 Robert A. M. Stern, "The Doubles of Post-Modern," *Harvard Architecture Review*, 1 (Spring 1980)

2 Abdel Wahed El-Wakil, architect's statement, in "Tradition and Architecture: Palaces, Public Buildings and Houses," *Architectural Design* 57 (May–June 1987): 53

3 Lucien Steil, "Tradition and Architecture: Palaces, Public Buildings and Houses" *op. cit.*: 5

4 Vincent Scully, "The Threat and the Promise of Urban Redevelopment in New Haven," *Zodiac* 17 (1967): 171

5 Lewis Mumford, *Sticks and Stones: A Study of American Architecture and Civilization, op. cit.*: 195–6

6 Charles W. Moore, "Hadrian's Villa," *Perspecta* 6 (1960)

7 Michael Graves, "The Swedish Connection," *The Journal of Architectural Education* 29 (September 1975)

8 Allan Greenberg, "Lutyens' Architecture Restudied," *Perspecta* 12 (1969)

9 Charles Jencks has made a similar analysis of the varying approaches to Classicism by con-

temporary architects in several books and articles, especially in *Free Style Classicism* (Profile 39, Architectural Design 52, January–February 1982) and, most recently, in *Post-Modernism: The New Classicism in Art and Architecture* (New York: Rizzoli, 1987; London: Academy Editions, 1987). The latter includes similar categories ("Fundamentalist Classicism" and "Urbanist Classicism" among them) and there are many thematic parallels, yet there are also distinct differences in our definitions of each approach and our interpretation of each architect's work

10 Robert Venturi, *Complexity and Contradiction in Architecture* (New York: Museum of Modern Art, 1966): 44

11 Robert Venturi, Denise Scott Brown, Steven Izenour, *Learning from Las Vegas* (Cambridge, Massachusetts: MIT Press, 1972): 64

12 Denise Scott Brown, "Learning the Wrong Lessons from the Beaux-Arts," *Architectural Design* 48 (November–December 1978): 33

13 Robert Venturi, *Complexity & Contradiction in Architecture, op. cit.*: 118

14 Prince Charles, quoted in "Controversy in London," *Architectural Record* 172 (August 1984): 55

15 Originally published in *Perspecta* 11 (1967), reprinted in a revised form as "Inclusive and Exclusive," in Charles Moore and Gerald Allen, *Dimensions* (New York: Architectural Record Books, 1976): 51

16 Charles Moore, quoted in Charles Jencks, Introduction, *Post-Modern Classicism: The New Synthesis*, edited by Charles Jencks, Profile 28, *Architectural Design* 50 (May–June, 1980): 9

17 Lebbeus Woods, letter to the editor, "Views—Magic Fountain: Back-Splash," *Progressive Architecture* 60 (January 1979): 8

18 Charles Jencks, *Post-Modern Classicism, op. cit.*: 9

19 Geoffrey Scott, *The Architecture of Humanism: A Study in the History of Taste, op. cit.*: 213

20 Philip Johnson, in *Architecture* 72 (July 1983): 64

21 Arata Isozaki, "The Ledoux Connection," *Free Style Classicism, op. cit.*: 28

22 Yukio Futagawa, "Interview with Arata Isozaki," *GA Document* 8 (October 1983): 4, 8, 10

23 Terry Farrell, quoted in Simon Jenkins, "The Picturesque Revival: Architecture of Terry Farrell," *Country Life* 179 (2 January, 1986): 34–6

24 Simon Jenkins, "The Picturesque Revival: Architecture of Terry Farrell," *op. cit.*: 36

25 Charles Jencks, *What is Post-Modernism?* (London: Academy Editions; New York: St Martin's Press, 1986): 14

26 Charles Jencks, "Star-Struck House," *House and Garden* 157 (April 1985): 121

27 James Stirling, quoted in *James Stirling, Buildings and Projects: James Stirling, Michael Wilford and Associates*, edited by Peter Arnell and Ted Bickford, introduction by Colin Rowe (London: The Architectural Press, 1984): 252

28 Mario Campi, quoted in "Within the Bounds of Reason," *Architectural Record* (July 1986): 88

29 Mario Botta, quoted in Livio Dimitriu, "Architecture and Morality: An Interview with Mario Botta," *Perspecta* 20 (1983): 12

30 Kevin Roche, in *Conversations with Architects*, John W. Cook and Heinrich Klotz (New York: Praeger 1973): 68–9

31 Kevin Roche, in "Symbol and Workplace: an Interview with Kevin Roche," Mildred F. Schmertz, *Architectural Record* 172 (September 1984): 106

32 *Ibid.*: 106

33 Aldo Rossi, The Architecture of the City (*L'Architettura della Città*), (Padua: Marsilio Editori, 1966; New York: Institute for Architecture and Urban Studies, Cambridge, Massachusetts and London: MIT Press, 1982): 46

34 Ignasi de Solà-Morales, "Neo-Rationalism & Figuration," Building and Rational Architecture, Profile 53, *Architectural Design* 54 (May–June, 1984): 18

35 Aldo Rossi, *A Scientific Autobiography*, translated by Lawrence Venuti (Published for the Graham Foundation for Advanced Studies in the Fine Arts, Chicago, Illinois, and The Institute for Architecture and Urban Studies, New York, by the MIT Press, Cambridge, Massachusetts and London, 1981)

36 *Ibid.*: 1

37 Aldo Rossi, "The Blue of the Sky: Modena Cemetery, 1971 and 1977," *Free Style Classicism, op. cit.*: 40

38 Architects' statement, in "A Landmark for the City: Office Building in Buenos Aires," *Lotus International* 42: 27

39 Rafael Moneo, *The Charlottesville Tapes*, transcript of the conference at the University of Virginia School of Architecture, Charlottesville, Virginia, 12–13 November 1982 (New York: Rizzoli, 1985): 77

40 José-Ignacio Linazasoro, "Ornament and Classical Order," *Classicism Is Not A Style*, Profile 41, *Architectural Design* 52 (May–June 1982): 23

41 Miguel Garay and José-Ignacio Linazasoro, "School at Ikastola," *Classicism Is Not a Style, op. cit.*: 80

42 Quoted in Charles K. Gandee, "Home is Where the Hut Is," *Architectural Record* 66 (November 1985): 132

43 Architect's statement, 1984

44 Demetri Porphyrios, introduction, *Classicism Is Not A Style, op. cit.*: 5

45 *Ibid.*: 51

46 Demetri Porphyrios, "Building and Rational Architecture," *Profile 53, Architectural Design* 54 (May–June 1984): 31

47 Demetri Porphyrios, "The Fitzwilliam Museum Extension," *Architectural Design* 56 (August 1986): 17

48 Raymond Erith, 1953, *in* Lucy Archer, *Raymond Erith, Architect* (Burford, Oxfordshire: The Cygnet Press, 1985): 34

49 Raymond Erith, "The Essential Qualities of Architecture," *The Architects' Journal* (15 January 1959): 85

50 Leon Krier, "Raymond Erith," *Art & Design* (May 1986): 5

51 Quinlan Terry, "Origins of the Orders," *Architectural Review* 173 (February 1983): 29

52 Raymond Erith, quoted in Lucy Archer, *Raymond Erith, Architect, op. cit.*: 88

53 Quinlan Terry, "A Question of Style," *Architectural Design* 49 (March–April 1979): 109

54 Clive Aslet, *Quinlan Terry: The Revival of Architecture* (New York: Viking, 1986): 194–5

55 Richard J. Betts, "Looking for America: Part I," *ACSA Forum*, Chicago, 2–3 October, 1986: 14

56 Architect's statement, January 1986: 2

57 There are many historic examples of this in American cities, perhaps most memorably the Standard Oil Building in downtown New York (Ebenezer L. Roberts, 1886; Carrère & Hastings, 1896; Shreve, Lamb & Blake, 1922–6)

58 Francesco Dal Co, *Kevin Roche* (New York: Rizzoli, 1985): 51

59 Robert Adam, in "Profile: Robert Adam," *Royal Institute of British Architects' Journal* 93 (March 1986): 6–7

60 John Outram, interviewed by David Pearce, "Profile: John Outram," *Royal Institute of British Architects' Journal* 93 (January 1986): 5

61 *Ibid.*: 7

62 *Ibid.*: 6

63 *Ibid.*: 6

64 Richard J. Betts, "Looking for America: Part I," *op. cit.*: 24, 26

65 Robert Venturi, *Complexity and Contradiction in Architecture, op. cit.*: 104

66 Vincent Scully, introduction, Robert Venturi, *Complexity and Contradiction in Architecture, op. cit.*: 9

67 Colin Rowe and Fred Koetter, *Collage City* (Cambridge, Massachusetts and London: MIT Press, 1978): 144–5

68 Alexander Tzonis and Liane LeFaivre, *Classical Architecture: The Poetics of Order, op. cit.*: 266

69 Christian Norberg-Schulz, "Towards an Authentic Architecture," in *The Presence of the Past: First International Exhibition of Architecture* (Venice: Edizioni La Biennale di Venezia 1980): 21

70 Leon Krier, "Leon Krier: School at St. Quentin-en-Yvelines, France, 1978," in "Classicism Is Not A Style," *op. cit.*: 69

71 Leon Krier, "The Reconstruction of Vernacular Building and Classical Architecture," *Architectural Journal* (September 1984): 56

72 Leon Krier, "Leon Krier: School at St. Quentin-en-Yvelines, France, 1978," *op. cit.*: 59

73 *Ibid.*: 64

74 Trevor Boddy, "The New Regionalism and Mississauga City Hall," in *Mississauga City Hall: A Canadian Competition* (New York: Rizzoli, 1984)

75 Interview with Charles Vandenhove in *Charles Vandenhove: Une Architecture de la densité*, edited by Pierre Mardaga, catalogue published in conjunction with the exposition presented by L'Institut Français d'Architecture (Liège and Brussels, Belgium: Pierre Mardaga, 1985): 18

("*Le danger, c'est de faire de grandes unités, de grands ensembles . . . il faut d'abord que ceux qui font la maison des autres aient du plaisir à le faire. Donc, il faut restaurer le savoir-faire de tous les artisans et des compagnons qui construisent une maison. . . . Et c'est là ou notre société déraille—Charlie Chaplin avait déja compris ça quand il montrait, dans ses films, des gens excédé par le travail à la chaine—il faut que chacun reprenne du plaisir à faire si on veut changer le société.*")

76 Paolo Portoghesi in *Bofill/Taller de Arquitectura: Los Espacios de Abraxas: El Palacio, El Theatro, El Arco*, edited by Annabelle d'Huart (Paris: Editions L'Equerre, 1981): 5

77 Ricardo Bofill, quoted in "Precast Classicism," by Deborah K. Dietsch, *Progressive Architecture* 174 (January 1986): 131

78 Paolo Portoghesi in *Bofill/Taller de Arquitectura: Los Espacios de Abraxas: El Palacio, El Theatro, El Arco*, *op. cit.*: 5

79 Bruce Graham quoted in "Land of No Discovery," by Catherine T. Ingraham, *Inland Architect* 30 (May–June 1986): 47

80 Catherine T. Ingraham, "Land of No Discovery," *op. cit.*: 53

INDEX

Page numbers in italic refer to the illustrations

ACKNOWLEDGMENTS

THE RISE OF MODERN CLASSICISM

Julie Ainsworth, 81; Albertina, Vienna, 48, 50; Archivi Alinari, Florence, 3, 5; American Battle Monuments Commission, Garches, 79, 80; Wayne Andrews, Chicago, 13, 33, 34, 39, 64, 65, 75, 98, 111; The Architectural Association, London, 38, 44, 55, 56, 77, 103 (F. R. Yerbury) 51, 93, 94; James Austin, Cambridge, 4, 9, 12, 25, 28; Tim Benton, London, 95; Bibliothèque Nationale, Paris, 11; Richard Bryant (Arcaid, Kingston-upon-Thames) 18; Bulloz, Paris, 27; Chicago Architectural Photographing Company, 31, 36, 37; Commonwealth War Graves Commission, Maidenhead, 58; Conway Library, Courtauld Institute, London, 53, 88; John Donat, London, 20, 96, 97; James Dunnett, London, 112, 113; Esto Photographics Inc., Mamaroneck, NY, 102, 110; Photographie Giraudon, 30, 32; Angelo Hornak, London, 19; Illustrated London News, 26; Italian State Tourist Office, London, 85; Philip Johnson, New York, 108, 109; A. F. Kersting, London, 29; Kunsthistorisches Institut, Kiel, 90; Ralph Lieberman, North Adams, MA, 7; University of Liverpool, 76; London Regional Transport, 54; Bildarchiv Foto Marburg, 22, 23, 41, 42, 45, 46, 47, 91; Museum of Modern Art, New York, 65, 66, 67, 70, 99, 100, 101; Tony Morrison, Suffolk, 104; National Monuments Record, London, 16; The New York Historical Society, 35; Edvard Primožič, Ljubljana, 59, 60, 61, 62; Roger-Viollet, Paris, 92; Helga Schmidt-Glassner, Stuttgart, 14; Sir John Soane's Museum, London, 17; Robert A. M. Stern Architects, New York, 57, 71, 72, 73, 74, 78, 82, 83, 84, 86, 105, 106; Swedish Museum of Architecture, Stockholm, 63; Ullstein Bilderdienst, 89; University of Virginia, 15; Virginia Division of Tourism, 107; Museen de Stadt Wien, 49; Frank Lloyd Wright Foundation, Taliesin, 69

The quotation on page 7 from *The Sacred Wood* by T. S. Eliot is reproduced by kind permission of Methuen and Co.

CURRENT CLASSICISM

Robert Adam (Winchester Design Partnership), 208; Atkin, Voith & Associates, Philadelphia, 155, 156; John Blatteau Associates, Philadelphia, 147, 148, 149, 150, 151, 294, 295; Ricardo Bofill/Taller de Arquitectura, Barcelona, 296, 298, 299, 301, 303; Mario Botta, Lugano (Lorenzo Bianda), 83; Henry Bowles, San Francisco, 242, 243, 244; Richard Bryant (Arcaid, Kingston-upon-Thames) 1, 47, 48, 54, 58, 59, 60, 62, 64, 234; Lluis Casals, Barcelona, 97, 100, 101, 102; Henry Cobb/I. M. Pei & Partners, New York, 152, 154 (Steve Oles), 153; Country Life, London, 132; Stéphane Couturier, Paris, 300; Tom Crane Photography, 145, 146; Espie Dods Architects, 123, 124, 125; Andres Duany and Elizabeth Plater-Zyberk, Architects, Miami, 86, 114, 115, 116, 117, 118, 282, 283, 284, 285; Eisenman Robertson Architects, Charlottesville (Joseph E. Garland, Charlottesville), 66, 67, 68; Erith and Terry Architects, Colchester, 131, 135, 136, 138, 139, 140, 141, 142, 143, 144; Esto Photographics Inc., Mamaroneck, New York, 174, 175, 176; Terry Farrell Partnership, London, 49, 50, 51, 52; The Frick Collection (Henry Hope Reed), 134; Miguel Garay, 103, 104, 105, 106; Frank O. Gehry & Associates, Venice CA., 35, 39; Michael Graves Architects, Princeton NJ, 192 (Peter Aaron), 188, (Esto Photographics) 187, 189 (Paschall/Taylor), 183, 184, 185, 186; Hammond Beeby and Babka, Architects, Chicago, 161, 162, 163, 164, 165, 166, 167, 168, 169, 170, 171, 172, 173; Paul Hester, Houston, 34; International Bauausstellung, Berlin, 262, 263, 264, 265, 266; Arata Isozaki & Associates, Tokyo (Retoria), 44, 45 (Yukio Futagawa), 41, 46 (The Japan Architect), 43; Franklin D. Israel, Beverly Hills, 56, 57; Charles Jencks, London, 53, 55, 256, 259; Jones & Kirkland Architects, Toronto, 286, 287; Alan Karchmer, New Orleans, 13, 18; R. M. Kliment and Frances Halsband, Architects, New York (Cervin Robinson© 1988), 198, 199, 200, 201, 202, 203, 204; Koetter, Kim & Associates, Boston, 76; Kohn Pedersen Fox Associates, New York, 178, 179, 180, 181, 182, (Jock Pottle), 177; Leon Krier, London, 267, 268, 269, 270, 271, 272, 273, 274, 275, 276, 277, 278, 279, 280; Christian Langlois, Paris, 157, 158; José-Ignacio Linazasoro, San Sebastian, 107, 108, 109, 110, 111, 112; Norman McGrath, New York, 17; James T. Maher, New York, 133; Manuel Manzano-Monís, Madrid, 159; Rafael Moneo, Madrid, 96, 98; Moore Ruble Yudell, Santa Monica, 16, 19, 20, 21, 22, 23, 24, 26, 27; Michael Moran, New York, 36, 37, 38, 40; John Outram, London, 160, 233, 235, 236, 237, 238, 239, 240, 241; Orr & Taylor, New Haven CT, 216, 217, 218, 219; Paschall/Taylor, 28; Richard Payne, Houston, 29, 32; P. Pennoyer, 258, 261; Peterson/Littenberg Architects, New York, 290, 291, 292, 293; Demetri Porphyrios, London, 126, 128, 129, 130; Paolo Portoghesi ed Associati, Rome, 253, 254; Cervin Robinson, New York, 30, 33; Kevin Roche John Dinkeloo and Associates, Hamden CT, 84, 85, 194, 195, 196, 197; Peter Rose, Architect, Montreal, 205, 206, 207; Aldo Rossi, Milan, 87, 88, 89, 90, 91, 92, 93, 94, 95; Colin Rowe, Ithaca NY, 251, 252; Steve Rosenthal, New York, 77, 78; Deidi von Shaewen, Paris, 297; Skidmore, Owings & Merrill, Chicago, 304; Thomas Gordon Smith, Chicago, 245, 246, 247, 248, 249, 257; Robert A. M. Stern Architects, New York, 7, 99, 220, 221, 222, 223, 224, 225, 226, 227, 228, 229, 230, 231, 232, 250, 255, 260, 302; James Stirling, Michael Wilford and Associates, London, 61 (John Donat), 63; Taft Architects, Houston, 65, 69, 70, 71, 72, 73, 74; Tigerman, Fugman, McCurry Architects, Chicago, 209, 210, 211, 212, 213; Alexander Tzannes, Sydney, 119, 120, 121, 122; Charles Vandenhove,, Liége, 288, 289; Venturi, Rauch and Scott Brown Inc., Philadelphia, 2, 3, 4, 5, 6, 8, 9, 10, 11, 12, 13, 14; Abdel Wahed el Wakil, 281; Paul Warchol, New York, 75, 80; Elizabeth Whiting Associates, London, 25, 113